HORSE TRIALS HORSES

Horse Trials Horses

VIVIEN BATCHELOR
JULIA LONGLAND

PELHAM BOOKS

First published in Great Britain by
PELHAM BOOKS
52 Bedford Square
London, W.C.1
1970

© 1970 by Vivien Batchelor and Julia Longland

7207 0397 2

Printed in Great Britain by
Northumberland Press Limited
Gateshead

Contents

Illustrations

Acknowledgements

The authors would like to thank all those who have helped in so many ways towards the publication of this book. Most important are the horses, whose brave and courageous exploits in terrible conditions have caused the book to exist at all. Then of course there are the riders and owners who have so kindly delved into their archives and their memories: namely: Mrs. Phyllis Tomkinson, Captain Martin Whiteley, Miss Shelagh Kesler, Major and Mrs. Derek Allhusen, Mrs. Gordon-Watson, Miss Jane Bullen, Lt.-Colonel Frank Weldon, Richard Walker, Mrs. Eileen Pitman, Richard Meade, Miss Kitty Clements, Miss Sheila Willcox, Anneli Drummond-Hay, Bill Roycroft, Jean-Jacques Guyon, Major Eddie Boylan, Miss Diana Mason, Bertie Hill, Major Laurence Rook, and Major James Templer.

In particular they acknowledge with deep gratitude assistance from colleagues: including Miss Jane Pontifex of The British Horse Society, Denis Blewett—*Daily Express* correspondent in Moscow, without whose tenacity the Russian chapter would never have been written; Roger-Louis Thomas of *L'Information Hippique*.

Lastly, especial thanks to publisher Mr. William Luscombe of Pelham Books for his unbelievable patience while waiting for the promised manuscript.

Vivien Batchelor
Julia Longland

London, 1970.

1 The Poacher

In the early 'sixties in the market place at Exeter a noted horsewoman, Shelagh Kesler, was wandering around looking at the horses up for sale.

Among them was a bay gelding, 16.2 hands, which she judged to be about four years old and which she thought to have the makings of a good horse. Inquiries made among the dealers elicited no information about his breeding. It was supposed he might have been bred in Ireland as many of the horses offered for sale in Exeter market were of Irish origin, but as far as any specific details went he might have been like Topsy and 'just growed'.

Shelagh backed her judgment and he was knocked down to her for a modest sum. She started schooling him and he at once displayed a phenomenal aptitude for jumping and an equally phenomenal bad temper. As Martin Whiteley, who later owned him, remarked: 'He kicked one end and bit the other. You almost needed a pitchfork when you went in to him in the stable.'

No one can account for this claustrophobic trait. Perhaps in the dim past when he was very young he was shut up in a loose box, or perhaps he had been beaten in a closed stable. Whatever happened, it left its mark.

After she had had him for a year Shelagh sold him to Mrs. Phyllis Tomkinson of Hook Norton, who hunted with the Heythrop. This great old lady, fearless and indomitable, who rode to hounds side-saddle immediately fell in love with 'Poach'. In her eyes he could do nothing wrong.

She said she wanted him for her son to ride, he being M.F.H. in Cheshire. Immediately she bought him she decided to ride him herself.

Shelagh, possibly with some unspoken misgiving, asked Mrs. Tomkinson to give her the chance to buy him back if she wanted to get rid of him.

Although Mrs. Tomkinson admits he was 'very naughty' in the stable ('almost savage' she went so far as to say once), her loyalty to him was unwavering. 'I knew he was out of the ordinary as soon as I saw him, and he was always very good with me. I never had any trouble with him, I never thought I would.'

Her close friends and relatives who knew Poach's reputation probably thought differently. Their consternation when this intrepid matron approached him with a side saddle can well be imagined. Perhaps, however, The Poacher instinctively recognised he had a rider of his own calibre. His later owner Martin Whiteley says of him he is a superb hunter provided you are going—and the indomitable Mrs. Tomkinson was nothing if not a goer. The pair got on famously for the two seasons in 1961 and 1962. And then disaster struck.

Out with the Heythrop, The Poacher with Mrs. Tomkinson firmly in the saddle took off over a hedge into a road. She did not see another woman rider whose horse was pretty well running away galloping full tilt towards her. The galloping horse cannoned into The Poacher and Mrs. Tomkinson was unseated and rolled into the side of the road. She broke an ankle and cracked her pelvis.

As it was obvious even to such an invincible rider that it would be a long time before she went hunting again she reluctantly decided to let Shelagh Kesler have the horse back. It was at this time that The Poacher began to gain a reputation of being an accident-prone animal.

Mrs. Tomkinson had him vetted before selling him and the

vet said he had a heart condition. So The Poacher went off to Cambridge to the Equine Research Laboratory for examination and was eventually passed fit, it being decided by the boffins that the particular condition they found would not affect him in the field. Indeed it does not appear to have done. So Shelagh became the owner of The Poacher for the second time, and decided to train him up for Eventing.

No sooner had she got him ready to enter the lists in this, for him, new field than he trod on a broken bottle and cut his stifle. Then she herself had a fall and was unable to ride him. Meanwhile Martin Whiteley, who had had his eye on him since he was five years old persuaded Shelagh to sell him.

So in the summer of 1964, Martin at last got the horse he had been wanting since it was a five-year-old.

That autumn Chatsworth was where the Golden Griffin Midland Bank Novice Championship was held. The Poacher won the Intermediate class ridden by Michael Herbert the Northamptonshire trainer who has schooled him ever since.

The following Spring Martin took him to Badminton and he won.

The Poacher had established himself as an outstanding Combined Training Event horse. Much of the credit was due then and later to Michael Herbert's unremitting patience. This is especially creditable because when Herbert first had The Poacher he did not really like him, according to his still most ardent admirer Mrs. Tomkinson.

As if she could scarcely believe what she was saying she told me, 'When he first had The Poacher he did not like him! He found him careless especially about his show-jumping!'

Mrs. Tomkinson cannot really believe that anyone can fail to fall in love with The Poacher on sight and develop, as she has done, a continuing love affair with the noble beast.

After The Poacher's win at Badminton he was put on the short list for training for the British Team which went to

Moscow—the first time a British team had taken on traditional masters of equestrianism.

The final selection for the team was made that year at Eridge Horse Trials in Kent and The Poacher stopped at a bank, so was dropped by the Committee.

In 1966 the weather in the early part of the year was so relentlessly appalling that the Duke of Beaufort in whose grounds at Badminton House at Gloucestershire the famous Trials are held, reluctantly decided to abandon the event. Many owners and riders were bitterly disappointed at the decision, but after all it was not their front garden that was being churned up by horses' hooves!

'Poach', as he is always called at home, had been prepared for Badminton. With the cancellation he went temporarily out of training. Martin Whiteley says he is soon got fit, but he also thinks that one Three-Day Event in a season is enough for him. He decided to get Poach ready for the World Championships at Burghley in the late summer of 1966.

It was here that this remarkable horse showed that his Badminton win the year before was no fluke. He never put a foot wrong and was finally placed fifth overall. He was the second among the British horses—beaten only by the great Barberry, who was placed second overall.

After the World Championships he had a Hobdey operation and so missed competing in the 1967 Badminton Trials.

He was selected as part of the British team to go to the European Championships at Punchestown later in the year. The British won and The Poacher was second in the individual placings. He and Martin Whiteley seemed to have worked out a perfect understanding with each other.

On the flight to Ireland Poach had yet another adventure which some might say proves he is an 'event' horse in more ways than one. In the next compartment to him on the plane which was specially converted with stalls for individual horses, a horse called Ballycarron, in the next stall to Poach, got loose and kicked her frightened way into his compartment. Poach, obviously disconcerted by the un-announced visitor who by this time had slipped and fallen so that her legs were entangled around his, at first showed signs of becoming restive or of kicking back. After all, he was the horse who earlier in his life had suffered from an obsession about confined spaces.

This was where Michael Herbert showed what a superb horseman he is and what a complete understanding he has of the animals under his charge. Realising that at any moment panic might break out among the horses and that a com-paratively small plane half-way over the Irish Sea is one of the least suitable venues for a stampede he got on The Poacher's back. Steadying the horse with language he understood and at the same time trying to soothe the fallen Ballycarron he sat on Poach's back, holding him still all the time for the rest of the flight. The journey must have seemed interminable.

But to Herbert's credit both horses arrived in Ireland unhurt and far calmer than anyone would have dreamed possible in the circumstances. 'It was the sort of incredible thing that could only happen to Poach,' Martin Whiteley told me when relating the incident much later.

After Britain won the European Championships of 1967 The Poacher was a natural for the short list for the Mexico Olympics and he and Martin went into training. It was at this time that Martin was offered a four-figure sum for his horse from a foreign buyer, but he refused the offer. He and Poach were going to represent Great Britain in Mexico unless something completely untoward cropped up.

The final selection of the team was announced after the Burghley Three-Day Event in September 1968 and of course it included Whiteley and The Poacher. But here that some-thing untoward which seems always to dog The Poacher did intervene. Martin sustained an injury to his back.

Many riders who through persistent hard work and deter-mination had reached so nearly to their goal would have been tempted to make light of the injury and hoped for the best.

Most probably they would have thought it would have held up on the day. But Martin Whiteley is a man of highest principle and great scruple. The back might not be all right on the day. It might cause him to let down both The Poacher and the other members of the British team. It might even cost us a medal.

So this generous man, whose lifetime's hopes of riding for his country in the greatest event of all amateur sport, the Olympic Games, had been so bitterly dashed, told the selectors he did not think he ought to go to Mexico. Even more generously, he offered his horse to the Committee with only one proviso—that it should be ridden by Sergeant Ben Jones.

It was a tremendous gesture, for there is no doubt that in experience The Poacher was, with Lochinvar, the sheet anchor of the team. Thus it happened that only a week before the Games were due The Poacher had a new rider in Ben Jones and the pair of them made their first public appearance together on the first day of the Combined Training Event —the dressage.

As if this was not enough, The Poacher had to add his own bit of drama to the proceedings. Shortly before the Dressage he got loose and, obviously over excited, started galloping about with stable hands and officials chasing after him. By the time he was caught it was nearly his turn to go into the ring. Then it was found he had lost a shoe and the farrier had to do a hasty job. This should have been enough to unnerve both the horse and the rider, who however experienced had never ridden this particular mount before.

It appeared, however, that the gallop had relaxed Poach or perhaps he felt pleased with being the centre of drama before he even entered the ring.

He did a very good Dressage, and was even better the next day in the cross-country where he had to swim through part of the course because of the storm floods. He and Sergeant. Jones were fifth overall in the individual placings.

On his return to this country from Mexico he was handed over to the Combined Training Committee by his owner Mr. Martin Whiteley.

The following year, 1969, again partnered by Sergeant Jones he was in the team which won the European Championships for Britain in Haras du Pin in northern France. During the following winter the Committee decided to try him with another rider. The rider they selected was Richard Meade who had ridden Cornishman V in the Mexico Olympic team but who was still without his own top class mount.

They made their debut at Badminton this year and as befitted such a Gold medal combination they won having led all the way. This was the second time The Poacher has been a winner at Badminton.

2 Lochinvar

'Have ye e'er heard of gallant like young Lochinvar?' So says the ballad and indeed, gallant could hardly be a more fitting description of that bright, bay steed who followed so faithfully in the footsteps of his namesake—the hero of the ballad—when he forded rivers in a strange continent to bring triumph and honour to his country.

And gallant would not come amiss either in an appraisal of Lochinvar's owner-rider, 55-year-old silver-haired grandfather Major Derek Allhusen, late of the 9th Lancers and now a Norfolk farmer.

Life is full of odd extremes, and it was curious that at Mexico the two highest individual awards ever won by Britain in the equestrian events of the Olympic Games should go to a pony prodigy and a man reaching his athletic prime in his middle fifties.

Since bringing home a Gold and Silver medal in October 1968 Derek Allhusen has become a favourite and familiar figure with the Press and the Public. They delighted in the 'galloping grandfather' image, and sympathised when he turned down the M.B.E. in the January 1969 Honours List. His refusal to accept was never officially confirmed by him, but he never denied it either, and it was an action typically altruistic of the man to refuse to take for himself an honour that his colleagues of that grim ride could not share.

Lochinvar too captured the fancy of the people—and conscious of this enthusiasm Derek Allhusen responded generously by parading the horse at banquets and on stage, for Pony Club lectures and Hunt suppers. After one of his nocturnal appearances the horse actually caught a severe chill which was probably the cause of the influenza virus that prevented him competing at Badminton, the following year. There are limits—even in the public duty of a famous horse!

To watch the ten-year-old Lochinvar, bulging muscles packed into a lean, glossy bodywork, suppling up for his least favourite occupation—a dressage test—suggests a defiant philanderer submitting to the strictures of authority with a sulky grace. His eyes and his ears roll backwards, and he swishes his tail with the rage of a thwarted cat—but I have recently discovered that the impression of virility is not a false one.

Derek Allhusen explained: 'Lochinvar is what is known as a rig—he was never cut properly by the Irish when he was a young colt, and I think he would be capable of serving mares —though I've never tried!'

Although Lochinvar could surely make a fortune today if he were ever chosen to advertise equine health foods, he made a very different picture nine years ago, when the Allhusens first saw him running out in a field at Gisburn, Lancashire, in June 1961. 'He was a great big skeleton of a horse,' Derek recalls. 'He looked very poor, like a hatrack, with no flesh or muscle on him anywhere, and very weak. The reason for his bad condition was that he had been broken and hunted as a two-year-old in Ireland, so had never had any opportunity to furnish. He was also smothered in warts, and I longed to get them attended to—there was one particularly bad one on the corner of his lip that would obviously have to be removed before he could be ridden.'

But the attraction between man and horse was instantaneous. 'We drove the car into the field,' Derek continued, 'and the horses came up—this three-year-old and a point-to-pointer. But this three-year-old, with all the inquisitiveness of a youngster, suddenly put his head in through the half-open window of the car and picked a glove up off the seat. And I thought: Well, that's an extraordinary thing for a horse to do—he must be rather intelligent. It was, so to speak, love at first sight.'

It takes a determined and knowledgeable man to chase a horse looking as vile as this one did—covered as he was in warts that extended over the corners of his mouth, his head, his face and his sheath. But both the Allhusens had been struck by this gaunt creature's intelligence and his independence of spirit, so decided it was worth going along with the owner's wish to leave the horse where he was for a few months, giving him a chance to fill out.

But they had reckoned without the warts. And when the owner, Tony Dickinson (whose brother, Michael, had been killed serving with Derek Allhusen's squadron in Italy during the War), rang up three months later, Lochinvar was still unrideable. Two more months went by during which time Derek had cause to be very grateful for his friendship with his former brother soldier's family—and to the honesty of Tony Dickinson himself.

Several other interested buyers, two of them extremely well-backed financially, had heard rumours of this promising young horse tucked away in a field, and had they become involved as well the price would have rocketed up. As it was, Dickinson held staunchly to his first refusal agreement and finally sold the horse for £500, one thick misty day in November. Derek describes his feelings on that first ride as if still amazed by the memory:

'He wouldn't take the bit because he was frightened in his mouth. I saw him jump a small fence and he jumped abominably, as if he was frightened of being caught in the back teeth. He got right up to the fence and sort of lurched over, he had no natural spring or parabola, and I said to Claude: (his wife) "I don't reckon much to his jumping." He'd been shockingly broken, and I didn't like him, but he was also a debility case. His back felt terribly weak, he had this overgrown frame still "unfurnished" and one of the warts on his mouth had still not healed. But Claude rode him too, and she loved him, his head, his temperament and his character.'

Back on their Norfolk farm the Allhusens found that the warts, loathsome though they were to look at, were the easiest problem to remove. The days of Mark Twain's celebrated Huckleberry Finn, who practised a macabre method of antagonising two cats with their tails tied together to scratch off warts in a graveyard at midnight, are long since gone. Lochinvar was liberated by the simple operation of a veterinary surgeon's scalpel.

More difficult by far to combat, if not irreparable, was the damage done to Lochinvar's back by some ignorant nagsman bumping up and down in the centre of that most delicate piece of equine mechanism—the back arch. Derek Allhusen became quite stirred up as he recalled watching, on a subsequent visit the same gentleman employing like tactics on another son of Battleburn. (Lochinvar is by Battleburn, out of a mare by Isolation.) 'I had the greatest difficulty in not being rather outspoken to the man, and I could see why Lochinvar had had such a miserable start to his training—there are certain things he has never really got over.

'Nothing is worse for a young horse in those initial stages of his training than for a rider to put too much weight on his back—it can do an awful lot of damage. Lochinvar has improved enormously, but he never got a natural parabola—the arch which a horse develops from using his hocks correctly. He never learnt to bend his back, like Sunsalve (the famous chestnut on whom David Broome won the King George V Gold Cup, and an Olympic Bronze Medal in 1960) —he always jumped with a hollow back.'

Over the years Derek tried many methods of treatment, in his search to alleviate the discomfort in Lochinvar's back —but the two really successful ones have been manipulation by Mr. Strong (who treats as many horses as humans) and heat treatment, called Faradism, which activates and pulsates the muscles through electrical impulses, dispersing fibrous tissue.

The winter of 1961 was a busy one for Lochinvar. Derek recalls, 'I re-broke him, lunged him a lot, put him on sidereins in the school, and kept off his back as much as I possibly could, because I find that is the best way of getting a horse that's spoilt to have confidence again, dissociated with the weight of the rider.'

The introduction to horse trials at Tweseldown, some nine months later, did not produce an auspicious start. Lochinvar was eliminated in the cross-country, and Derek wrote to Tony Dickinson: 'I don't think this horse will ever make either a jumper or a Three-Day Event horse,' but Claude had designs on him for dressage because he was 'so beautiful'. Derek himself was looking for a successor to Laurien (his famous eventing mare of the 'fifties), and after several days hunting with the Cottesmore he remembers thinking: 'He was both resentful and intelligent but I didn't know whether he had courage.'

At Tidworth—the military Three-Day Event—in May 1963 Lochinvar ran well, only dropping down to fourth place in his Novice section after hitting four fences in the final Jumping phase—a pattern that was to colour much of his later career. Arrangements for Burghley later that year were upset at the last moment when Derek tore a muscle: 'Lochinvar was in the habit of suddenly losing his confidence, and putting in a very quick short one in front of a fence, caused me to tear a muscle very badly in my groin and I couldn't ride,' he told me. But Shelagh Kesler stepped into the breach two days before the event started, and rode him to such good effect that the pair finished second, behind Ireland's Harry Freeman-Jackson on St. Finbarr. Derek recalls, 'We realised then we must have a very good horse.'

Half-way through his Badminton training the following spring Lochinvar, this time, came to grief. At Crookham Trials in March, he refused into a wall, got a splinter of wood into his fetlock and it blew up. Derek comments, 'He's a horse that gets infection through his skin to an incredible degree, and could get pressure bruising quite easily from being bandaged with cotton wool. I could never run him in over-reach boots because of his extraordinarily sensitive skin, so of course the splinter wound went septic, and Badminton was out.'

Derek's future team-mate, Richard Meade, became the new star after winning the event on Barberry, and storming his way into the Tokyo team. But the same problem that lost Richard a Gold Medal on the far side of the world—Barberry dropped from first to eighth in the final Jumping phase—was pursuing Derek at home. He met Richard Stillwell at a show near Chichester and asked him, 'I do wish you'd help me, I've just done a disastrous round on Lochinvar; what am I doing wrong?' He was told, 'Do you want the truth?' and answered, 'Yes, I'm prepared to take anything.' Richard, nothing if not truthful, came back, 'Well, everything's bloody well wrong!' Derek told him, 'Well, thank you very much. Will you please start to try and put it right?' and the reply: 'Yes, I will,' was the start of a new era for both horse and rider.

Firstly, it seemed, Derek was dropping the horse's head before a fence. 'You often see horses out hunting,' Derek told me, 'jumping without any contact from the reins—but Lochinvar had no confidence in his rider except in the cross-country when we were galloping, and he was terribly sensitive to a loss of contact in front of a fence. If this happened, he would think: "Good Lord, I'm out of touch with the rider," and he just put in a short one, and jumped flat—went through the bottom.'

1965 was European Championship year, and Russia, for the first time, was host nation. Despite yet another show-jumping lapse at Badminton (dropping from third to ninth) Lochinvar had impressed the Selectors. He represented his country for the first time on the Russian trip, accompanied

by Richard Meade with Barberry, Sergeant Ben Jones with
Master Bernard, Christine Sheppard with Fenjirao and Mary
Macdonell with Kilmacthomas as reserve.

Due mainly to a brilliant test by Master Bernard, the
British team stood first after the dressage, but dropped back
to finish third after too-slow cross-country times by Fenjirao
and Master Bernard. Lochinvar, at his worst in the dressage
arena, made up for his digression by returning the second
highest bonus of the event in the Endurance, and touching
only one fence in the show-jumping, to move up from
bottom to eighth. The winners, for the second time, were
Russia, and the runners-up Ireland.

The year 1966 was frustrating. In Europe swamp fever
crippled horse traffic and depleted teams for the Burghley
World Championships, while Badminton was cancelled
through wet weather. Lochinvar was prevented by a warble
from competing at Tidworth, and by a broken blood vessel
from running at Eridge in August. At Burghley in September
his individual bid was foiled when he took fright at a water-
fall fence cross-country, and skidded to a halt, hurling his
unfortunate rider into the water trough. Derek remembers:
'Fortunately the photographer who had caught us falling in
the water, took us again the second time!'

Since joining forces with Richard Stillwell both Derek and
Lochinvar had progressed at show-jumping—but still much
of the trouble was caused by discomfort in the horse's back
after a rigorous Endurance phase. And at Badminton in 1967
a chance of victory was thrown away when Lochinvar plum-
meted from top to eleventh place in the Jumping. Derek
shudders at the memory: 'It was the most shattering experience I've ever had in my life—I even remember the Queen
Mother sympathising!'

After that débacle there was an ominous silence from the
Selectors, grappling with weighty problems of lameness in
their chosen team for the Punchestown, Ireland, European
Championships in August. When, at the eleventh hour the

call came, Lochinvar, slightly unfit and therefore 'thick-winded' like many Battleburn horses, gave the impression of being 'gone in the wind' when galloping. But the Hob-deying operation turned out not to be necessary, for as he reached peak fitness he cleared his wind himself.

Punchestown was a triumph for the British team—although it did not start that way for Lochinvar—he finished the dressage one from bottom. Derek recalled: 'I nearly shot myself when I came out of the ring, I was so fed up, although I did think I had been toughly marked.' But again honour was redeemed in the Endurance when they recorded 31.2 bonus points on the Steeplechase (the course was over-measured by 500 yards, so this represented maximum bonus —the only pair to do so) and maximum bonus cross-country —superlative marks which moved them right up to fourth place. Better still for their improved image was the clear round show-jumping, and the eventual third Individual place at the finish. Added to Martin Whiteley's second Individual position on The Poacher (behind Eddie Boylan's Durlas Eile), Ben Jones' and Richard Meade's contributions on Foxdor and Barberry, the result was, as it turned out, an accurate pointer to Mexico.

At Burghley that year Lochinvar came fifth, as he did at Badminton the following April—and thus followed the Olympic short-list and Mexico. Much has been written of Avandaro—of the sun, the rain, the altitude, the horses lost, the riders' hopes and tragedies and the significance of one man's error in navigation. Suffice it to record here a few details of Lochinvar, from the West, who marked out the British trail to victory. As in the European Championships twelve months later (Haras du Pin, Britain's third consecutive team triumph), at Mexico Derek Allhusen and Lochinvar led the van. Their job was to get round the course safely and report back the condition of take-offs and landings, plus other dangers, to the team. Just as much as riding last this job carries heavy responsibility—and although Derek was criticised for his slow round at Haras du Pin, it would not have helped the British team had he fallen flat on his face trying to score more speed bonus points.

At Mexico he started ninth of the forty-nine competitors, escaping the torrential storm that drove in the faces of compatriots Richard Meade and Ben Jones. But although the sun shone, the air was stifling and humid and the ground treacherous and deceptively holding—Lochinvar's score of —40.61 at the start of the third day was a total to be proud of. And considering the set-backs of the past his clear round in the Jumping phase well-deserved the move up from fourth to second place. Whether the American horse, Kilkenny, who fell, or the Russian rider Deev, who lost his way, would have jumped clear—as they would have had to do to keep Lochinvar in fourth place—no one will ever know.

Lochinvar has now (February 1970) competed in twenty Three-Day Events. He has won the Calcutta Cup for points in horse trials, in 1965, 1967 and 1968, and his prize money totals about £1,250. His sense of humour is as sharp as ever— in October 1969 in the Final Cavalcade at the Horse of the Year Show, Wembley, he bucked his master off in front of the Royal Box. Derek, his arm in a sling from a dislocated shoulder, was, understandably, not very appreciative of the joke!

Derek Allhusen and Lochinvar have led the British team to three victories in five years. In 1968 Derek, who, incredibly, has never won a Three-Day Event, jettisoned what was probably the greatest chance he will ever have of such a victory at Burghley. In the lead on the final day he withdrew lest Lochinvar, passed by the vets but stiff and sore after the cross-country, should aggravate an injury in the final Jumping phase and damage himself before the Games.

The risk was slight—and the temptation to continue almost unbearable. Additionally, the Olympic team, due to leave in two and a half weeks, had not yet been named. What if the withdrawal prejudiced his chances? But the man who was awarded a Silver Star Medal for valour on the field of action, who is one of the Queen's Personal Bodyguard, had got his priorities right, determined that the work of years should not be wasted. He gambled for Gold—and the Trump card came up.

It was the sort of hand that supreme athlete and sportsman, Lord Exeter—creator of Burghley and one of Britain's most-celebrated Gold medallists—would have appreciated playing himself.

3 Cornishman V

On a stud farm in far west Cornwall in 1959 a well-known point-to-point mare, Polly Fourth, gave birth to a dark bay colt.

The sire was Golden Surprise, by Casanova, a son of the great Hyperion. Golden Surprise was the winner of seventeen steeplechases. If the breeding lines were anything to go by, the youngster looked set fair for a career in the steeplechase or the hunting field. It is unlikely that the man who bred him ever envisaged that he would one day represent Great Britain to help win an Olympic Gold Medal for Combined Training. But that is just what happened to Cornishman V at Mexico in 1968.

In spite of its mild climate, its warmer, softer airs, born of the prevailing west winds, Cornwall can be a hard place for livestock. The early springs may be ideal for flower growing, but the rocky soil with little deep lush grass makes tough nurturing for young livestock, except for those lucky enough to be reared in some of the more fertile acres. For many it can be a battle. And somehow, this battle is brought out in the character of the stock it produces—a strange mixture of the mild and wild, not found elsewhere. Certain it was so with Cornishman V as the handsome young colt was somewhat unimaginatively named.

There appeared also to have been little imagination and less sympathy shown in his breaking—a process which left a permanent scar on his temperament and took subsequent riders much time and patience to eradicate.

But though he was nervous and highly strung he grew into a beauty, an enormous, deep chested, beautifully proportioned animal standing 17 hands tall.

His breeder advertised him for sale.

It was at this time that Brigadier Gordon-Watson, a fine horseman and a great follower to hounds, was due to retire from the Army. 'I had always longed for a really top-class hunter,' he told me at Tidworth in 1969, 'and I decided to look around and see if I could find one.'

The Brigadier saw Cornishman advertised and liked the sound of his breeding. With a friend of his, a veterinary surgeon who at one time owned Highland Wedding, the 1969 Grand National winner, he journeyed to Cornwall to have a look at the four-year-old.

The great rangy animal was brought out of a stable, shaking and shying and ready to play up. The Brigadier said he would like to get a leg across him. Several stable hands looked dubious, but could not do otherwise than agree. Hardly had the Brigadier got a leg on his withers than the horse bolted forward like a shot from a gun, half climbing a pile of manure, and depositing the Brigadier in the yard.

But if Cornishman had a mind of his own about being ridden so had the Brigadier about riding him. 'Eventually, three men held his head while I got seated,' the Brigadier recalls. 'Then they let him go and he was away like a bronco.'

In spite of his nerves and temperament, the Brigadier liked the dark bay and he eventually changed hands for 525 guineas

At first he was so highly strung and unreliable that he put his new owner off no fewer than eight times. But he was already proving he was a natural jumper and kindness and gentling by Mrs. Gordon-Watson and their young daughter Mary gradually wrought a change in him. He began to realise the whole world was not out to do him down, though it was a very long time before he learned not to shrink back if anyone raised a hand to stroke him.

Early in his career at his new home in Dorset, Cornish-man formed a strange friendship with a ginger and white cat called Snowy. Snowy would sit for hours inside the stable or on the door and Cornishman would spend the time licking her and caressing her with his tongue. The friendship has grown with the years. This was another side of the Cornish-bred colt's temperament.

He has always got on well with others of his own species and can be turned out with the skittish Connemara ponies which Mrs. Gordon-Watson breeds and is as gentle and for-bearing with them as an old nannie.

He came to the Gordon-Watson family in a snowy winter and at first he was hunted by them in Dorset. Then he went to Leicester with the Quorn.

Brigadier Gordon-Watson rode him to win the Army Trophy in the Melton Cross Country. In 1966 it was decided to try him as an Event horse with Mary riding him. He had always gone well for Mary. In spite of his huge size and her slight almost delicate build the two seemed to have an affinity. The two went for training with Richard Stillwell at Wokingham.

Richard says he was not an easy horse to train. 'He soon gets bored, and it is best to give him a little work and then leave him for a while before going on again,' he says. 'He is a great natural jumper but is apt to be careless with his show-jumping unless you keep him concentrating. But he is a great horse,' he says.

In 1966 he competed as a novice at Wylye. When one considers that within two years from his first novice appear-ance he was in the gold medal winning team at the Olympics and was fourth in the world in the individual placings, one can get some idea of the great qualities and skill he possesses. If there is such a thing as a 'natural' in Combined Training, surely Cornishman is that.

In 1967 he won the Working Hunter class at the Royal

Windsor Horse Show and was subsequently runner-up to the Champion at the Horse of the Year Show at Wembley.

This was the year when he really began to make his mark as an Event horse. He scored his first big triumph at Tidworth when he won the Rover Division against a formidable field. This was the first time he had ever competed in a Three-Day trial.

In the late autumn of 1967 he had a Hobdey operation to help his wind. This seemed to have the required effect as he afterwards came second at Liphook and was placed ninth at Badminton, early in 1968. There was no idea at this stage, however, that he would end up in Mexico. Indeed, his career seemed to have come to a temporary halt when his partner Mary had the bad luck to break her leg at the Royal International Horse Show in the summer. While Mary ruefully hobbled around in plaster, Cornishman V was turned out in the field. Then, as so often happens in life, other people's destinies took a hand in his.

Staff-Sergeant 'Ben' Jones, incomparable horseman and a great friend of the Gordon-Watsons, who has many times ridden for Great Britain, was to have ridden Foxdor at Burghley Horse Trials. These would be the last before the selectors made their final announcement of the team which would go to Mexico.

Foxdor was in training, on the short list for the British Olympic team. He was owned by Mrs. A. B. Whiteley and had been one of the horses in the team which won the European Championships for Great Britain in Punchestown in 1967. In 1968, again ridden by Staff-Sergeant Jones, he had finished third at Badminton. Then tragedy struck. Just a few weeks before Burghley Foxdor dropped dead.

Brigadier Gordon-Watson was asked by the Combined Training Selection Committee of the British Horse Society if he would lend Cornishman V to Staff-Sergeant Jones as a substitute at Burghley for Foxdor and as a possible substitute for Mexico.

Very generously the Brigadier agreed.

Mrs. Gordon-Watson said to me much later, 'We did not really want him to go away from home. But we were very fond of Staff-Sergeant Jones and we could not see him without a horse. So he was brought in from the field and, with very scant preparation, competed at Burghley.'

The Gordon-Watsons were consoled that their great pet— for such he is—should have the honour of going to Mexico, even though they had not really wanted to let him leave home. But they realised that in the hands of Staff-Sergeant Jones he would be as well looked after as in their own.

Burghley, however, altered the fortunes of other riders who were on the short list for the Olympic Games.

Richard Meade, one of our greatest Combined Training riders, had two horses entered. The principal was his great horse Barberry. The two had been in the Olympic team at Tokyo in 1964 and had finished second in the World Championships at Burghley. The second horse was Lady Hugh Russell's Turnstone, which had finished second at Badminton 1968 but whose fitness was always a trifle suspect and made him unsuitable for a 'first stringer'.

Barberry seemed certain to be the choice—until disaster fell. He sustained a fall and injured himself, putting him quite out of the running to go to Mexico. This left one of our best riders without a mount.

The Fates had not yet finished at Burghley. Martin Whiteley was riding his horse The Poacher—of whom more in another chapter—on which he had been a member of the European Championship team. After Burghley, however, Martin felt he himself was not fit enough to go to Mexico. So he offered to lend The Poacher to the Selection Committee provided Staff-Sergeant Jones rode him.

The Committee was in quandary: Staff-Sergeant Jones had been offered two mounts, Richard Meade had none; the team was due to leave on September 23rd. Again they turned to Brigadier Gordon-Watson and asked if he would lend

The Poacher, with Captain Martin Whiteley riding him, splashes through the brook at one of the Badminton jumps on the cross-country phase of the Little Badminton Event which he won in 1965. He won Great Badminton in 1970. In 1968 he was in the Gold medal winning team in Mexico.

Lochinvar, ridden by Major Derek Allhusen, makes the leap of a lifetime at the Olympic Games in Mexico in 1968 to help Britain win the team Gold medal and to win the individual Silver for themselves. This was the treacherous flooding river at Fence 29 which took such toll of horses and riders. This picture was taken before the storm which broke in the middle of the cross-country section and shows the severity of the obstacles.

Cornishman V, ridden by Miss Mary Gordon-Watson, taking the oxer in the cross-country at the European championships at Haras du Pin in France in 1969. They became Individual European champions, although they were not members of the official British team. This jump had a back rail of 4 feet, a spread of 6 feet and a front rail of 3ft 6ins. Cornishman V was in the Gold medal winning Olympic team at Mexico when he was ridden by Richard Meade.

Cornishman V to Richard Meade. The Brigadier agreed. Thus, Cornishman found himself in the strange and unfamiliar surroundings of the plane for Mexico.

Back home in Dorset his 'family' followed his progress on the other side of the world with pride—and horror—when the full story of the atrocious conditions for the cross-country course became known. But he survived with distinction, helping Britain to win the gold medal and only narrowly missing an individual bronze.

On the dull November day when he was due back from Mexico all the Gordon-Watsons were on parade at London Airport at 4 o'clock in the morning to welcome their hero back. As part of the homecoming celebrations Peter Biegel was commissioned to paint his portrait.

Early in 1969, however, Mary and Cornishman got down to serious work together. They went for schooling to Richard Stillwell and spent two weeks in Norfolk with the Allhusens. At Crookham they were third and at Liphook they were second. Then they tackled Badminton and at the end of the second day were lying third, with only Richard Walker and the Australian Bill Roycroft in front of them. On the third day though Cornishman's show-jumping let him down—he refused and also knocked down a fence, ending up ninth. His show-jumping again was his weak point at Tidworth, when the weather and conditions on the ground must have reminded him of Mexico. But he did finish third.

Mary was determined to improve his show-jumping, so they went back to Richard Stillwell's for more schooling. She also entered him in Foxhunter classes for show-jumping and in the Grade C novice classes at the All England Jumping Course at Hickstead.

Cornishman was put on the short list for the European Championships British team which was to be chosen after Burghley. The championships were to be held in France, in Normandy at Haras du Pin.

On the way to Burghley Mary and Cornishman won the

Spillers Combined Training class at Kenilworth. When they reached Burghley, Cornishman had a slight swelling on his leg and did not compete in the cross-country section.

Although there was no doubt about the horse's experience the selectors decided Mary, whose slight, almost fragile figure belies considerable strength and toughness, was still lacking in top-class experience and they were not selected for the team. They did go, however, to compete as individuals. The result was a crowning triumph for Mary's hard work and persistence. They beat everybody and won the Individual European Championship—only the second time a woman has pulled off this feat.

There could have been no more fitting reward for the girl who generously let the British team borrow her beloved horse for the Olympic Games and help win a gold medal—and then had the disappointment of not being considered good enough to accompany her horse herself as part of the British team for Europe.

At Badminton 1970 they were placed third. Cornishman V is still only eleven and Mary twenty-one. A bright future surely lies before them.

4 Our Nobby

When the rest of the world's competitors gathered in Mexico for the Combined Training section of the Olympic Games in 1968 the arrival of the British team was awaited with much interest.

Britain had already won one Gold medal, at the Stockholm Olympics in 1956. She was the current holder of the European Championship from Punchestown in 1967 and since 1953 when she won the first European Championships for Combined Training ever held (at Badminton) she had won the title five times out of the eight times it had been staged, in many countries including Moscow in 1965—when incidentally we only managed to come third.

So the arrival of the British team would obviously give the foreigners the measure of what they had to contend with. Very little advance information could have leaked as the selectors themselves did not make up their minds until after the Burghley Horse Trials in September and the selected team left a few days later. However, all the foreign competitors knew that Britain had some of the toughest and strongest men and horses in the sport.

Imagine their reaction when the plane bringing the British team touched down and out of it stepped a young nurse, not yet twenty-one, whose mount was Our Nobby—only 15 hands high.

Indeed one competitor said to the nurse, (Jane Bullen): 'Only the mad British would send a girl and a pony for the

Three-Day Event at the Olympics!'

Actually, this was the first time we had included a woman rider. Not until 1964 had they been eligible for the Three-Day Event but our team then was all male.

At the time this was considered strange by many, as without doubt it was the prowess of British women riders in Combined Training which finally made the Olympic Committee change their minds and admit women to a section of the Games which hitherto had been considered altogether too tough for them.

It was the performance of Sheila Willcox at Badminton—acknowledged to be one of the world's toughest courses—which largely made them do so. Sheila is the only rider of either sex who has won the Badminton Trials three times in succession—on High and Mighty in 1957 and 1958 and on Airs and Graces in 1959. Then in 1962 Anneli Drummond-Hay took the laurels on Merely-a-Monarch.

However, whatever had gone on in the selectors' minds, there, in Mexico in 1968 was Our Nobby, to be ridden by the girl who always rode him, who had been given special leave by the Middlesex Hospital where she was training as a nurse, Jane Bullen. Even after they had completed their training there were some who shook their heads, and wondered. I remembered Lt.-Colonel Weldon at Badminton that year expressed grave doubts as to the desirability of sending a woman on such a tough mission. Not that he doubted their ability or keen spirit, but because it might be difficult for the other members of the team. He recalled how the Australians, who won the gold medal at Rome had got Bill Roycroft out of hospital and back to the saddle after he had been injured and half conscious from a fall.

'Who's going to be the brave man to do that to a woman?' asked Weldon.

However, such a grim situation did not arise as Our Nobby, although he made a couple of hashes which Jane says were entirely her fault but which were really due to the appalling going, proved himself to be the fastest cross-country horse of our team. His time on the cross-country phase was in fact the second fastest of any country.

Our Nobby is only 15 hands—pony sized—so those foreigners in Mexico could be excused for gaping.

It was not until he was nine years old—he was fourteen when he went to Mexico—that he officially achieved this height.

When he was six years old Jane was riding him in pony classes and he was certificated for life as height 14.2 hands. For three years, sometimes ridden by Jane's sister Jennie or brother Mike, he had a chequered career in the show world. Twice he was eliminated at Pony Club events for bad behaviour. Jane, who adores him and will hear no word against him, admits: 'He was getting very nappy and un-popular. Even we were beginning to get fed up with him—and he was beginning to be almost dangerous as a child's pony.'

So his career changed and he went into Working Pony classes and won everywhere, including the working pony class at Badminton (quite separate and nothing to do with the Three-Day Event).

But he was proving he could jump like a cat. One day, soon after he joined the Bullen family he took Mike over a solid 5 foot post and rails jump as if it had been a novice hurdle.

Then came a day at Slimbridge when Jane was riding him in a pony event and someone objected to him, saying he was over height. For three years he had been certified 14.2 hands, but now he was remeasured and to everyone's astonishment he was found to have grown and he measured 15 hands. It is most unusual for a horse to grow after six. Jane puts the phenomenon down to the fact that he was born three weeks prematurely.

He was not bred by the Bullens, who were then living at Didmarton in Gloucestershire. 'A man arrived with him one day in a trailer pulled by a Landrover and asked if we

would like to buy a five-year-old horse,' Jane told me. 'He
wanted £150 for him.'

The Bullens did not particularly want another horse; after
all, they already had about fifty at that time, but this one,
though in wretched condition, was classicly bred. He was by
Bewildered out of Lady Cecily. Bewildered was the sire of
those splendid 'chasers, Young Pretender and Chaos, so the
unprepossessing creature seemed like a bargain. The deal
was struck and Our Nobby was promptly nicknamed Loppy
because of his ears.

No sooner had he been installed at the Bullen home than
all the horses went down with the 'Canadian Pox'—a disease
comparatively rare among horses—and the source of
infection was traced directly to the 'bargain' newcomer. As
might be expected he was not at all popular, but the Bullens
fed him up and got him into shape. At first Jennie and Mike,
Jane's older brother and sister, rode him as he was considered
too nappy for Jane, who was then only eleven. It was about
this time that he achieved his famous post and rails jump
with the unsuspecting Mike.

Eventually Jane was allowed to take him in hand and from
the start the two found an affinity, though his propensity for
jumping and headstrong behaviour always made him a tough
proposition for a child to ride, and probably only children
like the Bullens who were practically born in the saddle
could ever have managed him. Jane even taught him a few
party tricks like shaking hands and nuzzling for Polo mints,
of which he is inordinately fond.

Jane also discovered that much of his apparent awkward-
ness was due to his sense of humour. 'He is a great joker,'
she declares. 'Often he will start to snort and shake, and put
on a great act of alarm just to tease and show off. He is a great
show-off and loves to know he is the centre of attraction.'

Probably this is the trait more than any other which made
him an Olympic horse. He does so well at the big moment
and before an audience. This must have stood in his stead

in place of experience, for the interesting thing is that he has only competed in five Three-Day Combined Training Events in his life including the Olympics. It was only the year before the Olympic Games that he first tried his luck at a Three-Day Event.

This was at Badminton in 1967—it was also Jane's first experience of Three-Day Eventing. The couple came fifth.

That same year he came third at Burghley and was put on the short list for the European Championships at Punchestown. Only ten days before Burghley Jane found him sweating and distressed in his box and it was found he had put his back out in three places. Equine osteopath Herrod Taylor managed to put things right, but it was not until the day before the Burghley Trials were due to start that Jane attempted to put even her slight weight on to his saddle.

An accident after Burghley that year prevented him going to Punchestown. 'We shall never know how it happened,' said Jane, 'but somehow he got himself caught up with a "saddle horse".' (The wooden stand used in most stables for keeping saddles on when they are not in use.) Undoubtedly genuinely frightened for one of the few times in his life, Our Nobby made off, dragging the 'saddle horse' with him. Still dragging it he jumped a fence, and although he was not seriously hurt the whole incident was enough to put him out of training, so he never made the European Championships in 1967.

Jane always said that whether he was selected to go to Mexico or not, Our Nobby would be retired at the end of 1969 when he would be fifteen.

She has kept her word—refusing an offer of £8,000 for the horse which once cost £150, and has won £650 in prize money—a record beaten only by the great Lochinvar whose story is told in another chapter.

Early in 1969 Jane was asked to take him to the Players' Theatre in Villiers Street at Charing Cross in London to appear in a charity appeal for the Sunshine Home for Blind

Babies. 'It was the first time anyone had suggested Our Nobby should appear on the stage and I wondered how he would react to the footlights and to the unfamiliar surroundings,' said Jane. 'But he simply loved it and behaved like a professional actor. He has always loved praise and applause.'

So now the Olympic 'pony' confines his public performances to appearing at charity appeals—always, as he has done throughout his life, giving a magnificent performance when the big moment comes.

5 Pasha

The Emperor Napoleon, marching from Elba to Paris at the start of his 100 days before Waterloo, is reported to have said, when the town of Grenoble surrendered without a shot: 'Before Grenoble I was an adventurer—at Grenoble I was a reigning prince.'

His fate was not a glorious one, yet history remembers him as a small, self-made man of genius who fought all the more fiercely to become great because of his diminutive size.

The prince of this story is also a small adventurer with humble origins, but his name, Pasha, is a Turkish title of honour. And the annals of Equine History will remember him with pride for the size of his heart not his lack of inches. A fourteen-year-old chestnut gelding, 15 hands 1 inch high, born of mixed parentage—his sire was an Arab stallion and his dam a Thoroughbred/Suffolk Punch mare—Pasha stormed the fortress of Badminton and it surrendered almost without a shot.

Pasha's jockey, eighteen-year-old student Richard Walker, was equally surprising. Born in Johannesburg of unusual parents—now teaching a Muscle Relaxation Technique in Putney, Richard was the current Junior European Champion and a real outsider beside four Olympic Gold Medallists. But victory brought recognition, and five months afterward Pasha represented his country in the European Championships, winning a Gold medal with the British team and the Individual Silver as well. The little horse who was sent home by the Duke of Beaufort for bad behaviour on the hunting field had come a long way.

At Waterstock, Oxfordshire, where Richard lives as a pupil of Swedish trainer Lars Sederholm, there was little to be learned of Pasha's background. 'I didn't ride him until he was nine years old,' Richard told me, 'so I don't know much about what happened to him before that. But there was a little old farmer fellow who appeared at the door to his stable at Badminton, and said he'd bred him, just about eight miles down the road. He was a little old boy, but I never got his name.'

Harry Matthews has rosy apple cheeks and bright blue eyes that considered me speculatively as I walked across his ploughed field at Doynton, Gloucestershire. He brought his tractor to a stop and politely took off his cap. 'Pasha's dam Prudence, was a right one,' he said, 'she was always difficult to get in foal, but I had had two foals from her and wanted a third. She didn't co-operate at all and after I had tried a couple of premium stallions I sent her to this little 13h. 2in. Arab called Rhudan, as a last resort.'

The passionate temperament of the East succeeded where British reserve had failed and the tiny chestnut colt was foaled in the late spring of 1956—the last of his line—for Prudence was found dead in the field not long afterwards. The big-boned, strongly-made mare of 16 hands had been a gift to Matthews from Mrs. Eileen Pitman across the road at Doynton House, and in the autumn of 1965 Squire Pitman was so attracted to the sprightly little colt that he walked across the road and offered Matthews £25 for him, thinking he might later suit his daughter, Valerie.

Matthews wouldn't sell, but Chris Pitman was determined to buy, and the following spring he tried again. 'I told Harry that as I had offered him £25 before the winter, and I reckoned it cost me about £12. 10s. to winter one of my heifers, I would up the offer to £37. 10s. He accepted.'

At two years old Pasha was backed and at three years the

Pitmans' groom, George Potter, started to break him in. 'He were a proper devil,' said George, 'and very naughty. He used to rear like blazes.' Perhaps Pasha did just that when eighteen-year-old Valerie rode out of the village bareback on him, and had the misfortune to run straight into the Beaufort hounds. Whatever happened that day, it was enough—no later training could persuade the hot-blooded Arab to understand the English passion, unlike his stout-hearted dam who had carried Mrs. Eileen Pitman through many seasons with the Beaufort.

Richard Walker, who never took the horse hunting because he knew him to be wild and uncontrollable, suggests that although 'he might have had a scare once ... it's probably just a little bit in his nature to be excited that way. He's really much better on his own.' British domination of the Three-Day Event may start on the hunting field—but not for those champions. Maybe Pasha is a throwback to his ancestors who travelled across the desert with a lone Bedouin for company.

Pasha learnt to jump with Mrs. Pam Carruthers (resident course-builder at Hickstead Show-jumping Centre) nearby at Nettleton, but even she remembers: 'Hunting him was such a nightmare that I used to turn round and go off in the opposite direction. But generally the fox did the same—and the field came back leaving us just as badly off as before!'

Her painstaking methods were sound. She taught him to extend over Cavaletti at the trot and to jump over raised ones still at the trot: 'I had been concentrating so hard on making him jump cleanly and properly from a trot that when I took him to a Foxhunter class at Wapley Show three months later, I believe I had only once jumped a fence with him from a canter.' He learnt how to bend his back, and today seldom hits a fence. Pam commented, 'I am delighted my methods worked so well—it makes all the difference to have a well-known horse to hold up as an example before my pupils!'

After a spell back with the Pitmans, Pasha was lent to Flavia Phillips not far away, and when she took him to Chippenham Show on August Bank Holiday in 1962 he was spotted by the Phillimore family from Sussex, as a pony for their eldest son, Francis—and changed hands again.

Richard Walker had been born and brought up in a big house in the suburbs of Johannesburg, learning to ride once a week at a local riding school next door to the stables of South Africa's famous international show-jumper, Bob Grayston (a coincidence). But in 1961 Richard's father—an exponent of the mysterious 'Alexander Technique'—brought his wife and five children home to England, and Richard was sent to prep school in London. 'I don't remember its name, but I know I disliked it intensely,' recalled Richard.

He joined the Cowdray Pony Club in Sussex through his father's long-time friendship with Claud Phillimore, and spent his holidays with his family in the Phillimores' gardener's cottage, riding in gymkhanas. When he had been in England three years, passing from another prep school at Liphook, near Haslemere, to St. Edwards School, Oxford, Francis Phillimore offered him Pasha. 'Francis was up at Cambridge,' Richard remembered, 'and preferred to spend his vacations sailing.'

The Cowdray Pony Club District Commissioner, Mrs. Marjorie Hance, had seen many children come and go during her time as Instructress—but this pupil was different. She taught him the elements of dressage, put him in the Event team shortly afterwards and watched him win the Individual award. At the championships at Burghley he and Pasha finished third out of 90 competitors, taking the cup for the best boy. Richard recalls: 'I don't think I ever really had a feel for dressage as such, in the Pony Club—I just know that when Mrs. Hance said I had the horse on the bit, I was doing all right.'

After winning a Cup for the best round by a hunt member in the Open Event at the Cowdray Hunter Trials the following spring (1966)—it had to be returned as Richard was only in the Pony Club—Mrs. Hance arranged for Richard and

Pasha to train during the summer holidays with Lars Seder-holm. Later in the autumn the partnership again won the Boys Cup at the Cheltenham Pony Club championships, also contributing to the team victory, and Richard decided to leave school—'I'd had quite enough!'—and make his career with horses.

He started at Waterstock in January 1967, and was joined in February by Pasha. 'Colonel Moseley wrote to my parents asking me to train for the British Junior Event Team, so they bought Pasha for me and sent him up to Oxfordshire,' Richard told me. 'It was wonderful to have a horse of my own at last.' Under the sharp eye of the Swede, horse and rider went from strength to strength, finishing second Individually in the Junior European championship at Eridge that August, and going on to win the Individual Title in 1968 at Craon, France, as well as finishing in the British team placed second. The faith of Marjorie Hance was well-justified—and by a strange coincidence the Pitmans' groom, George Potter, had been instructed by her husband the late Colonel Jack Hance, when serving with the King's Troop at Kirkee in India many years previously.

Badminton 1969 was described as a 'Vintage' year, yet the victor was the youngest in its nineteen year history. Placed ninth after the Dressage, Pasha moved up to take the lead when Australian veteran Bill Roycroft was penalised for a technical refusal at the Quarry on Warrathoola. The three other Gold Medallists had now dropped out, and the penalisation stood after a check by Control on closed circuit T.V., leaving Pasha in first place (plus 40.13) for the show-jumping —but less than one fence divided the first five horses. Waiting by the wings to jump the penultimate round was a test of nerves more-experienced men have often funked, but not this teenager Richard Walker.

Still cool and collected after one and a half hours, Richard and Pasha made no error and won the trophy. What was his worst moment, I wondered? Richard described it: 'I jumped the drop into Huntsman's Close but instead of going straight on, Pasha turned to the right. The rails he made for were the only part you could see between the trees, so he'd seen his line straight away. It wasn't the way I'd intended to go, and if the rails—about 5ft. 3in. had been more solid we would have turned over. As it was, I nearly came off the side door, and would have done if the crowd hadn't been stationed to the left. If he had gone left-handed instead of right-handed, I would have lost my balance and come right off instead of managing to scramble from half-way up his neck back to the saddle.'

He concluded: 'Pasha's a horse I get a real kick out of riding across country—and when I think that if I'd been on another horse at a moment of a nasty turn, then I know how lucky I am.'

There was a similar horror at the European Championships, Haras du Pin, France, in September 1969. Pasha jumped uninvited into a ditch at the foot of a bank topped by a rail-and-drop (Fence 8), jumped out again happily and on up the bank. The French course was the biggest many experienced riders had seen since Stockholm Olympics, 1956. But after a good Dressage of 62.51 (6th) Pasha went round the 17 mile Endurance phase as if it were a Pony Club event, to take the Individual lead when the six teams had finished, with the fastest round and a two-day total of plus 43.09.

Even when British Individual Mary Gordon-Watson on Cornishman V passed them by two points later on, Richard was enormously proud of 'my wonderful little horse', for the British team (Derek Allhusen-Lochinvar, Polly Hely Hutchinson-Count Jasper, Ben Jones-The Poacher) were leading. On the last day, the chance of another European Title came and went in the five seconds it took Pasha to reach the penultimate fence still clear, from the one before, hit it, and keep the position of runner-up, Individually. But to be the mainstay of the triumphant team was enough for Richard Walker.

Pasha, now retired from Eventing, is continuing with Combined Training (dressage and show-jumping) events. He is an enterprising little horse who runs his life on snap decisions—and Richard describes him as having: 'The speed of the Thoroughbred, the colour, looks and temperament of the Arab, and the shaggy coat of a Suffolk Punch in winter.'

As a working pupil Richard earns nothing and exists on pocket money from his parents. He has won scholarships, but: '£50 doesn't go a very long way with horses,' and how to remain amateur until Munich is the problem. 'My only hope,' he said, 'is to marry a rich girl—but rich girls who want to get married are difficult to find!'

The *Horse and Hound* advertisement (February 1st, 1969) listed the impressive achievements of the chestnut horse— the asking price, not published, was £900. Compared to the £19,000 paid for Ireland's Badminton and European champion Durlas Eile, £9,000 would have been cheap. I cannot help wondering if that man who turned up his nose at the offer isn't feeling very sore indeed.

6 Kilbarry

'A proper soldier's horse!'

That perhaps is the most fitting and sincere epitaph any soldier can speak of his charger. It is the epitaph of Kilbarry, probably one of the greatest Event horses of all time, spoken by his partner Lt.-Colonel Frank Weldon. Together they rode to so many triumphs between 1951 and the spring of 1957 when Kilbarry was tragically killed by breaking his neck at the first fence of his first One-Day Event of that Combined Training season.

'Others have inevitably taken the place where once he reigned supreme, but to those who knew him best there will never be another quite like him,' Lt.-Colonel Weldon wrote to me much later.

Certain it is that today's growing interest in Combined Training, both as a participator and a spectator sport, owes much to this Irish-bred bay gelding. Foaled in 1946, his sire was Malbrook and his dam Heligoland. Lt.-Colonel Weldon —then Major—bought him in 1951 from a Newark farmer, the late Roland Jarrow.

At that time Lt.-Colonel Weldon's only interest in competitive sport was in racing and he bought Kilbarry with a view to winning a race at the Grand Military Meeting at Sandown Park or the R.A. Gold Cup. But for a couple of unconnected accidents Kilbarry would probably have spent his life racing.

The first was an accident to Frank Weldon himself. He

had just been posted to command the King's Troop, Royal
Horse Artillery, and was wondering what worthwhile sport
he could think of for five young officers under him to take up
in their spare time. Racing was out of the question as they
had only their Government chargers, which although good
healthy animals were unlikely to be able to give highly bred
racehorses a run for their money.

Someone suggested Badminton to the Major. The now
famous Three-Day horse trials at the Duke of Beaufort's
beautiful estate in Gloucestershire had only just started.
Many keen and interested horsemen, including Major
Weldon, had never even heard of the trials, but when he did
Major Weldon thought they sounded worthwhile so the
following year two of the young officers, on their Government
chargers, and Major Weldon entered, on a mare called Liza
Mandy.

The two young officers got round the course safely and
returned to London delighted. Weldon finished up in
hospital after a stinking fall in the cross-country section. 'This
made me think that to do any good in this newfangled sport
I would have to take more trouble,' he said.

Kilbarry had started to show great promise in his first
point-to-points and hunting with the Belvoir and Quorn.
He jumped brilliantly, with great natural ability, and had
high courage. It occurred to Lt.-Colonel Weldon that Kilbarry
might be a better Event horse than Liza Mandy. Even so, he
might never have got launched on an Eventing career but for
a second mishap.

A severe coughing epidemic swept through the St. John's
Wood stable of the R.H.A. and although most of the troop
horses quickly recovered, Kilbarry was left with a permanent
thickening of the wind. He had a Hobdey operation, but
this was not completely successful and he was always 'noisy'
afterwards. This seemed to put paid to his hopes of a brilliant
racing career—although he did win a couple of small point-
to-points.

However, these two blows were to prove the start of a life for which it seemed he was obviously destined.

Lt.-Colonel Weldon now concentrated Kilbarry on Combined Training. In 1953, still a complete novice, he won the Open class at Stowell Park very early in the season, and then, with three other horses of Kings Troop he went to Badminton.

It so happened that this was a full-scale International event —the first European Championships ever held were being staged.

The night before the competition started the selectors of the British team changed their minds on its composition and Kilbarry was included. This was indeed both a compliment to the horse and a terrific chance to take on the part of the selectors. Kilbarry had never before competed in a Three-Day event. His earlier triumph at Stowell Park had been completed in one day. However, he soon had the critics silenced and the seal set on his own greatness. He came second overall and helped the British team win their first ever International Event in this sport.

During that year he won several One-Day events, and in 1954 started the season by again winning Stowell Park. He then went on to Badminton where a timekeeping error robbed him of first place. It was during the steeplechase phase and the error was of a whole minute. This robbed him of 24 bonus points, and made his final placing 3 points behind the winner, instead of putting him in the lead by 20 points. However, that is all part of life and Kilbarry that autumn made his first competition trip abroad to Basle in Switzerland.

He was a member of the British team which won their second European Championship and at the same time made history by winning first, second and third individual places.

Kilbarry was second, beaten by Crispin ridden by Bertie Hill.

In 1955 Kilbarry set up a record which no other horse has so far challenged. He was unbeaten in any competition that season great or small and he contested many.

They included show-jumping, hunter trials, a point-to-point and five One-Day trials. They also included the European Championships which were that year held in Windsor Park. Kilbarry took the Individual title, and was a member of the team which won the Championship for Great Britain, completing her hat-trick. He completed the season by winning the Harewood Three-Day Event in the autumn—an event which then was second only to Badminton in toughness and importance.

In 1956 he was on the short list for the Olympic Games which that year were held in Stockholm.

With the rest of the potential team he went to Badminton. Those who were fortunate enough to be at the Badminton trials that year will remember the neck and neck struggle for supremacy between Kilbarry and High and Mighty ridden by Sheila Willcox. After the dressage on the first day Kilbarry was fractionally ahead. Then on the second day, almost unbelievably, both horses scored maximum bonus points for time on all phases. On the third day, the show-jumping phase, Kilbarry could not afford to lose a mark if he were to hang on to his lead over High and Mighty. The crowd watched breathlessly, as he hung on to his lead and set up another record. He won a hat-trick of THREE Three-Day events in succession.

Six weeks later at the Olympic Games at Stockholm he was a member of the British team with Countryman, owned by the Queen and ridden by Bertie Hill, and Wild Venture owned by Mr. E. Marsh and ridden by Major Lawrence Rook. The team won the Gold medal—an amazing feat when one considers how new to Britain was the sport compared to many other countries.

Once again Kilbarry set up a record. He won the individual Bronze medal—the first time a British horse had ever won an individual medal at the Olympic Games.

The rest of the 1955 season was a blank one for Kilbarry

as Lt.-Colonel Weldon was fully occupied with the Suez crisis and could not compete.

The spring of 1957, which was to bring to such a tragic end the career of this brilliant horse, started off full of promise. Stationed in Kent, Lt.-Colonel Weldon entered him at some Hunter Trials and he won three classes in one day. A week later he was killed, taking a chance at a deceptively innocent-looking obstacle which experienced riders always say cause the worst falls.

'He died instantaneously of a broken neck. That was the only consolation,' said Lt.-Colonel Weldon much later. 'He went out like a lion in all his strength, tempestuously, as he had lived.'

For Kilbarry, as would be expected of a horse with his achievements, was a temperamental headstrong animal. 'A proper monkey,' is how Lt.-Colonel Weldon described him.

Out hunting he would buck and sidle prodigiously for the first half-hour, making determined efforts to roll in every puddle and also to catch his rider unawares—a characteristic which, according to Lt.-Colonel Weldon, never left him to the end of his days.

In the stable he was as good as gold with his own groom, but if a stranger were foolhardy enough to wander into the box he chased him forth, teeth bared and ears back, with the unfortunate intruder flying for his life.

Through his competitive career, which included racing, show-jumping, hunter trials—he won the Working Hunter Championship at the Richmond Royal Show one year—as well as Eventing, Kilbarry did his full daily duty as an Officer's Charger with the Kings Troop R.H.A. He took part in many ceremonial parades and Royal Salutes and in 1953 he did his full training for the Coronation Procession.

However, this was the year of his first attempt at Badminton and he returned to London so fit and full of himself that Lt.-Colonel Weldon decided to ride a less-pretentious horse for the great Coronation day. He had broken a bone in his neck steeplechasing and thought Kilbarry might be a bit hard to hold.

'I bitterly regretted it,' he said. 'I discovered that it took a horse with more courage than I thought to face the thousands of people thronging the streets of London, waving flags, papers and hats and cheering. Kilbarry would have done the job much better than the charger I took.'

Apart from his countless successes in home events, what a record this great horse leaves in international competition. A member of the British team which won the European Championships in 1953, 1954 and 1955 and the Gold medal at the Olympics in 1956. And in all these events never out of the first three individual places.

'There will never be another quite like him.'

7 Barberry

By rights, Barberry should have died as a five-year-old, been permanently maimed as an eight-year-old and put out of action through serious injury a score of times since. But his kind come tougher than they look. It is not so easy to get rid of one like him, who has as many lives as the most tenacious cat—a fact that Richard Meade, his rider, discovered over their long years together. For the partnership of horse and man were to set up a record of eight years in top-class Three-Day Event competition, and five years in succession with the British team—only being deprived of their second Olympics by a shock fall on a false take-off.

For one who started life as an undersized scrap, and seemed to have so little respect for his own skin, Barberry possessed an astonishing ability to cling on to life. For he was later to impale half his body on a wooden stake, nearly to bash a horse-box to pieces while travelling, to tear his elbow to ribbons on a tarmac road, to hang himself up in wire fences—and finally to fall into a ditch, breaking his sacroilium and three ribs.

But there is little thought that such incidents will deter his activities, although inevitably the last one curtailed his eventing career. Indeed, it looks as though, fit and ready to go for a season's hunting, he may even outlast his jockeys!

Barberry—who threw away a Gold medal at the Olympics through inexperience, who was Individual second at the World Championships, in the winning team at the European

Championships and triumphed at the Burghley Three-Day Event—was a most remarkably consistent performer. And for a horse described by his rider as a bad traveller, he put up an incredible total of miles on the log—Germany, Japan, Russia were all part of the itinerary.

But perhaps such stamina was to be expected, for he was bred both for speed and staying power. His sire, Beauford, by Fairford out of Carl Rosa, was a middle-distance horse who won six races, including the Irish Lincolnshire twice and the Priory Park Handicap at Goodwood. There, obviously, was the speed. But it was his dam, Caraway Seed, who provided the stamina, and incidentally the horticultural names, for her female antecedents ran back as Columbine, Olive and Blackberry—the last-mentioned deriving, delightfully, from Young Blossom and Plumpudding.

Caraway Seed came from a long line of light thoroughbred stock that had been bred in Co. Kildare for at least 100— probably 200—years, on an estate called Killadoon, the family home of Miss Kitty (short for Catharine) Clements. Caraway Seed, I learnt from Miss Clements, had been hunted for thirteen seasons by herself, as well as being driven in harness for two years in the War. She had won the Kildare Hunt members race in 1945, coming fourth in the Kildare Hunt Cup at Punchestown, and was described as being 'A small brown mare of great character and determination'.

Her brother, Buckthorn, raced by Miss Clements' brother, won two point-to-points and a hunters' chase in 1935, as well as eight steeplechases in England. All the mares seem to have been driven as well as ridden, including the delicious Blackberry, who was reputed to be 'The fastest driving mare in the country!'

The origins of this intrepid family, are unknown. All Miss Clements could tell me was when her grandfather inherited the Killadoon estate in 1878, the horses were already established there. Certainly the family tree is a distinctive one, featuring such immortals as St. Simon, who ran over all distances (he appears three times), Ormonde his great rival, Hampton, Bay Ronald, Galopin. With such a start to life, Barberry should surely not have lacked dash!

He was foaled at the Roristown Stud in Co. Meath, on Thursday May 12th, 1955, late in the evening. Miss Clements told me: 'I first saw him on Friday the 20th and was disappointed to find such a tiny foal with thin little legs like needles—no bone—but he was very shapely, rather like a little fairy foal!' By the time he came home to Killadoon on July 4th, however, he was already developing—and finally grew 'as fine a set of legs as anyone could wish for', as Miss Clements put it.

As a four-year-old Barberry was long-reined and backed by Miss Betty Hamilton, who was working at Killadoon at the time. Later he was sent to Mrs. Mainguy, whose groom Paddy McEntee brought him along slowly and took him hunting, declaring him to be 'The most marvellous horse that ever was born', and later still, at the end of the 59-60 season he was hunted by Miss Clements herself. She recalls:

'After a summer at home I thought experience of the Meath ditches would do him good, as he had mainly been out in the bank part of the Kildare country, so he went to Mary Rose Robinson (now Mrs. Seamus Hayes) who took him out first with the North Kildare Harriers. Having jumped the first few fences perfectly, she was filled with confidence and sailed away on her own at a straggly hedge into a lane. She said afterwards that Barberry took off perfectly, but seemed to check in mid-air—and they fell heavily into the lane.

'Barberry got up and then fell down again, and to her horror she saw a huge wooden stake embedded in his chest. She tried to pull it out but couldn't do so. Luckily her cries for help were heard by Lady Carew's groom, Tynan, who pulled out the stake, got Barberry to his feet and put him in someone's trailer to be driven back to his stable.

'But when the vet, Mr. Bryan Magee, was called, he found a lump in front of the saddle flap which he feared might be a broken rib. However, Mary Rose's mother had gone down to look at the place of the fall, and brought back the stake—the pointed head of which was broken off. Mr. Magee immediately operated and extracted the head from inside Barberry. Mrs. Robinson had an infra-red lamp set up in Barberry's stable, and for days he stood under it without moving while Mary Rose hand-fed him. Under her nursing and Bryan Magee's doctoring, he made a full recovery.'

Surprisingly, it was not the idea of hunting or jumping that upset Barberry afterwards—although it was decided that Mary Rose should start him off on dressage rather than continue hunting when his wound had healed. What he would not stand was travelling in a horse-box—and the memory of his nightmare ride home in the trailer with the stake embedded in his chest has remained with him for the rest of his life. He suffered from claustrophobia, and for a long time after the accident had to be ridden for hours before he would enter a horse-box.

After a summer's grass in 1961 Mary Rose Robinson was too busy to continue Barberry's education, so he went to Susan Lanigan O'Keefe. Miss Clements explained: 'I wanted to find a good home for him, but I did not want to sell him, although I had too many horses and knew we should part with him.'

Chance, in the guise of twenty-two-year-old Richard Meade, then intervened. Whilst stationed with the 11th Hussars in Northern Ireland Richard had often gone down to hunt with the Carews at Castletown—and Diana Conolly-Carew knew that Richard was looking for a horse. She suggested to Miss Clements that Richard was the man for Barberry, and Richard, now up at Cambridge, went across to Kildare to have a look.

'After watching the Rome Olympics, I was determined to find a horse for Tokyo,' Richard told me. 'Barberry was the fourth I saw, and I knew at once he was the one for me.' But their first jump together was not propitious. Barberry can-

tered up to a small artificially-built stone wall in the middle
of a field, stopped, then did such an almighty leap over it
that Richard was nearly jumped off. 'I thought he must really
have a jump in him to do that,' commented Richard. So the
deal was done, and the horse was permanently leased to
Richard on the understanding that when he retired he
should come home to Ireland.

Although his hunting had ended in such disaster, Barberry
had still learnt a great deal about self-preservation from
following hounds. Richard described him as a 'tremendously
suspicious horse. I found that when I rode him up to a puddle
he would stop and look. If he could see the bottom he would
walk through—if not, he'd jump it! And I think this careful-
ness stood him in good stead later on, for instead of getting
himself into trouble, he was able to anticipate difficulties'.

At the end of January 1962, Barberry, seven years old,
standing 16.0½ hands high cut rather a dashing figure with
his nearly black coat, when he arrived in Cambridge to take
over his new duties. But he had a lot to learn, particularly
about dressage, and when term ended Richard took himself
and the horse off to expert Paul Rodzianko, for some last-
minute schooling before Barberry's first event—Crookham
Horse Trials, Nr. Aldershot, at the end of March.

Altogether the pair competed in three novice one-day
events that Spring, coming sixth in one of them, before joining a team going to Amsterdam in the summer, for an international students rally organised by the Dutch. The British
student team won, but Richard remembers: 'It was not very
difficult!' That summer vacation was spent learning more
about eventing from two people who have given much of
their lives to encouraging horsemanship in others—Colonel
and the late Mrs. V. D. S. Williams. Greatly improved by their
tuition Richard and Barberry finished third at Eridge Horse
Trials in August, later winning the Open Event at Tweseldown, though still a novice, and also winning the Intermediate
Event at Chatsworth.

Before being laid off for the winter's rest Barberry went back to hunting, as the Cottesmore country where he was then kept was only an hour's drive from Cambridge, and happily there was no hangover from his previous experience. Badminton Three-Day Event in the Spring of 1963 was cancelled because of bad weather, but the organisers put on a Two-Day Event instead—in which Barberry came second. And at Munich later that year, where a form of unofficial international championship was held, it seemed inevitable that the promising young horse should combine his first Three-Day Event with his first appearance in a British team, going well enough to finish 15th.

Great Britain (James Templer and M'Lord Connolly, Susan Fleet and The Gladiator, Captain Jeremy Beale and Victoria Bridge and Richard with Barberry) came out as the winners—with Poland second and Germany third, while M'Lord Connolly walked away with his second successive international Individual title. But although ultimately a complete success, the journey across the Channel to the Continent had nearly been the end of Barberry.

While the horse-box was on the boat he got an acute attack of claustrophobia, smashing the partitions of the box and somehow managing to thrust his forefeet through the end, into the cubby-hole where the driver sits. The boat had no stabilisers, and no one could move him—so he had to be doped so that he could stay like that for the rest of the trip. It sounds horrible, yet Barberry's instinct for self-preservation had, if subconsciously, been working hard, and he suffered no damage to his legs which remained unblemished throughout his career.

Munich, however, had made such an impression on Richard that, as he had just left Cambridge and decided to devote a year to riding, he went back with Barberry to the riding school where the Event had been held—and spent three and a half months improving his technique. The instructor, Ottakar Pohlmann, had won the Harewood Three-Day

Event in 1958, and ridden in the victorious German team at the European Championships in 1959. 'He taught me a lot,' Richard remembers, 'and I felt that though we have all the facilities at home, and the best horses, one can learn an awful lot of the technical side from people on the Continent. I certainly found the experience of riding trained horses, as well as Barberry, invaluable.'

But at Badminton 1964, when British selectors were beginning to make a list for Tokyo, Richard's Olympic plans took a beating. He recalled: 'The going was very heavy, and I knew beforehand I hadn't given Barty (as he is known) enough fast work, but I didn't expect such disastrous results. Mistakenly, I rode for maximum bonus on the 'chase course —and blew him up. So he had a couple of stops and a fall across country.

'Up until then Barty had been regarded as an up-and-coming horse; but this performance, largely my fault, really put us out.' And at Tidworth in May an attempt to retrieve his reputation misfired completely.

'I had a very much fitter horse there,' Richard told me, 'But in trying to prove that he could go fast, we cut a corner and had a stupid fall, literally through taking a fence at an angle and hitting a grower in the middle of it. We turned turtle, and although we still got maximum bonus, that didn't help!' But there was still five months to go before Tokyo, and Richard refused to give up. 'I knew I should have to win Eridge or Burghley, or both, to have a chance,' he said.

The storm tactics worked. Barty won Eridge and Burghley, plus a place on the Olympic team with a fortnight's notice, joining Mike Bullen (Sea Breeze), Sergeant Ben Jones (Master Bernard) and James Templer (M'Lord Connolly)—a team to contend with, or so it seemed. But once more disaster struck, this time not on the journey, but on arrival. Barty got colic, and could not be ridden until just before the Games opened. Well behind in his work schedule, his fitness was much in doubt, and the decision to start him was not taken until a few hours prior to the initial ceremonies.

When Barberry went into the lead on the individual placings, after the cross-country on the second day, however, the
decision to run him would seem to have been vindicated. But
possibly the enforced rest beforehand at just the wrong time
exaggerated the effects of stiffness and exhaustion, and that,
combined with his inexperience in the show-jumping ring
made for too many troubles. Holding a tenuous $3\frac{1}{4}$ points
lead over Italian Mauro Checcoli on Surbean, Barberry made
three mistakes and dropped, with time faults, to eighth place.
Master Bernard did the same, dropping from fifth to ninth
place, as the final misfortune to a team already eliminated
the previous day.

Richard comments: 'The biggest disappointment was the
team—everything has to be geared to that, and individual
success comes by the way. One just hopes that one does so well
as a team that one gets first, second, third, individually! It
was very exciting to be in the lead, but I didn't find it affected
me particularly; I had been in the lead at Burghley a month
before, and jumped a clear round to win, but at Tokyo, it
just happened differently.

The following year, 1965, was uneventful for Britain.
Barberry and Richard Meade joined the British team for the
European Championships in Moscow, but the duellists proved
to be the Irish and the Russians—with victory finally taken
by the latter, leaving Britain in third place, and individual
honours going to Poland's veteran Marian Babierecki on Volt.

But 1966 was, for Barberry, another story. Richard had put
in some hard slogging on the show-jumping, and proved it
in public at Burghley in September, by jumping a clear
round to gain two places and win the individual Silver
Medallion in the World Championship. The British team,
with its preponderance of ladies—Richard was the odd man
out—was not a success; only Barberry and Christine Sheppard's Fenjirao (seventh) finishing the course.

Richard remembers particularly: 'At a party afterwards,

the Russians—whose team had unfortunately been eliminated by lameness—became very enthusiastic about Barberry,
and offered generously: "You give us four Barberrys, we
give you eight Pakets!"' (Paket is their magnificent stallion
who finished sixth.)

The European Championships at Punchestown in 1967
were notable for the British team victory. But Barberry fell
a victim to one of the steeplechase fences, dangerously
widened by the Technical Delegate, to look like a bank. Being
an Irish horse and used to changing feet on top, Barberry
tried to 'bank' this and, like many others, crashed heavily.
But horse and rider picked themselves up, plus broken collar-
bone for Richard, finishing the three-days in impeccable style
that included a maximum bonus cross-country. Unlike Bill
Roycroft in Rome, their score was not, eventually, needed—
but it could have been, and this is the essence of team riding—
to finish whatever.

The end, or almost the end of Barberry's career came
suddenly, and unexpectedly, a year later. Once more the
Olympic short-list were competing for a team place to
Mexico, at the Burghley Trials: but this time Barberry had
no need to gatecrash. As almost the last of the big entry to
start the testing course, he had the worst of the going—but
as a 'possible' he had been instructed to gallop on. At the
take-off to fence 23, a very awkward rails-in-a-dip followed by
a ditch, Barberry's feet slipped and gave beneath him as he
took off, somersaulting over the rails to land with his back on
the railway sleepers boarding the ditch on the far side. The
take-off, already battered to destruction by the many falls
and refusals, had given way completely.

And that was that. Four years of hoping, training and
saving energy for the big occasion were gone in seconds. Barberry had a broken sacroilium and three broken ribs.
Richard, who had commented beforehand, walking the
course: 'That's a good fence—I like a challenge,' said afterwards: 'If only I had known that the take-off was poached, I

would have taken off a stride further back—from the top of the bank.'

He was unlucky. Not being a championship, there were no runners posted to keep the starters informed of deterioration in the going.

Barberry took his last and final bow at Badminton the following Spring. After apparently a complete recovery, he started at Crookham in March, and seemed to be in no trouble. But when he stumbled, landing in the lake at Badminton, Richard pulled up and called it a day, realising that his back was painful over a drop fence. This was after a brilliant dressage test of 39 penalties, and a maximum bonus on the steeplechase course. What a horse! A video-tape recording showed that Barberry was not jumping with his usual spring —and Richard decided to retire him there and then.

Bold, tireless, highly strung, loyal and, above all, the owner of a gallant heart. What more could a man ask for in his horse? Richard sums him up: 'Barberry is very sensitive to touch. He always tries his best to do what you want—so long as you don't confuse him. This happened once at Burghley in the World Championships—he did a smashing first half of the dressage test, something confused him, and his concentration went—so he blew up.

'He's like an artist—temperamental. You have to play him like a highly tuned instrument.'

In the hands of a rider who understands opera as well as the delicate movements of the dressage test, or the leap through the air over solid timber—Barberry was fit to sing on any stage.

8 Paket

Murder, starvation, theft—these crimes become common-place in the lurid glow of gold. My story, however, concerns nothing so destructive, but it is still a tale of failure. Of a man who staked out his claim, only to take the wrong path to the mine.

Pavel Deev (pronounced Day-yev, and more correctly written in European form as Deyev), a popular and gifted Russian horseman, was not unique in his blunder at the Mexico Olympics. He joined the celebrated Harry Freeman-Jackson who lost his way on St. Finbarr at Rome, together with Irish hopes of a Bronze medal—but I believe Pavel Deyev to be the only man to lose an individual Gold medal in such a way.

The scene is a plateau, high up in the Mexican hinterland, at Avandaro. The painted jumps are laid out for the last act of the 1968 Olympic Three-Day Event. Perhaps 6,000 people are gathered round the attractive Golf Club to watch the final drama, and they are certainly not to be cheated of that.

The four chief actors—Frenchman Jean-Jacques Guyon with Pitou, American Jimmy Wofford with Kilkenny, Russian Pavel Deyev with Paket and Briton Derek Allhusen with Lochinvar, placed in that order—have scarcely the price of one fence to spare between them. It is asking a great deal of tired stiff horses to produce the suppleness necessary for an accurate round—and so it proves at first.

The American horse, revived with oxygen on the finishing line the previous day, is even more unlucky now. He

r Nobby, the Olympic pony
den by student nurse Jane
llen in the Gold medal win-
g British team at the Olympic
mes at Mexico in 1968. No
e else had ever ridden Our
bby since Jane reached adult
sses, and after the Olympics
e retired him although he was
l only fifteen. Jane was the
t woman to be in a British
mpic team.

ha, the part-bred Arab, with
hard Walker after they won
Badminton Trials in 1969
en Richard was only eighteen.
hard was then reigning Euro-
n Junior Champion and it is
only time a junior has
l the coveted trophy given
Whitbread's at Badminton.
ha has now retired, and while
ncess Anne was on the
tralian tour with her parents
y in 1970, Richard several
es rode Doublet, the Queen's
e which Princess Anne
ally rides.

Kilbarry, ridden by his owner Major Frank Weldon, who described his as 'a proper soldier's horse.' He was one of the greatest Event horses of the fifties and his untimely death after a fall was a sad loss to Britain as well as to his owner. He was the first British horse ever to win an individual Olympic medal—a bronze in Stockholm.

treads in a boggy patch half-way round the arena—staggers—
and falls. Finally he drops to sixth place. The Briton comes
and goes, swiftly and confidently, making no error in jumping
or time, his score stands at minus 40.61. Then comes the
Frenchman, who must be unpenalised to retain his lead, although he can afford some time penalties. All goes to plan
until the last, when perhaps he relaxes his concentration for a
moment, the fence falls—his penalty score leaps up by 10, to
minus 38.86 points. He has lost the medal.

The Russian pair, now claiming the Gold, have never made
a mistake in the show-jumping arena at an international
event. Now is not the time to break that record—they have
exactly .94 of a penalty point in hand—which allows them to
exceed the time allowed by 3 seconds. There is some delay
before the Judges give the signal to start—possibly the
Russian is nervous after the wait—the value of the stakes
would be enough to weigh on anybody's nerves. The signal
is given, the horse bounds forward. The French rider and
trainer, Jack Le Goff, writing in *L'Information Hippique*,
tells the tale from here:

'One single horse could beat Pitou—Paket, of the Russian
team, ridden by that great rider Pavel Deyev. He must not
make a single mistake, and cannot be penalised more than a
fraction for time. It was the second suspense of the day! I think
that we were all ready to applaud Paket and Deyev sportingly
and sincerely, because he is a very good horse ridden by a
first-class rider. Their round started with plenty of confidence.
The horse was controlled, going strongly, a little slowly, could
possibly collect time faults. And then the unbelievable error
of direction. I think that everybody cried out, or wanted to.
What happened? The only explanation is a lapse of memory.
Consternation was on everyone's face. One could not rejoice
at an incident of this sort, even when it meant that you won a
Gold medal, and Guyon, who benefited, would agree with
me. He was extremely upset. That is what matters, that kind
of generosity of spirit—perhaps that is why we so much

enjoy the atmosphere of Three-Day Events.'

Half-way round the course, going easily, clearing the fences without trouble, Deyev had turned the wrong way, missing out the 7th fence. Mary Gordon-Watson, owner of Cornishman V, recalled afterwards: 'I don't believe anybody made a sound—I remember only a stunned silence.'

Poor Deyev. There are no phrases in the Guide book to cover a situation like that. For not only had he eliminated himself; he had also eliminated the Russian team, in line for the Bronze medal. Already on the minimum of three horses after the loss of their fourth on the previous day, the U.S.S.R. were denied their reward. That is luck, and sport. As Jimmy Elder of the Canadian team told me after they won their show-jumping Gold: 'Everybody needs their little bit of luck.' I think the whole world, or everyone in the world who heard the story, must have felt the agony of that moment.

Outside the arena Jean-Jacques Guyon ran to apologise to Pavel Deyev, But the young Russian, who had dismounted, was suffering the desolation of defeat, from which there is no reprieve—and the Frenchman's apologies could be but a bitter comfort.

Deyev told me, through a translated interview, his feelings at that moment, in a single word: 'Horror! All the members of our team sympathised with me, and tried to calm me down,' but the memory of that mistake will live with him for ever. 'Mexico,' he said, 'was a moment in my life I shall never forget.'

Of the cross-country course, which he had ridden before the worst of the rain—recording a clear though slightly slow round (possibly because of the holding going), he commented: 'The course was complicated, but quite surmountable, and the ground was much better than at Tokyo. The difficulty arose when torrential rain flooded the ground in front of the jumps. But my impressions of the whole event were that it was well-organised, full of great sporting zest and the friendly atmosphere of the Olympics.'

Paket is a beautiful liver-chestnut stallion, about 15h. 3½in. high. He was foaled in 1960, at the Kirov National Stud, in the undulating steppe lands of the Rostov region to the north of the Black Sea. Rostov itself, where the mighty Don flows into the north-eastern corner of the Sea of Azov, faces the battle-scarred Crimean Peninsula. But the fertile Don delta, famous in the last century for its Cossack settlements, is quiet and peaceful. For the Cossack families living in its valleys, the river was a symbol of security—their songs describe it as 'gentle Don, our father dear,' who protected the children orphaned by war.

Paket's sire was an Arab stallion called Pomeranets and his dam a Trakehnen mare called Emblema. Pavel Deyev told me: 'Pomeranets was tested in flat racing at the Hippodrome at Rostov (the local racetrack) and showed good results for the Arab breed, but Emblema has no sporting record. The mating of the Trakehnen mare, Emblema, with the stallion Pomeranets was intended as an experiment, and so Paket, having had the Stud's training, and shown good racing qualities, was turned over to me for further testing in sport.'

He went on: 'The Stud have this training scheme for their young stock, which Paket underwent—it includes racing on the local track as two- and three-year-olds—until I took him over from the Kirov Stud as a four-year-old.'

Deyev taught Paket dressage and jumping with the help of Anton Zhagorov, described by him as 'merited Coach of the Russian Federation'. I asked him if Paket was difficult to train, and was told: 'Yes, he was at the beginning. His training demanded more strictness and perseverance than that of a gelding or a mare.'

However wild and headstrong Paket was to start with, he has perfect manners now, and must be light to handle, for Deyev tells me: 'My son, Victor, who was born in 1961, rides Paket after I finish the main exercises.' A fearless international star in the making, evidently! Paket, who is looked after entirely by Pavel Deyev himself, is obviously a family pet—

his nickname is Pashka, the familiar Russian type of diminutive for a favourite. Deyev adds: 'He loves sugar, and begs
for it.'

One is inclined to think of a stallion as temperamental and
over-excitable, but Paket, perhaps due to his Arab blood,
does not appear to have those characteristics. Although he
has already served mares, Deyev says, and will continue to do
so when he stops competing, he is very good-tempered. 'Strong
and agile, and he also has a well-balanced nervous system,'
added his rider.

Pavel Deyev, born in 1941 in the town of Novocherkassk.
near Rostov, is the son of a Russian working-class family. 'I
grew up in a peasant house called an "Izba",' he said, 'on the
outskirts of the town. I went to a Secondary school, but did
not go on to university or college. My favourite subject was
mathematics.' No excuse for incorrect sums during the
Endurance phase, then!

'I first got on a horse at the age of seven,' he said, 'but did not
learn to ride until I was fourteen years old, at a riding school.
There I tried various kinds of riding—dressage, concours
hippique (show-jumping) and natural fences across country.
My coach noticed my abilities and suggested that I take up
Three-Day Events as my main line. While performing in
Three-Day Events, I also took part in show-jumping and
steeplechases.

'My encouragement and inspiration came from my tutors,
the Olympic dressage champion, Ivan Kizimov, and the
Coach of the Russian Federation, Anton Zhagorov. From the
early days my hero has always been Ivan Kizimov. I was
determined to be like him, and tried to mould my riding
on his style.' Pavel Deyev now lives with his wife and son in
an apartment block at Rostov, and earns his living as a
mechanic of agricultural machinery. Paket lives at a riding
school in Rostov, and it is there that his training takes place.

'The school is called "Urozhai",' Deyev told me, 'which
means Harvest. It is run by the Rostov Regional Board of the

Agricultural Sports Society "Urozhai". Its director is Merited Coach of the Russian Federation, Anton Zhagorov. It has forty sporting horses, and is attended by 150 pupils, boys and girls from twelve to sixteen, and it has an advanced group from sixteen years of age onwards.'

On training for an international team, Deyev says: 'Every member of the U.S.S.R. national team trains in accordance with his individual plan, but that must be approved by the U.S.S.R. Coaches Board. As a rule the horses are initially selected by the Federation of studs, but there are instances when riders themselves select horses. When an international team is being chosen, the whole training process takes place mainly in the riding society to which the rider belongs—so the different team members train in different climes and areas. But before going abroad, the team assembles in Moscow.'

Breeding of event horses is now starting to become a specialised business, and the successful experiment of Paket has led to further Arab cross-Trakhenen horses. Deyev says: 'Stallions are used in sport (racing), to determine their sporting qualities, before they are used for breeding purposes.

Thus, Paket, who raced on the local racetrack with other Arabs as part of his early training, was not turned over immediately to breeding as he showed such promising potential. Deyev says: 'In Three-Day Events, pure-breds are mostly used, whereas in show-jumping half-breeds prevail.'

Of the forthcoming World Championships, Deyev comments: 'I did not take Paket to the European Championships at Haras du Pin in 1969, because I wanted to spare him and give him a rest. But I am planning to take him to the World Championships at Punchestown, in September 1970, and am preparing now, in accordance with the Three-Day Event programme.'

He says the two best horses he has ever ridden are Paket and Satrap (see later), but: 'I am also training on young horses for the future, and my reserve horse for Punchestown is a stallion called Akrobat, of the Trakhenen breed, who is now in training.'

There is, in Russia, an emphasis on a racing training which is inherent in the history of their eventing, because, Deyev told me, it was the Russian Racing Federation that first got the sport of eventing off the ground. 'After the first failure of our team in international Three-Day Events, (Helsinki, 1952 when it was eliminated (the U.S.S.R. Horse Racing Federation devoted a great deal of attention to this sport, conducted U.S.S.R. championships, according to the Olympic programme—hence our improved results! Three-Day Eventing has now become a very popular and growing sport among young Russians, we have four Three-Day Events a year, and I think our young team at Haras du Pin showed much promise.'

Deyev himself, Russian National Champion in 1965 on Paket and consistently in the line-up in the National Championships since 1962, first rode in a National Three-Day Event in 1957, when he was sixteen, achieving selection for the Russian team five years later, in 1962. That was the year their team came over to England, for the European Championships at Burghley—and they won. Deyev rode a horse called Satrap, ridden by Mursalimov at Rome and Chelenkov at Stockholm, and finished fifth individually.

At the Tokyo Olympics in 1964 the Russian team, consisting of Pavel Deyev on Satrap, Guerman Gaziumov on Granj, Boris Konkov on Rumb and Mursalimov on Dzhigit, finished fifth—the highest individual scorer being Gaziumov—who finished tenth. At the European Championships in 1965, Satrap had been retired but Paket was not quite ready for an international event, so Deyev was not part of the home side defending the European title in Moscow. Nevertheless, with the return of their great veteran Lev Baklychkin as captain, the title was successfully retained, Ireland and Britain taking second and third places.

In 1966 Deyev came to England for the second time, for

the World Championships, again at Burghley, and now he had Paket. The U.S.S.R. team, of Gaziumov with Gret, Baklychkin with Rulon, Konkov with Rumb and Deyev with Paket, were leading after the dressage, three of them being in the first seven. (Paket's score was 55 penalties, seventh place.) In the cross-country Paket refused at Fence 8, a nasty-looking birch pallisade with a hidden drop, thus collecting the extra 20 penalties, which, as it turned out, made the difference between third and sixth place. As it was, his 2-Day total of 23.4 put him in eighth place.

At the start of the third day, the Veterinary Inspection came as a great shock to the Russians, as the vets refused to pass Rumb, who was hopping lame. As Rulon (Baklychkin) had been eliminated during the cross-country, this meant that U.S.S.R., lying second as a team, were eliminated. I well remember the scene down at the stables that Saturday morning. Rumb, a ten-year-old stallion, very thin but hard and fit, had a beautiful bay coat with a silver blue metallic sheen I had never seen before. The morning sun caught these luminous panels over his back and quarters as he trotted up and back on three legs, and the Russians were running about as if demented, in their blue track suits, working up to an international incident. It appeared they had misunderstood the word 'fit' in the rules. Rumb, obviously 'fit' as opposed to 'soft' was not 'fit' to jump that day. I always wondered how they meant to jump him as he was! However, after a lot of explanations, equilibrium was restored.

Paket, moved up gratuitously to the seventh place vacated by Rumb, stepped up again to sixth after the final Jumping phase, in which he was clear. Christine Sheppard on Fenjirao (British team) collected 10 penalties and moved down one, Ireland won the team title, and Dr. Carlos Moratorio from the Argentine took the Individual on Chalan.

Outside in the collecting ring the teams were assembling for the Parade, but Paket, business over, had turned to pleasure—and was becoming very conscious of the ladies. Squeals and commotion could be heard even from the grandstand, and there were two men on his head trying to calm him down. As he came into the arena announced over the loud speaker, a lady outside made a plaintive call to her new suitor, and Paket gave an unmistakable stallion's scream, as he pranced round towards the grandstand, his glorious liver chestnut coat gleaming in the sun, his muscles rippling under the skin, the veins standing out in his neck.

He was indeed a proud sight, but the watchers in the stands were not sure whether to laugh or not. Some felt it was all rather indecent, that sex had no place in this setting, while others thought it a splendid joke and roared with laughter, especially when Prince Philip, trying to shake Deyev by the hand and give him his prize, found it almost impossible because of the stallion's cavortings. Deyev says of that day: 'I consider my placing of sixth in the World Championships as my greatest triumph so far.'

Which country, I asked him, did he prefer to compete in? 'I prefer competing in England, where good climate and soil contribute to one's successes.' The icy blasts of Russia, the torrents of Tokyo and Mexico, certainly, could make England sound a paradise! Deyev was also very complimentary about English riders: 'I have always regarded all British riders as the main rivals in events were I had to compete with them.' But he would not name any individual, British or otherwise, as being 'the greatest Three-Day Event rider in the world'.

'It is difficult for me to say who is the greatest Three-Day Event rider of all time, because my international record is not long. There have been, and there are, many excellent riders, but I am at a loss to say who is the greatest.' As he admits to following the results of events in Europe and the rest of the world, presumably from Russian magazines, I found that disappointing diplomacy indeed. But in truth, living, as he does, in such an isolated place, it must be difficult to give a fair assessment of riders and horses whom he hardly ever sees.

Paket's next international outing was not such a success,

Barberry, ridden by Richard Meade who were with the British team for international events for five successive years, Barberry won that Three-Day Event and a place in the Olympic team at Tokyo.

Paket, the Russian horse which was in their Olympic team at Mexico. He is ridden by Pavel Deyev and this picture of them is taken at the Urozhai Riding Club at Rostov-on-Don. This is probably the only picture of a competing Russian horse ever let out by the Russian Federation.

Gambit, the six-year-old grey owned and ridden by Sarah Roger Smith who is nineteen, clearing the Griffin fence on their way to win the valuable Novice Championship given by the Midland Bank at Chatsworth in 1969. This young couple are one of our bright hopes for the future of Eventing

but he was the only one of the Russian team at the 1967 European Championships, Punchestown, to finish the three days. Although a victim of the disastrous steeplechase course, where he had a nasty fall, the final placing of 22nd was not such a disgrace as it sounded. Due to the ill-designed additions to the steeplechase fences of take-off poles and extra gorse 'aprons' which looked solid but weren't, the steeplechase section caused massive destruction. Over half the entry had time penalties, there was no maximum bonus, one horse was killed, and about a quarter had crashing falls. The unhappy cause of this holocaust was Mr. Pedro Mayorga Equioiz, of Argentina, who—as Technical Delegate from the F.E.I.— decided to alter the obstacles. Paket, however, pulled himself together to record a faultless cross-country round, although slow, and a clear round in the show-jumping.

Although the last paragraph may infer the opposite, Pavel Deyev is, in fact, an extremely accomplished steeplechase rider! In 1965 he was third in the Grand Pardubice Steeplechase, and won the River Vaga Prize Steeplechase in Czechoslovakia. In 1966 he won both events plus a third—the Captain Popler Memorial Steeplechase—and went on, in 1967, to complete the hat-trick in the River Vaga. The Grand Pardubice is reputed to be almost as difficult as the Grand National course at Aintree. It apparently involves gigantic water jumps, far too wide to actually clear in a single leap. The horses jump over the big brush fence into the water and then swim for it—with or without their riders—and I understand that the winner seldom completes the course without falling off at least once!

Deyev commented: 'It is not that I prefer steeplechasing to show-jumping, but I think that taking part in steeplechases gives a Three-Day Event rider speed qualities, and an ability to use the horse's reserves of power correctly on the course.'

Russians and horses have always been associated in my mind with two things—romantic tröikas sliding through the snow to a jingle of bells and the dashing, though probably barbarous, Cossack legions of the past. Although Pavel Deyev insists that the Cossacks have not influenced riding in Russia today, I feel that their shadow is there whether he acknowledges it or not. Traditions still live on. There is the local horse-racing track, where countless breeds have their own races, and there is the indifference to falling off—shown by Deyev himself—said to be a very Cossack trait.

Deyev comments: 'Apart from daring and dash, the Cossacks have no influence on the classical riding sports because of the specific character of their riding postures, and the sports popular among them.'

The Cossacks, hundreds of thousands strong until finally decimated in the Revolution, whose families once congregated on the banks of the mighty blue Don near Pavel's home, have some interesting traditions as warriors. It is said that the Cossack father teaches his son the art of Cossack warfare in the streets and squares of Cossack towns. Double rows of saplings are set out, the father teaches his son how to gallop through these rows and cut the tops off the saplings with his sword. A man is said to attain perfection when, leaping over a stream on horseback, he can cleave the water with his sword without stirring any spray. This training is said to make a Cossack utterly fearless.

Pavel Deyev's favourite hobby is soccer—not so far removed, perhaps, in terms of daring and dash, from the Cossacks. Maybe he dreams of the football team famous for its speed and daring—the Moscow Dynamos—who can say? Deyev has, not unnaturally, one over-riding ambition! 'Mexico was the greatest disappointment of my life. I want, above all things, to regain my reputation, and win a medal at the Olympic Games.'

Perhaps, at the next Olympics, when he fights for the honour that could have been his, the fearless spirit of a young Don Cossack will run by his side to guide him to victory. For, as the old song says, the Don Cossacks knew only too well what could happen if they made a mistake in battle.

9 Gambit

One of the most promising young horses in the country today is a six-year-old grey gelding called Gambit.

Gambit is the only horse who went from novice class to senior Grade A in a single day's eventing. He did this by winning the Golden Griffin trophy given by the Midland Bank for the National Novice Horse Trials Championship at Chatsworth in October 1969. His owner and rider, nineteen-year-old Sarah Roger Smith from Priors Marston, Warwickshire, collected a handsome trophy, of a griffin surrounded by bezants (or guineas) specially designed by Alex Styles of Garrard the Crown Jewellers, plus £100 cash.

The day after the trials Gambit nearly knocked his stable door down banging at it to be let out. For, like all horses of star quality, he has his idiosyncracies. The morning after he returns from a show he refuses to stay in his stable and bangs and kicks at the door until he is let out to run in the field. At all other times he is well behaved and waits patiently in his stable until it is his turn for exercise.

Gambit who is by Gamesman II was bred by the Hon. Mrs. Williams and broken by Michael Herbert—the great trainer who schooled The Poacher which was in the gold medal winning team at Mexico, and who went to Mexico with the team.

Michael took him to one or two shows and he seemed to be a promising youngster. He was four when Sarah, who was looking for a new horse for adult classes which she was then just old enough to enter, went to see him and fell in love with him.

Like her elder sister Althea, Sarah had been riding since she was a tiny child.

When she was only thirteen she was eventing with a horse called Foxtrot on whom she twice represented Britain in international Junior Show-Jumping team events. She also won many open hunter trials with him—all before she was old enough for senior classes. In 1965 she was Junior European Show-Jumping Champion.

The first season she had Gambit she hunted him with the Grafton and an excellent schooling it proved for him. He proved himself a great all-rounder and in 1968 he qualified for the Spillers' Combination Event at Wembley and for the Foxhunter novice jumping.

At the beginning of 1969 he was still a 'dual' horse, showing equal promise in both show-jumping and Eventing.

Then came the announcement by the Midland Bank that they were to further develop their interest in horse sports by sponsoring a national championship for novice Combined Training horses.

The Bank had the previous year become the first bank to sponsor top-level show-jumping by sponsoring the King George V Gold Cup international championship for men riders and the Queen Elizabeth II Cup for ladies at the Royal International Show.

The new championship for Combined Training was named the Midland Bank Novice Championship, and carried the Golden Griffin (the symbol of the Midland Bank) trophy plus £100 first prize.

In all, the bank provided more than £3,000 in prize money. The qualifying rounds took place at more than thirty-five official Horse Trials which carried some fifty divisions in all parts of Britain. The winners of each division qualified to enter for the championship which was held at Chatsworth in the beautiful grounds of the Duke and Duchess of Devonshire. During the season of 1969 about 2,000 competitors took part in novice classes, so those who finally got to Chatsworth, whether they qualified for eventual prize money or not proved that they were horses with a good potential. The winner had his feet set well along the road to fame. It will be interesting to watch his progress as he is still very young indeed, as is his rider.

Gambit's win is all the more creditable because many of the horses, although themselves novices, were ridden by experienced trials riders including some who had been members of Olympic teams. Throughout the season of 1969 he had been gaining an international reputation as a show jumper.

At the July meeting at the All England Jumping Course at Hickstead which was a warm-up for many horses and riders for the Royal International Horse Show at Wembley, and where the crack men riders were gathered for the Men's European Championship, Gambit won two classes in fine style, beating many international horses.

In August he and Sarah went to Dinard where she won the title 'Leading Lady Rider'—a title she also won after Chatsworth in Vienna.

At the Chatsworth championships Gambit did the first clear round in the show-jumping section, and the fastest time in the cross-country with a penalty score of 34 points. Sarah had given him careful schooling in dressage and although this was not his strongest point he did well enough.

It is obvious that given a fair amount of progress, and that never-to-be-discounted-element, luck, Gambit is likely to be in the selectors' minds for the Munich Olympics. At present Sarah favours concentrating him on Eventing; but who knows? On the showing at the time of going to press there is no great choice in either the Eventing or the Show-Jumping field. If Gambit continues his progress in both fields he is likely to give the selectors a headache deciding into which category to include him.

Whatever happens he has already proved to be a horse with

the temperament for the big event. He dislikes fuss—hates to be fawned over even by his rider after a spectacular success —and never appears to be ruffled by a big audience. He loves free style jumping but at the same time has already proved himself amenable to the strict discipline of the dressage ring. Barring accidents he looks to be one of the brightest stars in this country's immediate firmament.

Before the start of the 1969 novice season, when the Midland Bank first announced their participation, Major Derek Allhusen, the Silver Individual Medallist of the Mexico Olympic Three-Day Event, said:

'We shall be starting to look for young riders and young horses to make sure that we win another Gold medal in Munich in 1972. This Novice Championship has produced the very competition we needed. The Final at Chatsworth will be over a bigger course and will definitely produce the sort of horse and rider we require.'

10 High and Mighty

He was not very big, just under 16 hands. He had an eel mark down his back and 'donkey' markings on his front legs. He was an odd dun colour. Not a very beautiful horse at all.

That was the first impression which Sheila Willcox received of High and Mighty when she collected him from the train in Lancashire whence he had travelled from Sussex, in 1954. But he also looked lively and appeared to be taking a keen interest in what was happening around him; and he had an air about him which is never missing from a good horse, an unmistakable aura which those who have to deal with horses can nearly always recognise.

He was destined to make horse trials history for both himself and his young owner (Sheila then was still in her teens) and to set up a record of winning Badminton for two years in succession in 1957 and 1958, a record which still stands. Sheila was to go further and be the only rider ever to complete the hat-trick by winning three successive Badmintons, as she also won in 1959 riding another horse Airs and Graces, after High and Mighty had retired from the Eventing world to concentrate on dressage.

Sheila acquired High and Mighty—whom she always called Chips—through an advertisement for a potential event horse.

He had been bred in Ireland by Mrs. Lake who eventually brought him over to Sussex. He was by a thoroughbred sire and a part Highland mare and was originally called

Sanction. When Sheila bought him he was seven and he cost her under £200.

Eventing was a new form of sport for Sheila, who up to that time had concentrated on hacks—and had won the hack championship at the White City in 1954 with a hack called Blithe Spirit. So the pair of them set about training for this new sport together. And the training and the partnership nearly came to a tragic and untimely end.

They were out on the marshes behind Lytham St. Anne's and were in a field which was cut by a tidal creek. Chips tried to jump across the stream but missed the bank and fell back into the muddy ooze. Immediately he started to sink and the more he and Sheila struggled to get him out the further he submerged. Sheila could see he was not only tiring but was giving up. So she dashed across the field to a farm. Breathlessly she told the farmer about Chips' plight and begged him to lend a tractor.

The obliging man went back with her to the now almost totally submerged horse and a rope was got round him. Sheila had to hold his head out of the mud while the tractor pulled. It was a near thing. Eventually he was got safely out, none the worse physically for his adventure.

Understandably however, he had a marked aversion to water after that and it took all Sheila's firmness and patience to overcome this and get him across water at the many fences he was later to encounter. Fortunately he was a very obedient horse. In fact, Sheila herself maintains that he was always more obedient than brave. Certainly he had an absolute trust in her—a trust manifestly lacking when it was attempted to train him for the Olympic Games with another rider.

When Sheila first started to train him he did not take too kindly to jumping. It took her some time to teach him what was expected of him, but when once he had got the idea he never looked back. In fact, but for his unfortunate experience at the creek, he never fell. As he gained experience he became very clever at knowing just the best part of a fence to get over most easily.

After one or two try-outs at one-day events, High and Mighty made his debut in Three-Day Eventing at Windsor in 1955. This was the year when the Queen lent Windsor Park for the official European Horse Trials Championships and the best riders and horses from five countries were competing. There were altogether fifty-four starters and the course was tough. One horse in fact broke its back and had to be destroyed at a particularly nasty fence in the cross-country phase. Apart from the British team which won the championship, only the Swiss international team finished the course.

High and Mighty was 13th in the final placing—a gallant and highly creditable feat for a first effort in formidable company and over a gruelling course.

Later in the year Sheila and High and Mighty entered for the Three-Day Trials at Harewood in Yorkshire. These trials are now no longer held and have been replaced by Burghley Horse Trials in Lincolnshire—but the course was as tough and rugged as Badminton—some say even tougher. The Harewood Event ran from 1953 to 1959 when a full-scale European Championship was held there.

On this particular year, 1955, when the winner was Kilbarry one of the greatest event horses ever, High and Mighty was placed 4th. He had definitely arrived in the eventing world.

After this reassuring performance which proved that his Windsor placing was not beginner's luck—High and Mighty and Sheila were invited to train for possible inclusion in the British team to go to Turin for a European international event—Concours Complet Internationale, i.e. not an official championship. That had already been held for the current year at Windsor.

But there were more international teams competing than had been at Windsor including entries from Italy, Switzerland, Germany, Turkey and France.

High and Mighty made the team, and off went the couple in their first foreign venture in the sport in which they were still both only in their first full year.

The Germans had been favourites to win the first place, the odds being in favour of their leading trials rider Lütke-Westhues, but High and Mighty beat them all. He was the leading individual horse, and in addition Britain won the team event.

By now the name of this horse was on everybody's lips, both at home and on the Continent. This was the year before the Olympic Games and Sheila received handsome offers from more than one foreigner for her oddly-marked dun gelding. She refused them all and the pair returned to Lancashire.

At this time in equestrian history no woman was allowed to ride in the Three-Day Event at the Olympic Games, and Sheila, who had made the horse and had built up such a perfect partnership with him was determined that if the international rules said she could not compete, then neither could her horse. Above all things, she would not see her horse competing for a foreign country.

So came 1956 the year when the main Olympic Games were to be held in Melbourne, but because of Australian equine quarantine rules the equestrian events were to be held in Stockholm.

Plans for the team which was to represent Britain had gone awry because of sales of horses, inexperience or unfitness. There were only two horses, Kilbarry and Countryman which seemed 'certs' and nowhere did there seem to be a horse of Olympic calibre.

Except High and Mighty. But the selectors had reckoned without Miss Willcox. She adamantly refused to let the horse be taken over. There was of course a great deal to be said on her side. She knew that she was as much to do with High and Mighty's success as the horse itself, and that it was unlikely a horse used to being ridden by a young girl would have the same response for a man.

All sorts of pressures were brought to bear on Sheila. The selectors alternately pleaded and bullied. An outsider could see their point of view. Here was Britain trying to scratch a team which could worthily represent her at the Olympic Games—and here was one of the most brilliant event horses since the sport began, which with Kilbarry and Countryman would make a really strong team, and a slip of a girl was standing in their way.

Eventually Sheila gave way. She did not lend High and Mighty. She sold him to Mr. Eddie Marsh who was a noted event riding enthusiast and a great patron of the sport. Mr. Marsh promised her she could ride the horse the following season after the Games.

So it was 'Goodbye, Mr. Chips' for Sheila and off went High and Mighty to go into training for the Olympics as the mount of Michael Naylor-Leyland. For Mr. Marsh generously handed over his purchase to the Olympic British team selectors together with one of his own promising horses Wild Venture.

But whether it was simply fate or whether Sheila had really had a sub-conscious hunch she was proved right. High and Mighty and Michael Naylor-Leyland did not get on very well together and finally the horse went lame. So after all the heart-searching and the drama High and Mighty never did after all get to the Olympics and the following year Sheila bought him back from Mr. Marsh and one can imagine the joyful reunion of the pair.

Any recriminations which there might have been from the Olympic selectors were offset by the fact that after all Britain won the Gold medal for the team award and a bronze for the Individual. (Won by Kilbarry.)

Meanwhile High and Mighty and Sheila got over their separation and into training for Badminton 1957.

The win at Turin may have carried international fame and prestige, but at home in Britain the Badminton Horse Trials have always been something special—and to win it has, and still does, imbue the winner with a status of its own.

That year High and Mighty won Badminton and even the harshest critics of 1956 had to agree that perhaps he was, as Sheila had always maintained him to be, a one-woman horse.

His win was specially noteworthy because he finished the three days with a plus score of 79.37—a score far better than any other winner had scored since Badminton began.

In the October of that year the European Championships were held in Copenhagen and this time Sheila and High and Mighty were in the team.

The other horses were Wild Venture, Laurien, and Pampas Cat, with Just William as Reserve.

Other countries which sent teams were Germany, Sweden, Denmark, France and Poland.

In the dressage section High and Mighty scored second best individual points to the German horse Franko II—which was the saving of the British team as the rest of them had disastrous marks.

After the second day the German horse was still in the lead from High and Mighty but only by 7.34 points—and High and Mighty finished the day in better shape than Franko for the jumping phase on the last day. Even so, he incurred 20 faults in the jumping by knocking down one fence and having a foot in the water at the water jump. Franko, however, knocked down three fences and incurred a time penalty. So High and Mighty became the reigning individual European champion—actually his second European championship although Turin did not count officially.

The British team also won the team championship, High and Mighty's performance beating Major Allhusen's efforts on Laurien, who had a clear round in the show-jumping although incurring lost points for time.

This was the fourth official international Three-Day Event championship in succession to be won by the British.

In the following spring of 1958 High and Mighty won Badminton for the second time.

Much to the surprise of many of his staunchest followers Sheila then decided to retire him from eventing. She concentrated him on dressage and for a time he did very well but never had the spectacular successes of his Three-Day Event days.

Finally, leaving the dressage world he retired from competitive life and had a happy time in the hunting field.

Not until 1969, when he was twenty-two-years-old, did Sheila decide it was time to say the last farewell—'Goodbye, Mr. Chips'. This was just before the Horse of the Year Show at Wembley, and at the same time she had to put down a promising young eventer Fair and Square who had never really recovered from an accident at Badminton. It was a sad Wembley for Sheila. She has produced a number of good horses since, the best probably being Airs and Graces on which she completed her hat-trick at Badminton, but so far she has not found a horse of the calibre of High and Mighty, who is sure of his place in the halls of eventing fame. In all the intervening years since the height of his career there have been few to equal him.

11 Laurien

Like a fire-engine on call, Derek Allhusen's celebrated mare Laurien had two speeds—flat-out and stop. Happily she possessed manoeuvrability and her brakes were in fairly good repair, but inevitably there was an occasion when they failed. The result was disastrous. Her long-suffering owner-rider recovered his wits and his health in hospital.

But then, everything about Laurien was a little different from the usual pattern. To start with, she was female, and as such one of the tiny minority ever to run successfully in top-class Three-Day Events, or indeed any top competition. The female of the species may be more deadly, but it can certainly be less reliable!

Her parentage was possibly a unique blend of beautiful temperament, determination, stamina and speed, that resulted in her using her heart more than her head. Her dam was a German transport mare, captured by the 8th Army in northern Italy, at the end of the War. Her sire was a famous steeplechaser called Davy Jones, who lost the 1936 Grand National to Reynoldstown at the last fence, when his rein broke.

Laurien herself, who, in the words of her owner, 'never gave less than her best,' always seemed to be that little bit unlucky, doomed eternally to second place. Second at Badminton, second at Harewood, winner of the Bronze medallion (third) at the 1959 European Championships, winner of the Silver medallion (second) with the British team on the same occasion. Her one great victory was winner, with the team, of the Gold medallion in the 1957 European Title—an historic moment for Britain, who, having reigned supreme in Europe and the world for four successive years, was not to regain her mastery for a decade.

At the end of the War, Derek Allhusen, a Major in the 9th Lancers, was stationed with his squadron near Padua, in the north of Italy. On hearing that a packed Transport Group which was being demobilised, had some good horses on offer to the rest of the 8th Army, Derek went down to Riccione on the Adriatic to investigate. He recalls: 'Riccione is the place where Mussolini used to go as a child. He had a villa there. Now, it's a tremendous place for cheap package tours.'

Tied up to a bar behind the stable building of a Riccione hotel, Derek picked out a bay, light-draught mare that he rather liked the look of. 'She was being groomed at the time,' he remembers, 'and she had an air about her, of intelligence, that appealed to me. She was a German mare who had worked in the Transport division of the German army, and the 8th Army had captured her to use themselves. But when the officers and men were sent home to England, the horses were distributed to other parts of the Army.

'She hadn't got any stud brand on her,' Derek told me, 'which was interesting, so she wasn't pure Hanoverian. And she'd already been taught to jump quite successfully, a good sort of B & C Grade Jumper. I paid £50 for her, and that included paying for her and transporting her home to Melton Mowbray, where the Remount Depot was. I paid £50 because she was under nine years old. Her name was Laura.'

Derek's other cut-price bargain was even cheaper—£37. 10s. for a horse called Lancer. 'The best buys I ever had!' he says. The two horses did not travel straight home, however; Derek stayed on in Europe with other sections of the Army, clearing up after the War. So Laura and Lancer went too, getting in some useful show-jumping in Italy and Austria on the way.

'We had enormous numbers of German horses,' Derek recalled. 'The Germans had twenty Divisions, but only two motorised ones—the rest were all on a horse basis. So all their Divisions were supplied, instead of by lorries, like ours, by horse transport. We had two German Cavalry Divisions surrender to us on the borders of Italy and Austria—they'd have 20,000 horses in each—and Laura was one of those.'

Derek Allhusen became famous to millions of people during the 1968 Mexico Olympics, when he led the British Three-Day Event team to a Gold medal victory, in a torrential rainstorm. He himself, then fifty-four years old, and riding a horse called Lochinvar, also won the Individual Silver medal. But what most of the televiewers did not know was that the gallant Major had already ridden for Britain at the Olympic Games—twenty years before, in the British Pentathlon team at the 1948 Winter Olympics.

Now, in the 1970's, Derek Allhusen is a man of tremendous activity, who likes to keep several pots boiling at once. In 1947/48, when he was stationed in Lanarkshire with Laura and Lancer and training for the Pentathlon team—which required expertise in Downhill Ski-ing, Long Distance Ski-ing, Shooting, Fencing and Riding—I can only guess that the atmosphere around him must have been positively radio-active!

Derek did so well in this multi-sided sport, finishing individually 6th, that he was asked to train for the Summer Pentathlon team, part of the London Olympics at Wembley Stadium. For this he was sent to train at Aldershot—and found himself living in the Officers Mess with rooms next door to General Linkenbach, winner of a Gold medal in Dressage at the 1928 Amsterdam Olympics. But Linkenbach was at Aldershot to train the Three-Day Event team for Britain, and Derek struck up a friendship with him that was to last many years and exercise a powerful influence on his future success in Three-Day Events.

Also training at Aldershot, of course, were Col. Harry

High and Mighty, ridden in this picture by Sheila Willcox at Badminton, is one of only three horses ever to win Badminton twice. The way he is taking the water here is a tribute to her skill and training as after a mishap in his early days when he was nearly drowned, he always hated water.

Laurien, ridden by Major Derek Allhusen at Badminton in 1958, when Laurien finished second to High and Mighty. Out of a German-bred mare captured by the 8th Army during the war, who Major Allhusen bought at the end of the war for £50—which included her transport home. She was a great Event horse in the fifties and in 1958 won the Calcutta Cup for the horse with the best trials record of the year.

Merely-a-Monarch, with Anneli Drummond-Hay in the days when he was a great Event horse and before he began his present glorious career as a show jumper. Here they are on their way to victory at Badminton in 1962—when they not only won but finished 42 points ahead of their nearest rivals.

M'Lord Connolly, who was eventually sold to the United States, was ridden for this country by Captain James Templer. In this picture he is taking the water at Burghley in 1962, when he became individual European champion, not having been selected for the British team on the grounds of inexperience.

Llewellyn, Major Arthur Carr and Col. H. M. V. Nicholl—
with Foxhunter, Kilgeddin and Monty—who were destined
to win a Bronze medal for show-jumping at Wembley, in
preparation for a Gold at Helsinki. Derek recalls: 'I used to
go and watch the show-jumpers and the eventers in their
basic training near Tweseldown, and I became very interested
in the idea of eventing, as well as learning a great deal from
them.'

Going on at about that time was the Military Tournament,
so Derek rode Laura and Lancer in the Kings Cup, eventually
won by Laurence Rook (of the 1956 Stockholm Gold medal
team). And then, two weeks before the Pentathlon team was
finally chosen, came trouble—Laura went lame with tendon
injuries, was sent back to Lanark to be fired, and was therefore
no more good for Derek's Pentathlon training, in which swimming and cross-country running were substituted for the two
kinds of ski-ing.

Deprived of his trustworthy mare, Derek was then dependent on the extremely moderate horses allotted for the actual
Pentathlon itself. He remembers with awful truth the horse
given to him to ride: 'It was the sort of horse who was out to
get you, whatever you did, a really nasty-minded type. We
were asked to hump a large solid fence with a 4ft. spread,
and I don't know what happened, but the horse went straight
through it. It was a slow, stinking fall, made ten times
worse by the horse rolling on me, and treading on my shoulder
—I've had trouble with it ever since. I lay on the ground,
and can just remember Joe Dudgeon bending anxiously over
me! (The famous Irish rider.)

'Unfortunately, when I was X-rayed at the Military
Hospital, it was found that I had a dislocated left shoulder,
and so I couldn't be part of the Pentathlon team, but I was
reserve.'

In June 1950, Laurien was foaled at the Allhusens' home,
Claxton, near Norwich. She was the first foal from Laura, and
probably the last service that Davy Jones ever had. As a

three-year-old, Laurien was broken in, and given some dressage training by General Linkenbach, who had returned to England and was helping the Allhusens to build an indoor riding school. Two years later Laurien was launched on her eventing career—at a one-day event in Malton, Yorkshire.

After two more novice events that autumn, including Tweseldown, Nr. Aldershot, Laurien had made such progress that Derek decided to try her at Badminton in the following spring, 1956. But that fell through, when she cut her leg rather badly at an event at Stowell Park, in the Cotswolds, shortly beforehand—so her first Three-Day Event was Harewood, in the autumn.

Although popular with the riders, this great course, generously lent by H. R. H. The Princess Royal, never really caught on with the public and in 1959 it closed, to be succeeded by Burghley in 1961.

But Harewood in the fifties was a hotbed of talent, and attracted many riders from the Continent. In 1956, Laurien finished fourth—a fact that few noticed. The interest of the Eventing world was fixed on the dramas and glories of Stockholm.

And then the next spring came the moment every Event rider marks with a big red cross in his diary—his (or her) first Badminton. But it was not an auspicious initiation for Derek or his courageous little bay mare.

He recalled: 'Laurien loved to go—and she really could gallop—but she hadn't learnt how to conserve her strength. Unfortunately, it was impossible to strike a half-way speed with her; she just used to go flat out! But at Badminton she went too fast round the first circuit of the steeplechase course, and the second time round galloped straight through the bottom of a big brush spread. I landed up in hospital!'

Notwithstanding such a setback, however, the British Selectors were impressed by Laurien's obvious quality, even if her brilliance was somewhat erratic. She was chosen for the British team defending the European Championship title, at Copenhagen in October 1957; other team members were: Sheila Willcox (High and Mighty) Mr. E. E. Marsh (Wild Venture) and Kit Tatham-Warter (Pampas Cat).

On the final day, when the Germans were just in front of Britain, only to drop back with poor show-jumping, Laurien excelled herself with a dazzling clear round to ensure a British victory. The Individual title went to High and Mighty, and Laurien finished fifth—evidently she was learning fast.

In 1958 she did even better, finishing second at Badminton to High and Mighty, and in front of Pluto, ridden by Anneli Drummond-Hay. After also coming second at Harewood to the German Ottakar Pohlmann on Polarfuchs, and winning the Combined Training Championship (Dressage and Show-jumping) at the Horse of the Year Show, Laurien crowned a consistent year by being awarded the British Horse Trials Championship—the Calcutta Cup. This is for the horse with the best record in horse trials that year.

And again, 1959 was almost a repetition. Fourth at Badminton, and a Bronze medallion for Individual third place at the European Championships, Harewood. But the British team of Col. Frank Weldon (Samuel Johnson), Jeremy Beale (Fulmer Folly), Sheila Willcox (Airs and Graces) and Laurien, were defeated by Germany, who had just a fraction of a mark to spare. And Laurien again left her mark on the British records, with a second presentation of the Calcutta Cup. This trophy has, by now, been won by Derek Allhusen no fewer than five times, a score that includes three victories by Lochinvar; a feat no other rider has even approached.

It would have been reasonable, for anybody with a horse as talented as Laurien, now to hope for a place in the Olympic team, assembling in the spring of 1960, for Rome. But it was not to be. And Derek was destined to wait eight more years before his ambition was finally realised.

For in February of 1960 Laurien developed a strange and mysterious lameness that was never really diagnosed. All the Allhusens know is that it seemed to start after she galloped through Claxton village. They describe it as something wrong with the lymph glands, or some liver disorder causing poison to go into her system. Badminton, of course, was out.

But Laurien just as mysteriously recovered afterwards, in time for the Selection Committee to try and commandeer her services for Rome. Derek fought the request, feeling, not unnaturally, that if anyone rode her it should be himself—and knowing also that hers was an especial kind of brilliance that needed much acquaintanceship and understanding.

The Committee had their way, but it did them no good at all. The very first time Frank Weldon tried Laurien out, she jumped him straight off; the combination was not a success —and since the Games were to start in three weeks, Frank Weldon reverted to the horse he knew, Samuel Johnson.

Laurien's swansong came in 1961, at Badminton. Derek says of that last, rather sad occasion: 'She is tremendously brave, but she was not right and not fit. She refused at the last fence in the cross-country, and I just took her out, and retired. I was so upset at her not being right that I decided instantly that that was her last event.'

Courage, they say, is inherited. And if so, then Laurien took a good lump of it from her sire, Davy Jones. His story is one that ranks alongside such dramas as Devon Loch, but he was less lucky than Mandarin.

Reynoldstown had won the National in 1935, ridden by Frank Furlong, who was in Derek's regiment. But the next year he couldn't make the weight, so Fulke Walwyn, whose troop Derek took over in the 9th Lancers, replaced him, and Davy Jones was ridden by that great accident-prone amateur, Lord Mildmay. Davy Jones was leading by three lengths, but coming into the last but one Fulke Walwyn saw Mildmay using his whip to try and scoop up the end of the rein which had come apart at the buckle. The left rein had fallen on the ground, and with his whip he was trying to recover the end into his hand.

Fulke Walwyn therefore brought Reynoldstown up on the

off side, because he didn't want to be carried out by the horse, but of course that aggravated the trouble for his opponent, and Davy Jones ran out at the last fence. Reynoldstown went on to win his second successive Grand National.

That was thirty-five years ago, and Davy Jones has long since gone. But his line survives, for his daughter reigns supreme as matriarch of The Manor House, Claxton, producing progeny to fill the Badmintons of the future—Laureate, by Carnival Boy; Laurieston, by Happy Monarch; and one still unborn, from Question—sire of the 1969 Grand National winner, Highland Wedding.

Laurien's prize money totalled about £1,000—a fair-sized sum at any time for an event horse, but considerable for ten years ago. It shows that even though she was thought to be unreliable, she made an astonishingly convincing display of being just the opposite.

How like a woman; to be misleading, too!

12 Merely-a-Monarch

At the far end of an enormous field strewn with bits of glass, strands of barbed wire and broken-down Nissen huts, grazed a horse that was to become a legend throughout the horse-fanciers of the world—a tall black gelding of three years old, without a name.

Winner of the Grand National, the Cheltenham Gold Cup, Olympic Gold medallist in Three-Day Eventing, Show-jumping, Dressage—name it—and he could have done it. But he didn't—he achieved none of these things, and probably never will, for time is running out. The clock will beat him in the end.

His record, nevertheless, is no mean one. As a Three-Day Eventer he won the Burghley-Badminton double in seven months, as a show-jumper he has won the European Championship, six Grand Prix, and other trophies and championships too numerous to list.

Anneli Drummond-Hay first saw the horse that was to become Merely-a-Monarch in the Autumn of 1958, but she was not over-impressed by the meeting. In fact, the future partnership might never have existed had it not been for the presence of Major Derek Allhusen, who fell in love with the horse himself and bought it two days later.

Anneli recalls: 'I'd advertised several months before, I wanted a four- or five-year-old. I'd had about eighty answers, but none of them was any good. Mostly they were too expensive, or I didn't really believe what they had to say. I went to see quite a lot of them, but I wasn't inspired—and I was committed a certain amount over the price!'

On the way up to Harewood Three-Day Event in Yorkshire Anneli, who was riding a horse belonging to Derek Allhusen (Dachs), asked if they might stop off at Tadcaster, to see another answer to her advertisement, from a Mrs. Steele. The three-year-old, who had been unsuccessfully broken and hunted the previous year, had, they discovered, learnt two things in his short life: to mistrust humans and get them off his back as quick as he could.

But he was quiet in hand, Derek Allhusen remembers: 'I was very impressed when he was caught, and lunged on the end of a bit of old ploughline, that he took no notice at all of the other horses galloping past.' For both Anneli and Derek, however, the asking price of £300 seemed a lot of money for an ignorant, high-minded three-year-old with bad habits, and they drove on to Harewood.

But during the three days there, at the end of which Derek was to finish second on Laurien and Anneli third on Dachs, Mr. Steele appeared at Harewood from Tadcaster to find out what was going on. So the deal was done—Derek bought the horse, and told Anneli: 'I'll buy him and you can ride him. If you like him enough to buy him later on, you can. But if you don't want him, then I shall keep him, I think he's the most wonderful horse I've ever seen.'

Anneli's problem at this stage was money. Her family said the price was much too expensive, that they would have to sell capital, that the horse was too young. What Anneli's family didn't know, however, was that he was worth every penny of that £300, and was later to be worth about eighty times as much.

On the way home from Harewood to Norfolk the Allhusens' horse-box stopped to pick up the new addition to the stables. Anneli remembers: 'He promptly started to smash the box to pieces. I thought he must be a complete maniac! When we got home, I remember looking over the stable door about five minutes later, and there he was, boxing the wall on the far side! I had already had a horse by the same sire as this one (Happy Monarch), which really was a maniac—it had to be shot, it was so mad. Then I peered in again, and he turned round and started kicking his haynet! He still does that even now, if he gets particularly cross.'

Derek Allhusen kept the young horse for nearly a year on his farm near Norwich, but his hopes of riding his new property diminished daily. For Anneli, who was living with the Allhusens at the time, was fast realising that she had stumbled on a miracle. But even miracles need a name, and this christening was the responsibility of Derek's wife, Claude.

By Happy Monarch, the three-year-old was out of a hot-blooded 14.3 hands high pony hunter—herself by a premium stallion called Merely-a-Minor. Thus, Merely-a-Monarch was born.

Early training was a problem, and Monarch was so nappy that eventually Derek called in dressage expert Robert Hall to advise Anneli on tactics. They found that the most successful method was that of long-reining the horse whenever he rebelled: but that the other problem could only be solved by constant applications of glue! Anneli remembers: 'All he'd learnt to do was to buck people off. He discovered he could do it, and he's never grown out of it. But, quite honestly, I've yet to find a really good horse that hasn't got a bit of character, especially if they've got the guts to do what you ask them to do.'

During the winter of 1958-59 Anneli was sometimes away and Monarch roughed it out with the cattle. 'He had a passion for eating the sugar-beet tops—the crowns—which are very sugary,' Derek recalls, 'But when the weather got better he liked to lie down by one of our dykes, on the warm bare earth where the cattle had been resting. I can see him now, rolling over towards the side of the marsh, and being constantly

Pitou from France, ridden by Adjutant-Chef Jean-Jacques Guyon. At the Olympic Games in Mexico they won the Individual Gold medal. Here they are on their way to finishing 4th individually at the European Championships Punchestown in 1967.

Durlas Eile, one of the great Irish Event horses, with Major Eddie Boylan in the saddle, takes the vicarage ditch at Badminton which he won in 1965. He was in the winning Irish world championship team and an individual European championship winner. A majestic horse he stands 17.1 hh—one of the biggest horses in the sport.

Tramella, with her owner and rider Miss Diana Mason, wait their turn for an international Dressage contest. Tramella is the only British horse ever to be in a winning team in European championships for both Three-Day Events and Dressage. Now retired she still makes an occasional public appearance although she is twenty-three years old.

terrified that he would roll over into the dyke by mistake—but he never did!'

Anneli was chosen, later on in 1959, as reserve to the British team for the European Championships at Harewood—with a grey gelding called Perhaps. She told me: 'I bought Perhaps for £20 in 1957—he was a Belsen case. But he was so pathetic and he had such a sweet face that I couldn't resist him. When I bought him as a three-year-old, he was 15.1, and by the time he was 6 years old he was 16.2. I have two pictures, before and after. That's why I called him Perhaps—I didn't know if he would survive or not.'

In fact Perhaps, as reserve, was not called on to jump—although six months later Anneli sold him to the Swiss after finishing third at Badminton. But the nine international teams assembled at Harewood that September had a glimpse of the horse that was to become the most widely discussed eventer and show-jumper of the next decade. Sailing over a fence in a practice ring was Monarch, already at four years old showing a tremendous spring. And it was exactly a year after she had first seen him in that Yorkshire field that Anneli finally bought Monarch from Derek Allhusen, for the same amount as he had originally paid—£300.

After a season's hunting—'I always like a young horse to have just that one season with hounds, it teaches him to look after himself,' Anneli told me—Monarch was ready for his first event. But Anneli also found that she had to keep her wits about her if she was to look after herself as well. From being overgrown at three years, the five-year-old, now 16.3 hands high, was fast finding his strength.

And at the first two events Monarch stopped. His rider told me: 'The first time I didn't take much notice—he stopped going into a ha-ha, and sort of fell with his chest against it. The second time was a rail-and-ditch, I knew he'd spook at it—he was going too fast really to stop. He put his front feet over, stopped dead, and I went straight over his head into the water! That was the only time he ever stopped on a cross-country course.'

That spring Monarch got into the money at three One-Day Events, but in the Autumn he did even better. At the Horse of the Year Show in October he won the Combined Training Championship (dressage and show-jumping), came third in the Working Hunter and fourth in the *Daily Express* Foxhunter Championship.

But by now he had learned how to gallop, and it was almost inevitable with a horse of his calibre that the following year Anneli's thoughts should turn to the racetrack. At Ivor Herbert's training stables, in a trial gallop with a well-known fast-miler, Monarch gave such a good account of himself that Anneli almost decided to put him into training. She remembers the head lad rushing in to say that 'somebody had offered £6,000 for him!' A likely tale, perhaps—only with an animal who looks and moves as Monarch does—such stories are apt to be true!

Anneli, however, was not to be tempted. She turned from the heights and went back to eventing, determined to finish what she had set out to do. At Sherborne that year, 1961, Monarch won the Intermediate; came third in the Open at Dunster, and was placed first in the 'Bulford' at Tidworth (he didn't start in the other phases).

In August, Monarch took part in a Three-Day Event in Geneva, which was so unimportant that it is generally forgotten, but is, in fact, worth recording for the one reason that, for the first and last time in his life, Monarch represented his country in a Three-Day Event. The team consisted of Michael Bullen with Sea Breeze, Susan Fleet with The Gladiator and Monarch. Anneli recalls: 'I thought we were going to the European Championships, but I couldn't have been more wrong, it was a kind of Pony Club course!' They finished third individually, and sailed on in triumph to Burghley—the magnificent new course lent by the Marquis of Exeter in Lincolnshire.

And what a triumph it was. Unchallenged, Monarch coasted 30 points into the lead after the Dressage, and was never headed. Anneli remembers: 'It was very exciting to win Burghley, because I was a complete nonentity. I had entered Monarch just by chance, but I wasn't expecting to ride him because I was supposed to be riding O'Malley's Tango. That fell through, so I thought I might as well ride Monarch.'

Badminton was, for Anneli, another story. She had more or less decided, by the Spring of 1962, to turn Monarch over to show-jumping, but: 'I was determined to win one Badminton,' she says, 'because I had slogged away at it for a few years.' Being hot favourite was, however, not so easy to cope with.

'In order to make certain that Monarch was never beaten in Dressage,' Anneli told me, 'I had to threaten being more dominating, which I didn't like. It slightly put me off eventing, after I'd won Badminton, when I realised I had been a much more dominating rider than I am now. I suddenly knew that the horse has got to think for himself—I like a horse to have more of its own personality. I think Monarch, really, made me realise this because he has such a personality that it amused me—and I didn't want to take it away.'

Like David Broome, Anneli prefers to 'come up from behind' in an event, but this was impossible as a hot favourite running to form. 'I think possibly at Badminton I had over-trained Monarch,' Anneli confesses now, 'and it sounds awful to say this, but I didn't really get such a thrill from winning there. I felt Monarch was so much more superior than the others that he jolly well ought to win easily.

'The trouble was this. I didn't want to risk Monarch any more eventing—he was miles ahead of everybody else—and I didn't get enough kick out of beating everybody by 30, 40, 50 points, or whatever; I like to be able to struggle for what I get. It was not enough of a struggle for him, and also horses get worn out eventing.'

Anneli's predicament was one that not many sportsmen or women find themselves troubled by, but it is easy to understand. Someone with that kind of determination to win must pass on to other fields, when one has conquered so absolutely. She and Monarch had, after all, won Burghley by 32 points, and Badminton by 42 points—and ladies were still, in 1962, barred from the Olympic Three-Day Event team. Perhaps if they hadn't been, or if there had been stronger competition about—there was, unfortunately, a dearth of British talent just then—her decision might have been different.

And so Monarch and Anneli turned to show-jumping. 'I'd always wanted to, all my life,' Anneli told me, 'but you've got to have a top-class horse, and I hadn't that kind of money. You can get to the top in Eventing if you work hard enough with a horse that is not top-class—I say, at the top—but I wasn't necessarily at the top. I was there or thereabouts with ordinary, honest horses. It's all up to how hard you work, how hard you train him—if you've got the article there, you can train him.

'There's a lot of different ways of approaching Eventing. There's one way, which is to be completely dominating. With an Event horse, if he's bold, you can afford to dominate him to the extent that you can almost take his personality away— of which I don't approve. But if you want to be sure of getting to a certain level, you can take a horse and force it up to a certain point, to perform a particular standard of dressage.

'The Three-Day Event standard isn't very high—and you can then make him obedient so that he daren't stop across country, if he's a reasonable enough jumper, and the show-jumping's nothing much. The horse has to be able to gallop fast enough—and the rest of your problem is getting the horse fit.

'But there is another way, which is, I think, the one that most people use in this country. That is to form the normal partnership of horse and rider, which often means sacrificing a certain standard of dressage, but gaining much more on the cross-country. The trouble is, if you get the partnership where the rider is not so dominant, sometimes the horse lets you down and blows up in the dressage.'

After winning Badminton Anneli was asked if she would consider training Monarch for the Dressage team, but turned it down. She explains: 'I'd probably trained thirty-odd horses before I got Monarch, and by this time I'd begun to realise what a quality horse was, and what points to appreciate. Monarch had just such fantastic qualities, compared to the horses I had had before, that I was terrified of hurting them. He was outstanding at dressage, but I thought that was a bit quiet at that time, and he was obviously a fantastic show-jumper. He was Grade A when he won Burghley and Badminton—so it wasn't really such a quick change.'

At the International Horse Show in July 1962, Merely-a-Monarch won two competitions, attracted a great deal of publicity and became, overnight, a public figure. The foreign riders, at the White City for the Men's European Championships, clamoured for possession. They offered £15,000, £20,000, £25,000, but Monarch, then owned jointly by Anneli and Mrs. Gilroy, secretary of the Perth Hunt Pony Club, was not for sale. Anneli recalls: 'Quite honestly, these tremendous sums didn't mean anything to me. I said, "No this was the horse I'd waited for all my life, and you can't buy everything." '

But at the Horse of the Year Show that October, Monarch was sold—to wealthy Yorkshire industrialist Bob Hanson—for £7,000—with a legal agreement that Anneli should ride him. The next year he swept the board. British teams, nations cups, championships, he was almost invincible—and Tokyo seemed a foregone conclusion. Naturally, however, it wasn't.

In 1964, Mister Softee went lame, Monarch started refusing, O'Malley and Firecrest were off form—the Tokyo team for the 1964 Olympics had disintegrated. At Aachen in June, Monarch went so badly that everyone thought he was finished. But Anneli, on their return, found that something really was wrong. A blood test showed that his blood was full of infection, and his coat was dull and staring.

Drama succeeded drama, however, when Bob Hanson, suspicious at the latest discovery, whipped the horse off, and produced him ten days later at the Royal International, with David Broome as jockey. Disaster fell there, too. Monarch, sick and off form, gave poor David an experience in the ring that is only remembered with a shudder, for its terrible number of faults. Anneli's mother, Lady Margaret Drummond-Hay, then stepped in to the fight. She took the matter to Court, and won a Court Injunction ordering Monarch to be sent home to Anneli. But Bob Hanson asked for the return of his £7,000—and Anneli had virtually spent it all! However, she found the money, and kept the horse.

Treatment for the blood infection followed, as also for the abcess in Monarch's groin that Anneli had discovered one morning, and quite soon he was back jumping like his usual self. Only Tokyo was out—Monarch was not considered a safe bet—a decision which, I hope, the Selectors regretted later.

In 1965, Monarch made a brief come-back to eventing. Anneli says: 'I wanted to regain confidence in myself and the horse. We had leapt to the top of the show-jumping tree very fast, and fallen down very hard.' They won Crookham, but once more Fate was against them. Four days before Badminton, Monarch broke a blood vessel behind his eye in the final gallop—and nearly lost the sight of his eye. Anneli remembers: 'He was very lucky to get it back at all.'

Munich approaches—but what will have happened to Merely-a-Monarch by then? Anneli admits: 'Yes, I should like to go to the Olympics very much, but there's nothing I should hate more than to go when I'm not in form. It's very sad really that Monarch is probably the only horse I shall ever have of that calibre—and he will be seventeen years old by then, rather old.'

But for Anneli, her dream horse—indeed Monarch of all he surveys—(as the poet says) will never be old. 'It's difficult to explain,' she says, 'but he's rather like—I don't know if you've ever driven a really super car—he's like a Rolls-Royce.'

13 Our Solo

As a circus pony Our Solo had all the right attributes—a clever logical mind, a fine sense of balance, a swift turn of foot, a sense of humour, adaptability and the litheness of a cat. But although he could sit down and shake hands as well as the next pony, he was never called upon to do it for a living. His owner taught him for the fun of it.

For Bill Roycroft, however, a lean Australian agriculturalist from Victoria, the pony's versatile brain proved to be a spur that would send them both thousands of miles across the sea to the ultimate honour in the sporting world—a Gold medal at the Olympic Games.

Perhaps the best victories are the unorthodox ones. Certainly Bill Roycroft's contribution to the Australian team's Gold medal in the Three-Day Event at Rome in the 1960 Olympics was so wonderfully full of daring that it captured the imagination of the world. Bill, then forty-six, and with less flesh on him than a greyhound, came in for a great deal of favourable comment and admiration—fully deserved. But the one who rather got missed out in the building of the legend was Bill's partner: the 15 hands high Our Solo, sometime circus pony, polo-crosse pony, stock pony, show-jumper, show hack and winner of five Three-Day Events (including Badminton) plus a Gold medal.

Since winning Badminton in 1960 Bill has been back to England twice, with different horses—once after Tokyo and again after the Mexico Olympics. It was twelve months after

Mexico that I talked with him in the cabin of a Blue Star Line cargo boat berthed in the Royal Albert Dock, London, hours before he sailed for home in charge of three horses.

'I bought Our Solo in 1957 from a chap that had already bought him for his children, and he was a bit difficult— threw the children off a few times—so he sold him to me. He was a thoroughbred, foaled in 1950 by Royal Welcon out of a thoroughbred mare. I never got to know what the mare's name was, but I believe the blood went back to Carbine, and that was supposed to be the best blood ever, Carbine blood; it came from England originally.'

But Solo's owner, intent on a sale, put in quite a bit of hard work before Bill could be persuaded to buy. 'This chap I bought him from,' recalled Bill. 'He was some five miles from me, and he used to follow me round the shows and say: "Look, I've got a better horse than you've got, come and have a look at him." I had so many horses I wasn't terribly worried about buying another one at the time, but when I did go and ride him—he could buck a little, could Solo—I was very impressed and bought him for £50.'

Solo's original owner and breeder was a man who used to race ponies, a popular sport in the area at that time, but Solo grew 2 inches too big to 15 hands (the limit was 14.2.) and never went on to the racetrack. Used mainly for stockwork on the farm, he also became a family pet.

'He was taught to do circus tricks, more or less,' Bill told me. 'I think the chap was just gifted in this way of making horses learn tricks. Some people seem to have no trouble whatsoever in making a horse sit down or lie down, but I never tried them on Solo, I was too busy making an event horse out of him. I think this chap just loved doing this sort of thing, and used to get him to lie down so that the kids would sit all over him—make him sit up and all that sort of tricky business. Yet you'd turn him out for two or three days spell, and put the saddle on him and he used to put up a beautiful exhibition of bucking. I don't think he'd been taught to buck; he just had a cold back, a bit girth-shy perhaps.'

After joining the Roycroft home at Boonabaroo, Solo continued with his stock work at first, winning a lot of stock horse classes at shows, and being a very pretty-looking little horse also won a number of hack events. But his training rounding up the cattle and sheep had made him quick on his feet and handy to turn about—perfect for another national sport, polo-crosse.

'I used to play polo-crosse with him, a good game something between lacrosse and polo. I enjoy it and I played it for eight years straight. I was still playing it when I started eventing,' said Bill.

I asked him what made him think that Solo could turn to eventing.

'Well, naturally enough, everywhere I went on my place I used to jump something—you know—jump for joy, as Pat Smythe would say, and he used really to like this, going across country, ditches, anything you liked to put him at. And our team had been to Stockholm at that stage and were just back, so I thought I'd like to have a go if I had the horse—and Solo was it!'

As a show-jumper, Solo had shown a lot of promise, and although he was never top-class material he was already Grade A. Bill himself had been show-jumping 'right from the days when we used to go round over the old straight fences. I think probably John Shedden (the first ever Badminton winner on Golden Willow, 1949) coming to Australia more or less started off Olympic-type show-jumping back in about 1955. But it didn't spread to the country where I was until about 1958.'

The biggest drawback to Bill's plans to go eventing was a complete lack of knowledge about the vital preliminary stage —Dressage. Although he had ridden since he was a small child, to and from school on a pony, and most of his life (he was then forty-two) had been spent on horseback, he had never had a riding lesson, so it was back to school for Bill Roycroft.

'I learned myself dressage from one of Wynmalen's books* and this I continued with until Franz Mairinger took over to come to the Games, in 1958. Well, I did go to one school of ten days then, I think, but that was the only one before we left at the end of 1959 for Rome.' That simple truth must, I think, finally give the lie to the old adage: 'You can't learn how to ride by reading books.'

Bill went on: 'My own trouble in teaching Solo dressage was this: He was such a beautifully balanced little horse that if you wanted to change direction on him, naturally enough he'd change legs to the direction he was going, and I spent many months trying to get him to contra-canter, which you had to do in Three-Day Eventing, around those sharp corners in the dressage arena.' (Contra-canter being the same as counter-canter, two movements in the F.E.I. dressage test, where the horse must canter (a) to the right with the near-fore leading and (b) vice versa.)

Both pupils graduated successfully and by 1958 were ready for their first Three-Day Event in Melbourne, at a place called Oakleigh—they came second. Although Bill stands about 6ft., and Solo a mere 15 hands, Bill was never struck by the incongruity of their appearance. 'I never thought so much about it in those days because I suppose I did ride a lot of small horses, and Solo didn't really seem small to me. When you got on him and moved him up he gave you a big horse's feel. He carried himself high, and a very powerful short coupled-up little horse he was. But I guess I did look rather large on top, because I remember when I started to wear a top hat, our manager said to me: 'Bill, you know, you should get rid of that top hat—you with your head in the clouds and your feet on the ground on that little horse looks funny!'

In 1959 Solo was again second at Melbourne, and went on

* *Equitation*, Henry Wynmalen, *Country Life* 30s.

to win the Sydney and Gawler Three-Day Events (the latter equivalent to Badminton). On this showing they were selected for the Olympic team, travelling to England with the captain, Laurie Morgan and Salad Days, plus Neil Lavis and Mirrabooka and Brian Crago with Sabre.

In the Spring of 1960, Badminton, the testing-ground for the Olympics, was a scene of speculation, in which the Australians played a decisive part. Our Solo, 8th after Dressage moved up to 2nd after the Speed and Endurance (a maximum bonus on steeplechase and cross-country gave him 33.27 bonus) and finally won with a clear round in the show-jumping. In second place, a bare 3½ points behind, came Bill's team captain and big rival, Laurie Morgan on Salad Days, in third place was Anneli Drummond-Hay on Perhaps, and in fourth place was Mirrabooka. And in the event, that dress-rehearsal proved as true a forecast as there probably ever has been.

Bill Roycroft commented: 'The course at Badminton was similar to our courses at home. But I feel that our courses early on in Australia, when we started Three-Day Eventing, were bigger than they are now, because our chaps had come back with Stockholm fresh in their mind—and they built courses big thinking that that's what we would have to face at the next Games. Today they seem to have slipped back a bit; the courses are not as big or as testing.

'I suppose this could have had something to do with my winning at Badminton, but he was rather a terrific little machine, Solo. You could liken him to Our Nobby, a horse with a mighty lot of go. He gave you a big horse's feel to ride, a big-striding horse with a great depth of girth and great stamina. I think at Badminton he got full bonus with 22 seconds to spare on the cross-country.'

The Three-Day Event at Rome that started on September 7th, 1960, has now passed into history, and for two-thirds of the eighteen nations present it is a chapter I feel they would prefer to forget. Only six nations finished. Of the five countries ahead of Australia after the dressage, four were later eliminated in the cross-country. When a third of the horses had completed the cross-country, Roycroft and Our Solo—first of the Australian team and eighth of the 73 starters—were in the individual lead with a score of -118.33. But Bill, unfortunately, was in hospital with a broken shoulder after a fall at the drain-pipes (Fence 31). Bill described his disaster:

'Unfortunately you approached these pipes looking through them—I imagine that the horses looked through them and downhill as it was on the other side, and didn't see the little thin lip of concrete at the top. A lot of horses came to grief here, in that they just galloped straight through the fence as if they couldn't see it. There was a black French horse ahead of me—I saw the fellow later on—and he just galloped straight through those pipes as if they weren't there. I was following him and did exactly the same thing, only Solo came down on top of me, and ironed me out somewhat, and galloped away.'

The horse was retrieved, an unconscious Bill kicked to his feet and put back in the saddle to finish the four remaining fences on the course—a feat which, not surprisingly, he has no recollection of performing. Solo must have been doing a wonderful round, because even with that fall and some minutes lost while he was caught, Bill still received some 60 bonus points cross-country.

Whereas it has become accepted that a *man* can be kicked in the ribs to save his country's honour, there has recently been fierce argument as to the rights and wrongs of the same treatment to a girl. Colonel Frank Weldon commented, after Jane Bullen had won the 1968 Badminton: 'If it was a fragile girl lying on the ground instead, I would much rather someone else's toe did the kicking.' In 1960, girls were barred from Three-Day Events at the Olympics—but by 1964, they were in. Bill's views were typically hard: 'I would be just the same way as Frank Weldon. I revert back to Mexico now, with the Irish girl when she had her fall, Penny, at a simple fence, but she had a nasty fall and broke three ribs. Unfortunately the horse was destroyed, but had it not been injured and thus able to go on, nobody would have put Penny Moreton back on that horse and sent her on—but they would a man, they would expect a man to do it.

'I think probably in most things women can hold their own with a man and in lots of cases beat them, but when it comes to being cruel to the extent of sending them on, it's a man's job. In future, perhaps, one girl. You've got three men to kick about—but I wouldn't have a team, as Ireland did, of three girls. Most times, I suppose, nothing happens, but when you've gone to so much trouble to send a team a long way at great expense, you've got to be prepared to put up with quite a bit. No, I don't believe in girls in Olympic Three-Day eventing, because at the Games they must go on, hurt or otherwise, if they're capable of sitting on a horse again.'

The burden here is on the rider not on the horse. Commented Bill: 'It's hard for me to sit here and say the horses can't go if they're injured—I know they can do it. It's not the point that they can, or can't do it—it's the fact that if they get hurt you won't ask or expect them to do it.'

At Rome, 73 horses started the event, but only some 33 were left on the final day. 'Rome, was the biggest course I'd jumped,' said Bill, 'but then it was perfect going. I suppose it was the big flimsy fences combined with the fast going that caused the massacre of horses.'

Although the Australian quartet had got better and better —first Neil Lavis and Mirrabooka then Brian Crago and finally Laurie Morgan had all taken the lead in turn after Our Solo, there was a crisis. Sabre, who actually belonged to Bill Roycroft, but was ridden by Brian Crago, had broken down badly five fences from home, but nevertheless galloped on to get full bonus points cross-country, obviously, could not be brought out to pass the vet in the morning. But Australia had a lead of 140 points for the Gold medal, and there was only one way to keep it—retrieve Bill Roycroft from hospital! Bill recalls:

'Straight after the accident they flew me down to the Rome hospital in a helicopter—always wanted to ride in one of those things—but unfortunately I don't remember much about that trip! But when I had to get out, this was a bit cagey, because they said I wasn't fit to leave and they weren't going to let me leave. And I said: "I'm going," so they immediately took my clothes, and in desperation I said: "Well, look, if you don't give me back my clothes, I'm just walking out of this place with nothing on!"'

'This threw them into a bit of a panic and they brought the head man, who let me sign papers that I left at my own risk, and away I went.' In the Piazza di Siena off came the strapping—'after all, the jumping only lasts a couple of minutes,' and Bill Roycroft recorded a perfect clear round—'thanks to my good horse Solo' to finish individually seventh, behind Laurie Morgan's Individual Gold on Salad Days and Neil Lavis's Individual Silver on Mirrabooka.

Undoubtedly, a broken shoulder-bone, dislocated shoulder-joint, and dislocated collar-bone both ends—'... just a little bit of ... trouble' (Bill's description) was a small price to pay for his team's Gold medal.

On returning home to Australia, Solo came second in the 1961 Sydney Three-Day Event and retired in 1962 after winning the Pony Club championships with Bill's eldest son, Barry. After a spell of polo-crosse he now does light stock work at the age of twenty, on a stud farm at Mortlake, some twenty miles from the Roycroft property.

In 1965 Bill had another go at Badminton, bringing three horses, Eldorado (2nd), Avatar (2nd in Little Badminton) and Stoney Crossing, into the money—he was fifty-one years old, or should I say, young, because he also rode Stoney Crossing into 3rd place in the Cheltenham Gold Cup the same year, as well as riding with the show-jumping team (which included his son, Barry) in the London and Dublin Nations Cups, his mount there being Eldorado. They finished 3rd both times.

In 1969, after riding to a team Bronze medal with his son, Wayne, Jim Scanlon and Brian Cobcroft at Mexico the previous October, Bill collected 3rd and 4th places at Badminton on Warrathoola and Furtive.

The future for Australian eventing looks rosy, but Bill is a little pessimistic: 'We have a high standard in Australia, but I think perhaps we're slipping back a little. The young, who should be riding horses and enjoying it, are doing other, more exciting things like water-ski-ing—it's a mechanised age now. And kiddies no longer have to go to school on ponies— they're picked up in buses—and where they would normally have learnt to ride a horse, they are now sitting on motor bikes and driving jeeps.'

What was it, I wonder, that made Bill Roycroft take up eventing? Was it perhaps to pick up a challenge thrown down by Laurie Morgan, almost exactly the same age as himself, who came back from a successful individual tour of Europe in 1957?

Bill's reply came back: 'Well, nothing had been done in Australia before they sent that team to Stockholm, but when the team got home it became sort of a craze, and everybody wanted to event. And I thought, perhaps, well, I could sit on a horse, perhaps I would make the Games, and to this end I set my hat...'

That poor discarded titfer, lying forsaken in a dusty cupboard, has much to answer for.

14 Pitou

A small athletic figure wearing the azure-blue kepi of the French Army stood stiffly to attention on the rostrum at the XIXth Olympiad as the Marseillaise rolled out over the Mexican hills. Waiting impatiently behind him stood a chestnut horse.

Dependent one upon the other for success, their victory ride had been a shared honour—and although the Gold medal was awarded to the man rather than the horse—it was seen minutes later dangling from the horse's halter.

Jean-Jacques Guyon, 5ft.6½in. tall, weighing just nine and a half stone, is the most Gallic-looking Frenchman I have ever seen, with his military crew-cut and roguish eyes. When I talked to him a year after that great day, it was for him as if it had just happened—his pride in his 'Pitou' had not lessened a whit. 'He is very courageous,' Guyon told me, 'and especially bold jumping across country. It was my luck to be riding him.'

We were talking in the indoor riding school at Haras du Pin, Normandy—the French National Stud famous for its Percheron stallions. This was the venue, in September 1969, of the European Three-Day Event Championships—and Guyon was not competing since he had found no replacement then for Pitou, retired from eventing after Mexico.

'Pitou,' he told me, 'is a half-bred chestnut gelding foaled in 1959 in the northern coastal district of Normandy called "La Manche". By the half-bred stallion Plein D'Espoir,

property of the French National stud—Haras de Saint-Lo—
Pitou is out of Lakmé, a half-bred mare by the thoroughbred
Foudroyant and out of Vaudoise. There is talent on both
sides of the family, for while Plein D'Espoir is responsible
for many successful event and competition horses, Lakmé is a
full sister of Kenavo D, the horse that Janou Lefebvre rode
in the French Silver medal show-jumping team at Tokyo.'

As a three-year-old Pitou was sent to the Angers Veterinary Centre, where he was bought twelve months later from
the Remount Depot by Colonel Boyer (now Technical
Director of French Equestrian Sport) for around £28. Taken
to St. Cyr, he was taught dressage by a military colleague of
Guyon's, Adj. Chef Donnard, to whom Guyon paid an especial
tribute during the radio and T.V. broadcast following his
Mexico triumph.

Jean-Jacques Guyon was born in Paris on December 21st,
1932—but by origin he is a Poitevin. At two-years-old he
went with his parents to the warmer climate of Poitou where
he lived until he was twenty-one, going to school at L'Ecole
Saint-Germain, followed by Poitiers University where he
studied technology. But he learnt to ride back in Paris with
his uncle, M. Vivenot, who ran a riding school in the Bois de
Boulogne and was pleased to teach his twelve-year-old nephew
in the school holidays.

Military service followed university, and in 1951 Guyon
was sent to Tarbes in the Hautes Pyrenees, a garrison town
between Toulouse and the French border. But his love of
horses was as strong as ever and when offered the chance of
studying equitation under the auspices of the Army, he
decided on a military career. Posted north to Saumur, the
famous French Cavalry School (not very far from his home at
Poitiers) he concentrated on steeplechasing: 'It was my first
real chance to learn how to ride natural fences at speed across
country,' he said.

During the next few years he rode in many military races
as well as those for amateur riders, competing in the Prix de

France at Auteuil in the latter category. But after three years at Saumur, his initiation into the art of higher equitation had progressed so much that he was given the post of Assistant Instructor in the legendary Cadre Noir—the magnificent group of selected horsemen in the Cavalry School who practise High School riding in accordance with the classical French tradition.

Founded in 1771 by the Duke of Choiseul, the Academy of Saumur was the direct successor to the School of Versailles started by Louis XIV. In the middle of the last century the classical equitation was modernised and adapted, so as to include the necessities of modern riding—especially jumping, hunting, cross-country riding and steeplechasing.

In 1964 Guyon, who had by this time started competing in combined training events, was reassigned to the Special Military School of St. Cyr-Coetquidan, (north-west of Saumur) with the more responsible post of Chief Instructor. And there it was that he met the horse who would fulfil his one ambition —Pitou—who was taken over by him at the suggestion of Colonel Boyer, as he was now specialising in combined training. In 1965 Pitou entered his first novice event, won it, and repeated his success in the three other novice Two-Day Events he started in that year.

Guyon comments: 'For the first time in my life I was forming a partnership with a horse in whom I had complete confidence—and he had confidence in me. I had never owned a horse of my own, but although Pitou belonged to the Army, I was allowed to do what I liked with him. At first I was afraid that the Army would take him away from me, and give him to somebody else—that often happens—but then, when I began to do well with him, he was handed over to me completely to train. He jumps superbly, and I have never had a stop with him. He has only once fallen with me, and that was when he slipped up on the flat.'

In the autumn of 1965 Guyon, still wearing the black tunic of Saumur, but an unknown outsider, created a big impact on the riding scene by winning the French National Three-Day Event Championship on Mon Clos (a member of the 1964 Tokyo team and National Champion in 1963). The pair also achieved the impressive record of standing first in all three phases.

But by the following year Pitou also was becoming known. He started in five Two-Day Events, winning four of them, and ended the year by finishing 4th in the National Championship. Already the young horse was showing considerable potential—a fact that was not lost on the military and equestrian authorities choosing a team for the 1967 European Championships at Punchestown. As France had not sent a team to Moscow in 1965 or Burghley in 1966, this was a last possible try-out for Mexico.

On October 1st, 1966, Guyon was posted to the Equestrian Centre at Fontainebleau and Pitou followed suit. A year later the French team of Guyon and Pitou, Michael Cochenet and Artaban, Daniel le Chevallier and Opera, and Henri Michel with Ouragan finished third in Ireland—Pitou coming individually fourth, after faultless steeplechase, cross-country and show-jumping rounds (-43.3). A good showing for his first international event, and interesting to find that twelve months later Pitou reversed the first four positions with a vengeance: Durlas Eile, The Poacher and Lochinvar.

After Punchestown a disease which had been evident for some time started to become extremely troublesome—lumbar arthritis. And in fact, although Pitou was treated in Mexico and miraculously 'came good' for the event, Guyon told me that he will almost certainly never contest one again. 'It is too difficult to keep him sound,' he said. 'He suffers terribly from arthritis now, and I'm certain I would not be so lucky again, but I aim to try some show-jumping with him.'

At Mexico, Colonel Boyer noted in the Diary he wrote for the French magazine L'Information Hippique: 'Pitou has spent the last few months alternating between hope and despair. It was obvious that his lumbar arthritis was causing trouble, from the way he kicked out when he was tied up. But a remarkable treatment by Dr. Pradier allowed him to escape from his misery for the last few days—and we have benefited from it.' He added: '...But, in spite of his victory, I still think that we must look for our event horses in breeds nearer to pure thoroughbred—for Pitou is a single instance, and one cannot base a policy on an individual.'

The French team at Mexico—Olivette (Andre le Goupil) Quel Feu (Adj. Jean-Louis Martin) Joburg (Jean Sarrazin) and Pitou—lay in fourth place after the Dressage. Pitou's performance had visibly improved in the twelve months since Punchestown, and he scored -73.01 penalties as opposed to -82.5 previously. Colonel Boyer wrote in his Diary: 'Pitou was impressive for his precision in all the movements—only his stride left something to be desired.'

After a steady steeplechase, collecting 10 points under maximum bonus, (27.2), he set off on the cross-country course—second of the French team and fourteenth of the 49 competitors—but the sky, still a beautiful harmless blue, was to prove later the old sailors' warning: 'The bluer the sky, the harder it rains.' And when the rains did come the ground, already soft, became treacherous, the river gradually spread farther and farther until there was water everywhere. Boyer noted: 'Guyon was remarkable for the way in which he kept his accuracy and balance all through the difficult course.'

Pitou also kept his accuracy, making no mistake and answering his rider's demands with great willingness, and a steady stride. Guyon told me: 'The cross-country was just as arduous for the riders as for the horses! The altitude certainly accounted for some of the trouble, but the appalling weather was far more to blame, as certain obstacles presented a real danger.'

He went on: 'I had a lot of luck on the cross-country. I rode the course very carefully, but I still could have been carried away by the flooding river, as happened to my opponents.'

And indeed, as happened to the fourth member of the French team, Jean Sarrazin and Joburg (the former tragically killed in a motor accident at Christmas, 1969).

By going early in the day Pitou is thought to have had some advantage—and it is certainly interesting to note that Cornishman V (Richard Meade, G.B.) who started 34th, with the worst conditions, recorded a faster steeplechase than Pitou, and an identical cross-country marking (clear with 17.2 bonus). But by achieving a good dressage mark, Pitou led at the start by 12 points over Lochinvar (-85.01), by 35 points over the Bronze Medallist, Michael Page and Foster (U.S.A.), and by 25 points over Cornishman V who finished fourth. The balance lay, therefore, with the all-rounder, rather than the specialist.

Of the final lap, when Guyon held on to his nerve, his patience but nearly lost his lead to the Russian Pavel Deyev on Paket (who lost his way and eliminated himself), Guyon recalled: 'I did everything I could to ensure victory—but that did not prevent me from making a stupid mistake at the last fence. Admittedly the going was terrible, and it was not easy to get out of it without tripping up.' That final error in the 'unforgiving minute' nearly cost him the Gold medal, so close were the placings. But Deyev jumped the wrong fence—leaving Guyon as the second Frenchman in 20 years (Bernard Chevalier was the first, at London 1948) to win the Individual Olympic Three-Day Event Gold medal.

Of the Russian's mistake, Guyon commented: 'It was not right. I would have preferred to win in another way—it was a false victory.' His life's ambition had suddenly gone sour.

Of the Endurance test, which had claimed two horses as victims, he recalled: 'The ground was deceptive. Pitou stumbled, righted himself, stumbled. Towards the end I felt him weaken beneath me, but I never doubted him. He is trustworthy, staunch and strong. Above all, he has a great faith in me. Now I can hardly believe it is over—one trains for such a long time and then everything happens so quickly.'

Of Eventing in France he comments: 'The future is uncertain. Many people do not want to bother with all the hard
work involved. They want quick results.'

In October 1969, Jean-Jacques Guyon left the Army, but
still lives at the Equestrian Centre, Fontainbleau, with his
wife and daughter Cecile (born in 1967) and, of course, Pitou.
As I drove Jean-Jacques Guyon in my car up to the steeplechase course at Haras du Pin, where the final jumping phase
of the Championships was held, I wondered if perhaps Pitou
and his master share the same sense of *very* French humour:

When Guyon spotted the endless crocodile of cars creeping up the track, nothing would satisfy him but that I should
manoeuvre my car over a ditch on to the wide grassy verge.
Bumping up and down like a Dodgem car we cheated the
whole streaming crawling queue, and at that moment he was
as delighted as any small schoolboy!

Here was a man neither too grand to succumb to an impish
prank, nor too proud to admit to fear. 'I lived through
frightening minutes at Mexico,' he said, 'minutes I shall
never forget. But to win a medal, that is something—non?'

Pitou, former property of the French Army, has been presented to Jean-Jacques Guyon in honour of his historic
victory. The Concours Complet, as it is called in France,
demands men and horses made of iron. To Pitou, of the valiant
heart, and Jean-Jacques, of the tenacious nature, I say:
'Bravo!'

15 Durlas Eile

Like Geoffrey Chaucer's 'fair prelate' in *The Canterbury Tales*, Father Sweeney from Tipperary kept a good stable. But as almost invariably happens to producers of high-quality bloodstock, Father Sweeney sold his masterpiece in a moment of aberration while preparing for the priesthood—and has probably spent the rest of his life regretting it. Alas for the sporting cleric. Although he tried his hardest to buy the horse back, it was too late. The chance of a lifetime had gone for good, destined for a far more glittering future than ever the Irish priest could have given him.

Durlas Eile (pronounced Tur—Lus, and Eile to rhyme with sailor) took his name from Thurles in Co. Tipperary, home of the Sweeney family, where he was born. It was a simple beginning for a horse who was later to become Badminton champion, team winner at the World Championships, individual winner at the European Championships and create a world record market price before the Mexico Olympics.

But perhaps the end results were not so surprising after a closer look at Durlas Eile's parentage. He was sired by Artist's Son, a stallion standing in Ireland at that time by the immortal Gainsborough. Apart from several good steeplechasers Artist's Son was responsible for the 1955 Grand National winner Quare Times, and a brilliantly courageous Irish mare called Height O'Fashion—winner of six steeplechases and eight hurdle races, who came dramatically close to beating the mighty Arkle in the 1964 Irish Grand National. In fact Height O'Fashion was only caught at the last fence, and the finishing distance at the post was a bare 1¼ lengths.

On the side of the dam, Durlas Eile does not boast quite so much—although the mare, Royal Cob (by King Cob out of Royal Gem) came from good stock. She was seventeen years old in 1956 when the big colt was foaled, (she lived to be twenty-six), but as Father Sweeney was getting ready for his priesthood just then, the mare and foal were looked after by his brother Mr. Phil Sweeney.

Left to his own devices the colt grew to a tremendous size —eventually reaching 17.1 hands high—and like all really big horses needed (and was given) plenty of time to develop. Broken and taught to jump by the Sweeneys he was finally sold as a five-year-old, showing great jumping ability, to the Irish Army Equitation School at McKee Barracks in Dublin.

Durlas Eile, as he was now called, had inherited the formidable stamina of his family—as the Army officers found to their delight when they queued up to take him hunting— but he had not got the finishing speed, so the racetrack was out. And his placid temperament was thought, after experiment, to be rather a disadvantage in the international show-jumping ring, although he could jump a considerable height. So when the Army invited tenders for his purchase, in 1964, Durlas Eile, already eight years old, was still a great big promising horse that hadn't done much out of the ordinary.

Father Sweeney, now Curate of Knocklong in Co. Limerick, then came back into the story. At dinner with Thady Ryan, Master of the 'Black and Tans'—the Scarteen Hunt whose kennels are close to Knocklong, he told his host that if he had his way he would 'sell everything he had' to buy back a horse that was at present with the Army.

This very Irish statement, plus the accompanying history of the horse, convinced Thady Ryan, also chairman of the Training and Selection Committee of the Irish Olympic Horse Society, that this was the horse already described to him by

Major Eddie Boylan, and he determined to go up to Dublin and find out for himself.

It was the same horse—and in talking of it Father Sweeney had unwittingly written his own death warrant, in so far as his hopes were concerned. Aided by Thady Ryan, Eddie Boylan bought Durlas Eile to train for Three-Day Eventing— and a new era for Ireland had begun.

Eddie Boylan is a tall active ex-Gunner officer, much addicted like the Australian medallist Bill Roycroft, to polo. In eventing he believes he has found the complete answer to competitive all-round horsemanship, but still likes to keep his hand in at other equestrian sports—such as show-jumping, hunting, hacking and dressage. Having joined the Army in the War, just in time for the Crossing of the Rhine, he afterwards went to St. John's Wood with the Riding Troop, Royal Horse Artillery, and bought a multi-purpose horse called Cool Star, who later took him to his first Three-Day Event— the original Badminton—in 1949.

But when Cool Star was subsequently sold to H.R.H. Prince Bernhard of the Netherlands, who rode him in show-jumping and dressage events in Holland, Eddie Boylan disappeared from the eventing scene for eight years, only returning when he was stationed back in England again, at Shoeburyness in Kent. After two seasons hunting, show-jumping and eventing on a borrowed horse—Ballyhoo—he went back home to Hilltown, Drogheda, Co. Meath, with one overwhelming ambition—to get into the Irish team for the 1960 Rome Olympics. This he very nearly achieved, being selected as reserve rider with his new horse, Corrigneagh, on whom he had finished fifteenth at Badminton that year.

The fate of most reserve riders is to sit drumming their feet on the sidelines, and for Eddie Boylan this is the nearest he has yet got to his Olympic goal (at the time of writing). But, due to another horse going lame, Corrigneagh was taken over by team rider Ian Dudgeon just forty-eight hours before the start—and except for some appalling bad luck befalling the captain, Harry Freeman-Jackson, on the final day, Ireland would have taken the Bronze medal.

Although Corrigneagh went on to win the Open Event at Aldershot that year, his early promise was never to be fulfilled, for he died of a ruptured stomach during an attack of colic that November.

Eddie Boylan's next horse was a mare called Josephine (by Napoleon Bonaparte, dam by Match) who won him the Castledown Open Event, but she was eventually sold to Dr. Mikio Chiba, of Japan, before the 1967 European Championship. And then came Durlas Eile.

Horse and rider did not come together for training until July 12th, 1964, but with all the unshakable optimism of his countrymen, Eddie Boylan was convinced he could make the Tokyo Olympics in October. Eddie recalls at this stage: 'I soon found that his hunting experience needed no improvement, but that my task was to improve his dressage, and to get to know his capabilities.' But unexpectedly at the Eridge Two-Day Event in August, where the Irish short-list were trying out, Durlas Eile had a rare fall (his only one in competition) at a drop fence—probably weakening his chances considerably for team selection.

By the beginning of September, however, the new combination was making up ground fast. Eddie and Durlas Eile, after two months' acquaintanceship, finished fourth at Burghley—a performance good enough to jolt the ideas of any Olympic selector, except, it seemed, the Irish ones. Even though he had been placed sixth in the dressage and made up two places on the cross-country, Durlas Eile was considered too green for the Olympics. Eddie comments sadly: 'It might have been a "flash in the pan", though I certainly did not think so—but of course I was biased!'

How much difference Durlas Eile's contribution would have made at Tokyo no one, of course, will ever know, for the Irish finished fourth as a team. But it is curious here to remember that of the two really outstanding Event horses in the sixties, Merely-a-Monarch and Durlas Eile, neither was ever to gain the Olympic honours he deserved—the former because he became a show-jumper and the latter because he changed hands.

Throughout the winter of 1964-65, Eddie, greatly aided and encouraged by Mr. E. Schmit-Jensen, the international Dressage judge, continued to school his 'dark horse' at home in Drogheda. Most competitive riders have one 'Advice Bureau' where they go with their problems—and Eddie Boylan was no exception. As a man who followed the traditional military methods of Weedon himself, it was a broad but possible step to the continental teaching that combined the best of German, French and Spanish schools.

Of Schmit-Jensen, Eddie says simply: 'I think he is the best and most experienced teacher of Dressage I know. He deserves all the credit for any achievements that I have had in Dressage. He does not simply teach "The German school, the French school or the Spanish school"—but he has a real knowledge of all the old masters—and in my humble opinion is himself not just an instructor, but a real Riding Master.'

As a dairy farmer running a property of some 1,000 acres, and joint-owner with his brother of a poultry farm—his family have lived at Hilltown for at least 260 years—Eddie believes in working his horses during the morning's farm business. He explains: 'I like to keep an experienced horse in stables round the year and, when not actually preparing for an Event, just ten or twenty minutes every day helps to continue to improve his ability—both Dressage and jumping. You then start preparation for an Event with the horse in good condition, with his muscles well toned-up and ready to start the longer work to get fit for the second day of an Event. As a farmer, I combine farming with training.'

In this way of keeping a horse 'up' all the year he differs somewhat from the accepted routine of turning out rough a horse that competes in the summer for some of the winter months, only getting him 'up' again in time to start serious training in, say, late January or early February, to reach peak fitness in the Spring.

But in the case of the big bay gelding, as obviously with other Hilltown trainees, the method paid off handsomely. At Badminton in April 1965 Durlas Eile became a star overnight, taking the lead on the first day, never to be headed. Eddie recalls: 'Although I thought he was capable of being placed, he was a "dark horse" in more ways than one to everyone else. I do remember that Harry Freeman-Jackson (the great Irish rider, veteran of their team at Rome and Tokyo Olympics) wished me luck before the Dressage and asked how he was going that morning. I was very pleased with him, and said that I hoped he would get "in the forties"—which I think surprised Harry—but he said: "I hope you do."'

As it turned out, it was Eddie Boylan who surprised himself with the accuracy of his own forecast. Fulfilling Schmit-Jensen's teachings with telling precision, the pair recorded a *well* in the forties score of 45.5, to take the lead three points above Sheila Willcox (then Waddington) on Glenamoy. On the second day this lead was increased to 16.6 points, after an imposing journey through the Speed and Endurance phase, but the cards nearly fell for Ireland in the show-jumping ring. Two mistakes there cost 20 penalties, but luckily for Durlas Eile his downfall was Glenamoy's also—and victory went to the Irish Republic for the second time since 1949.

Now the Selectors could have no doubts, and five months later Durlas Eile was representing his country for the first time, at the European Championships in Moscow. Narrowly leading after the cross-country the Irish team of Boylan (Durlas Eile), Penny Moreton (Loughlin), Tony Cameron (Lough Druid) and Virginia Freeman-Jackson (Sam Weller) forfeited victory on the third day to the Russians, after some faulty show-jumping principally by Sam Weller, plus one mistake by Durlas Eile.

Many top event riders in the past have been criticised for

neglecting the dull but important show-jumping aspect, but Eddie Boylan could scarcely have been credited with that. In 1966, year of non-Badminton and Swamp Fever, Eddie took his last chance to jump at the Royal Tournament, winning the Kings Cup on Durlas Eile, which his father had won forty years earlier.

The World Championships at Burghley two months later were rather depleted in numbers after the Ministry of Agriculture's Swamp Fever ban, but nevertheless five nations started. The Irish team, with Tommy Brennan and Kilkenny replacing Tony Cameron and Lough Druid, then set out to exact their revenge for the Moscow defeat in a truly majestic manner—coasting home 300 points ahead of the only other finishers—the Argentine.

Durlas Eile, lying sixth after a competent dressage of 54 penalties, effortlessly caught up three places across country, but dropped, with Sam Weller, to fourth and third respectively after a mistake show-jumping. Victor was the Argentinian Carlos Moratorio on his Tokyo Silver medallist, Chalan, with runner-up Richard Meade on Barberry.

After losing the Whitbread Trophy at Badminton in 1967 to Celia Ross-Taylor's Jonathan, merely through two mistakes in the show-jumping ring, Eddie attacked the weakness once more. At White City's Royal International Durlas Eile, finishing second in the Intermediate Dressage, was the only horse also to compete in some International show-jumping. At Dublin in August he finished sixth in an International jumping event, only losing the National Championship by a foot in the water, in the second jump-off, to Seamus Hayes—indeed an honourable defeat.

Thus Punchestown, later that month, found Durlas Eile at the peak of his career for the European title fight. His exhibition of Dressage—for that is what it really was—is thought to rate as the best ever seen in an international Three-Day Event. Schmit-Jensen, standing on the sidelines, must have been a proud man. Durlas Eile's 33 penalties put him so far ahead of his rivals that he had no need to extend himself on the steeplechase (where he nearly fell) or the cross-country. The only challenge came from Martin Whiteley and The Poacher (of the victorious British team) but this evaporated after two mistakes in the show-jumping. Durlas Eile, it need hardly be said, was beyond all earthly error at this moment, and strode onwards in majesty to his throne, without the shadow of a fault in the show-jumping arena.

Eddie comments here: 'Durlas Eile had a wonderful temperament. He was an excellent traveller and a good "doer", but his easy-going temper was a disadvantage in the show-jumping ring. The cross-country, however, made him very keen, and in fact I used to delay mounting him until about 20-30 seconds before his time to start. I remember once at Badminton, as soon as I got up he started to do the Piaffe round "the Box" (the starting place for the cross-country). Someone shouted to me: "No, Eddie, you have got it all wrong—the Dressage was yesterday!" He had a long stride, and when he got going, could carry on for ages. He did not have much finishing speed, but his great willingness made him a lovely horse to ride over the country—fast or slow.'

Both visually and statistically this regal champion had dwarfed his rivals on the green bowl of Punchestown race-course—and by giving himself as he did Durlas Eile showed that he was mentally and physically capable of supreme exertion. Two writers, Lt.-Col. Frank Weldon (*Horse and Hound*) and Lt.-Col. Charles Hope (*Horse Trials Story**) considered that the horse who might have 'given him a run for his money' at that time was Merely-a-Monarch—but unfortunately for posterity these two giants were never to meet.

And, disastrously for Ireland, Durlas Eile was then sold to Canada for the Mexico Olympics, fetching a record price for a Three-Day Eventer, of £19,000. At Avandaro in 1968, the young and inexperienced Canadian Barry Sonshine made a gallant attempt to do justice to his horse in the worst of the

* Pelham Books, London.

weather conditions, but the pair finished down the line, after a fall, in thirty-third place.

What made Eddie Boylan sell the goose that laid the golden egg? He told me in Dublin in August, 1968: 'It was too much money to refuse. Had I done so, the horse would probably have injured himself irreparably in the field the following day.'

Fourteen months after Mexico, Eddie wrote: 'I have always had the ambition to ride in an Irish team in the Olympic Games, and help to win a medal for Ireland. I have missed the opportunity on two occasions—but I certainly hope to have a horse for Munich; I am sure that we shall have an experienced Irish team by then.'

To be offered a King's Ransom for a horse in a thousand, like Durlas Eile was at his best, is a frightening thought, for he could only move in one direction—downwards. There is inevitably great loss, therefore, for the owner in either decision: to lose his horse and the possible medal, but keep the money—or lose the money, keep the horse and hope it stays sound to win the medal. It sounds like one of those terrible tongue-twisters where you go round and round searching for the right answer—which is, of course, one only the inner man of the man concerned could say.

Did Eddie Boylan feel a pang at the thought of the honours he and his great horse might have won at Mexico? Perhaps—for he, better than anyone else, must know how long are the odds against finding another champion from the same street.

Countryman, the Queen's horse in the Gold medal winning British team at the Olympic Games equestrian section at Stockholm in 1956, ridden by Bertie Hill, here takes one of the third day show jumping fences. On the steeplechase phase he was the only horse to gain bonus points so greatly helping his country's chances.

Starlight, one of the most brilliant horses on his day in the earlier days of Eventing in Great Britain. He was in the British team which went to the Olympic Games at Helsinki in 1952, but the following year was dropped from the British team at Badminton. However, partnered by Major Lawrence Rook he won overall. In the picture he is taking one of the show jumps on the third day of that year.

Chalan, the World Champion of 1966 and one of the few foreign bred horses to achieve international fame in Eventing. He was bred in the Argentine and and was ridden by Captain Moratorio when he won the World title at Burghley. Later he was bought by the American rider Bill Haggard who is riding him in this picture, again at Burghley, in 1967.

Doublet, owned and bred by the Queen and ridden by H.R.H. Princess Anne during 1969, her first full season at Eventing, qualified for the Midland Bank Novice championship at Chatsworth. Here she is taking the Midland Money-box fence at Eridge Horse Trials near Tunbridge Wells.

16 Tramella

In the Parade of the Horse Personalities of 1969 at the Horse of the Year Show at Wembley was a little bay mare called Tramella. Only 15 hands high, her gleaming bay coat, lively step and bright intelligent eye made it almost impossible to realise that she was now twenty-three years old.

Tramella had come to Wembley from her home in Locksley in Warwickshire with Miss Diana Mason who bought her as a four-year-old. Together they rose to fame in the Combined Training field, and later, to even greater fame as a Dressage combination. Tramella in her time was one of the greatest Dressage horses produced in this country since World War II. With her adaptability and her quick capacity for learning 'tricks' she might well have become a circus horse.

The audience at Wembley in 1969 applauded nightly as she did her party piece of going down on one knee and bowing to the royal box. Not many knew the story behind this little trick.

When she first started to train her Diana taught her to stand on her hind legs and wave her front feet—she scarcely needed any training in fact, the trick came to her, it seemed, naturally.

In 1953 when Tramella was competing at the horse trials at Badminton and was stabled in the magnificent stalls adjoining the Duke of Beaufort's home, the royal party including Princess Margaret were making their customary round of the stables to visit the competing horses.

As Princess Margaret approached Tramella the little horse decided to do her party piece in honour of the distinguished visitor. But possibly her intention was misunderstood. The Princess drew back in some alarm and hastily passed on.

'I decided Tramella must be taught some other way to receive a royal visitor, so I set about teaching her to go down on one knee,' said Diana.

The following year, when Tramella was again competing at Badminton and the royal party paid her a visit, she bowed and bent her knee, to the great delight of all.

Tramella seems to be a horse with a penchant for royalty. When she was in training with the British team for the European Combined Training Championship at Basle she was quartered with the rest of the team at the Royal Mews in Windsor which the Queen had lent as a headquarters.

One day when Diana was doing out her loose box, (Diana always 'does' her own horses, often getting up at 5 a.m.) and had propped the door partly open with a wheelbarrow, she turned her back for a moment. Before Diana realised what was happening Tramella had neatly cleared the wheelbarrow and was briskly trotting away towards the Castle. 'She seemed to have decided to pay a visit to the Queen,' said Diana.

Tramella has always found an open door or gate irresistible. The trait almost made Diana decide not to keep her when she first bought her in Gloucestershire as a four-year-old.

'I noticed that when I went to look at her they led her right to the other side of the field before they opened the gate. As she flew across I soon knew why. I was not very keen on her at first as you could not ride her away from home. She was never nasty but very determined. She would keep turning for home and it took some time to break her of the habit.'

The two soon settled down together and later Tramella was to have the unique distinction of being the only horse ever to have been part of the winning British team in both European Combined Training and Dressage championships. The former was at Basle in 1954 and the latter in Copenhagen in 1963. She also won an Individual International Dressage competition at Aachen in 1964—beating the kings of Dressage, the Germans, on their own ground.

Through Tramella, whom nobody else has ever ridden, Diana became the first woman rider ever to be included in a British Combined Training team at an International Event —at Basle.

But they first started together in Small Hunter and Hack classes, and although graduating to Combined Training, and even having a go at show-jumping, and getting as far as the finals of the *Evening Standard* Foxhunter Jumping Championship having won a section in 1955, they never really forsook the hunter ring.

In varying years at the Horse of the Year Show Tramella was runner-up in the Working Hunter of the Year, runner-up and third in the Small Hack of the Year and third in the Small Hunter of the Year classes.

She was also Combined Training Horse of the Year in 1954 and 1955 at Harringay.

With such an all-round record it is not surprising that when a suitable signature tune was being thought of for Tramella in the 1969 Parade the one chosen was 'Anything you Can Do I Can Do Better.'

When Tramella was five Diana became taken with the idea of Eventing. 'It sounded fun and I thought we would have a go,' she said.

So in the summer of 1952 the young horse and her pretty dark-haired young partner had a go at a One-Day Event at Melton Mowbray and came first—beating another horse who was also making his first appearance and was later to become world famous, the incomparable Kilbarry.

They continued competing, often winning, and always gaining experience at Events up and down the country.

The next year they appeared for the first time at Badminton, putting up a very creditable performance particularly in the Dressage section. More wins at One-Day Events followed and their understanding of each other increased all the time, making itself most apparent in the Dressage sections at which they were fast becoming one of the most formidable combinations in the country.

So came 1954, the year that was in many ways to be the year of Tramella's greatest distinction. That year the European Championships for Combined Training were to be held at Basle in October, and the Badminton Trials were to be used by the selectors to choose a short list of likely members of the British team.

Women riders had of course competed at Badminton since the first Trials in 1949 and had gradually been making their mark. Men had ceased regarding them with an indulgent eye and, admiring their pluck, had come to regard them as worthy adversaries. But so far a woman had never been selected to represent her country in a Combined Training team.

In 1954 a woman, Miss Margaret Hough riding Bambi, won Badminton for the first time. Her triumph was slightly marred by a mix-up in the timekeeping for Kilbarry on the steeplechase phase which many said robbed him of first place. Whatever the rights or wrongs of this the fact remained that on the final day for the show-jumping Bambi needed and achieved a clear round to win while Kilbarry knocked down two fences.

Tramella ended only just behind them—a well placed third.

Both Bambi and Tramella were selected for the short list for the European Championship to go into training in the summer at Windsor with Kilbarry, Starlight and Crispin. Shortly before the final selection of the team, Tramella won her first Combined Training Horse of the Year title and so was included in the team. And to her owner went the honour of becoming the first woman to be included in a British team.

In spite of many forbodings when they first saw the

Olympic proportions of the course at Basle the team were easy winners. Tramella was to provide a gratifying surprise for the British and a real shaker for the foreigners.

Up till now British horses had conspicuously lagged behind the continentals in the Dressage section. Somehow they seemed to lack the sparkling movement and often gave the impression of being plodding and heavy.

But at Basle Tramella beat the lot, winning the section with a score of only 79.6.

The next day on the cross-country phase she was not so lucky. Turning too sharply after a fence she dislodged Diana and so lost points.

In the show-jumping, which was not confined to a flat central course as normally but included an up and down route as well, Tramella had ten faults. Her final placing was 7th which when one remembers that of the twenty-eight starters at Basle eleven were eliminated and two failed the third day veterinary test is no mean feat. Tramella came home in triumph. The other three members of the team were in the first three places but they had all been given a head start by Tramella's dressage.

In 1955 she again became Combined Training Horse of the Year.

This same year, however, at Windsor again in the European Championship team for Britain she had a bad fall and Diana decided she had had enough of Eventing and would in future concentrate on what had always been her strong suit, Dressage.

She rapidly became a regular member of the British dressage team going abroad every year with the team, which was all the time improving.

In 1960 Tramella was reserve horse for the Rome Olympics.

Although we as a nation still had room for improvement in Dressage we had long ago left behind the clumsy plodding image of the early 'fifties. Not only Tramella, but horses like Pilgrim and Little Model, owned by the late Mrs. Brenda Williams who twice rode in the Olympic Games when already a grandmother in her sixties, had all contributed to raising the British standard.

In 1963 we sent a team including Tramella to Copenhagen and here the British scored a triumph to win.

Thus Tramella became the first horse to be in a winning team for Combined Training and Dressage—a record so far unequalled.

The following year, 1964, when Tramella was already eighteen she won the international Individual Dressage competition at Aachen and Diana decided she should rest on her laurels.

'She had earned a rest,' says Diana. 'I shall never have another horse like her I am certain.'

So now Tramella divided her time between field and stable —and a highlight trip to London, still young at heart and a credit to Diana. Diana once decided to breed from her but Tramella, a real career girl, would have none of it. Her immortality is a place in the history of the international rise in the prestige of the British horse.

17 Countryman

'He's no good to you,' the fellow said—but he was wrong. Countryman did come good, and like the little girl in the nursery rhyme, 'When he was good, he was very, very good'. But first of all, he was bad—and then, without a doubt, he was horrid.

Eventually to be owned by The Queen and the Queen Mother as their first and only (but, hopefully, not their last) entrant at an Olympic Games, Countryman was a wild rascally Irishman from the bogs of County Cork, who was to win, with the British team, a European Championship and an Olympic Gold medal. While not one of the original 'adventurers' in British Three-Day Eventing like Starlight, his name will be remembered for ever, along with the other 'greats' of that era—Kilbarry and Wild Venture. These were the horses that put British eventing on the Map of the World, at Stockholm, in 1956, with a Gold medal for the best team performance.

And what a performance it was! From all accounts it was the toughest and the largest course ever built at an Olympic Games. The question was not how to get a clear round, but, simply, how to get round at all!

Countryman was foaled in the year of the first Olympics to be held after the War, 1948, at Wembley Stadium, London. He was by Sandyman, who was standing with Battleburn in County Cork at that time, out of a mare by Within-the-Law. Bertie Hill, a young Devonshire farmer already making quite a name for himself as an Event rider—he had finished seventh at the 1952 Helsinki Olympics—and a point-to-point rider, discovered him as a four-year-old in an Exeter dealer's yard late in 1952.

'I went there to buy a horse for my sister,' Bertie told me when I went to see him at his South Molton home. 'We didn't deal on this particular horse—and as I was coming away, a horse stuck his head out of a box. Countryman, I've always reckoned, had the best head of any horse I've ever seen—and he stuck his head out, and I said to the fellow: 'What's that?'

On being assured that the horse was no good to him, Bertie replied: 'Why not?' 'Well,' said the fellow, 'this is my trouble.' Bertie continues: 'And he was limping badly on two sticks, and I said, "Well, what's the trouble, does he buck a bit?" "Oh, does he buck!" said the fellow. So I said: "Can we see him out?" and he said: "Well, he's no good to you, anyway,"; so I said: "Why not?" and he told me: "He's got two shocking curbs". So then I began to think that the price might be right, within my bracket, and we pulled him out— and I liked him the moment I saw him.'

Bertie continued: 'And I said, "How bad is he?" and he said, "Well, it's like this: I bought him in Ireland as a quiet horse, but I've discovered since why they didn't ride him with a saddle. A chap rode him over half a dozen stone walls and went absolutely superbly with him, jumping like a buck —without a saddle—and I bought him.

'"I brought him back and put a saddle on, and he spent half an hour trying to get the saddle off. Well, we got over that, and I got on his back, and no sooner had I started to walk than he did this: he froze up and then when he moved he sent me to kingdom come!" I said, "Well, this is just too bad."'

The asking price of £175 seems almost ridiculously small nearly twenty years later. But Bertie Hill, then in his early twenties, was well able to meet the dealer on his own ground. He told him: 'Well, that's no good—two curbs and can't ride it,' and left for home.

The next morning before breakfast the dealer's wife rang up: 'Bertie, what did you bid my husband last night for that horse?' Bertie told her: '£90.' The answer was straight: 'You come and fetch him—he'll kill him else.' The dealer Bertie remembers as being aged about sixty-five years, and it is easy to sympathise with his wife's determination to get rid of the four-year-old!

But Bertie still hesitated, not wanting to force his friend into a sale. 'Are you sure?' he asked the wife—and the reply came: 'You'd better come and fetch him.' Bertie demurred: 'Are you sure about this? Does the Guv'nor say that it's O.K.?' And the Guv'nor's wife settled the matter for once and all: 'The Guv'nor's got to say it's O.K. I say that he's not riding it—you're having it!'

Bertie soon found that his friend the dealer had not exaggerated. 'They were quite right,' Bertie told me, 'he was a devil. It took me a long time to get him so that I could ride him. Every time you went from a walk into a trot, he'd turn himself inside out. When you went from a trot into a canter, it was very bad. Well, the hills were what did him in. We've got a very steep cleave, so I used to take him to the bottom and start to walk him up—get half-way up, and then start to trot.

'He couldn't buck up the hill, it was so steep—3 in 1—and eventually by the time I got to the top he was quite blown. But then, to start with, I used to jump off and lead him down, and come up again—and eventually it got so that when I got to the top I could canter because he was puffing and blowing. I went a little bit farther and a little bit farther before he finally gave it up altogether.'

Quite apart from the stimulating battle of wills, Countryman and his owner must have become superlatively fit by the time the former capitulated! A very dark brown horse, standing 16.2 hands high, he was some adversary. Bertie recalls:

'It was the speed of his reactions that had caught out so

many people. When I first got on him, he'd whip round with you and turn himself inside out. But coming up the hill was coming towards home, so he got to know that, and you could keep him going straight. But we have heard since from the Irish boys, two brothers, that they once drove Countryman for the whole of one day on long reins, over every kind of bank they could find in every ploughed field, and they were on their benders, but the horse could still do what he liked with them after they'd finished with him.

'It was in County Cork, where they were breaking him in— and they could back him without a saddle, but that was all. He was a real outlaw when I had him, but a terrific character.'

Bertie Hill has probably won more point-to-point races than anyone else in the West Country, and certainly more than any other event rider. In 1965 he topped the list for Amateurs with twelve victories, but was forced to give up after a bad fall. 'My neck was giving me a lot of trouble,' he told me, 'it wasn't too strong, and they told me that two vertebrae were badly damaged. I was very lucky not to be more badly hurt. I'd got two very good young horses, and I'd won eight races on one, and three on another, and I won one other race. I was riding this novice five-year-old, and another horse came across in front of it—and that was the end of my racing career. So I turned professional. I never had before, for the simple reason that if I had, I couldn't ride in races.'

Bertie's total was 166 wins—a figure only exceeded in this country by Major Guy Cunard, Frank Ryall and John Daniell.

Inevitably, Countryman took his turn on the racecourse. Bertie remembers: 'It was about three months before we got him going properly, and then, when he came, he came good and terribly quickly. As a five-year-old we raced him over banks—he ran three times, was second twice, and won a race. That taught him an awful lot, and in fact he would have made a good racehorse. The Queen Mother was in two minds, after the Olympic Games, about having him as a 'chaser, on purpose for Aintree.'

What a unique double that would have been—a Gold medal for Three-Day Eventing, and the Aintree Grand National! Obviously, because of the 2-mile Steeplechase and the (approx.) 5-mile cross-country course that requires about thirty fences to be taken at speed, there is a marked affinity between the horses and principals of the Eventing world, and those in the Steeplechasing world. But, so far, no horse has reached the top of both careers.

After his season's racing, and I suspect that had Bertie been a little bit older Countryman might have ended up winning the Foxhunter's Steeplechase at Cheltenham instead of a Gold medal, the business of Eventing came into view.

In 1964, Countryman started in two One-Day Events, winning one of them; at Stowell Park, the event that used to be run in Gloucestershire by John Shedden (the winner of the first-ever Badminton in 1949 on Golden Willow), he made a tremendous impression on that pioneer of top-class dressage in Britain—the late Mrs. V. D. S. Williams. Bertie remembers: 'Mrs. Williams liked the look of him a lot, and said she'd have him for me. We swapped horses, actually, I had a horse of hers to get ready for racing, a mad rascal, a very good horse but completely mad. And she got the dressage good on Countryman, which was an enormous help.'

Countryman, by now six years old, was promising material for Three-Day Event prospects at Stockholm in two years' time. But Bertie Hill was way ahead of his horse. After his good finish of seventh place at Helsinki, on Colonel John Miller's Stella, he had ridden with the British team again a year later, in 1953, at the first-ever European Championships, at Badminton. His mount then was Bambi, owned by Miss Margaret Hough—together with Major Reg. Hindley on Speculation and Frank Weldon on Kilbarry—and the team won.

And a year later British supremacy still held. Major Frank

Weldon and Kilbarry, Major Lawrence Rook and Starlight, Bertie Hill and Crispin (belonging to Mr. E. E. Marsh) and Miss Diana Mason with Tramella won the second European Championship, at Basle, coming home in triumph with the Individual title as well (Crispin).

The following year Badminton moved to Windsor, and the British team defending their European title pulled off the hat-trick. 1955 was also Countryman's debut in the international arena, and that, too, was a success. Riding in the British team with Kilbarry, Starlight and Tramella, Bertie and Countryman finished third individually, behind Kilbarry (1st) and Lt.-Commander Oram on Radar. Bertie remembers: 'Windsor was what I consider as difficult a course as we'd ever had here—it was quite an event.'

By 1956, Stockholm had virtually arrived. Bertie recalled: 'Mind you, there weren't so many horses, then, to pick from as there are now—and we'd got three very high-class horses in Kilbarry, Wild Venture and Countryman. But if one of them went wrong, we were in the soup!' Wild Venture was a horse belonging to Mr. E. E. Marsh who took over Starlight's place, and was ridden by Lawrence Rook.

But a short time after Windsor, Bertie had had his own problems of ownership. He had just got married and started a farm, and money was scarce. He found he could not afford to keep Countryman in top-class training, and decided he would have to sell him. The Swiss, who'd seen him at Windsor, offered a very big price, fortunately to no avail. Bertie comments: 'In order to ride him, it was better to sell him to The Queen. I was told that if I sold him here, I could ride him as the Olympics were coming up, so I sold him for £1,000, which would be a gift horse in these days. They thought it was a lot of money then, and to me it was a lot of money, I must say—for the Events were very few and far between, just Badminton and Harewood.'

Conditions at Stockholm in June 1956 were expected to be perfect—and so indeed they were for the dressage. But then the rains came, and quite soon the crumbling slippery take-offs were causing a lot of grief, especially the steep downhill bank of Fence 22, a post-and-rails in a deep dip.

The British team, marginally in the lead from Germany after the dressage, seemed to be holding their own, after a good round (with one refusal) from Wild Venture, and a promising one by Countryman—well up on time at the three-quarter mark on the cross-country. And then came trouble. Bertie described it to me: 'I got hung up on this Fence 22. It was one where you go partly down and then jump across on to another bank. Walking round the course, I had wanted to jump from bank to bank—there was only one other fellow who did, and that was Harry Freeman-Jackson. He'd got a horse that was another Countryman, a racehorse. Countryman would have stepped across it if he'd been allowed to go on, but we were told not to—to take it steadily because it had been so wet, which was fair enough. That's what a trainer's for.

'And it was just darned bad luck that the very spot that I'd chosen to approach the fence at had become very very slippery, because a horse had just been pulled out dead there. As Countryman took off, the bank gave way ... and as he was sliding to the bottom he lurched himself at the other side, literally threw himself. We've got a film of it—his hind legs drop back into the ditch and his forelegs straddle the top rail.

'Well, there he was. About twenty soldiers came and tried to lift him over, and out, but they couldn't. I jumped off and we all tried to throw him back, but that didn't work either. Then, fortunately I remembered that this had happened here at home with a bullock, not long before—it had got caught in a gate, same sort of thing, and I had got hold of its leg: as it tried to straighten itself, I held it and it pushed itself back. Just the same thing happened with Countryman. I held his leg, just like giving someone a lift into the saddle—held the back up—then when he struggled he tried to straighten it, and he threw himself back over. He was submerged in the water in the bottom of this dyke, which was supposed to be dry, and went under completely—then turned around in the water (he'd gone in on his back). I was never more thankful to see a horse come upright in my life.

'I went back, got on, and the saddle—everything—was nothing but a slimy mess. At about twenty lengths back I turned him round, he pricked his ears and jumped from bank to bank as if nothing had happened, as if saying: "O.K., Guv, let's go." What an incredible horse.'

To a cheer from the bystanders the brave pair sped onwards safely, to victory. Amazing to think that Britain could still win, with two run-outs and that fall, which cost Countryman 80 penalties, (20 for a refusal and 60 for the fall). But although he was terribly unlucky to have the fall, he was lucky to escape—for nearly a third of the fifty-six riders had trouble at that fence.

Short of disaster, Britain had the Gold medal in the bag, with a generous allowance of four fences down per horse in the show-jumping ring, equal to 120 points, over Germany: and they made it easily, Kilbarry winning the Individual Bronze medal as well. Bertie Hill describes the cross-country with feeling:

'My God, it was a course—very, very tough. The boys laughed at me when I said (in Mexico) "You haven't seen a real one yet." Every one except Derek (Allhusen) who said: "He's quite right." He kept telling Ben Jones: "We shan't see what we saw in Stockholm", because Derek was there—and that was when there were only three in the team, three had to finish, a very dodgy situation.

'In fact, there was so much trouble with the Course, and the horses killed, that it was said there was going to be an inquiry into it. But by daylight the next day there wasn't a single pole left in sight. Everything had been cleared off during the night by the army boys; everything was gone. People went back to measure, and see how high it was—and it was all gone—cleared by the Swedes.'

It was four years before Bertie rode Countryman again—at a try out for the next Olympics at Rome. But it was too late. He was no longer the same bold-hearted horse who had ignored danger four years previously. Too many long hours of dressage training had taken away his spirit, and it never came back. Bertie says sadly: 'I must confess that it does hurt to think that I sold him, afterwards, because he could have done another Olympics—he was only eight at Stockholm.

'The Queen would have sold him back to me, but unfortunately I didn't have the money—and so the Duke of Beaufort bought him for David Somerset. He did a great job as a hunter, but he could have done anything.'

Although David Somerset did ride Countryman at Badminton in 1957, 1958 and 1959, progressing from 23rd, initially, to second in 1959 to Sheila Willcox on Airs and Graces, thus keeping the Event side going, Bertie found him 'dead' in 1960. The dressage expert who had given him two hours, instead of ten minutes, a day had done his job too thoroughly, not realising, perhaps, that such a fine, rare spirit can never be subdued or dominated—only broken.

For Bertie Hill that heartbreaking experience could not even be obliterated with victory in Rome. Competing in his third successive Olympics, this time on Wild Venture, he again came to grief at a crumbling bank. Although the pair did finish the course, France beat Britain for the Bronze medal by half a mark.

After turning professional, Bertie trained the British team for their European and Olympic victories, in 1967 and 1968. And without a doubt the will to win is just as strong in him now as it was when he drove Countryman tirelessly up and down the Devon hills. The horse and the man were two of a kind—gifted naturals who followed their instincts through a mechanised age.

18 Starlight

One of the most brilliant but mercurial horses of the earlier days of Three-Day Events was Starlight XV, a 16 h.h. bay who was ridden to fame by Major Lawrence Rook, then in the Guards and now farming at Tetbury in Gloucestershire.

Looking back recently over a gap of sixteen years Major Rook described Starlight as 'A real bastard of a horse'. But he said it with an affectionate gleam in his eye and went on to recall his good points rather than the bad.

The late Hylton Cleaver, of the *Evening Standard* who in his day was one of the most authoritative writers in Fleet Street on equestrian affairs, described Starlight as 'Great-hearted, but too temperamental.'

Bred from Trappeur II out of a point-to-point mare called Dawn, Starlight was bought as a wedding present to his wife by the late Mr. J. R. Baker in Devon. He was intended as a steeplechaser. Mr. Baker then had a horse of his own racing and thought it would be fun for his wife to have one too. He was sent to the late Gerald Balding for training. From the start Starlight was a problem. If he had a mind to it he could jump like a Guy Fawkes cracker, but he was completely undisciplined and, it seemed, untrainable.

He passed to another trainer, Dick Hern, who used to train the Astors' horses, but he still did not settle down to chasing.

At about this time, the late 1940s and early 1950s, the idea of Combined Training as a serious sport was just taking shape in Britain. The Duke of Beaufort had decided he could put on as good a show in the grounds of his home at Badminton in Gloucester as had been put on for the Olympic Games at Aldershot in 1948, and the British Horse Society had agreed to back him, at least until a team for the Olympic Games in Helsinki in 1952 could be decided upon. So started the Badminton Horse Trials—and the bright if somewhat flickering career of Starlight.

Dick Hern was at Porlock visiting the establishment of the late Tony Collings, who had recently set up the Porlock Vale Riding School and was looking for suitable horses for Badminton. It was suggested that Starlight might benefit from the discipline of Combined Training. So he went to Porlock and Major Duggie Stewart who had been a member of the 1948 team at Aldershot took him over. Later Major Stewart was to go to Helsinki as did Starlight. But by this time the Major had transferred to show-jumping and Starlight was ridden by Major Rook.

During his days of training for eventing Starlight gave those about him many headaches. For instance, the sight of a vet drove him nearly berserk. No one really knows what was the origin of this aversion. One theory is that he was never properly gelded and the sight of a vet brought back painful memories. It is thought by some that this also explained his erratic behaviour.

Whatever the reason the fact remained that before a vet could go into his stable even for the most cursory visual inspection the horse had to be blindfolded. Yet at this time he was looked after by a girl, Pip Rankin, who could do almost anything with him and with whom he was as gentle as a lamb.

After some preliminary training he was tried out at a One-Day Event in 1950 at Wellesbourne, ridden by Major Duggie Stewart. He shaped up quite well and was taken for a second outing to a One-Day event in 1951 at Great Auclum.

So came the New Year of 1952. The year of the Olympic Games at Helsinki—and the year that the general public, even though only on a small scale then, first took an interest in the Three-Day Event section of the Games. Major Lawrence Rook was on the short list as one of Britain's riders and it was decided to send him to Porlock to see how he got on with Starlight.

They got on extremely well. Starlight was a tremendous jumper and full of courage. Although he took a lot of holding and firm riding, Major Rook says that as soon as he came near a jump 'you could ride him with your little finger'.

Eight horses were at Porlock for preliminary training for the Olympics by Tony Collings. They had been selected after the One-Day Event at Great Auclum where the course, built by Neil Gardiner, another early event enthusiast, had been reckoned by many to be suicidal. It was certainly nearer to an Olympic course than had been seen often in this country before—and probably never seen at a One-Day Event. Gardiner, however, rode over the course himself—and in due time those who eventually got to Helsinki said it had been the most useful pre-Olympic trial of all.

Of those eight horses none was very remarkable except Starlight. He had already started to show that brilliance which in spite of his being so unpredictable has earned him a place among the greats. He was not originally selected from the string in training at Porlock as one of the final members of the British team. But shortly before they were due to leave for the Games one of the team members, Major Michael Naylor-Leyland, fell ill, so his place was given to Major Lawrence Rook who by this time was firmly in the saddle with Starlight. Unfortunately, he did not remain firmly enough in the saddle to win an individual gold which was well within their reach until near the end of the cross-country.

The misfortune came about when Starlight, going so fast that his British supporters including the Duke of Beaufort could hardly believe that it was really him, fell into a deep ditch and unseated his rider. This did not cost him penalty points as he was outside the penalty area. Major Rook, had however, gone down with great force and was obviously dazed and stunned.

The British supporters at the spot quickly caught Starlight before he had time to make off. Others heaved Major Rook to his feet, shook him back to semi-consciousness and watched him remount. The pair, still both not really knowing what they were doing, set off down the track and jumped the last fence. Then they went on the wrong side of the last flag and were eliminated. Up till then Starlight had been in the running for being the highest placed individual horse.

When Starlight returned from Helsinki he went back to Devon, to his owners the Bakers, and was turned out for a rest after the strenuous training for the Olympics and the journey to and from the Games.

Even on his journeys abroad he just had to be different. In those days flying horses from one country to another for a show was a great novelty, and not nearly so much was known as to how a horse would react to the strange experience and how to cope with it. When it came to flying Starlight Major Rook was extremely dubious and eventually insisted that when the horses were landed Starlight should not have to be cooped up in a horse-box with other horses immediately after the flight. He was so claustrophobic that Major Rook feared he would become completely unbalanced if he were transferred immediately from the confined conditions of an aeroplane to those of a communal horse-box.

When this situation was put to the authorities on the destination side they agreed to make special arrangements for Starlight to travel from the airport to the stables where the visiting competitors were being housed.

These 'special arrangements' turned out to be an open-topped, gate-sided knacker's cart.

There was Starlight with Major Rook and his groom driving ignominiously through the streets in the open truck looking much more like a couple taking a broken-down horse off to the knackers than the proud representatives of Great

Britain in the leading equestrian event.

After a rest with his owners it was decided to keep him Eventing for a little time more, especially after his by-no-means-disgraceful performance at Helsinki, so he went to Count Orssich for further schooling.

So came 1953, with Starlight much improved and steadier. This year the Badminton Trials were truly international top-grade horses from France, Holland, Poland, Ireland, Sweden and Switzerland. It was decided that Britain must be strongly represented. After much discussion and argument it was decided to drop Starlight from the official team and make him reserve.

Almost as if he understood the situation, Starlight proceeded to mop up all the opposition—ably assisted by his rider, who once again was Lawrence Rook.

In the Dressage phase he collected second-best marks of the day—to the astonishment of his many detractors and supporters alike, the difference being in the reactions of the two factions.

He sailed through the speed and endurance tests, and the cross-country and put on maximum bonus points. Finally, at the end of the third day and the show-jumping phase, he and his rider emerged as the clear winners of the individual prize.

After this brilliant display he was kept in training for Eventing although it had been intended to return him to racing. He was in the British team which won the European Championship at Basle in 1954 and his final placing was third, just behind Kilbarry. When he returned from Basle, by now a seasoned traveller, he went for a rest to his owners the Bakers down in Devon. But he came back again to Major Rook for the European Championships held in Windsor Park in 1955 and was selected for the British team. Britain again won the championship but it was noticed by everyone that Starlight was entirely lacking in 'go'. It was as if he had become bored with the whole business and preferred to leave it to some other horse.

In the words of the man who knew him best, Lawrence Rook, he had 'gone sour'. He was a potential for the 1956 Olympics but never made the short list nor regained his zest.

It was decided that the time had come to return him to 'chasing and he was given to Toby Balding. Toby qualified him for point-to-pointing and rode him at Larkhill. But it was sadly obvious that his competition days were over. He was then fourteen. The following year he died.

19 Chalan

Broadly speaking the horses which have most distinguished themselves in the field of the Three-Day Event have been of English or Irish origin. The Germans and the Swiss have of course produced some excellent horses, but their best products go back to before the second world war, which was before the sport had really been introduced to this country. Even horses which have made a name on the other side of the Atlantic have often been bred on this side.

There are, of course, notable exceptions, one of which is Chalan, who was bred in the Argentine from a sire called Encarté and foaled in 1956. When he was ten years old he became World Champion—at Burghley.

Chalan, a handsome chestnut gelding is almost always referred to as a 'little' horse, but he was in fact officially measured at 16.2 hands. He is so compact with such a sturdy neck and shoulders that he never looks as big as he really is.

He first made the international headlines when he was seven, being one of the horses in the Argentine team for the 1963 Pan-American Games which were held in Brazil at Sao Paulo. These Games are roughly the equivalent of our European championships, and in this particular year the Argentine, Brazil, Mexico and the United States of America were competing.

His rider was Captain Carlos Moratorio of the Argentine,

and the pair were another of those perfect combinations—
although at the end of the Games they had not achieved
the promise they had shown at the beginning, their progress
being dogged by ill luck.

This was the first time the Games had been held in Brazil
and the Brazilians arranged all the events—including the
Three-Day Event—to be held within the compass of their
largest city. The cross-country course was laid out close to the
airport, the start and finish being at the Ippico Santo Amore
club. The course was a difficult one to follow and four of the
fifteen starters were eliminated for taking the wrong course.

Chalan did a good dressage test in company with the
Americans and another Argentine horse.

At the end of the second day he was only marginally behind
Grasshopper, ridden by Michael Page for the United States.
(This horse was in fact a former Irish Olympic horse under
its original name of Copper Coin.) Indeed, only two points
separated the two. In the last phase, the show-jumping Grasshopper had 22 faults and it seemed as if Chalan must win,
but by a stroke of bad luck he slipped as he turned into
one jump and fell. Thus he ended the Games in third place.
Nevertheless he had 'arrived'. He had shown he had that star
quality of the great Three-Day Event horses.

The following year was the year of the Olympic Games at
Tokyo, and Chalan, ridden by Captain Moratorio, was in the
Argentine team. Eleven other countries were competing.

At the end of the dressage phase Chalan was third. A
German horse Donkosak was in the lead and Master Bernard
for Great Britain was second.

On the cross-country course, which brought disaster to
many horses (and indeed put Britain out of the Games), the
Argentinians fell back to seventh place as a team but Chalan
had done brilliantly with only one jumping mistake and had
fallen back only one place ending the day fourth. The leaders
were all very close together in marks there being only 21

points between the leading horse (Barberry of Great Britain) and the eighth horse (Black Salmon of Eire).

The jumping course for the third day was a difficult one with maximum sized jumps and perilously sharp changes of direction.

Chalan had a clear round. He had jumped like a cat, and as his rider remarked, 'I purred like one'—but as soon as they left the ring began their greatest suspense. Comparing their score with the horses which had gone before them it was obvious they must end in the first three—either a gold, silver or bronze medal. And the two horses yet to go were Donkosak, who had finished the second day in third place just ahead of Chalan and Surbean (Italy), who was second. (Barberry had alas come to grief in the show-jumping and was out of the running).

Surbean, doubtless fired by the challenge of Chalan, did a clear round and clinched the individual gold medal. Capt. Moratorio confessed he could barely watch the German Donkosak as he set off to tackle the course. As it happened, Donkosak knocked down the combination and so had to be content with third place.

Chalan had secured the individual silver medal for the Argentine.

Captain Moratorio said afterwards that Chalan's masterly performance in the show-jumping phase did not surprise him as 'little' Chalan had started life as a show-jumper in the Argentine.

In this respect Chalan was rather exceptional. It is much more usual for a horse to graduate to show-jumping from eventing (as did Merely-a-Monarch) than the other way round.

It was to be more than a year after the Tokyo Olympics before spectators of the sport in Britain were to have a chance to see Chalan—in 1966 at Burghley. That was the year when Burghley was selected as the centre of the World Championship Three-Day Event. It was a most unfortunate year for any British centre to have been chosen. For that was the year when equine swamp fever hit Europe and all movement of horses between Britain and the rest of the continent was halted unless a period of quarantine was observed. This meant that countries like Germany, France and Switzerland could not compete. But countries beyond the Atlantic, the United States of America and the Argentine came over, and Russia—which was beyond the limit of the quarantine ban—also competed. Ireland also sent a strong team.

Chalan made his mark from the first. He did a superb dressage test, scoring 76.8%, and being almost entirely responsible for the Argentine being in second place after the first day. On the second day he again ended streets ahead of his rivals. Across a course which most competitors and officials admitted was tougher than that at Tokyo he gained 78 bonus points and ended with a score of plus 73.1 well ahead of any other competitor.

Britain and America were eliminated after the second day and Russia joined them at the veterinary inspection before the show-jumping when one of their remaining three horses went lame.

Chalan had a commanding lead individually, although the Argentine team was well behind the Irish. However, possibly because he sensed the tension of his rider who admitted to feeling a trifle more nervous than was his wont, he knocked down a fence. He could afford to do so however, and still became World Champion, 1966. This performance, together with that at the Tokyo Olympics and at the Pan-American Games, has put him among the all-time greats of the Event horse world. But sadness was to follow.

Chalan had always been owned by the Argentine government and now they decided to sell him. The price asked was understandably high—far beyond the means of Capt. Moratorio to whose skilful riding Chalan owed much of his success. These two had an affinity such as Lt.-Colonel Weldon had with Kilbarry, Sheila Willcox had with High and Mighty, and Jane Bullen with Our Nobby.

It must have been one of the worst moments of Capt. Moratorio's life when he realised that the authorities had really determined to sell the horse which had been so much part of his life. But a soldier knows how to obey orders and Chalan and his rider parted company. The price has not been officially stated but rumour had it that it went into five figures.

Chalan's buyer was Bill Haggard of the United States—a wealthy man and a keen event rider who had already been seen on this side of the Atlantic. Mr. Haggard brought Chalan over to Britain in 1968 to compete at Badminton with the rest of the proposed United States team for the Mexico Olympics later that year.

None of the Americans went full out as this Badminton was to be a sort of dress rehearsal for Mexico. But still their showing, including that of Chalan, was not inspiring. They were not in the first eight, all of which places went to Britain.

Haggard tried him a few times more but it was obvious that the two did not get on. It was difficult to believe he was the same horse as when he had been ridden by Moratorio.

Being a sensible as well as a generous man Bill Haggard did not wish to see the horse wasted and thought he might do better with another rider. So he presented him to the United States Equestrian Team, and he became the mount of one of their most experienced and brilliant riders, Kevin Freeman for the Olympic Games.

Alas, although the United States team won the silver medal for the team event it was without the assistance of Chalan. On the second day, in appalling weather conditions, he was eliminated during the cross-country.

It really seemed that this was a case of one horse, one rider. Some might say it served the Argentine right for parting with him as they have done little in the event field since.

He is now fifteen and obviously his best days are past. But

in spite of the disappointment he must have proved to the Americans, Chalan has earned his niche in equine history. He was a Tokyo Olympic silver medallist, and won the 1966 World Championship.

20 M'Lord Connolly

Even today few people who remember the bay gelding Anglo-Arab M'Lord Connolly at his best can make up their minds whether there was a streak of weakness in him, whether he lacked courage, or whether the faults were possibly in the way he was ridden. Discussions and arguments, especially those conducted from a long period of time, are fruitless and inconclusive.

Whatever the reason, the fact remains that this brilliant horse—owned by Capt. James Templer who always rode him —who went right to the top in three years failed at the supreme moment, in the Olympic Games in Tokyo in 1964. In the cross-country on the second day, at what seemed a comparatively easy fence, certainly one which had given little trouble to most of the other horses, he suddenly gave up. No efforts could make him have a go at it and he was eliminated, and with him went Britain's hopes of any success. Some said he was ridden too hard in the early stages, especially in the steeplechase, though his time for that was five seconds below the time allowed for a maximum bonus. Others said the horse was not fit enough for the gruelling Olympic test. Some shook their heads and remembered that in 1962 at Badminton he had missed being placed first in the Little Badminton Event because of a fault at the last fence. Perhaps he was just an unlucky horse.

Although he just missed first place in the Little Badminton Event the rest of 1962 was a brilliant year for him. He went on to win at Sherbourne and Eridge and then came Burghley. On this, the second year of the Burghley Horse Trials, it was chosen to stage the European Horse Trials championship —the sixth to be held.

There was considerable interest in this championship mainly because the Russians sent over a team. No one thought much of their chances—to British eyes the horses looked too lean and not fit. The western world was soon shaken out of its complacency when the Russian team won a convincing victory. Of the British team one was eliminated on the cross-country, another had two refusals and a fall and the third had a refusal and a fall.

M'Lord Connolly had not been selected for the team in spite of his growing reputation as the selectors felt he had not had enough experience. So Capt. Templer, a young gunnery officer went it alone.

And alone he did it, winning the individual championship and putting the Russian rider Gaziumov into second individual place. So M'Lord Connolly salvaged something of our national pride and became one of our most-fancied Three-Day Event horses.

The following year in the spring the rain poured day after day and the ground in Gloucestershire was reduced to a quagmire. Reluctantly the Duke of Beaufort had to cancel the Three-Day Event. The ground on his estate simply would not stand up to it. Not only was there the churning up of horses hooves to consider but the thousands of cars and wheeled vehicles which would also pound into the ground.

But in this particular year there was an international Three-Day Event held in Munich. Although not an official championship it had the same standing and prestige and six nations entered teams.

This time M'Lord Connolly was in the British team. He had won the Liphook trials earlier in the year which seemed to have served to limber him up. His performance at Munich was brilliant. Although after the dressage the Germans were

in the lead by more than 60 points, on the second day M'Lord
Connolly raced into the lead with the other members of the
British team well up. They were Richard Meade and Barberry, Jeremy Beale and Victoria Bridge, and Susan Fleet
and The Gladiator.

At the end of the three days Britain had won the team
prize and M'Lord Connolly the individual competition.

In 1964 he won the Badminton Three-Day Event.

This was the year of the Tokyo Olympics and he became
a virtual certainty for the British Olympic team. So much
so that at Burghley in the September, when the selectors
still had not finalised the list, he and Sea Breeze (a horse
ridden by Michael Bullen brother of Mexico Olympic rider
Jane) were only required to run hors concours.

The final choice of team was M'Lord Connolly, Sea Breeze,
Master Bernard (ridden by Sgt. Ben Jones) and Barberry
ridden by Richard Meade. All four horses arrived safely by
air in Tokyo after special wide stalls had been provided on
the plane. Sending horses by air is not the simple matter it
sounds.

The atmospheric changes and the noise can have the same
effect on horses as on humans, and any air turbulence can be
even more unnerving to a highly strung horse than to a
human. After all, you can explain to a human what is happening and the cause. Even the most intelligent horse cannot
grasp the principles of air travel. Two countries lost horses
during the long flight to the Games—Chile and the U.S.A.—
the latter losing one of their best horses, Markham, which
got into such a panic that he had to be shot.

On the first day of the Games the British team started well
in the Dressage. Master Bernard was second and M'Lord
Connolly was fourth, with Barberry and Sea Breeze gaining
quite good scores. At the end of the day Britain was in the
lead by a small margin from America and Germany.

Torrential rain on the second day made the going tough
and caused havoc among several teams. The steeplechase

course was a tough one and seemed to take more out of some of the horses than had been bargained for. M'Lord Connolly got round the steeplechase, as was said earlier, in only five seconds more than the time allowed for a maximum bonus. Then came his disastrous refusal in the cross-country and his elimination.

He was not the only British horse eliminated that day. Sea Breeze was eliminated for a refusal at the 25th fence during the cross-country—but he had been badly shaken by two crashing falls, one in the steeplechase and one at the fourth fence of the cross-country. At the first fall both the horse and Michael Bullen, the rider, were severely shaken, Bullen's shoulder was badly hurt.

Those who watched the event in Tokyo said it was a great tribute to the courage of Sea Breeze that he went on to tackle the cross-country at all after his crash in the steeplechase. Of course he had to do so if Britain were to stay in the event after M'Lord Connolly's elimination. With Sea Breeze's elimination our hopes had gone and the Games were over for us. Other eliminated nations were Japan and Korea.

Soon after the Tokyo Olympics M'Lord Connolly was sold to America. Here he became the mount of Kevin Freeman, a member of the U.S.A. equestrian team.

He returned to Britain with Kevin to take part in the world championships at Burghley in 1966. His final placing in these was ninth, which considering he had a fall in the cross-country was fair. Although he was one of the ten horses on the short-list to represent the United States at the Mexico Olympic Games he was not finally selected and now at the age of more than 15 it must seem his heyday is over. James Templer, who rode him for all of his career in Britain and representing Britain, now has a new young horse which has already made a promising beginning in trials in the Midland Bank novice championships at Chatsworth.

21 The Royal Family and Combined Training

From the earliest days of Badminton and the awakening of public interest in Combined Training, the Queen and other members of the Royal Family have taken the most active interest in the sport.

There have been few years when the Queen and the Queen Mother and members of the Family have not been guests of the Duke of Beaufort at his country seat for the now world-famous Three-Day Event. While she is there, the Queen often strolls round the stables which adjoin the house, chatting to the competitors and showing not only interest but a shrewd knowledge of their problems in tackling the course.

It is probably true to say that at the beginning as many members of the public flocked to Badminton in the hope of getting an informal glimpse of the Queen or Princess Margaret as did those who went to follow the Event. Gradually, with the help of Press and television, the spectators became more aware of what was going on, and better able to follow the complicated system of marking for the different phases—and increasingly familiar with the names of horses and riders. The thousands who today travel to horse trials, not only at Badminton but in all parts of the country are now knowledgeable and informed. But to the Queen must go much of the credit for firing the public's imagination and interest in this fast-growing sport.

In 1954, when the selectors for the British team which was to go to the European Championships at Basle were wondering where they could get the horses and riders together for intensive training, the Queen suggested that they should go to Windsor. She lent stables at the Royal Mews at the Castle, and placed Windsor Great Park with its marvellous facilities for training at the team's disposal. During the time the team was there she took the keenest interest in the riders progress and in the final selection of the official three.

The British team triumphed at Basle, and the Queen was so delighted that when Britain was officially allocated the 1955 European Horse Trials Championship she at once suggested to the organisers that the event should be staged in Windsor Great Park.

Next year, 1956, was Olympic year and the Games were held in Melbourne. But because of the Australian equine quarantine laws it was decided to hold the equestrian events in Stockholm. In the British team was a horse belonging to the Queen, Countryman III. It was ridden by Bertie Hill, one of the keenest and most brilliant event riders of the 'fifties and trainer and adviser to our gold medal winning Olympic team in Mexico in 1968. So, appropriately, the Queen had not only a patriotic but a personal interest in the progress of the team in the sport she so enjoyed. She visited Stockholm for the opening of the Games which were a triumph for Britian.

Our team won the Gold medal (does Bertie Hill have a Midas touch?), and Colonel Weldon of Kilbarry won the Individual Bronze.

As the years passed the Queen's interest remained undiminished, and now another member of the family was coming along; one who did not only share the Queen's enthusiasm, but was to become an active participant: Princess Anne.

While she was still a child she made her first public appearance in the show ring in the children's pony class at Badminton. Her name had not appeared in the programme, but, with that uncanny instinct which a crowd has for sensing when something is going on, by the time the Princess rode into the arena the spectators were about six deep around the perimeter. The Princess was completely calm and was placed first. After that she competed in a number of pony club events and was a keen member of the Garth and South Berks Pony Club.

At school at Benenden she took riding as an extra subject, and with the Battle Riding Club she was in the team which in 1968 won its way through to the Horse of the Year Show at Wembley for the finals of the Eldonian Quadrille.

But already her principal interest in riding events had turned to Combined Training. In July 1969, just before she left school, she won the senior individual Combined Training cup at the riding school display. At the One-Day horse trials at Windsor in the Pony Club classes she came seventh out of thirty-one. This was her first attempt in open competition, albeit for pony club classes, and the result was creditable.

It is interesting to note that at this time the Princess was riding a horse called Purple Star.

Purple Star was bred by the Queen's Equerry Colonel John Miller out of a mare called Stella which he had owned while a Major in the Welsh Guards, and which had been one of the horses in the British team at the Olympic Games at Helsinki in 1952—ridden by Bertie Hill. The pair were placed seventh individually, which considering that as a nation we were very much in the novice stage of Combined Training was a gallant effort.

In 1968 the Princess rode in the Two-Day trials at Eridge in the grounds of the Marquess of Abergavenny near Tunbridge Wells, and the Queen drove over from Goodwood to watch. In 1969 the Queen was at a number of horse trials at different parts of the country, on private visits to watch her daughter's progress.

By 1969 the Princess was riding two more horses—Doublet and Royal Ocean.

Doublet is owned and bred by the Queen, and is out of a polo mare called Doubtless. The chestnut gelding was intended as a polo pony but grew too big so was handed over to Princess Anne to see what she could make of him eventing.

Royal Ocean, which is the Princess's own horse, was bred in Ireland from racing stock. It is by Guersant out of a mare called Santa Baby, a descendant of Ocean Swell. It was schooled and hunted in Ireland and raced a little before it joined the Royal stable as an eight-year-old.

The year 1969 could be called the Princess's first full season at eventing. Between April 2nd and October 18th she competed in no fewer than twenty trials, sometimes riding Doublet, sometimes Royal Ocean and sometimes both.

During the season she qualified both horses for the finals of the Midland Bank National Novice championship which was held at Chatsworth.

Royal Ocean qualified at Windsor in April, and Doublet at Osberton in July. Only the winning horse at each of the selected trials qualified for Chatsworth. The Princess had other wins during the season, the most important being the Combined Training meeting at Stokenchurch in April where she had two firsts and a second and the Dressage meeting at Basingstoke where again she had two firsts and a second.

Three times she was only narrowly beaten into second place; at Powderham Castle in Devon, at Stoneleigh Abbey in Warwickshire, and at Wylye. At Wylye she had a nasty fall, but having finished the course slightly dazed she had a cup of coffee and completed the course a second time for final second placing. At this trial she was competing in intermediate classes against much tougher opposition.

Much of the credit for her first season's success must go to Alison Oliver, wife of show jumper Alan Oliver, who has carefully coached the Princess.

The Queen went to Chatsworth to watch the finals of the

novice championship and to see Princess Anne placed sixth.

So ended her first complete season in the competitive world of equestrian sport, a world where no quarter is given and none asked. If her public duties allow, it is quite likely that eventually we shall see her among the top flight of competition riders, in the years to come.

22 The Principal Horse Trials

In spite of the fast growing popularity of Combined Training as a sport, there are still only three major Three-Day Events held in Britain.

They are Badminton, Burghley and Tidworth. At first this seems strange, and anyone might be excused for wondering what all the fuss is about for a sport which has only three major 'meetings' in the year. But a little thought for what is entailed in organising a Three-Day Event soon makes it clear why there are not more.

In the first place a suitable course must be found. There must be room to lay out a full-scale dressage ring, a jumping ring, and a steeplechase course of two miles, another course of up to ten miles of roads and tracks and finally a cross-country course of up to five miles which includes thirty-four jumps over fixed obstacles, so that penalties are incurred only for refusals and falls. These jumps must conform to international regulations and include banks, ditches and water as added hazards.

There are few places in the whole of Britain where such a course can be laid out. Most probably the difficulties of finding a suitable place to stage a Three-Day Event accounts for the fact that up until the Second World War Combined Training was known as 'The Military' and was staged by the

Army on Army training grounds like Aldershot.

Only an organisation like the Army with the grounds at its command could begin to provide the facilities for such an event—and in those days there were few members of the public to cater for. The sport was essentially confined to a select band of horsemen and the mounted regiments.

To put on Three-Day Horse Trials as a public spectator sport as well as to provide the necessary conditions for testing horses and riders up to international standards needed the co-operation and generosity of one of the few remaining landed gentry with huge private estates at his command.

Such a one was the Duke of Beaufort, with his great estate at Badminton in Gloucestershire. After he had watched the Olympic events at the 1948 Games at Aldershot (the other sections were held in London), with especial interest in the Combined Training sections, he decided that he could put on as good a show at Badminton and at the same time British riders could begin to be selected and trained for the 1952 Olympic Games.

The Duke approached the British Horse Society, who gladly agreed to back him in the venture—and in 1949 the first Badminton Horse Trials were held.

There was already a steeplechase course on the Duke's estate which was used for that phase, and the cross-country course was largely laid out by the Duke himself and by Colonel Trevor Horn who lived near-by and who shared the Duke's enthusiasm for the project.

The dressage ring was laid out in front of the great house which dates back to the 17th century, and it continued there for many years, until terrible weather in 1959 softened the ground to such an extent that what had once been gracious green sward became a sea of mud which took several seasons to recover. The dressage ring was moved away beyond the lake and above it, and remains so placed today.

At first the Duke of Beaufort's venture was looked upon with mixed feelings by the horse-riding world. Some were enthusiastic, some sceptical. The latter were mostly doubtful about the ability of British horses to accomplish dressage. They looked upon this as some exotic foreign nonsense—quite unnecessary for a good hunter, which at that time was the only type of horse likely to enter for the Three-Day Event. It was not long, however, before some British horses at least were proving that they could master this 'foreign nonsense' very well indeed, and by the middle fifties horses like Tramella were beating their continental competitors at what had always been considered their own game. Even the most sceptical were beginning to realise the value of dressage in producing obedience, balance and suppleness even in the most brilliant goer across country.

So Badminton became not just a training for the 1952 Olympics but a great event in every horseman's calendar—and the greatest in the fast-growing numbers converted to this new great sport.

Meanwhile other Three-Day Events came into being.

In the early days a frequent member of the Royal house party at Badminton House for the trials was the Princess Royal, Princess Mary, whose home was one of the greatest estates of the north, Harewood House.

The Princess was fired with the idea of holding a similar event to Badminton for the benefit of those in the north, in her beautiful grounds in Yorkshire. The British Horse Society were entirely in favour, and in the autumn of 1953, the second Three-Day Event came into being as an annual function. A magnificent cross-country course was laid out up to full international standards, and many horses who later achieved world fame started their winning careers at Harewood.

Yet somehow, although everything seemed to be in its favour, Harewood never quite caught the public imagination as did Badminton. Perhaps the people of Yorkshire found the sport too long winded and 'highbrow'—and those of the south and west found the distance to the North Riding too great. Whatever the reason, there were never the entries nor the spectators which it had been hoped to attract. But it went out with a flourish. In 1959 the European championships were held there (the team event won by Germany and the individual by Switzerland with Britain second for both awards), and after that it was announced that owing to a change in agricultural policy on the estate the trials would no longer be held.

The following year the British Horse Society were in a quandary—back to the one major Three-Day Event at Badminton. This was a pity as the sport had grown and prospered and there was an increasing number of One-Day Events on the calendar.

But at Tidworth in Wiltshire, the Army, under the auspices of the Army Saddle Clubs' Association and the British Horse Society had started a One-Day Event in 1958. It proved a resounding success and in 1959 it was extended to a Two-Day Event, which was a specially devised 'concertinaed' version of the usual Three-Days. Dressage and show-jumping were held on the first day and the speed, endurance and cross-country on the second. The aim was to give the chance of experienced riders to bring on young horses of promise, and to give horses ready for Badminton but not very experienced a chance to graduate from the One-Day to the Three-Day event.

In 1960, the year after Harewood finished and before another full-scale international course could be found, the Army Horse Trials (in which there are as many civilian as military entries) were raised to a Three-Day Event but graded by the British Horse Society as Restricted because the fully fledged international horse was still barred. Qualifications for entry were, however, raised from having completed a single One-Day Event to having completed two.

The following year Tidworth became Unrestricted. The qualifications for entry remained the same, but the horses which had won the most prize money competed for the Tidworth Event and those with less competed for the Bulford

Event.

By 1965, owing to sponsorship by Courage, the brewers, and the Rover car company, the two events were renamed after the sponsors. By 1969 the trials at Tidworth had grown into three sections, the third being sponsored by the firm of Joseph Lucas Limited.

Sponsorship in Combined Training has made a lot of difference to the promoters of the big Three-Day Events, as the higher prize money it enables to be offered, attracts more high-quality entries and more from overseas.

For some years Whitbreads have sponsored the Badminton trials, for which in 1969 the first prize was £200 in cash plus a magnificent trophy down to £12 in cash and a replica of the trophy for the horse and rider coming 12th. They also sponsor the show-jumping classes.

But the search for an alternative ground for a full-scale autumn meeting to take the place of Harewood went on through 1960. In the following year one was found. The Marquess of Exeter, who as Lord Burghley had himself won an Olympic Gold Medal and Silver Medal for hurdling before the Second World War, and is a member of the International Olympic Committee, offered the park of Burghley, his Elizabethan home at Stamford in Lincolnshire.

From the start Burghley caught on with the public and with riders. It has now become as important an event as Badminton—indeed some would say more so, as it was selected as the venue of the World Championships in 1966.

At Burghley sponsorship also plays an important part. Again it is the brewers which put up most of the prize money—there must be an affinity between horses and brewers probably going back to the days of brewers' drays—this time Bass Charrington put up the prize money and the Bass Trophy in the form of a Queen Anne Silver Tankard.

Because they take place in September, the Burghley trials have on several occasions been used as the final test before the selectors picked a team to represent Britain abroad. This was so in 1968 before the Mexico Olympics and again in 1969 before the European championships in France.

After these three main Three-Day Events come the Two-Day trials which may at some time in the future become upgraded to Three-Day Events. The two principal Two-Day trials are at Eridge in Sussex in the grounds of the estate of the Marquess of Abergavenny, which are held at the beginning of August, and the Wylye Wiltshire trials in the grounds of Bathampton House, Wylye, the home of Lord Hugh and Lady Russell.

23 How They Score to Win

Although this book is primarily concerned with the horses that have made their mark in Events, it might be of interest to readers to know the rudiments of how they score.

The most complicated phase to follow is the dressage. This is because there are various standards of tests, from that for novices to that for a full-scale international event. Between these two are a number of intermediate score-tables and the main difference between all of them is in the number of movements required and the standard of marking.

All competitors, in whichever class they compete, must conform to a set standard whether it be the British Horse Society Novice dressage test or the highest test of the Fédération Equestre Internationale.

These standards are rigid, so there can be no question of one set of judges being more lenient than another.

There is neither space nor place here to go into all the variations of the dressage test. As most of the horses, included in these pages have been of international or Olympic repute it will perhaps be sufficient to give the scale of marking for the F.E.I. Three-Day Event Dressage Test (1963) which is used at Badminton and at most international events.

There are nineteen movements in the test and each movement is marked from o to 6 good marks by each of the judges.

There are also four notes for general impression, also scored at from 0 to 6—giving a maximum of 138 good (or plus) marks from each judge. In this test there are three judges. If the rider takes a wrong course, or exceeds the time allowed, the penalty marks are deducted from each judge's sheet. The total marks of the three judges are then averaged. The good marks so obtained are then subtracted from 138 and the result expressed in penalty points.

Each rider is allowed seven and a half minutes to complete the test, and for every second taken over that time a time fault of half a mark is incurred.

Each test must be carried out from memory and an error or wrong sequence of movements, whether corrected or not, are penalised: first error, 2 marks; second error, 5 marks; third error, 10 marks; and the fourth means elimination.

The course is always displayed near the collecting ring and if you are watching a test it is a good idea to study this before the start so that you will have a better idea of what is going on. Very often the programme will give you details of the test, but the organisers of smaller events are not always able to arrange for this.

THE F.E.I. THREE-DAY EVENT DRESSAGE TEST (1963)
(Ridden in a snaffle or double bridle)

Arena: 6om × 2om

Movement	Test
1.	Enter at collected canter. Halt, and salute.
2.	Proceed at ordinary trot (sitting). Track to right. Change rein at extended trot (rising).
3.	Ordinary trot (sitting). Change rein at extended trot (rising).
4.	Ordinary trot (rising).
5.	Turn right at ordinary trot (sitting). Halt. Immobility for five seconds. Move off at

collected trot (sitting), track to left. Collected
trot (sitting).

6. On two tracks (one direction). On two tracks (in
alternate direction).

7. Ordinary walk. Change rein at extended walk.

8. Collected trot (sitting). On two tracks (one
direction). On two tracks (alternate direction).

9. Halt. Rein back six steps. Move off at ordinary
walk without halting.

10. Ordinary walk. Collected canter to the right.

11. Half circle, ten metres diameter. Counter-
canter.

12. Ordinary trot (sitting). Collected canter to the
left.

13. Half-circle. Ten metres diameter. Counter-
canter.

14. Ordinary trot (sitting). Collected canter to the
right.

15. Extended canter.

16. Ordinary walk. Change rein at extended walk.

17. Collected canter to the left. Extended canter.

18. Ordinary trot (sitting).

19. Collected canter to the left. Down centre line,
Halt. Salute. Leave arena at free walk.

The four sections for the judges' general impressions are:
regularity of the paces; impulsion; lightness, freedom and
submission of the horse; position and seat of the rider, correct
application of the aids.

On the second day the tests are designed to prove the speed,
jumping ability, training and condition, and the endurance
of the horse. There are four phases, each marked separately,
but following one another, and performed at a stretch, with
the exception of a ten minute compulsory break before the
cross-country. During this break a vet and two judges examine
the horse to decide whether it is fit to tackle the cross-country

course, which usually has 34 jumps many of which make the Grand National look like a novice course and all of which must be completed within a given time.

The first and third phase consist of several miles of roads and tracks which must be completed in an exact time. No marks are awarded for completing the phase in less than the allowed time, but one penalty mark is awarded to a rider for each second he takes over the time up to the time limit, after which he is eliminated. This limit is usually between five and six minutes.

Between these two phases come the steeplechase. This entails ten jumps and a distance of roughly two-and-a-quarter miles and must be completed in a specified time. On both the steeplechase and the cross-country (always the last phase) bonus marks can be earned by the rider for completing the course in less than the specified time. Again the maximum bonus is specified, so that no rider shall be tempted to try to take his horse too fast.

The following table shows how faults at obstacles are penalised if they occur in an area known as the Penalty Zone surrounding each obstacle:

First refusal, run-out, circle of horse at obstacle	20 penalties
Second refusal etc: at the same obstacle	40 penalties
Third refusal etc: at the same obstacle	Elimination
Fall of horse or rider or both at obstacle	60 penalties
Second fall of horse and/or rider during the steeplechase phase	Elimination
Third fall of horse and/or rider during the cross-country phase	Elimination
Knocking down a red or white flag	4 penalties
Omission of obstacle or red or white flag	Elimination
Retaking an obstacle already jumped	Elimination
Jumping obstacle in wrong order	Elimination

All penalties are cumulative and elimination from any one

phase means elimination from the whole contest. A competitor is also eliminated if he receives any outside assistance whether solicited or not, or if anyone intervenes with the object of helping the horse or rider. He may, however, receive outside help to catch his horse and help him adjust his saddlery and remount after a fall.

Before the final phase on the third day, the show-jumping, the horse must pass a strict veterinary test. This always takes place in the morning after the horse has had a chance to rest from his exertions of the second day.

Faults at Obstacles:

First refusal	10 penalties
Knocking down an obstacle	10 penalties
Touching boundary mark, or feet in the water or in the ditch	10 penalties
Second refusal in the whole test	20 penalties
Third refusal in the whole test	Elimination
Jumping a fence in the wrong order	Elimination
Fall of horse and/or rider	30 penalties
Knocking down a red or white flag	2 penalties

Ideally the ratio of importance of the three tests are Dressage 3; Speed and Endurance 12; Jumping 2. What this means is that a competitor's performance on the Speed and Endurance tests should have four times more influence on his final placing than his performance at Dressage and six times more than the final jumping test.

To try to keep this balance the rules allow the Ground Jury to make an adjustment, using what is known as the Multiplying Factor, to the Dressage markings. According to how severe they consider the second day's tests will be, so they order a Multiplying Factor of 1, 1.5, or 2. Although this will make no difference to the relative placings of each competitor in the dressage test it does increase the spread of penalty points between the best and the worst, and also increases these incurred by the best, making his task in keeping his lead on the second day proportionately harder. There has been much criticism of this Multiplying Factor system of marking but so far no one has come up with a better idea.

After all, a Three-Day Event is to test the 'all roundness' of each horse and it would be wrong for a horse that was brilliant at Dressage but poor at cross-country to ensure a top placing simply by building up an unassailable lead on the first day. Such a horse should be left to concentrate on Dressage alone, for which there is of course ample opportunity and international and Olympic competition.

At least two of our top Eventers whose stories are told in this volume, Tramella and High and Mighty, eventually did retire from Three-Day Eventing to concentrate solely on Dressage and won international honours to follow up those they won in Three-Day Events.

Appendix

RESULTS TABLES

WINNERS OF THE BADMINTON THREE-DAY EVENT

Year	Horse	Rider	Owner
1949	Golden Willow	Mr John Shedden	Mrs. Home Kidson
1950	Remus	Capt. J. A. Collings	Miss G. H. Crystal
1951	Vae Victis	Capt. H. Schwarzenbach	Switzerland
1952	Emily Little	Capt. M. A. Q. Darley	rider
1953	Starlight	Major Lawrence Rook	Mrs. J. R. Baker
1954	Bambi	Miss Margaret Hough	rider
1955 Windsor	Kilbarry	Major Frank Weldon	rider
1956	Kilbarry	Major Frank Weldon	rider
1957	High and Mighty	Miss Sheila Willcox	rider
1958	High and Mighty	Miss Sheila Willcox	rider
1959	Airs and Graces	Mrs. J. Waddington (Miss Sheila Willcox)	rider
1960 } Gt. Badminton	Our Solo	Mr. W. Roycroft	Australia
1960 } Lt. Badminton	Peggoty	Capt. Martin Whiteley	rider

Year		Horse	Rider	Owner
1961	Gt. Badminton	Salad Days	Mr. L. R. Morgan	Australia
	Lt. Badminton	Mr. Wilson	Capt. J. P. E. Welch	rider
1962	Gt. Badminton	Merely-a-Monarch	Miss Anneli Drummond-Hay	rider
	Lt. Badminton	Priam	Mrs. P. M. Crofts	Mr. H. Graham-Clark
1963		No Three-Day Event		
1964	Gt. Badminton	M'Lord Connolly	Capt. James Templer	rider
	Lt. Badminton	Glenamoy	Mrs. J. Waddington	rider
1965	Gt. Badminton	Durlas Eile	Major Eddie Boylan	Ireland
	Lt. Badminton	The Poacher	Capt. Martin Whiteley	rider
1966		No Three-Day Event		
1967		Jonathan	Miss Celia Ross-Taylor	rider
1968		Our Nobby	Miss Jane Bullen	rider
1969		Pasha	Richard Walker	rider

WINNERS OF THE HAREWOOD HORSE TRIALS

Year	Horse	Rider	Owner
1953	Neptune	Miss Vivien Machin-Goodall	rider
1954	Carmena	Miss Penelope Molteno	rider
1955	Kilbarry	Lt. Col. Frank Weldon	rider
1956	High and Mighty	Miss Sheila Willcox	rider
1957	Charleville	Mr. Ian Hume-Dudgeon	Ireland
1958	Polarfuchs	Ottokar Pohlmann	Germany
1959 } The European Championship	Burn Trout	Major H. Schwarzenbach	Switzerland

WINNERS OF THE BURGHLEY HORSE TRIALS

Year	Horse	Rider	Owner
1961	Merely-a-Monarch	Miss Anneli Drummond-Hay	rider
1962	M'Lord Connolly	Capt. James Templer	rider
1963	St. Finbarr	Capt. H. Freeman-Jackson	rider
1964	Barberry	Richard Meade	rider
1965	Victoria Bridge	Capt. J. Beale	rider
1966 } World Championship	Chalan	Capt. Carlos Moratorio	Argentine
1967	Popadom	Miss Lorna Sutherland	rider
1968	Fair and Square	Miss Sheila Willcox	rider
1969	Shaitan	Miss Gillian Watson	Mrs. M. Stinton and Mr. and Mrs. and Miss Smallwood

WINNERS OF THE ARMY HORSE TRIALS TIDWORTH

Year	Section	Horse	Rider	Owner
1958	Tidworth	Fermoy	Lt.-Col. Frank Weldon	rider
	Military	Stafford	Major M. W. S. Fleming	rider
1959	Tidworth	By Golly	Officer-Cadet J. Smith-Bingham	rider
	Military	By Golly	Officer-Cadet J. Smith-Bingham	rider
1960	Tidworth	The Gladiator	Miss Susan Fleet	rider
	Military	Alpine Princess	Mr. R. E. Curnock	Queen's Own Hussars
1961	Tidworth	High Jinks	Mr. P. V. Hervey	15/19th King's Royal Hussars
	Bulford	Merely-a-Monarch	Miss Anneli Drummond-Hay	Mr. J. R. Hindley
	Military	High Jinks	Mr. P. V. Hervey	15/19th King's Royal Hussars
1962	Tidworth	Finjarao	Miss Christine Sheppard	rider
	Bulford	Drambuie	Miss Susan Fleet	rider
	Military	By Golly	Lt. J. Smith-Bingham	rider
1963	Tidworth	By Golly	Lt. J. Smith-Bingham	rider
	Bulford	Donahoney	Mr. R. Vines	rider
	Military	By Golly	Lt. J. Smith-Bingham	rider

Year	Section	Horse	Rider	Owner
1964	Tidworth	Mannikin	Miss M. Wettern	Miss S. Whitmore
	Bulford	Blue Commando	Mr. E. Thompson	Miss V. Nicholl
	Military	Victoria Bridge	Mr. J. J. Beale	4th/7th Royal Dragoon Guards
1965	Courage	Viscount	Mr. L. Sederholm	Mr. N. P. Gold
	Rover	Bugle March	Sub.-Lieut. E. C. Atkinson	Royal Navy
	Military	Bugle March	Sub.-Lieut. E. C. Atkinson	Royal Navy
1966	Courage	Jonathon	Miss Celia Ross-Taylor	rider
	Rover	P.J.-L.L. Esq.	Miss C. Corser	Benenden Riding Est.
	Military	Evening Echo	Capt. T. W. Ritson	Queen's Own Hussars
1967	Courage	Call Me Madam	Capt. P. V. Hervey	15/19th King's Royal Hussars
	Rover	Cornishman V	Miss M. Gordon-Watson	Brig. Gordon Watson
	Military	Call Me Madam	Capt. P. V. Hervey	15/19th King's Royal Hussars
1968	Courage	True Flash	Mrs. O. Fox-Pitt	rider
	Rover	Corinthian	Mrs. B. Parker	Miss P. Hely-Hutchinson
	Military	Magic Carpet	Lt. E. C. Atkinson	Royal Navy

EUROPEAN CHAMPIONSHIP

Year	Venue	Team winner	Individual winner
1953	Badminton	Gt. Britain	Major A. L. Rook on Starlight
1954	Basle	Gt. Britain	Mr. A. E. (Bertie) Hill on Crispin
1955	Windsor	Gt. Britain	Maj. Frank Weldon on Kilbarry
1957	Copenhagen	Gt. Britain	Sheila Willcox on High & Mighty
1959	Harewood	Germany	Maj. H. Schwarzenbach on Burn Trout
1962	Burghley	U.S.S.R.	Capt. James Templer on M'Lord Connolly
1965	Moscow	U.S.S.R.	M. Babirecki on Volt (Poland)
1966	Burghley (World Champion)	Eire	Carlos Moratorio on Chalan
1967	Punchestown	Gt. Britain	Major Eddie Boylan on Durlas Eile
1969	Haras du Pin	Gt. Britain	Mary Gordon-Watson on Cornishman V

PAN-AMERICAN GAMES

Year	Venue	Team winner	Individual winner
1955	Mexico	Mexico	Walter Staley on Mud Dauber (U.S.)
1959	Chicago	Canada	Michael Page on Grasshopper (U.S.)
1963	Sao Paulo	U.S.A.	Michael Page on Grasshopper (U.S.)
1967	Winnipeg	U.S.A.	Michael Plum on Plain Sailing (U.S.A.)

OLYMPIC GAMES

POST-LAST-WAR RESULTS

Year	Place		Gold	Silver	Bronze
1948	London	Team	U.S.A.	Sweden	Mexico
		Individual	Capt. Bernard Chevalier on Aiglonne (Fr.)	Lt. Col. F. S. Henry on Swing Low (U.S.A.)	Capt. J. R. Selfet on Claque (Swe.)
1952	Helsinki	Team	Sweden	Germany	U.S.A.
		Individual	Capt. H. G. von Blixen-Finecke on Jubal (Swe.)	Capt. Guy Lefrant on Verdun (Fr.)	Willy Busing on Hubertus (Ger.)
1956	Stockholm	Team	Great Britain	Germany	Canada
		Individual	P. Kastenman on Illuster (Swe.)	August Lütke-Westhues on Trux von Kamax (Ger.)	Maj. F. W. C. Weldon on Kilbarry (G.B.)
1960	Rome	Team	Australia	Switzerland	France
		Individual	Laurie Morgan on Salad Days (Aust.)	Neil Lavis on Mirrabooka (Aust.)	Anton Buhler on Gay Spark (Switz.)
1964	Tokyo	Team	Italy	U.S.A.	Germany
		Individual	Mauro Checcoli on Surbean (It.)	Capt. Carlos Moratorio on Chalan (Arg.)	Fritz Ligges on Donkosak (Ger.)
1968	Mexico	Team	Great Britain	U.S.A.	Australia
		Individual	Adj. Chef. Jean-Jacques Guyon on Pitou (Fr.)	Major Derek Allhusen on Lochinvar (G.B.)	Michael Page on Foster (U.S.A.)

Index

SAPPER MARTIN

Tickled to Death to Go

Veterans: The Last Survivors of the Great War

Prisoners of the Kaiser

The Trench

Last Man Standing

All Quiet on the Home Front

Boy Soldiers of the Great War

Britain's Last Tommies

The Last Fighting Tommy
(with Harry Patch)

Famous

The Soldier's War: The Great War Through Veterans' Eyes

SAPPER MARTIN

The Secret Great War Diary of Jack Martin

Edited by
Richard van Emden

B L O O M S B U R Y
LONDON · BERLIN · NEW YORK

First published in Great Britain 2009

Diaries copyright © Laurence Martin, Anna Morrison, Mary Wren, Shelagh Martin 2009
Introduction and Notes copyright © Richard van Emden 2009

The photographs reproduced in this book are courtesy of
Peter Martin except where credited otherwise

Bloomsbury Publishing Plc
36 Soho Square
London W1D 3QY

www.bloomsbury.com

Bloomsbury Publishing, London, New York and Berlin
A CIP catalogue record for this book is available from the British Library

ISBN 978 1 4088 0267 0

10 9 8 7 6 5 4 3 2

Typeset by Hewer Text UK Ltd, Edinburgh
Printed in Great Britain by Clays Ltd, St Ives plc

FSC Mixed Sources
Product group from well-managed
forests and other controlled sources
www.fsc.org Cert no. SGS-COC-2061
© 1996 Forest Stewardship Council

Dedicated to Peter and Maggie Barton
and Jeremy and Clair Banning

I am now on night duty. Sitting by the firelight has grown oppressive so I have lit a precious candle to enable me to pass the time in writing. I have been outside the billet and the silence is the sort that can be felt. People who live under modern conditions of civilisation can scarcely comprehend the meaning of absolute silence. And the silence of the trenches among the mountains is almost palpable.

Outside the billet I looked towards the line and listened for any sounds of war of contending armies but the absolute quiet was not broken even by a 'beetles droning flight'. There is not the least sign of life or activity and the winking stars look down like the cynical eyes of cruel gods ready to laugh at human suffering and misery. Yet you know well enough that away in front men are ceaselessly watching ready to give the alarm at the first sign of animation on the enemy's lines; and there are rifles and machines guns and trench mortars and field guns and howitzers of all kinds and sizes ready to break forth into a clamorous roaring and screeching at any moment. And there may be added the drone of aeroplanes and the rushing of wagons and motor lorries and the rattle and banging of railway trains and many other incidental noises.

You know that all this noise is possible and the Silence makes you shudder. It feels uncanny. It oppresses you. You whistle for sake of company but your own whistle makes you start and the Silence following the momentary break seems stranger and more awesome than before. So you creep back into your billet with cold shivering down your spine and a dull nervousness in your heart. And there you have a light and you see your comrades asleep, and hear their snorings and inarticulate grunting and you feel like being at home once more. Your spine becomes warm and erect – your heart steady and brave, and you say 'Bah! I wasn't afraid; I was only interested.'

Jack Martin, 9/1/18

CONTENTS

INTRODUCTION

Is it simply too easy to suggest that a man who fought on and survived the Western Front was 'lucky'? The word appears to offer a quick, casual distinction between those who were killed or seriously wounded and those who came home apparently whole. How can 'lucky' begin truly to explain an individual's remarkable escape from shell splinters that fell next to, or ripped past, his body? How can 'luck' justly explain the bullets that cracked past his head, time and time again, never finding their mark, belying all the apparent odds? Yet it is the right word, because there is no rational explanation. In the end only 'luck' amply explains the sheer randomness and utter injustice of war that could leave a man standing after four years of fighting, and take another who had only just arrived in the trenches.

In January 1917, Sapper Albert (Jack) Martin, four months into his service on the Western Front, wondered at his luck when a shell just skimmed the top of the dugout in which he had been sitting and exploded in a neighbouring one, killing a fellow Royal Engineer. 'A piece of the shell [had] passed clean through his body close to his heart,' Martin noted in his private diary. 'He had only come out just before Xmas and his comrades had envied him as having a safe "cushy" job.'

Jack Martin was to remain a lucky man. He managed to survive more than two uninterrupted years on the Western and Italian fronts, and received nothing more than a 'cat's claw' scratch in all the time he was in or near the front line during some of the most intense battles of the Great War. Perhaps he was luckiest of all in that he was constitutionally a man who could compartmentalise his war, able to move on from all that he had experienced, all the degradation and suffering he had witnessed, to live a contented and fulfilled life. For this reason alone, he was one of the Great War's true survivors, damaged neither physically nor mentally; he was not obsessive about his service, unlike so many others, did not flail about in his sleep, or jump or duck at the backfiring of a car. He did not suddenly weep, or moodily sulk. His temper remained even; he was happy.

This is not to say that Jack Martin forgot his past. He remembered his comrades on Armistice Day but then moved on. According to his surviving son, Peter, an eighty-eight-year-old veteran of the Second World War, he tried to put the Great War at the back of his mind, not always successfully, but he certainly escaped its malign influence that haunted so many others for the rest of their days.

His lasting contribution to the memory of the war is in the form of twelve diaries of exceptional quality and depth. Like all diaries illicitly kept by both officers and soldiers during the war (for they were, like cameras, banned), it was not meant for public consumption but was left as a meticulous record of one man's service. Was it written for his family, or was it a way of putting his war to bed, once and for all? Nobody knows, for he never spoke about it. From the date that he transcribed his diaries (probably in 1922) until his death, the diaries remained hidden and were never mentioned to family or friends. In fact, even after Jack Martin's death nearly forty years ago, the diaries did not immediately come to light. Bundled up with a heap of odds and ends, they were kept in a large black plastic bin bag, undiscovered until a decade ago when Peter found and read them.

The original wartime diaries were apparently not preserved, and in fact very little was known of Jack Martin's war. No discharge papers survived and only two photographs, one taken shortly before Jack left for France, the other in post-war Germany where Jack served briefly with the Army of Occupation. Even his two service medals have disappeared.

Jack was born Albert John Martin at Fakenham, near the north Norfolk coast, on 3 September 1884, one of three brothers and four sisters. He was a sickly infant. He was once given up for dead when he was just a few months old, and his parents drew the blinds as an indication to the outside world that somebody had died. No one now knows what his illness was.

His father was a Methodist minister who, in that capacity, moved his family around Britain every three years to a new circuit. The upheaval was considerable, the family moving from as far away as a mining village in South Wales to Gravesend in Kent. Jack's father, according to his grandson Peter, 'was probably pacifist and very liberal, at least he liked to think he was liberal, liberal in a way, but fierce at home where he was a strict disciplinarian. A self-righteous man, his evils were debt, dirt, drink and the Devil . . . and the *Daily Mail*.'

Comics were utterly prohibited when Jack was a boy; his father, a humourless man, would not have them in the house. Playtime at school was being marched around by the local recruiting sergeant, though at home toy soldiers were forbidden by his father. Jack's humour came from his mother, who was an altogether different personality; she wrote poems and she had emotions that were quite different from those of her husband.

As a young boy, Jack learnt to play the piano and then played the harmonium for his father's Sunday services; he had to listen to the same sermon three times a day at different churches. Peter commented that his father later called himself a nonconformist but wasn't aligned to any church in particular.

Jack's father died in August 1916; his relationship with his son had never been close. Nevertheless, Jack was like the older man in one way: he was a believer in self-help and, although he left school at fourteen, he educated himself. He had some lessons on the piano, but was largely self-taught; he also taught himself law and accountancy even though he had no further formal teaching at all. Financial circumstances meant there was never any possibility of his going to university.

When he left school, Jack was persuaded to take the Civil Service Boys' Exam and went into the Admiralty, presumably as a clerk. As a young man in London, he lived with Mr and Mrs Berwick, who owned a boarding house. He became good friends with them and frequently noted their generosity in his diaries, receiving a number of letters and food parcels while serving overseas.

Apart from his immediate family and the Berwicks, Jack refers in his diaries most often to Elsie. Jack met Elsie Kate Brewster in London around 1910 and they were engaged, but did not marry until June 1919. Their son Peter suspects that they thought it wasn't right to get married just because war was coming, and they would see it through, as they did. Perhaps, too, Jack did not wish to leave Elsie a war widow, a plight suffered by so many others.

Jack joined the army in early 1916, and felt it right that he should go. Aged thirty-one, he was a patriotic man, firmly patriotic, clearly feeling that the British nation was a cut above everyone else. He was the only member of the family to serve; one brother died before the war and the other was in a reserved occupation. It is probably fair to say that he did not like the army, he did not like most officers, he did not like being told what to do by people he felt were his mental inferiors. His son does not think that he ever sought promotion or was ever particularly offered it, although he ended the war as a lance corporal.

Jack Martin made a reluctant but idiosyncratic soldier. He played the organ, quoted from *Tristram Shandy* and carried a copy of Shakespeare's *The Merchant of Venice* for preferred reading. He was chosen to stage-manage army events when out of the front line, and, when time and a cloudless sky permitted, he waxed lyrical to anyone who would listen, about astronomy and the constellations they could see: he was, it is fair to say, no ordinary Tommy.

Yet, at the same time, that is exactly what he was. Sapper Martin, a sometimes grumbling, grousing 'other rank'; a man who stood by his mates through the worst that war could throw at him. At times he kept going although shell-shocked, with shaking hand, gaunt face and a profound depth of fatigue that haunted his waking hours. When finally relieved he slept, indifferent to the chaos of his surroundings, unruffled by the discomfort of his 'bed'.

Sapper Martin belied his lowly rank. Erudite and articulate, he kept his diary throughout his service in France from the moment he left Great Britain to the moment of demobilisation two and a half years later. Despite the ban on soldiers keeping diaries, a restriction that was widely broken, he carefully noted the day's events in notebooks that grew in number from one to twelve, rarely missing a day.

Probably owing to his obvious intelligence, he was chosen to be a signaller in the Royal Engineers, and a very proficient one he turned out to be. His job did not consist merely of taking encoded messages sent from various parts of the line; he was frequently expected to leave the dugout and pass across the battlefield, maintaining communications when telephone lines had been cut in many places by shell fragments.

The diary reflected each day. Nevertheless, it would be surprising if, during the intense horror of an attack, he wrote much about his experiences; indeed, it would have been a dereliction of duty had he done so. After all, the lives of hundreds if not thousands of men were held in the balance, and success or failure in an attack could depend on the one intact telephone line that led back from a muddy hole in a battle-scarred wasteland all the way to Corps Headquarters. For that reason, he regularly updated his diary, sometimes days later, going back over recent events. In the main, however, he sought out quiet moments when he could jot down his thoughts, sometimes, when times were quiet, at a length of several pages.

There are some frustrating aspects to the story. Did Jack actually know that soldiers were forbidden to keep diaries during the war? If so, did he go to great pains to hide the fact that he was keeping one? It would not have been easy, given the amount that he managed to write, and it is possible his Commanding Officer chose to turn a blind eye. Certainly, he took risks: he divulged information that might have been useful to the enemy, giving, for example, the names of towns and villages, and repeating conversations he heard between senior officers. It is possible, of course, that he originally used a code, especially as he records using one in his letters to Elsie, letting her know in this way where he was at the time. As the original diaries have not survived, we shall never know.

Sadly, Jack Martin's enlistment papers no longer exist, either. Around 70 per cent of all records were destroyed in an enemy raid in the Second World War (the remainder are held at the National Archives) so details of precisely when he enlisted are not known, nor even where

he trained. It is very likely that he enlisted either under the Derby
Scheme (a scheme by which men could volunteer and then return to
civilian employment until required) or that he was called up shortly
after conscription was introduced in January 1916. He had no previous
knowledge of or training in signals (he was never a member of the
Scouts, for example) and so he must surely have received a minimum
of six months' instruction before being ordered overseas.

During his army career, Jack was particularly close to Private
Stuart Thomas Glasspoole, known as Tom, who, like Jack, had been
a clerk, working for the Pearl Assurance Company in London. Jack
refers to Glasspoole throughout his diary, with obvious affection.
He was ten years younger than Jack, and was only twenty-two when
he arrived in France. He had enlisted in the Surrey Yeomanry in
1913 and transferred to the 12th Battalion East Surrey Regiment
after the outbreak of war. We do not know whether Jack knew Tom
before their service overseas. However, they embarked within five
days of each other in September 1916 and were demobbed within
ten days of each other in February 1919.

Perhaps the most interesting relationship that Jack Martin had was
with his Commanding Officer, Lieutenant, later Captain, Buchanan.
Fletcher Gordon Buchanan came from Glasgow and went to France
in May 1916, aged twenty-seven. He served with the 122nd Infantry
Brigade Signals, to which Martin was sent, until he was transferred to
39th Division Headquarters as a signalling officer in July 1917. His
sojourn there was short, as he was injured only three weeks later when
he was knocked off his motorcycle by a shell explosion. He received
shrapnel wounds to head, arm and leg, though none was considered
serious. We do not know whether he returned to France. However, he
was forced to resign his commission in January 1919 owing to ill health.
Lieutenant Buchanan had, as Jack Martin's diary shows, made an offer
to the men under his command that if they needed help after the war
they were to call on him at his business address and he would endeavour
to do what he could for them. It is not clear exactly what Buchanan did,
but it appears that he had business interests in eastern India.

Jack's relationship with Buchanan was fraught. His attitude to officers, especially those who did not come up to the mark, was ambiguous to say the least. However, Jack respected Buchanan but could not understand why his Commanding Officer was difficult with him, always pointing out supposed errors or failures. Normally, Jack would have cared little for what an officer thought but with Buchanan it was different. The desire to win this officer's commendation was strong and when Buchanan finally accepted him, the depth of feeling elicited from Jack was unprecedented.

Unlike some veterans who walked away from all connections to their service, Jack was friendly for many years with his comrades in arms. Jack's son Peter met up with several: Glasspoole was one, and there was another from Halifax. With one old friend he actually crossed the Channel and went back to Belgium; it was against his own wishes and all his inclinations, as Peter recalls. 'Jack didn't want to go, but he went just to please this man. They were there only a day and possibly a night and they came back, and he had not enjoyed it. "What's the point?" he said. It didn't do anything for him.' He never went again.

He thought about the war, Peter remembers, but he didn't want to think about it. 'It was an aspect of his life that he had not exactly turned his back on but wanted to ignore, to forget about. He was quite keen on respecting Armistice Day, though he didn't go to church then. Nor did he ever wear his medals, definitely not. We don't know what happened to them but I suspect he just threw them away; I've never come across them. As for the diaries: I suppose he wanted me and my children to know about what it was like.

'I asked him one or two things but he never opened up. The diaries were how he communicated his feelings. I knew hardly anything, except that he was on the Somme and that he had gone to Italy. I knew he'd seen tanks, and that gas had been blown into the trenches where he was, but they had a damp blanket across the doorway to keep it out. I don't think he minded me asking, but he was not naturally forthcoming about it. Reading the diaries I found he didn't come across as any different from the man I knew. He may have mellowed in the 1920s, he may have been less uptight. He could just close the door on that part of his life and start again with my mother's help.'

What would he feel about his diaries being published? 'I don't think he would care one way or the other; he wouldn't be embarrassed, in fact on the whole I think he would be pleased but I don't think he would be overjoyed. He didn't express much emotion. He never said "I love you" to me, like I do to my children, and I didn't hear him say that to my mother although he must have loved her. That was his innate nature, the war had not taken emotion from him. He was very much his own man.'

After Jack Martin returned to civilian life he took a job in Beckenham, Kent, with a company that made electrical motors. It was not a long-term job. In the spirit of self-education to which Martin had always subscribed, he studied and qualified as a certified accountant, before becoming self-employed in the late 1920s. He set up a practice, eventually taking his only child, Peter, into partnership. He continued to work until shortly after his wife Elsie died in January 1964, retiring the following year aged eighty. Jack then lived with his son's family in Basingstoke. He died on 24 April 1970 aged eighty-five.

Jack Martin has made my job as editor not only a highly enjoyable one, for he is such a good writer, but also a relatively easy one. His stories are frequently self-explanatory and at times I have had little more to do than to clarify abbreviations. While editing the book, (about a third of the original text has been deleted), it was evident which passages might be cut to avoid repetition and only during the third and final fine cut did the process prove at all tricky.

As editor I had to make the decision when to interject into proceedings and whether my words would seem more like an interruption than a help. In the end I felt that my role was to let Jack tell his story in as pure a way as possible and so I have restricted myself to a full introduction and then, as far as the text is concerned, simply setting Jack's words into their historical context.

There are, of course, many well-written diaries about the Great War, from the classics by Graves and Sassoon to lesser known ones that were nevertheless beautifully written. They are, in the main, written by officers. Far fewer are by other ranks, and, of those that exist, none, to my knowledge, are written by Royal Engineers, except for this one. But here is a brilliantly written book, penned, unusually, by another rank who happened to be a signaller. However, what gives this book an extra dimension is the beguiling character of the man himself, a cautious and meticulous character who wrote diaries of remarkable insight and sensitivity but also, perhaps most surprisingly, of easy and natural humour. Jack Martin was a man brimming with curiosity, full of life and vigour; a man who was utterly honest in what he wrote. The old adage 'still waters run deep' was never better exemplified than in him.

Jack Martin served with the 122nd Infantry Brigade Signal Company, part of the 41st Division. He wore the camp badge of the Royal Engineers, perhaps one of the most overlooked regiments of the British Army when it comes to written history. This is ironic for they were never overlooked during the Great War. On the contrary, their presence on the battlefield was absolutely vital not just for the successful prosecution of war but for war to be waged at all. As the conflict grew increasingly industrial in nature, so the regiments that reflected that change grew as a proportion of the army as a whole. For example, Heavy Artillery grew from 1.3 per cent of the army's strength to over 8.5 per cent by 1918; the Royal Engineers grew from roughly 6 to 12 per cent. Conversely, the cavalry shrank from 10 to just 2 per cent and even the infantry, their numbers swelled by voluntary enlistment and conscription, shrank as a proportion of the army from 65 to 50 per cent.

The REs grew from a little over 25,000 officers and men in August 1914, including regular, reserve and territorial troops, to over 295,000 just three years later. Of these, 19,794 were to die in the war and sixteen Victoria Crosses were won.

It was, and remains, a simple fact that the British Army could not function without the Royal Engineers. They acted as the glue that kept the army's constituent parts together, and the oil to ensure that all parts worked well. Their motto *Ubique* (Everywhere) amply described their presence on the battlefield, both in the front line, building and reconstructing (as well as demolishing) positions and fortifications, transporting and constructing pontoons and bridges, very often under intense fire, and, behind the front line, building and maintaining roads, railways and waterways.

As well as being ultimately responsible for the large-scale infrastructure of the battlefield, they maintained key elements vital to the army's overall success. They were responsible for all communications, maintaining telephone lines, wireless and all other equipment used for signalling. They ensured a water supply to the trenches through miles of pipes, hundreds of water tanks and butts filled from temporary reservoirs supplied from bore holes. In the line, they were in charge of tunnelling operations, digging shafts and burrowing deep beneath the ground to lay explosives under enemy trenches. Field Survey companies located enemy positions, through sound ranging and flash spotting, so that accurate fire could be laid down, and, after the enemy's first use of poison gas, special gas companies were formed to engage the enemy in the deadly art of gas warfare.

The Royal Engineers quarried, drained and bored; they surveyed the topography of the ground, and studied meteorology, forecasting the weather for the senior command. They were responsible for forestry, chopping down trees for myriad purposes, including the duckboard tracks that wended their way across the battlefield, the assault ladders that would take the men over the top, and the wood used to line and prop a trench.

Everything that was used to construct the defences upon which the infantry relied was tried and tested by the Royal Engineers, right down to the strength and durability of the nails that held everything together: the list goes on and on. It is hardly surprising, then, that the Royal Engineers grew in number throughout the war as their overall remit was massively expanded.

Sapper Martin was the smallest cog in an enormous and expanding wheel. But his job, as a signaller with Brigade Headquarters, was more important than that of any corresponding infantryman, trooper or gunner, for the lives of hundreds, perhaps thousands, of men could rely on his accurate message taking, on his courage to mend a telephone line cut by shrapnel, or his willingness to stay awake and mentally alert when his body craved sleep. It was a heavy responsibility, and he knew it and responded to the challenge.

THE DIARY

1916

Sunday 17.9.16
Left Hitchin just before 9 a.m. Saw Elsie at her window as we marched to the station. Embarked at Southampton at 4 p.m.

18.9.16
Disembarked at Rouen about 6 a.m. Marched past numbers of German prisoners working in the streets, to a barbed-wire compound where we got some breakfast at a YMCA hut. Crowded with men either going up to or coming down from the line. Played a number of ragtime choruses on the piano. Later I was fetched to play hymns for a service. The chaplain me gave a Testament that I retained until sent home for demobilisation. Medical exam and then entrained.

19.9.16
Arrived at Abbeville after a most uncomfortable journey (thirty-six in a truck) early in the morning. Marched to the Signal Depot where we caught up some of the men who had left Hitchin a few days before we did.

20.9.16–22.9.16
Did not have much to do at Abbeville and each evening we were allowed out. Could not go in the Cathedral but saw the massive doors which are its pride. Don't think much of the city – some parts are very low, and probably the present circumstances of being a military centre have dragged it lower.

23.9.16
This morning my name appeared on orders to proceed to the 41st Division. I leave tonight and anticipate finding myself on the Somme tomorrow.

The Battle of the Somme was a campaign essentially conceived out of political necessity. The idea was to show that the British and French could not only launch a successful campaign together but that they could fight alongside one another in a show of military solidarity. That was the primary reason why, in late 1915, the gently rolling chalk downland of the Somme region was chosen as the 'best' place to force a decision on the Western Front in 1916. Hitherto, the area had been little more than a Franco-German backwater where little actual fighting had taken place.

The British had arrived in the summer of 1915, not necessarily to fight in the region but rather to take over more of the front line that stretched all the way from the Belgian coast to the Swiss Alps. The French had been holding by far the greater proportion and as the number of British troops serving overseas grew exponentially in the spring and summer of 1915, so it was felt appropriate that Britain should shoulder a greater responsibility not just in terms of fighting but simply holding the line. Only after the British had arrived on the Somme did the idea of a joint offensive begin to germinate. In February 1916 the Germans attacked the French at Verdun and, as more and more French servicemen were drawn into the fighting further south, so their commitment to a Somme offensive was much curtailed. Indeed, such was the ferocity of the fighting at Verdun that the British were increasingly urged, then implored, to fight at the earliest possible moment so as to draw off German forces from the beleaguered town. The British would put an enormous effort into what optimistically became known as the 'Big Push'. A huge preliminary bombardment followed by a heavy infantry assault would, over days and then weeks, throw back the Germans across French-held territory. The outcome, as it was sold to the British public, was that this was an offensive that might end the war.

Reality was rarely the equal of expectation in the Great War and a catastrophic failure on the first day of the battle was only partially redeemed by limited success in the weeks and months that followed. Success would soon be measured in hundreds of yards rather than in dozens of miles, as each wood, each village and each roadway was contested by British troops determined to take the land in equal proportion to the Germans' desire not to relinquish it.

In September 1916 the British introduced a new secret weapon, the tank. This seemed to hold out the prospect of renewed success, but although the Germans were taken by surprise at its appearance, once again the battle stalled. It was just days after the advent of the tank that Jack Martin arrived in France, to be quickly sent forward to join his unit in the line. As a signaller with the 41st Division, a unit used in some of the tanks' first assaults, he would quickly get to see all the horror of modern warfare and the skeletal debris of both man and knocked-out tank close to the front line.

24.9.16

Travelling. We left Abbeville in the usual crowded cattle trucks at 9.30 last night. In the morning we were near Amiens. Progress is frightfully slow. Sometimes there were as many as five trains all crawling close behind each other. There may have been more round the bends. Every time we stopped near any orchards some of the fellows would jump out and fetch apples. Two or three got left behind just as we entered the tunnel before Amiens but they walked over the top and caught us up at the other end. Stace, another fellow named Morgan, and I were booked for the 41st Division. We were told to get out at Edge Hill which is the railhead. We found a Middlesex guide who said he would take us to our Division. He walked us right up to Fricourt where we saw the big guns in action for the first time, but after tramping about for some time without finding any trace of the Div. we decided to pad it back to Edge Hill – jumped a lorry part of the way. Some cooks at Edge Hill gave us tea and we learnt from a motorcyclist that the 41st Div. was at Ribemont, a few km further back. We jumped a train but it only took us a few yards. After waiting ¾ hour we decided to walk to Mericourt where the RTO [Railway Transport Officer] put us into a Rest Camp and promised us some breakfast.

26.9.16

Today I am posted to the 122nd Infantry Brigade, and Stace to the 124th Inf. Bde. We're taken up on a limber. Found the 122 encamped in tents and bivvies on the heights at Dernancourt overlooking Albert. Reported to the Signal Officer who seems pretty supercilious. His name is Buchanan. I'm in amongst a crowd of Scotsmen from the wilds of Glasgow and they don't exactly open their arms and embrace me.

27.9.16–1.10.16

These few days I have done nothing in particular except run messages and have two journeys to the baths at Méaulte. We have to walk about a mile each day to get an ordinary wash in the River Ancre. Talked to a German prisoner who is confident that the Germans will win in the end.

2.10.16

Up early and dismantled the camp. About 9 a.m. we moved off to go up the line. Since I left England the weather has been fine, but today it started to rain about 11 a.m. and it continued to pour throughout the march. We were soon wet to the skin, the water trickled down our bodies and into our boots. We arrived at the remains of Mametz Wood, all trenches and shell holes and mud, and after erecting tents for the officers were given bivvy sheets and left to make ourselves comfortable. Hetherington, Bennett and I selected an excavation where Fritz had started to make a dugout, put branches across it and spread over the bivvy. Then we collected the driest wood we could find, lit a fire close to the entrance to our 'home', took off our clothes and dried them one by one as much as we could, tipped the water out of our boots, wrapped ourselves up and went to sleep. At 2.30 a.m. I was called to go on wagon guard for half an hour, during which time I wrote one or two letters huddled up under a tarpaulin.

3.10.16

The rain had ceased when we got up but the roadways are swimming
in liquid mud. They look nice and level but really they are full of
big holes, and although usually the mud is not above the ankles yet
every now and then you go in up to the knee. Horses and mules
fall down every few yards. After a few miles of this we left the
road and went along a track over open country. The going soon
proved too heavy for the mules, and also we were getting into the
danger region so we unloaded the limber, each man taking as much
as he could carry – the rest we left to be fetched later on. So we
went across country, worming our way between guns of all sorts
and sizes till we came to a trench called Fish Alley. Down this we
went a long way to Ferret Trench which was our destination. The
Signal Office and Officers' Quarters were down a deep dugout. Our
billet was an old German dugout, dug in the face of a high bank,
and, of course, facing the line. The village of Flers is close by and a
crippled, battered tank, one of the first used in war, is lying almost
opposite. Field batteries are all round us and this seems a pretty
warm shop. Our dugout is filthy – lice and flies by the million
and the stench of dead bodies makes one sick. One of our orderlies
started to dig a hole in the bank to put his equipment in and came
across a boot. He pulled it and a leg came with it.

4.10.16

This morning I was the first one up and went outside to get a
breath of comparatively fresh air. Found Macdougall, the acting
cook, astir, but he had no water. I offered to try to get some. There
are wells in Flers but Fritz has got the range of each one. Although
the journey was only a few hundred yards it took some time,
dodging shell holes and bits of trenches and gun emplacements.
Two RFA [Royal Field Artillery] men arrived at the well at the
same time as I did, fortunately, for it was three men's work to get
the water up. The winch was broken and we lowered our petrol
cans by means of a length of telephone wire. It took a long time to
fill up, meanwhile Fritz was getting busy and we had only just got

away when he began to drop 'em all round the well. While I was
gone the Sergeant (Twycross) came round and found out what had
happened. He stormed and raved and cursed Macdougall for letting
a man go singly to such a spot but I got back safely with the two
petrol cans of water and so we had some tea, which otherwise we
might have whistled for.

5.10.16 and 6.10.16

The Signal Officer, who hasn't taken very kindly to me, doesn't
consider that I am capable of taking over regular duties in such a
strenuous period, so I am on all sorts of odd jobs. Rations are scarce —
we get only two meals a day each, consisting of a half-pint of tea, one
or two biscuits and a piece of bully or a little jam. Some of us have
been out on the scrounge; we found some cases of bully and biscuits
and brought back as much as we could carry. The rations are brought
up to the dump, a few hundred yards away, each night, but Fritz
generally manages to blow some of them into the air. Ours went west
one night but two men who were guarding them didn't get touched.

Spent some hours on the parapet this evening trying to get visual
communication with the Hants [Hampshire Regiment]. Raining
all the time. All our pigeon baskets got blown to bits, but there
were no birds in them and one shell landed right in our trench
a few yards away from me and wrecked an Artillery Observation
Post. One man (RFA) was wounded and buried, but he was got
out all right. Another shell landed on top of an Artillery dugout
close to ours and a young fellow came running and screaming up
to us. He wasn't wounded but had been badly shaken so I took
him along to where there had been a Dressing Station, but that
had gone so I took him back along the trench and he was crying
loudly all the time and calling out 'Oh my mother, oh my mother'.
I could get nothing out of him and when I had got him back as far
as Longueval I laid him on a truck to wait for an ambulance to pick
him up. I could do no more.

I've had a most welcome parcel from Lil — never did good food
taste so really good — but oh for a good drink of pure water. A

pint of petrol-tainted tea a day is all we get. We have used the water from our bottles sparingly and guarded it almost savagely – so easily does the primal instinct of self-preservation rise above all the teaching and training of centuries of civilisation. Bennett and I went back a couple of miles risking shells and bullets all the way in the hope of filling our bottles. It was a journey in vain although some RFA men gave us a drink out of their scanty store. A big shell landed just outside our dugout and made a hole big enough to take a General Service wagon. Another blew up six dead Germans to add to the intolerable stench. You can hardly go ten yards in any direction without coming across dead bodies or parts of bodies – an arm here, and a leg there. In trying to cross a very muddy track I stepped on what appeared to be a white stone – it was a skull. Buchanan unbent far enough to ask me what I thought of modern warfare, I told him 'not much'.

7.10.16

All this morning Fritz continued his strafing but at 2.30 p.m. we launched an attack. Then he stopped shelling us and gave his attention to the front line. The infantry only got about 100 yards – in some places not so far. They got mown down by machine-gun fire. The attack was a failure. In the evening I had to go to Tock Esses (= TS = Test Station) with Southwood so that I may know the way as I may be wanted to guide some officers up there later on. Davidson, Carter, O'Brien and McLachlan were there. It was difficult going owing to the large numbers of wounded who were coming down.

8.10.16

I waited till 3 a.m. in the trench by the Signal Office but nobody came along so I was allowed to go to my billet. The shelling was not so bad this morning. Both sides seem tired after the exertions of yesterday. Early in the afternoon I managed to get a bit of a wash and a shave, the first I have had for six days. Then a number of us were sent for and told to find our way to Carlton Trench. In addition to our overcoats and equipment we were loaded up with all manner of Signal Stores, so much so that my knees quavered under me. We split up in two or three groups – Dickson, Brady and I were together – we progressed in easy stages along Fish Alley stumbling along the duckboards, but the real trouble began when we got out into the open with nothing but mud and shell holes. In attempting to step across a bit of trench I slipped and fell; and it was some minutes before I could get up. I now know what exhaustion means. Passed by a dead body in a shell hole that must have been laid there for weeks – couldn't tell if it were British or German. A little further on we look off all our clobber and had a rest on an old parapet. Once at Carlton Trench we soon got rid of our excess luggage and scrounged round for somewhere to sleep. Dickson and I found a sandbag shelter roofed with corrugated iron and settled ourselves in it. We can sit up in it and that's all. The 123rd Brigade are here and we went to their cook and begged a mug of tea and a slice of bread and jam. Dickson had a couple of parcels this morning and we had a feed of cold sausages and cake. This is the largest amount of food I have had in any one day since we left Dernancourt. Just before dusk we were called out to unload a wagon that had come up the transport track. This is one of the tracks that cut across country just anywhere and have not been made up at all; consequently it is knee-deep in mud. Even by picking your steps carefully you can't avoid going in over your ankles. They put as many as fourteen horses on an ammunition wagon and even then the poor beasts collapse and can't get up – and, of course, the wagon standing still gradually sinks deeper and deeper into the mud. I was ankle-deep when I stood by the wagon. They dumped a heavy officer's valise on to my shoulders and it pushed me further into the mud – up to my knees in fact – and I couldn't move. They removed the valise and I pulled myself out and after considerable struggling managed to get away with my load. Later in the evening I was told off for duty as 'check' at the Staff Office. All I did was to hang about the trench shivering and hungry for three or four hours. The Officers' cookhouse was close by and the smell of roasting meat made me ravenous, but it is worse than sacrilege to go

near the Officers' cookhouse except on business. One man noticed
me and I suppose I looked gaunt and hungry for he offered to try
and get me something to eat. Presently he came back with a hunk of
bread which I fairly gobbled up. But it was a long way from being
sufficient and when the cooks shut up the cookhouse and went to
bed, temptation was too strong for me – I broke into that cookhouse
and hacked off a great lump of roast beef with my jackknife, grabbed
a lump of bread, shoved both into my pocket and then returned to
my post. I ate all that meat, fat, gristle and everything, and felt all
the better for it. I shall always feel a deep sympathy with the man
who steals food because he is starving.

12.10.16

About four o'clock I woke up feeling very queer. Got up and went
outside but everything swam round and round and I clutched hold
of the bivvy pole or I should have fallen. After a time I crawled back
and got a little more sleep. After breakfast we marched down to the
railhead, which has been pushed up this far since we were here ten
days ago. We entrained and were taken as far as Méaulte, where a
small party of us were immediately despatched to the old camping
ground at Dernancourt to erect tents and get things ready for the
others. I am sharing a bivvy with Dickson and McCormack.

15.10.16

This morning the Divisional Commander (General Lawford)
reviewed the Brigade. Before he turned up, General Towsey (our
Brigadier) said a few words to us about the recent stunt. The 11th
Royal West Kents were the only battalion on the whole of the
attacking front who dug themselves in in advance of the original
line, but even this bit of trench was lost by the battalion which
relieved them. So much for that victorious onslaught!

16.10.16

Up early, struck camp and marched to Mericourt where, after
waiting some hours, we were packed into railway trucks – about

thirty-five or forty men in each truck – barely room to stand. Made the usual steady progress and cheered ourselves by singing and making a great deal of noise. But after nightfall our spirits flagged and we wished to rest. We curled ourselves up as well as we could, legs and feet and heads and arms were all mixed up in a horrible jumble and every now and then there was a hearty cursing when somebody got another man's boot in his eye. It would have been impossible to tell which legs belonged to which head or which head was the owner of a certain pair of arms.

17.10.16

After travelling about twenty-five kms in eighteen hours we arrived at Oisemont just after dawn and then marched several miles to a chateau. I'm not very certain as to whereabouts we are but it's somewhere in the neighbourhood of Abbeville. Soon after leaving Oisemont it came on to rain and we got pretty wet. I was glad to dry my clothes at the transport cook's fire. Our billet is a sort of loft approached by a rickety ladder but the straw is a luxury after so much of mother earth, and also we have been issued with a blanket. We had them given to us when we got back to Dernancourt – and that was not before we needed them.

20.10.16

Up long before daybreak and started a long march by the light of the moon and without any breakfast. It was very exhausting – twelve miles on an empty stomach, and carrying about 80lbs of equipment is a pretty stiff task. McCormack was pushing a bike and he offered to strap my rifle to it but I declined. About 9 a.m. we arrived at Longpré station where the cooks, who had come in advance with the transport, had prepared our breakfast, but before we could touch it we had to get the horses and mules and weapons loaded up. Then we moved off through Abbeville, Etaples, Boulogne, and St Omer to Caestre where we arrived after dark. The journey was considerably swifter than any other I have had in France. From Caestre we marched to Eecke where we were billeted in a big room with a large fireplace. I was among the last to get up the ladder and so lost a position against the walls and had to make up my bed with three or four others in the middle of the room where we ran a certain risk of being walked on.

21.10.16

Eecke is not a bad little village. The church is just opposite our billet and our Signal Office is in the Tower. Spent the afternoon in the billet writing letters. Frank Wallace came in rather the worse for liquor and started doing and saying silly things. When he began to be abusive to Sgt Oxley I thought it was time to clear out – wish I had done so sooner, for later on Buchanan met me and told me that I should be wanted to give evidence. Don't relish this at all. These Scotsmen don't like Oxley and if my evidence goes against Wallace it will be all the harder for me to make friends with them. They are terribly clannish and don't take to strangers in the least. Had my hair cut by a woman barber.

24.10.16

After a short spell on wagon guard I took a short stroll through the military-infested village and was then put on guard over Frank Wallace. This duty lasted all night but, of course, prisoner and guard both had a good night's sleep. Our bed during this night was the uneven, badly worn brick floor of a brewery. With only a groundsheet to lie on it was the most uncomfortable bed I ever laid on, but nevertheless we slept.

25.10.16

Crossed the Franco-Belgian border east of Abeele. Into camp at Zevecoten, just outside Reninghelst. Took over from an Australian Brigade who left the huts very dirty. These huts are ancient, leaky buildings made of wood, roof felting and tar – they are practically all roof. The one I am in boasts a door. There are a number of beds, wooden frames with wire netting stretched across and supported

by four legs, more or less rickety. My immediate neighbours
are McCormack on my right and Dickson on my left. There are
plenty of rats.

29.10.16

Had a brainwave – discovered a brilliant way to let Elsie know my
whereabouts. Told her to get a *Daily Mail* Birdseye Map of the
British Front and later in the letter gave an answer to a mythical
problem in terms of figures which appear on the map. I think she
will twig it all right. Andy McCormack has been on the scrounge
and brought home a stove which we have rigged up and, although
fuel is scarce, we have a fire each evening and generally one of us
does some washing. I did some socks and handkerchiefs last night,
but dispensed with the starching and ironing.

1.11.16

Had a lovely parcel from Elsie and there are some others on the
way from Mother, Lil and Ada. Have managed to get a soft cap at
last – been wearing a tin hat ever since we were on the Somme, as
I put my soft one on the GS wagon when we went into action. The
wagon got 'done in' and a lot of stores were lost including the mail,
though parts of this arrived before we finally left Dernancourt.

The housing problem is an acute one for the civilian population
for there are so many refugees who fled before the German
onslaught in 1914 and have just taken what shelter they could find.
Just outside Abbeville I saw a 'home' which was only a wretched
wooden shed about eight feet square, certainly no more than ten.
In this single room lived a woman and four children. The husband
was at the front.

2.11.16

Steady downpour all day long. Weather is worse than we get in
England. No wonder Uncle Toby in *Tristram Shandy* said 'our
armies swore terribly in Flanders'. They had the same sort of
weather and probably less comfort. Was on duty this afternoon

and now (7 p.m.) the rain has ceased and the moon is shining brightly. My mug of water is boiling on the stove so I must make my Oxo and then get to bed.

4.11.16
Quite a fine day. This afternoon I sat outdoors and wrote letters. A parcel arrived from Mrs Berwick which she posted on 22 September, six weeks ago – but the grub was all good – also a parcel from Ada. Sergeant Twycross is irreverently known as 'Callipers' owing to the shape of his legs.

5.11.16
Frank Wallace had his court martial and has no hope of acquittal. It's a crime to be drunk – there are no degrees of intoxication – you are either drunk or sober in the army. Evidence of your having had ½ a glass of watered beer is sufficient to prove that you were drunk and your punishment would be the same as if you had had a barrel and were right royally and nobly 'blind'.

6.11.16
Wallace was sentenced to two years' hard labour, but this was subsequently reduced to ninety days' Field Punishment No. 1. He has been returned to Division to undergo his sentence.

7.11.16
Vile weather. Haven't been outside my hut all day except to go to the Signal Office or to the cookhouse. Sent a parcel of odds and ends off to Mrs Berwick together with A Girl of the Limberlost for Elsie. I have made dots under a lot of letters commencing on p. 140 which when sorted out will provide interesting information of my doings.

8.11.16
Soon after breakfast we marched off to Dickebusch where our headquarters are at the burgomaster's farm. We came up through Ouderdom and right through the village of Dickebusch which is

very much battered. It consists of one street with just a few outlying houses and a church. Every building is in ruins. Burgomaster's farm is in front of the village nearer to the line and is practically unharmed. The burgomaster and his wife, both old people, still live there although for over two years they have been in continual and very real danger. The Officers live in the farmhouse, all except Buchanan, and he has a dugout next to the Signal Office. This latter is a pretty strong dugout camouflaged to represent a straw stack, but is generally known as the 'Haystack'. The men are accommodated in a number of small dugouts ranged along two sides of the field.

12.11.16

Well, this is the most comfortable billet I have struck since I left England, and so long as old Fritz keeps as quiet as he is at present I shall be able to stick this for a long while. The dugouts are old and frail and you can only stand up straight in certain places but we can make them warm and comparatively dry. The men who were in here last built a brick fireplace and we have got a home-made table and stools. It's a bit of a business to keep the fire going – we have to scrounge the wood, bring it in and chop it up. Yesterday I spent a lot of time wrestling with a young tree – broke a felling axe and gave myself a whack on the knee – it's a bit painful but we've got the wood. My letters are now coming with a rush. In the last two days I have had twelve letters and three parcels. My comrades in this dugout are Capt. J.C. Hamilton, Cpl Davidson and Andy McCormack. There is room for one or two more, so we are not overcrowded. Three of our men, Cpl Davidson, Jack Carter and John O'Brien, have been awarded the Military Medal for work done on the Somme. Have just heard a little incident that happened on the Somme. Tom McLaughlin was cooking some potatoes up at his Test Station and to get a better blaze he picked up what he thought was a rocket but what was really a German bomb – an oval-shaped missile slightly larger than a duck's egg attached to a wooden shaft about eighteen inches long. The shaft he pushed into the fire – soon the bomb began to sizzle – but he just coolly pulled it out of the fire and stamped it in the mud. 'I didn't want to lose the totties,' he explained.

13.11.16

I think we are likely to stay here for about three weeks as a start off. After that it will be a week in and a week out. This is a pretty wet part of the globe — 'water, water everywhere, but never a drop to drink' until it has been boiled, although we get it out of the pump at the farm, for it has a vile smell and the place swarms with rats — millions of them — 'they chase the dogs and kill the cats, make nests inside the ladies' hats' etc etc. (I've forgotten the rest and I fancy it ought to be 'men's Sunday hats', but the Pied Piper could have the time of his life and there's plenty of water to drown them in — but I don't believe rats can be drowned.)

20.11.16

Elsie doesn't seem to have tumbled to my little ruse for letting her know my whereabouts by means of dots under letters in *A Girl of the Limberlost*. She says she has already read the book, but I have told her to read it again, or at any rate to read the passage I referred to. We have had a few fine days with frosty nights, and yesterday morning we woke to find a thin coating of snow on the ground but it soon became milder and commenced to rain and we are ankle-deep in mud once more.

24.11.16

I have had several attacks of toothache lately, due, I think, to wet feet. My boots are worn and let in the damp, and I shan't be able to change them until we get back to Reninghelst. Have finished the phospherine tablets which Elsie sent me and have also had some tablets out of the Medicine Chest which Buchanan supplied when the Division came out to France.

29.11.16

Shivered with cold all night — all the other men were the same — these huts are wretchedly cold and draughty after the comparative

comforts of the little dugouts. Haven't had neuralgia for three days
– touch wood!

30.11.16
Night shift last night – the stove we have in the Signal Office is
a very sorry affair. It either smokes or goes out, and the question
is whether to sit and shiver or sit and choke. Make my first essay
with a 'Gong' Soup Square – Mother and Lil have sent me several.
I couldn't get enough heat out of the fire to boil the water, but all
the same the attempt was quite successful.

4.12.16
We have been issued out with leather jerkins. Some of the men
have furry ones and look like bears but I have a plain brown
one; when dressed up with tin hat, jerkin and gumboots my
closest friends at home would hardly recognise me – I only need
a spear and a shield to transform me into a medieval warrior.
Last night I talked music for nearly two hours to Davidson and
McCormack and managed to keep them interested, which is
rather wonderful.

11.12.16
Went down the town this afternoon and bought a few trinkets at a
little shop opposite the church for Xmas presents. Cost nearly 50
francs which is a large sum in these days. Haven't been able to get
my wristwatch to go ever since that turn on the Somme. Think it's
got shell shock.

13.12.16
Labelled each of my Xmas presents, packed them up and sent
them to Elsie for distribution. Sent my watch also so that it can
be repaired. I have been doing postman's duties today for the first
time, adding another 'profession, occupation or calling' to the long
list that I have followed since I joined the army.

15.12.16

Back to Dickebusch again this morning. Everything quite normal. We always carry out these reliefs in broad daylight and I can't make out why Fritz leaves us alone, for he can't help seeing us. Still I don't mind him not taking any notice. He throws a few shrapnel over now and again and once in a while we get a whizzbang or two, but nothing to worry us. Just as we were about to leave Reninghelst the mail came up and I had a parcel from Mrs Berwick. The wagon was loaded and tied down so I had to carry it, but I didn't mind that. Remarkable how anxious some of the fellows were to help me do the carrying.

16.12.16

We have just about denuded the broken-down dugout. It is waterlogged but we have torn down all the dry wood and used it for our fires. A Belgian soldier came there while Andy and I were pulling it to bits. He told us that it had been their cookhouse until it was struck by a shell. He had come over to find a sack of coal but as this had been transformed into heat and smoke I was unable to enlighten him as to its whereabouts. We had previously imagined that the Belgians had occupied it because we found a pair of wooden shoes such as the native peasants wear. I had thought of sending them home as souvenirs but they were rather bulky and not very handsome – besides there was no telling what sort of feet had been in them. This soldier belonged to a Belgian battery of field artillery which is close by and covers part of our front. They take matters very casually – only fire a few rounds now and again, then retire to their dugout and amuse themselves with a piano and concertina, which they have scrounged from somewhere or other, probably from the big house close to the church. This house is very much in ruins and is another source of supply for firewood, but we have to be careful when we go up there because it is forbidden ground and if any officer or MP catches us we shall be for it.

17.12.16

Buchanan is going to censor our letters. It has been done hitherto by the chaplain and I don't welcome the change, for I don't like the idea of him prying into my correspondence. He doesn't take to me any more kindly. Every time he comes into the Signal Office he watches me most intently and if I make any little error or slip I hear all about it. But I don't let it worry me – I simply listen to his remonstrances apathetically – I am not in the army to make a living so he can bluster. I shan't be greatly perturbed. As far as I can make out, the reason for all this is merely a dislike of new faces. On the other hand, he is a good officer – he keeps us all up to scratch and he won't let any other officers interfere with us and that's something to be thankful for. Even the Staff Captain and Brigade Major are afraid to give us any orders without his permission. He is a good athletic figure – an Oxford Double Blue according to reports. In time his dislike may disappear – meanwhile, I shall jog along as usual.

18.12.16

Last night I was on duty and spent a lot of the time in letter writing in the hope that they will be in time for Xmas. Also addressed and sent off eighteen Xmas cards. Elsie hasn't discovered my message in *The Girl of the Limberlost* so I have had to urge her to look at it again. Paid seven francs towards our Xmas dinner. Sgt Oxley and Andy McCormack have gone to Bailleul today to buy the poultry, vegetables etc for the dinner which we anticipate will be the first thundering good meal we have had since we left England. The Germans have made some peace proposals but I bet they are rejected. It takes longer to end a war than to start it.

The Battle of the Somme had been officially closed down on 18 November. The onset of winter and the dire nature of the ground meant that further operations were pointless. The British and German armies had fought each other to a standstill but it was Germany who could ill afford the losses it had sustained. The battle might not have liberated much French soil in terms of square miles, but the effort had begun to underline an unpalatable fact for the Germans: they were being slowly outmuscled. British aircraft had temporary mastery of the skies, with the introduction of more advanced planes, but, more importantly, they had gained mastery (permanently) of firepower, and in particular artillery, the war's greatest killer.

The winter of 1916–17 was the worst in recent memory. Over Christmas and the New Year, the soldiers alternately froze or found themselves wading through mud, sludge and slop as snow and ice melted, then refroze. There was no fighting to speak of, but the Germans had not been idle. Throughout the autumn and winter months, they had been busy building a new defensive position, known as the Hindenburg Line, to which their troops would retire in the spring. The new positions would hopefully hold the Allies in the west while Germany aggressively fought in the east, but crucially, too, it would help the Germans to shorten the line their weary and overburdened soldiers would have to hold. This was vital, for the Allies' intention to maintain an offensive spirit in the west was consuming vast numbers of German men and vast volumes of raw material. When the Allies launched another offensive at Arras in April and May 1917, the German army was once again forced to use every ounce of its strength to hold the line. There is perhaps nothing more depressing than for an army to be almost permanently on the back foot, and for half of 1916 and the whole of 1917 that was the reality faced by the German soldier.

22.12.16

In the towns and villages which lie a few miles behind the lines a great business is done by the native trades people (reinforced by refugees who live in the shanties made of wood and old biscuit tins) in selling souvenirs of one description of another, the majority being of a semi-religious or ecclesiastical nature. Rosaries seem to be sold in pretty large numbers and one can now get pendants bearing ecclesiastical emblems such as the Lion of St Mark, the Lamb of St John etc. Favourite souvenirs are rings made from the aluminium portions of exploded shells and I have seen some very nice antique silver cups, saucers, serviette rings etc but besides being expensive they invariably bear the crest and name of some town or district and therefore cannot be sent home by post. A big trade is also being done in Xmas cards; not the sort we usually have in Blighty but gaudy things with a bunch of flowers and 'A Merry Christmas' or something of that sort worked in highly coloured silks, something like the things our grandmothers did in their youth – the Lord's Prayer or the Ten Commandments worked in wool, framed and hung up over the mantelpiece.

The little bit of frost and snow didn't last long. We have only one standard type of weather, it is rain and leaden skies – any variation is only of a very temporary nature. It is pouring with rain and everywhere is ankle-deep in mud. Even the duckboards are becoming submerged in it. Bill Rogers computes that already there are several million of them beneath the surface in Flanders. I thought the 21st was the shortest day but my diary lays the blame on the 22nd. Still no matter, they are both pretty short. After I got to bed last night the Surreys' band played a few Xmas hymns and carols. It is not a very strong band at present as most of its members became casualties in the Somme fighting.

25.12.16

Christmas Day. I was on duty at 8 a.m. but didn't turn out of bed till 7.40 a.m. – so I took my breakfast with me and had it in the Signal Office where it is usually a bit warmer than in the huts. The holiday spirit was prevalent and there was precious little work to do. I washed and shaved at leisure, received and sent a few complimentary messages and wrote to Elsie. Meanwhile Sgt Twycross' gramophone was going at full tilt, one man was chopping up wood with a blunt axe, others were doing juggling tricks with oranges and some were trying to pile up oranges and apples on plates to make them look like they do in fruiterers' windows, but their attempts were not as successful. The gramophone is a good one and there are some excellent records but they are usually spoilt by some fellow or other humming, whistling or barking out the tune and so the brave endeavours of the instrument are spoilt.

During the morning I received letters from Mother, Elsie, her mother and a card from Edith. Finished duty at 1 p.m., had a cup of tea and some bread and pozzy [jam] and then got ready for the Great Feed. All day long the men not on duty were making the necessary preparations. All of the beds had been taken out of one of the huts, a long table and forms fixed up and a platform built at one end. All the food and drink had been collected and the rather large-sized difficulty of getting it cooked had been overcome by the discovery that in one of the outhouses of the little farm just behind us there is a baker's oven and the farmer knows how to work it. Getting the stuff across to the hut was rather perilous because we had to get through a hedge, scramble up and down a bank and all in the dark. However, there were no accidents and we all sat down to a first course of turkey, ham, beef, mashed potatoes, cabbage and plenty of stuffing. Everything was excellently cooked and delightfully tender. We especially enjoyed the cabbage for we get very little green stuff in the ordinary course. After the poultry came the Xmas pudding, custard, jellies and tinned peaches and pineapple. Apples, oranges and nuts came as dessert and there were cigars and cigarettes for everybody and beer and wine for those who desired either.

Dinner was finished about 6.30 p.m. Then we started a concert. A programme had been arranged and everybody had to do something, each one being referred to by his nickname, mine being 'Tin Hat Joe', generally abbreviated into Joe. This name was conferred upon me when I had lost my cloth cap and couldn't get another and was consequently compelled to go everywhere tin-hatted. My contribution to the programme was 'Widdicombe Fair'. We had no instrumental accompaniment but that didn't prevent us from enjoying ourselves. At 9.30 we had an interval for light refreshments – jam tarts! Large ones called 'church windows' because they had strips of pastry latticed across the jam, cakes, biscuits etc. The Signal Office was closed all the evening except that one man had to be on duty. This resolved itself into a number of us doing ½ hour shifts so that no one was away from the merry-making for long. After the 'cakes and ale' the concert was resumed and lasted until midnight. Buchanan is on leave but the Staff Captain (Capt. Ainger) came in and stayed a few minutes. At midnight we sang 'Auld Lang Syne' and were served with sandwiches made up with what was left of the poultry and meat. These were not exactly drawing-room sandwiches. The bread was cut about ¾ inch thick, generously coated with butter and between the two slices was loaded (that's the only word) a quantity of turkey, beef, ham and stuffing – the whole sandwich being anything from two to three inches thick, but they were jolly good. My turn on the programme was rather late and after 'Widdicombe Fair' I gave them 'I Love My Gal Across the Water' as an encore. Both were applauded tumultuously, partly because they were liked and partly because the men had arrived at that stage when they will applaud anything. I heard no gunfire at all on Xmas Day but they got going again sharp at midnight.

26.12 16
After the concert it was my luck, with McCormack, to be on night duty. Didn't feel very much like it. I sat up on the table with my back in the corner and slept from 1 till 4.30 when Andy roused me and we changed places. I had a rare job to wake any of the men for duty at 8. I called them at 7, at 7.10, at 7.20 and 7.30 but it was 20 to 8 before I got any of them on the move; only one managed to be punctual at his job. Brady and Coultherd were supposed to take a class of battalion signallers at 8 but each time I shook them Brady said 'Is Bob up yet?' and Coultherd said 'Jim up yet?' The battalion men were not very late considering the day but their class didn't get going until 9. I was the only one who had any breakfast and I made this meal of cold turkey and ham. Afterwards I was quite busy taking cups of tea to men who were not on duty and who were still inclined for slumber. Then I turned in and slept till dinnertime. Apparently everything was not devoured at last night's gorge because today's dinner was made up of ham and little pieces of turkey etc.

28.12.16
Elsie still has failed to discover my message so I have told her straight that I have marked certain passages so now I hope she

will find it all right. Talked astronomy to George Henderson (from Ascot Post Office) and got him quite interested.

Feel as if I would like a real good bath – one I could lie in and soak. Whenever we are out of the line we get a bath (army type) but that's more in the nature of a lick and a promise. We are marched down to the Brasserie which has been converted into baths; before entering we start to disrobe for an RAMC [Royal Army Medical Corps] man who stands at the door yelling 'Take your boots and puttees off outside!' This done, 'St Peter of the boots and puttees off outside' admits us by batches into an ante-room where we stow away our boots, puttees, overcoat, cap etc in places where we hope to be able to find them later on, jostling all the time with another crowd who have had their bath and are now trying to find their clobber. From here we go into another chamber and finish undressing. Finally we arrive at the bathroom which is stone-paved, the hot water being supplied in showers from pipes running across the room about seven feet up. Under these showers we scrub ourselves as well as we can, taking turns at 'doing' each other's backs. Of course there is a bath attendant who hurries us up and we get back into the dressing room and dry ourselves, or at least do our best at it, with our dirty towels. Being fairly dry and shivery we pick up our dirty underclothing and trot to the Exchange Room where, if we are lucky, we get a clean article for each dirty one we hand in. Generally, there are 'No clean shirts' or 'No clean pants' or 'No clean socks' and to get a clean towel is an occasion to be marked as a red-letter day, while a complete change is almost unheard of. When we get back to the boot and puttee room we come under the attention of Mr Peter again who sternly admonishes us to hurry up and put our boots and puttees on outside.

Physically, this country resembles the eastern counties of England. Birds and plants are the same but I have seen more magpies in two to three days than I have in England in two to three years. A number of sinister looking carrion crows haunt the neighbourhood of our huts getting fat on garbage and filth. As for rats, they are as the sands of the seashore for multitude and cannot be numbered.

They swarm everywhere and run over our bodies when we are in bed. They have taught me how to sleep with my head under the blanket. Up at Dickebusch they run along a beam, over the head of my bed and then over the middle of Davidson's bed and so to various holes which take them out of the dugout. My head lies directly in the track and after two or three had trotted across my face I soon became able to breathe with my head covered up.

In the huts here at Reninghelst they jump up from the floor and sit on our bodies or legs. They come with a 'plop' which is sufficient to wake me up and then with a violent kick upwards I send them flying, but they are slow at taking lessons and I generally have this exercise two or three times each night. At Dickebusch we have both rats and mice in our dugout which I believe is rather unusual as I have often heard it said that rats and mice will not live together. Also, I fancy, fleas will not live where lice abound – we get plenty of the latter but seldom see any of the former. In the neighbourhood of our dugouts live a number of half-wild cats, something like those that may be found around many English farmhouses. They hide themselves away in the daytime but at night we hear them having fierce battles with the rats.

The Belgians are more phlegmatic than the French: they are not so excitable and gesticulatory and to hear them talking casually one might easily think that they were speaking some dialect of our own language. But there is no need to try to understand them for nearly all of them can speak and understand English even though they get all the dialects from Cornwall to Caithness hurled at them. I quite marvel at some of them, particularly one young woman in a book, paper, postcard and general assortment shop for she understands some of the Scotch and North Country dialects better than I do. And little street urchins jabber away indiscriminately in both Flemish and English. All this, I imagine, is due in some measure to the masterful British nature. To us these people are foreigners and therefore our inferiors – why should we stoop to learn their language? It is up to them to understand what we say in our own language. And so, unconsciously perhaps, we impose our will on theirs and take the place of top-sawyer as by divine right. And the natives seem quite content and accept the situation quite placidly. In some districts, we have gone so far as to obliterate all the original street names and replace them by English ones such as Station Road, Carlyle Road, Piccadilly Circus etc. The way of Englishmen with people of other nations, even on the latter's own soil, makes you feel rather proud of your nationality. I've written enough for one day so will shut up. We move up the line tomorrow so, of course, Andy and I are on night duty tonight.

30.12.16

Been thinking of making a collection of Soldiers' Songs, but it's a difficult job as it is seldom that they are sung through from beginning to end. I dare say some enterprising blighters are making exhaustive collections and some no doubt will reach the dignity of print, but a good many never will; they are not sufficiently polite and it is a fact that those which are the most typical, the most forceful, with the most 'character' and the most wit are easily the most unprintable. So far I have only managed to get snatches here and there – a man may start a verse and leave off in the middle, or start in the middle and finish just anywhere or sing a few words and whistle the remainder or make inarticulate gurgles to fill the place of words he has forgotten. This is sung to the hymn tune 'Aurelia':

> We are Fred Karno's Army
> The gallant RE Boys
> We cannot fight, we cannot shoot
> No earthly good are we
> And when we get to Berlin
> The Kaiser he will say
> 'Hoch, Hoch, mein Gott
> What a bally fine lot
> Are the Boys of the Old RE!'

31.12.16

This being the last day of the year, the Scotsmen, who barely understood Christmas and had never heard a carol, are in a state of excitement. They jabber about Hogmanay with the accent on the 'ay', and have promised that I shall learn what it means. I look forward to tonight with certain qualms and misgivings.

1917

1.1.17

Hogmanay is an excuse for mirth, merriment and jollification degenerating into rowdyism and horseplay. I protested that it had no interest for me and accordingly went to bed at 10 p.m. Andy looked on me with a mixture of sorrow and disgust while Davidson and Hamilton declared they would have me out of bed before midnight. I lay and read and smoked, then, about 11 p.m., Andy started to prepare the feast. I had received a parcel from Elsie; Davidson also had one which contained the necessary shortbread which is the Scotsman's Passover Cake at this season. Andy spread a newspaper over the table and arranged all the eatables and got the water boiling for the cocoa. There was a certain something in the atmosphere which caused me to think it expedient to rise and join in the festivities. At midnight we rose, shook hands all round, wished each other a happy new year and sang 'Auld Lang Syne'. Then we trooped out of our dugout and visited all the others, waking up everybody who was asleep and compelling them to shake hands with us. The various Scotsmen, of course, were up celebrating the occasion and the Englishmen took the commotion and disturbance in good part, with the exception of Billy Gould, our irascible cook. He would have slain the lot of us gladly and reached his hand out to find something to throw at us, but he could reach nothing but his pipe, and that was too precious to lose. So we let him go to sleep but went back an hour or so later and woke him up again. We finished up at the Sergeants' dugout where we indulged in gramophone, cigarettes and a bottle of port till nearly 2 a.m. The night was moonlight but muddy.

2.1.17

Had a rare old beat-up with Buchanan this evening – the other day Sgt Twycross had to fill up a form with all sorts of particulars of each of us including our civil occupations. I said, 'Shove me down as a clerk or an accountant.' He thought accountant sounded better and so put that down. Buchanan apparently had perused this list and when he found me on duty he started asking a lot of impertinent questions which I resented. I gave him some information about Chartered Accountants but told him I was not one. Then he said, 'Oh, I suppose you are a clerk in a chartered accountant's office?' I replied 'No, I am not,' quite respectfully having regard to his dignity as an officer. But so decidedly that even a rhinoceros would have considered himself told off. He turned away, picked up a paper, and a terrible tense silence fell on the place. Brady looked aghast while Andy almost fainted, for they had never heard a mere man talk to Buchanan like that. They sighed great sighs of relief when B went out, and they told me that I was in for it now. Well, if I am it can't be helped – I can't be punished for what I said, but I suppose he'll get his own back in some way or other.

3.1.17

Ha ha! Buchanan has done it. Just before 10 o/c last night when I was preparing to go off duty Sgt Twycross came into the office and told me that I am to go to the Transport for a week. We came back to Reninghelst today, and tomorrow I have to report myself to driver O'Gorman for instruction in horse riding and transport duties. Ever since I have been in the army I have declared my absolute ignorance of horses – and Buchanan has remembered it.

4.1.17

This morning at 9 o/c I reported myself to O'Gorman for instruction in the care and management of horses. He didn't want to be worried with me, so he set me on cleaning his harness – I made such a mess of it that he soon told me to leave it alone. His chief interest seemed to be to get rid of me – so I just mooned about keeping out of the way of any stray officers until 12 o/c when we knocked off for dinner. The afternoon was much the same.

5.1.17
I've been given one of McHowell's horses to look after, a quiet lazy old creature. Actually, I don't do anything more than look at it, but I haven't been quite so lazy today for we have made a roadway down to the Quarter Master Stores with bits of brick and old bully beef tins.

6.1.17
This morning McHowell and I saddled up Robin, our ancient and steady old beast, which has never been known to raise more than a gentle trot, and only this by dint of much goading, shouting and whipping. I trotted up through La Clytte towards Hemmel and back again. When I dismounted, McHowell said, 'Don't tell me you've never ridden a horse before.' I replied, 'On my honour I haven't – since I've been in the army.' He smiled and said no more. When I got back from dinner McGovern and McHowell were asleep and O'Gorman was writing a letter so I just lounged up against the doorway and smoked. All at once Buchanan appeared without any warning. He strafed us without any mercy – it was a 'fair cop'. What had brought him over was the fact that the new stables were ready for occupation and all the other drivers had got their horses into the best places while ours were still resting in the old ramshackle shelter across the field. We rushed across to our horses and Buchanan gave mine a smack – the dust flew out and he demanded to know when I last groomed it. 'This morning, sir,' I replied looking up accusingly at the dusty dirty roof. Military training makes one a very ready liar.

7.1.17

Had another trot on Robin and finished my transport training for the present as tomorrow we move up the line and I don't suppose for one moment that I shall be left behind. Had a letter from Elsie saying that she had discovered my message in *A Girl of the Limberlost* so now she knows where I am.

8.1.17

Back to Dickebusch. The Maltese Cart [a lightweight, two-wheeled cart pulled by one horse, pony or mule] got stuck in a ditch about 200 yards from our dugouts. The wretched old horse (the one I didn't groom) is a frightful jibber, and when the cart stuck it just sat back in the breaching strap and took things easy. No amount of cajoling or thrashing would get it to budge. We tied the big black mule on to the cart, but the rope came away with a swish and caught McGovern on the legs so he had to be taken away to hospital. Eventually we got the cart out but had to unload all the clobber the rest of the way. This particular ditch is only a little one and we have to cross it to get to our dugouts. In one or two places it has been partly filled in so that any sort of horse transport can get across if they go at it with a will, but our old gee-gee is one of the tired sort.

9.1.17

This evening a parcel came from Elsie and it contains a lovely Xmas pudding. I still have the one which Mrs Berwick sent me the other day. This is going to be warmed up for supper tonight and tomorrow I shall put Elsie's in the basin that now contains Mrs Berwick's – so we are all right for suppers for two nights. The grub we get from home is more acceptable than can be imagined by anybody who has not been compelled to the monotony of army dietry. Bacon, meat, potatoes, bread and jam day after day, with hardly any variation, make us appreciate as luxuries the little things which we took for granted in civil life.

11.1.17

A 'tin hat' inverted and pressed down into the mud just outside the door serves us for a washing basin. Last night and the night before it also served as a saucepan with the top of a biscuit tin for a lid. In it I boiled up the puddings which Elsie and Mrs Berwick had sent me. The bread ration was short so the puddings were doubly welcome.

13.1.17

Every day we think we have reached the limit of vile weather, but each succeeding day proves us mistaken. The most vivid imagination could scarcely picture anything more wretched than the weather we are getting today. Rain, hail, snow – water and mud worse than ever and most of the dugouts flooded. Woke this morning to find a little water in and around the door but it was soon baled out – and every now and then we have to do a little baling just outside the door or it would be in again. Wood scrounging is impossible, but fortunately we have enough to keep us going till tomorrow. We always try to keep a day's supply in hand to meet occasions like this.

17.1.17

Buchanan has not been censoring all the letters, as I understood he was going to do some time ago but now there has been a shake-up in the Censor's Department and he is to do it in future. Incidentally, we are getting rebuked for writing so many letters and at too great length. We had a rather exciting entry into the line on the 8th inst. It was a clear day and by way of a change Fritz took more notice of the 'change-over' than usual. The mules with the limber crossed over the ditch quite easily but the Maltese Cart, of course, got stuck and the wretched old horse just sat back and blinked placidly. Fritz had opened up a general sort of 'strafe' and we felt very uneasy for he could see us quite plainly. The only thing to do was to unload the cart and carry the things to the dugouts. I had made one journey and was back for a second when a shell dropped quite close to us but did no damage. At the same time Fritz put several round about the dugouts. O'Gorman had unloaded and had drawn his limber behind the cookhouse to be safely out of view but a shell dropped right against the gate and so frightened the mules that they bolted all round the mud track by the duckboards and so past the moat and the farm, up the avenue into the main road, O'Gorman hanging on for his life and quite unable to stop them. We watched them go and wondered if it were safer to stop where we were or go on with the carrying business. As this was a question that we could not answer, we just carried on. When we got to the dugouts we found that one of the shells had just skimmed the top of our dugout and gone clean through the next one between us and the cookhouse. This was inhabited by a 'runner' from the Field Ambulance and one from the Field Coy, RE. They were both inside at the time – the ambulance man was wounded and the RE was killed outright, a piece of the shell having passed clean through his body close to his heart. This man had only come out just before Xmas and his comrades had envied him as having a safe 'cushy' job.

As soon as we had pulled the cart out of the ditch (the horse refused to do it even when the cart was empty), I had a bit of bread and bully before going on duty in the Haystack. Fritz kept up his 'strafe' and another shell fell between our dugout and the Haystack, missing the duckboards by a few inches. As the bits settled I made a dash for it and got into the Haystack dugout quite safely. Hamilton followed me and a 'five-nine', which landed a few yards from the door, caused him to come in head first without any ceremony. After this the shelling subsided. The mail came up later on and I had a parcel from Mrs Berwick which, after examining, I carefully tied up again, a very wise course for when I came off duty just after 5 p.m. it was so dark that I tripped over the duckboards and fell full length into the soft juicy mud. During the evening two RAMC men came to take away the body of the RE. Davidson and I helped them to get the body out of the dugout and on to a stretcher. The next day (9.1.17) Buchanan vacated his dugout. Ours had been a good bit shaken and we had been busy patching it up, but B sent word that we could have his old one. We didn't give anybody else a chance to get into it and started to move straightaway although it was pitch-dark. Our new home was absolutely bare, so we had to knock down our old beds and cart them away and re-erect them.

21.1.17
The weather is now very cold – 17 degrees of frost last night – the huts are white inside as well as out, but the ground is firm and hard and this weather is infinitely preferable to the rain and mud we have endured for so long.

25.1.17
The hard frost continues and, generally speaking, things are quiet from a warfare point of view. There are occasional raids by one side or the other at various parts of the line, but beyond a little shrapnel now and then Fritz leaves us alone. He pays more attention to the batteries which are all round us but not so close as to bring the enemy's attentions to our little corner. For this we offer up thanks.

31.1.17
Have had a little more snow. The ground is white everywhere and at night time it shows up a remarkable reflection from the Verey lights [flares fired from a pistol] although they are four or five miles away in a straight line. The signs of the times seem to point towards increased activity on this front in the spring. A great deal of work is being done in this neighbourhood in the way of dump-making and laying railway tracks. A broad-gauge track is being brought up right through Reninghelst to Ouderdom. Of course, nobody knows what it all means – we can only guess.

Have had some lively arguments lately regarding the termination of the war. It is interesting to notice how desires form into opinions. Quite a number of the fellows reckon on March or April seeing the end. I laugh at them and say '1929' but in serious argument I say that the war may last until 1920. So I am looked on as a miserable pessimist but despite all my hopes and desires I cannot imagine the war finishing this year. The people who are running the war are not doing any of the fighting!

6.2.17

Last night was a blighter – the thermometer has touched zero once or twice lately and last night it went below. I was on night duty in the Haystack (where we have a switchboard now that the Signal Office has been transferred to the Farm Cellar). Harvey Dale was the runner on duty with me and we shivered with cold all night long. A wood fire was impossible because there is no fireplace or stove and no ventilation other than the door. Charcoal was not to be got or we would have had a fire in the petrol-can brazier. So we just had to stamp about all night long. About 3 a.m. I got out my Tommy's Cooker, boiled up some water and made a pint of soup. This was very welcome but we could have done with a gallon. Cpl Cole (motorcyclist) has had his skates sent out and spends his spare time skating about the moat. Incidentally, the ice on the moat provides us with a short cut to the Farm. The other day a game of hockey was played on Dickebusch Lake. Fritz took no notice but the next day he put a few big shells into it.

9.2.17

Last night the Kents carried out a raid – the preliminary bombardment was very heavy and the raid was quite successful from a military point of view. A party of REs went over with them to do demolition work. I went on night duty in the Signal Office at 10 p.m. and about midnight twelve German prisoners were brought into the Brigade Offices. They were a mixed lot but most were fairly well built. The Brigade Major got a little information out of them – they were all jolly well fed up and glad that they had finished with the fighting, albeit a bit apprehensive as to their immediate fate. Subsequently they were taken by motor lorry back to Division.

While the raid was on I was busy taking messages – Buchanan and Ainger (Staff Capt.) and Reap (Intelligence Officer) were all in a state of excitement, particularly the latter two – Buchanan never shows much excitement. They came buzzing around me, causing me to get unnecessarily flurried. The messages were coming off in code and it's not an easy matter to receive when three or four officers are crowding round you watching each letter that you write and grabbing the form before you have finished writing. However, the man who was sending to me was a better operator than most and I got his messages correctly. But presently Buchanan came down and said, 'This is wrong, Martin, why don't you pay more attention to your work?' I looked at the message and replied, 'That's exactly as it was sent.' 'No it isn't,' he said, 'get it sent over again.' So I had to call them up and get them to repeat – it came through just as before – still Buchanan was not satisfied, so I had to get it repeated three times, and B went off in a huff. He hadn't been able to find fault with me. Later, after the prisoners had gone and the Brigadier and Brigade Major had retired, he sent for me to go up to the Officers' Mess, gave me a dose of rum and asked me if I knew anything about lighting fires. I said I had lit a few since I had been in France so he asked me (not ordered) to have a try at lighting his. So I obliged and then retired to the Signal Office. While I was lighting the fire, one of the Kents' officers came in and related sundry incidents that occurred during the raid. The Kents tried another raid later on but found Jerry ready for them and had to retire.

11.2.17

Buchanan gave me a fatherly lecture – says that the duties of a signaller demand resource and initiative, and that there are times when he must act on his own and not be bound by the rigidity of Army Rules and Regulations – he may be praised or he may 'get hell' for it, that just depends on how things turn out, but he's got to risk that. Also my demeanour is rather 'off-handish' and I continually appear to be thinking about things other than my work. I listened very attentively till he had finished, then said 'Very good, sir', saluted, turned round and gave myself a smile.

16.2.17

Been feeling very depressed and miserable so that for two whole days I refrained from writing any letters at all, but today I bought two green envelopes from one of the runners for a franc and have written a long letter to Elsie. It has done me good and I feel in better spirits. But oh, the utter desolation of this life out here. Absolutely helpless and impotent, we feel ourselves to be the wretched tools of an inexorable fate. It is bad for us to sit down and think – we become morbid. No wonder that the majority of the men, as soon as we get out of the line, turn their attention to estaminets and vin blanc.

18.2.17

Had a parcel, containing a nice lot of fruit from Mrs Berwick; also enclosed was a copy of a very painful pamphlet prophesying all sorts of terrible things about the war, and based on the books of Daniel and Revelation and on the movements of the sun, moon and planets. Quite amusing reading, especially as already a good many of the predictions have failed in fulfilment. Its chief point of interest, however, is in the prophecy that this war will last till 1929; then we shall have two years of peace, after which will break out a war more terrible and awful than this one, and it will be engineered and ordered by the present Crown Prince.

23.2.17

Didn't get any mail at all for three days and now it's coming in with a rush. I shall have a busy time answering them all. My watch is going all right but seems to have a pain inside it because it groans a bit when I wind it up.

1.3.17

A fine spring morning, and a blackbird came outside my dugout and sang just like the one that frequents the tall elm tree at the back of my house at Ealing, and used to wake me up with his whistling. This weather, the sweet spirit of spring swells in the hearts of men, and fills us with hopes and longings for something better than this sordid existence. In this way, perhaps, it makes us feel more discontented than we were in the very bad weather.

10.3.17
Snow yesterday, rain during the night and now the thermometer has made a big jump upward. Have done quite a lot of letter writing during this spell out of the line.

14.3.17
Wrote five letters, the first for several days as I have been in a very 'pippy' frame of mind. – I am thoroughly 'fed up and far from home'. The absurdity and utter imbecility of war only becomes more apparent the longer one is out here.

22.3.17
Woke up to find about two inches of snow on the ground. Then the sun came out and melted it but all day long we have been getting fierce blizzards of snow with biting cold winds, and in the intervals the sun has shone out of a deep blue sky flecked with a few white feathery clouds in regular spring fashion. According to the Almanac, spring started at 4.27 a.m. yesterday but tonight it doesn't feel very springlike. This evening I've been trying to warm up the hut, but as soon as the fire goes out it will be bitterly cold. My illumination is a solitary candle stuck on top of an empty rum jar and I'm sitting on the end of Colin Veitch's bed because that's the nearest point to the fire. Otherwise it is not a very comfortable seat as it is not joiner made and nails stick up in such profusion as to demand considerable care in sitting on it. Now I am going to pack up and get into bed for tomorrow we are off to Dickebusch again.

23.3.17
Arrived at Dickebusch safely. Had a parcel from Lil containing a body belt folded up just as she had bought it. When I unfolded it a piece of paper dropped out – I picked it up and read this:

Miss Dulcie Bennett
111 Mansfield Road
Nottingham
Wishes the boy who receives this belt the best of luck and a safe
return to Blighty. XXXX for luck

Oh, Dulcinea, I am no Don Quixote so I vulgarly displayed your
missive to other eyes and there was quite a competition between
several fellows as to who should have it and write to you. I even
cruelly left them to settle the matter between themselves. But
listen, Dulcie, one of these young men makes quite a profession
of answering little notes of this sort and already he has a large
collection of photos he has written to.

24.3.17
Fritz has been pretty quiet all this month but has gradually
increased his activity till this evening he burst out ferociously. I
was on 5–10 p.m. duty in the Signal Office. About 7 o/c a violent
bombardment was going on on our front and Fritz was shelling
all round us pretty liberally. When I came off duty at 10 p.m. the
bombardment had slackened down almost to normal on the front
line but Fritz kept plugging us with his heavy black shrapnel.
He sends them over in threes with about two-minute intervals. I
waited till one triplet had burst and the pieces settled, then made
a bolt for my dugout which I reached only just in time to avoid the
next issue. A West Kent private, by name W. Taylor, was buried
up to his neck by a 'Minnie' [nickname for the *Minenwerfer*, or
trench mortar]. A party of men were going to dig him out but he
shouted that he could stay where he was until the fire slackened.
Eventually he was rescued uninjured. For this he was rewarded
with the Military Medal.

28.3.17
Looking across the moat into the Farm Garden I noticed some
crocuses in bloom. Called out all the dugout to see them and we

nearly went barmy with excitement for they are the first flowers we have seen since we left Eecke on 25 October last.

1.4.17

Palm Sunday. The Belgians observe this day by taking big lumps of box tree to church.

Haven't seen any of the usual palm which graces this season in Blighty. Men, women and children were all carrying lumps of box down to the church this morning and looked quite serious over it. This plant grows into bushes and small trees out here – it is not trimmed down into a garden border as it used to be at home. I suppose it's the Belgian equivalent of the Judean Palm. The weather is not much like April, cold winds and blizzards of snow, so of course I've clicked for an outdoor job. Brady, Coultherd, McCormack and I have been told off for practice in signalling to aeroplanes. Each morning and afternoon we proceed with our 'flapper' [white-painted canvas used to signal] to an appointed spot in a field just off the Wesboutre Road. There we are joined by men from each of the battalions similarly equipped. Lieut. Walker (commonly known as 'Hookey' or 'Shugley') of the East Surreys is in charge. We adopt various methods of keeping ourselves comparatively warm until the 'Contact' aeroplane arrives when we can send and receive a few practice messages.

9.4.17

Originally there were only five of us in our dugout, but when two or three of the others started to collapse a few weeks ago we found shelter for two more, to wit, O'Brien and Robertson. Now we feel rather crowded but, of the seven, two of us are English and four are Scotch while O'Brien is cosmopolitan – Irish parentage, born in Glasgow, lived some time in London, and is very keen in argument, so keen, in fact, that he varies his nationality according to the turn of the argument. If anything good has been done by Scotsmen, he is a Scot, if by Irishmen, then he's Irish and the same with the English. If anything derogatory to one nation is mentioned, well, he belongs to one of the others. On Sundays, out of the line, he and Brady are Catholics because, being so few in number, they don't have Church Parade. Robertson is the baby of the section, both in years and appearance. He is round all over, round face, round body and round legs. Probably known as 'Fatty' in his schooldays. He and O'Brien are bosom pals and, as such, are constantly quarrelling but it's fatal to take sides with either for then they immediately unite and present a solid front to the common enemy. Dagnall is the other Englishman – comes from Cheshire and is a foreman of Post Office linemen. He is grandfather of the dugout, I am father, the rest being children of twenty to twenty-four except McCormack, who is twenty-six and is affectionately styled Mrs McCormack because he acts as housekeeper and looks after the rations and performs all the maternal duties of the establishment. Aitken is the 'Cheese King' – has ideas of settling down in Cheddar after the war. He has toasted cheese for breakfast, dinner, tea and supper and frequently between meals, generally drops more into the fire than he succeeds in cooking. Also he is the most neatly groomed person in the section – seems to take a pride in his personal appearance – even cleans his boots and buttons and brushes his hair when there is no need for it at all. Frequently been known to wash twice in one day. Otherwise intelligent and a very decent fellow.

Davidson is the terror of the dugout and, indeed, of the whole section. A big, strong, fair-haired young giant with a voice, yes, yes, with a voice. Has got a lot of reserve energy which he endeavours to dispose of by vocal effort. When he discovered that I was musical he asked for my opinion on his voice. He was insistent but I remained polite for many days. At last I was driven to tell him that he was one of those blighters with music in his soul but precious little in his voice. Then I bolted, but he took it as a good joke, didn't feel ticked off in the least, and now he warbles away, more than ever. Repertoire very limited. Knows a lot of tunes but only a few words of each. This is how he sings one called 'The Five-Fifteen':

Lumpty-umpty-umpty-um five-fifteen
Lumpty-umpty-umpty-um five-fifteen
Lumpty-umpty-umpty-um five-fifteen
Lumpty-umpty-umpty-um five-fifteen.

O'Brien likes the words of this song so well that he usually calls for a second verse. Davidson starts to warble as soon as he wakes in the morning and is quite impervious to all threats, pleadings, cajoling and ridicule. I got so annoyed the other morning that I thought if he could be so cheerful it was really time he got up. But he wouldn't be persuaded and at last, greatly daring, I reached over and took hold of his nose very firmly and pulled; he came out of bed with a jerk. I didn't know that he had a terribly sore nose, but he wouldn't accept any apologies, so, out of bed I came, blankets and all and was rolled on the floor of the dugout. He is always the last to get to bed and keeps lullabying from about 10 till midnight, but nothing short of absolute destruction will keep him quiet — sleep only brings a change of utterance, for no matter how often we wake during the night, Davidson is yap-yap-yapping away about something or somebody. The only gratifying aspect of it is that he doesn't sing in his sleep. And he is going to get married after the war! Poor wee wife!

10.4.17

We are having a very busy turn in the line again. In the ordinary course I should only have been on duty for four hours today but I was operating the telephone switchboard from 8 a.m. to 10 p.m. with only brief reliefs for dinner and tea. Had a beat-up with an officer. Oh how cocky and important some of these creatures become as soon as they get into officers' uniforms! Lieut. Hogg, the Divisional Observation Officer, called me up and asked for one of his Observation Posts so I put him through without any trouble, but when he had finished he called me up and let drive without any warning. Said that he had been calling for ten minutes before he got an answer. I told him I answered directly he called. He cursed and swore and called me a liar and sundry other nice kind names, took my name and number and said he would report me to the Staff Captain and see that I got properly punished. When he had finished I got hold of Sgt Twycross and told him my version. I didn't fear much because this is the sort of affair in which Buchanan will stand by me. He may strafe me himself but he won't let Staff Captains or Divisional OOs or anybody else interfere with his section. However, there was no need to trouble at all for only a few minutes later Hogg called me up again and made a really handsome apology saying that the trouble was due to a loose wire at his end which resulted in only intermittent connection. So now I can sleep in peace. Later in the evening he came into the Haystack for no apparent reason at all, was very nice and affable and gave me a cigarette. Suppose he only wanted to see who I was.

13.4.17

Back to Reninghelst. We had just got settled in and had tea when there was the sound of a shell burst. This was most extraordinary as Fritz has never dropped any shells in this neighbourhood. We all rushed out of our huts to see what was up when there was a terrific whizz and a thud and lumps of dirt and mud flew up all over us. A shell had pitched close to the door of the Officers' Kitchen only a few yards from where we were standing. The Brigade Major came out and ordered us to disperse, so we cleared off in all directions but we saw another shell burst behind the Post Office Hut and one in the direction of the Ouderdom Dump. The shelling was only a spasm, however, and soon everything was normal again.

14.4.17

Some Artillery Officers have been up to examine the shell hole. It turns out that although it landed with a deuce of a roar it didn't explode. If it had done it would have accounted for the best part of Brigade HQ. Fortunately it struck a deep bed of soft mud which was insufficient to explode it. The hole at the top is about four or five feet across and about five feet down it becomes just a hole twelve or fifteen inches in diameter. We probed this hole with long poles but couldn't touch the bottom. The Artillery Officers say that it is an armour-piercing shell from a long-range high-velocity naval gun firing probably from a distance of fifteen miles. They would like to have dug up the shell, but that would take a battalion of men about a week. It was jolly lucky that it struck that very soft patch instead of coming a few feet further on and striking the comparatively hard surface of the lane. However, the powers that be have gained certain information as to the direction and distance from which the gun is firing.

15.4.17

We hear that our aeroplanes have spotted Fritz's long-range gun and they or our artillery have put it out of action. It was fifteen miles away from us and right on the other side of the sector. Very glad to know it's knocked out as we had thought it very unkind of old Fritz, after giving us a very lively time in the line, not to leave us alone when we got out here. Went down and had a look at the shell hole by the Post Office. It's a big one, almost as big as the one outside our dugout on the Somme. It fairly put the wind up Smithey and Peter Kenny, who, although they have been out here since 1914, have always been in safe places. This is about the first shell they have seen burst.

16.4.17

Heard a humorous tale about Sgt Maton, Brigade Vet. Sgt. He wrote a letter which somehow or other fell into the hands of some of the men in his hut. Being short of news he drew on his imagination and gave an extraordinarily detailed account of how, for the past six weeks, he and his comrades had been building themselves a dugout under terrific shellfire and he enlarged on the danger of his ordinary duties by telling how he had crawled into no-man's-land to minister to a wounded horse! And three days ago he had never seen a shell burst except 'Archies' [anti-aircraft fire]. This romancing is rather common amongst certain types of men. One fellow thought it a great joke when he told his parents that he had saved his Sgt Major's life and had been rewarded with a packet of fags. This same man went a bit further and told them that when he went over the top he came to a German dugout. He looked in and was greeted immediately with cries of 'Kamerade'. 'All right,' he said, 'come out, you blighters', and out trooped a hundred and fifty of them. He was taking them back when he met an officer who took charge of the party and subsequently laid claim to having captured them himself, but the man protested and the result was that neither of them got the VC!

17.4.17

In these huts I am not associated with the same bedmates as at Dickebusch. There are only five of us in this hut and we get all the disadvantages of open-air treatment without any of its compensations. Charlie Werry is another youngster something like Robertson – round all over – and he's infernally lazy but very cheerful withal; therefore he is one of those persons one gets on with very well, but would like to kick or turn out of bed and shake. It's very hard to rouse him to a sense of his responsibility for the care and cleanliness of the hut but on the rare occasions when he does wake up he will chop wood till the perspiration is trickling all down his body and oozing out of his boots. This is good for him, keeps him fit, so once started, we encourage him to keep on at it. His home is at Chichester. Colin Veitch is a canny Scot from Fife and was in Egypt and Gallipoli before he came to France. He bustles about and cleans up and generally acts a mother, always keeping an eye on the rations and the fuel and estimating if they will last us till the next issue is due. Dickson has several elder sisters but no brothers, therefore it's taking him a long time to get over the fondling and attention to which he was accustomed in civilian life. He is one of those blithe spirits who has never been known to smile and if he is a little out of sorts, dwells on the hardness of his lot a bit too much. He is the parcel specialist of the section. Nobody has been able accurately to reckon up how many parcels he gets in a month, but what with all his sisters, his parents and sundry other fond relations who think the poor lad is suffering untold privations and must be fed bountifully from home, there are times when he gets parcels nearly every day. In this respect, of course, he is a desirable acquisition to our hut.

Hetherington, a North Countryman, is one of those rare geniuses who only once in a thousand years flash through the pages of history with the brilliance of a mighty meteor on a moonless night. He is a musician of no mean order and an artist who scorns to exhibit his paintings to the criticising and unappreciative public. So all these treasures he has locked away to be seen by no mortal eye until he returns to Blighty. His knowledge and grasp of social economics and politics are something beyond the ken of ordinary mortals; and time out of number he has addressed audiences of thousands and swayed them backwards and forwards by his incomparable eloquence, and has played on their emotions with the same skill and effect as he plays on the violin. There are a lot of other things at which he excels, indeed it is impossible for him to make a bungle of anything; and whatever he attempts he excels at immediately with that ease and grace which cannot be acquired but which are natural to him. Remarkable, but nevertheless true, because he keeps on telling us so. Incidentally, he is the section's appetite and if ever there is a mysterious shortage of grub we know where to lay the blame. One day I saw him eat a one pound tin of jam straight off in about three gulps.

A few weeks ago I was down by Reninghelst church when I saw a rural Belgian funeral. Apparently it was the funeral of an elderly man, and his widow and grown-up children were the mourners. The hearse was a farm wagon (not much like a modern English one, more like those in Constable's pictures) drawn by two heavy draught horses, well-groomed and fitted with well-polished harness. This feature was noteworthy because ordinarily the Belgians don't give much attention to 'poshing up' their horses and harness. Over the wagon was the coffin together with two or three chairs occupied by the bereaved daughters. But the widow had the seat of honour in front of the wagon, low down, almost on the shafts and just behind the horses' tails. From this position she directed all the operations with just that amount of regal dignity which was appropriate to the occasion. The Belgians spitting here there and everywhere is not very pleasant especially when you see the women spitting on the floor and rubbing it out with their boots or wooden clogs, or the men doing it and the women running round mopping it up after them. I have an idea that social position goes by the number of times a man can spit in the same place. If he can make a cross without once misfiring he becomes a councillor and the man who can weave the most intricate pattern is made a burgomaster.

Back in January I was getting fed up with the army baths and, as I had collected three changes of fairly decent underclothing, I looked out for a chance of getting a private bath somewhere or other where I could have a good scrub down and leave my dirty clothes to be washed. I went up the La Clytte Road and crossed the fields to a little group of cottages where I found one with an 'Authorised to wash for Soldiers' notice in the window. An old lady answered my knock. 'Good morning, Madame, can you let me have a bath?' 'No compree,' she replied. I discovered that I had struck one of the few Belgians who couldn't speak any English. I don't know any Flemish so I tried 'Lavez?' – 'No compree' – 'Bathez?' 'No compree.' I began to get rather desperate so I rubbed my hands over my body and made various other antics intended to resemble a person having a bath, and then threw out my last word, 'Washez?' – 'Ja, Ja,' she replied, and her wrinkled features brightened up with intelligent comprehension. I sat down in the kitchen while she made the water hot in a great big kettle and prepared the ablution chamber. This chamber is a shed at the back of the cottage. The bath is a round wooden washing tub. I have a pailful of hot water and ditto of cold. The old dame provides a chair and I take my own time over my ablutions. When finished, I hand over my dirty clothes and get back the lot I left for washing on the previous occasion.

The woman does a lot of washing but has some system of marking so that she always brings out the right set. Only once have I had any trouble, and that was over a pair of socks – I got the wrong ones, but she soon put that little matter right. She knows me as 'Telefon' because my blue and white armlet declares me to be a Signaller.

All this winter we have realised that we have had a quiet time. Both sides have been quite content to hold on just where they were – and except for occasional raids into each other's territory, and a few artillery strafes just by way of keeping things from going to sleep altogether, we have not done much more than play at war. But things have livened up considerably during the last four or five weeks and we look forward to spring with very mixed feelings. It is evident that the Big Push is going to take place somewhere in this sector, but when and how and by whom are matters that lie in the laps of the gods. Many rumours are current but I have had so much experience of the birth and growth of rumours since I've been out here that I don't pay much attention to them. Yet I think it is pretty well settled that we are to go out for our long overdue rest. The 124th Brigade has had one and the 123rd are now having theirs in the St Omer region. Whether we are coming back to this neighbourhood to take part in the push, nobody knows.

In the camp just mentioned we passed a number of large wooden posts with ropes attached. This is where men, who are fighting for a country in which probably they have no interest except that Fate ordained that they should be born there, are tied up like slaves for two hours a day and in other ways punished for all sorts of trivial offences. Prussianism is not confined to the Germans. Our own military system is out and out Prussianism. I suppose the only way to persuade men to face the horrors and vileness of war is to drive them at the point of the bayonet, and mete out to them all manner of cruel punishments, holding over their heads the murderous threat of being shot at dawn. Such is the fierce, brutal discipline under which we live. The 'is and is not' of the King's Regulations and the various Army Acts are very definite and are interpreted in the most rigid Roman fashion – and of course the host of young schoolboys, clerks, counterjumpers and the like who have managed to fall into commissions, like to exert the authority reposed in them. Never having been in the position to order or command, and suddenly finding themselves possessed of power over their fellow men, they become snobs and tyrants of the worst description. Fortunately for us, Buchanan is not one of this class. Although for some reason or other he hasn't taken kindly to me yet, I must admit that he is a good officer: he looks after his men and he knows his work, and the best thing about him is that he won't let anybody else interfere with us.

23.4.17

A Corporal Flynn and two Signallers of the 23rd Middlesex have been left behind by the 123rd Brigade to instruct us in the use of the new portable directional Wireless Set. This morning we established two stations and got through several messages, but I can see there is going to be more holiday about this course than serious business. Flynn says this Wireless Set is the only one of its kind in France at present – it is a big advance on anything similar, the chief novelty being the use of 'valves', little bulbs like incandescent electric light bulbs but containing wires other than the filament.

Mulligan was billeted in a cottage near the village with a couple of MPs [Military Policemen]. They had a bare room, and slept on the floor. M. discovered a spare bedroom in the farm and got permission to take it. It's a small room with a single bedstead, dressing table etc and family photographs on the walls. All very nice and comfy. I helped him get his kit down there and the farm girls asked me if I were the Sergeants' domestique! We had some coffee and sat talking for about ¾ of an hour when we decided it was time to get back to our posts previous to packing up for dinner. In the afternoon we had a lamp-reading test which was quite easy but John O'Brien cursed it – said he was an instrument repairer not an operator – so I read for him as well as myself but he thought it advisable to put a few extra mistakes of his own so as to avoid suspicion. Heard the cuckoo for the first time this year.

In the evening Horace (a Kent Signaller, don't know his other name) and I took a walk into the forest. We went along the road past a number of cottages when suddenly we met some Germans. It gave us a bit of a start because we thought we had left them a long way behind. It turned out they are prisoners located in a cottage right on the edge of the forest — a much better billet than we have got. They are guarded by a few French soldiers and are employed in tree-felling. The forest is on a hill and we climbed up through it till we reached a road — went along this for half a mile or so and then turned back into the forest and soon lost our bearings — climbed up a tree to get a look over the countryside and so found the direction to take. The other fellows laughed when we told them we had seen the wily Hun — they won't believe us.

24.4.17

A little more wireless — also coffee — this morning, and this afternoon 'visual'. I was in charge of one station with the three Surreymen. Going to take up our position, I noticed a hen sitting in the ditch. Said nothing, but later I heard a clucking, went back and discovered four eggs which, in accordance with the best traditions of the service, I promptly commandeered. We had one each for tea. This evening I was taking a quiet stroll when I saw Glasspoole and Cheesman going across the fields obviously on the track of the Hun, so I hailed them and conducted them to the cottage where some of the prisoners were just returning from their day's work and others were busy in the garden. So now, they believe us.

27.4.17

This week has been the easiest one I have spent in the army. It has been a regular holiday. Walker has troubled us but very little — about ten minutes a day on average. Twice we have had a lecture on wireless in the village schoolroom. It was a job to squeeze into the little desks but we managed it. The walls are decorated with the same sort of pictures of birds and animals and scriptural subjects as those at home except that the Bible pictures here have a flavour of Catholicism. Each evening I have been down to the farm and had coffee. Lucienne speaks a little English and I speak less French so we get on all right. Two or three times I have bought eggs there and they have boiled them hard for me so that I could bring them back and eat them for supper. The family at the farm consists of the farmer, his wife, Lucienne (their eldest daughter, about eighteen) another daughter about fourteen, and a miscellaneous assortment of small children.

29.4.17

Now that I am so far from the line, in a spot where the heavy guns can only be heard when the wind is in the right direction, where there is no sign of war, and where the rural occupations of peacetime plod steadily along as if totally unconscious of the awful horrors that are taking place only a few leagues away, I feel my old love for the countryside reviving. I was half afraid it was dead, killed by spending so many months in about the most monotonous and soul-destroying region imaginable. It may be quite passable in peacetime, but war annihilates everything. Devastation and suffering are forced into one's mind and with these things uppermost it is almost impossible to appreciate nature even in her most glorious moods. Now I am longing for Blighty – but oh, the heaviness of longing and waiting! I grow impatient and rebellious at times – although I know perfectly well that it is all to no purpose for we are very much the creatures of circumstance – paltry pieces on 'this chequer board of nights and days'. I slept this morning but got up for dinner, then did some writing but was interrupted with the call for Church Parade. This caused a bit of excitement as it is the first one we have had since the middle of October – the weather today is glorious – just as it was on this particular Sunday five months ago. The sun is bright and warm though there is a little chilliness in the wind and the birds are singing gaily.

2.5.17

Spring has burst upon us quite suddenly. Cuckoos, swallows, primrose, butterflies all seem to have come with a rush, and last night I heard the nightingale. I have just written seven letters, and am sitting on a big stone in the farmyard with my back against the wall. The sun is going down and a cuckoo is calling in the distance. Everything is absolutely peaceful. The only sign of war is an anti-aircraft gun which stands in the roadway close to the Signal Office – it comes up on a lorry every morning and goes away in the evening. It is manned by artillerymen who are suffering from nerves or who are otherwise temporarily unfit for the strenuous life of active warfare up the line. Another sign of spring – a bee has just come buzzing round my head.

6.5.17

A 'rest' in the army does not mean the same thing as it does in civilian life. It really means a change of occupation: instead of fighting, we have innumerable parades, inspections, route marches, field days and the like – anything to prevent us from idling half an hour away. We have a continual round of duties so that I get precious little time for letter writing or reading.

12.5.17

Thank heaven we are having things a bit easier today. The last four days have knocked the stuffing out of me, particularly yesterday when it was very hot and we had a full dress rehearsal of the attack we are going to make when we get back in the line. I was at an advanced Signal Station when Buchanan came up and asked if anybody had any tobacco. I offered him my pouch and said, 'It is only Waverley' – 'Well, what's the matter with that?' he asked. I nearly said, 'Oh it's only boys' tobacco', but changed my mind and said, 'It's not very strong.' When he had gone, MacDougall told me that Waverley is B's favourite tobacco. Glad I changed my mind.

13.5.17

Buchanan had us all out (including the 'Forward Party') and gave us a little lecture on what is going to happen. We are going back to our old sector to make a big attack. The 123rd and 124th Brigades are going over first – we follow and take over from them on the

Damstrasse then push on the final objective – presuming, of course, that Jerry doesn't protest too vigorously. We don't look forward to it with any particular joy.

Just south-east of the city of Ypres was the strategically important Messines Ridge. This naturally important position dominated the landscape and had been in German hands since the early fighting around Ypres in October and November 1914. Since then, the British had not seriously contested the strongpoint in the German line. However, since mid-1916 plans had been undertaken to take the ridge by literally blowing the enemy off it. In great secrecy, twenty-one mines would be dug underneath the German lines and exploded simultaneously. Those Germans left alive – indeed any who still retained any faculty for thought – would be assailed by infantry supported by artillery, tanks and gas.

The work to dig the mines took over a year and involved thousands of men not only to dig the tunnels but also to remove the vast amount of spoil. In the end eight kilometres of tunnels were dug; at the end of each were laid explosives that cumulatively weighed 600 tons. Only one of the twenty-one mines was discovered; the other twenty were primed to go. Then, at 3.10 a.m. on 7 June, the mines were detonated; only two failed to explode. The explosion could be heard in London, while on the ridge the Germans were not only stunned but stupefied, 10,000 being killed in the opening moments of the battle. The British forces advanced and in the main suffered relatively few casualties for the significance of the prize. German counterattacks could only be organised the following day and failed entirely.

31.5.17

After seven weeks I am back in Dickebusch once again but the aspect of the country has changed. It is crowded with gunpits. Gordon Farm, which lies on the other side of Dickebusch Lake and a little nearer the line, has been inhabited by civilians until a few days ago. It has also been the HQ of an artillery brigade. The civilians were removed on account of the impending attack and within three days of their leaving Fritz had set fire to the place and razed it to the ground. It is now only a smouldering pile of rubbish and ammunition dumps. The derelict, waterlogged dugouts round the lake have been restored and now house one of our battalions. There is much more bite and sting in the shellfire and it is not safe to wander about as we used to do.

5.6.17

We are now at the Micmac Camp – came here this afternoon – the few days we spent at Dickebusch were not exactly pleasant, for Jerry is giving all his attention to the back areas, and the actual front line is peaceful. Our bombardment has been continual and terrific beyond imagination, and against it Fritz's retaliation, though pretty hot, can only be described as a bit troublesome. Once on the night of 29–30 May I was on night duty in the Haystack, Southwood was the runner with me. About 11 o/c I heard a Boche aeroplane flying about. This is the first time I have actually heard any night-flying although I have heard of it, even as long ago as last October on the Somme, when we had returned from the trenches and made up a big camp fire and had a 'sing-song'. We were advised to put it out as only a night or two previously the Hun had been over dropping bombs. I looked outside the Haystack and although it was bright moonlight I could see nothing. Later, about midnight, Southwood had fallen asleep on the doorstep, when I heard a shell fall a little nearer than is comfortable. It didn't make much of a noise and I concluded it was a dud. But it was quickly followed by another and another and then lots more all of the same score. Gas shells explode with a gentle 'plop' just like a dud 'five-nine' [5.9-inch shell] (that's why Fritz mixes them). So I sniffed the air and there was no doubt about it. I woke Southwood, told him to go round and warn all the dugouts, phoned through to the Signal Office and told them – looked round for my gas mask and found I had left it in my dugout – the first time I have ever done it – so I rushed out to get it. The gas shells were now coming over in a continual shower, and with my hand over my mouth and nose I ran to the dugout, alarmed them all and got my mask on and returned to my post. It was a rotten business working a telephone switchboard with a gas helmet on. As much as possible I 'buzzed' but every now and then I had to loosen my mask and talk and then the gas got into my throat and made my eyes water terribly. After two or three hours of it Jamieson came running into the Haystack saying that his dugout had been hit, but fortunately no one was hurt. As these dugouts are such frail structures the men soon came trooping down to the greater security of the Haystack. There was one terrific explosion which nearly shook the dugout down on top of us. The candle was blown out and the place fairly rocked. We thought a shell had struck the top of the dugout but later we learnt that it was a 'toffee-apple' dump [two-inch mortars shaped like a ball on a stick] blown up on the other side of the lake. Fritz kept on with his gas shells and a few heavies until daylight.

6.6.17

This afternoon we were all ordered to pack everything in our valises, except fighting kit, and hand them to the care of the QM [Quarter Master]. At 6 p.m. L/Cpl Aitken, L/Cpl Dagnall, Coultherd, Brady, MacDougall, Paterson, Robertson and I joined the Forward Party and moved up the line. We went by a newly made cavalry track, skirting Dickebusch on the north, and so past Scottish Wood into the trenches. In the shelter of some trees were a number of tanks in readiness for the attack. It was 9 p.m. before we were in our allotted positions in the support trenches. The front line trenches were manned by the 123rd and 124th Brigades. It was a wretched night – the strain of waiting was great – our guns were going continually – Fritz was 'nervy' and in addition to throwing over trench mortars and the like, kept his guns traversing our trench all the time. He had got it taped to a nicety and as the trench was so crowded there were a good many casualties. We (the Forward Party) had twelve men wounded, one having his left arm blown off – but none of the REs were hurt although for a few seconds I was given up for lost. I was crouched down in the trench with my back to Jerry when a small shell landed almost on the parapet a matter of only inches from my head. The trench came in on top of me and, but for the fact that it was strongly revetted, I should have been completely buried. When the smoke and dirt had cleared away, the other fellows were surprised to see me pick myself up unhurt. Aitken said, 'That one had got your name on it, Joe.' 'Yes,' I replied, 'but it was the wrong number.' It gave me a terrible shaking but it might have been much worse.

7.6.17

The night wore on with a miserable slowness but towards dawn the fire on both sides slackened and just before 3 a.m. we were ordered to leave the trench and lie out in the open. It was an impressive time – the gunfire ceased altogether with the exception of an occasional shell here and there – a thick mist was over the land and we had to lie full length, partly because of the shock that would result from the explosion of the mines and partly to prevent Fritz seeing us in the growing dawn. There was a strange groaning and rumbling from behind us and presently, looming out of the mist, came a tank, moving straight towards us. We began to scramble out of its way, but it turned off to the left and was soon buried again in the mist. Out of the silence came the sound of blackbirds from a clump of battered trees a little way back only to be rudely silenced at 3.10 a.m. by the tumultuous explosion of nineteen mines. This will probably be accounted as the greatest artificial explosion in recorded history. For several minutes the earth rocked to and fro oscillating quite twelve inches. It was an experience which I shall remember very vividly for the rest of my life – all the phases of the preliminary bombardment, the calm silence that succeeded them suddenly broken by a most terrific uproar, the weird sights of moving men and things in the semi-darkness, the rolling clouds of smoke picked out every now and then with shooting tongues of flame, all formed a tremendously wonderful sight. It was stupendous beyond the imagination.

The blowing up of the mines was the signal for all the guns on the front to open out. The noise rendered talking or shouting impossible. Every type of gun was in action, from immense howitzers to machine guns which were arrayed some little distance behind us and carried out a barrage all on their own. A few minutes later the 123rd and 124th Brigades went over and we returned to the trench. As daylight increased I looked directly on to the line that was being battered and the sight was so awfully impressive that the real horror of it all was temporarily quite obliterated. On our left, Fritz was sending over cloud gas – he also had an observation balloon up but this was soon put out of action by our aeroplanes. The prisoners came over in dozens and scores and passed behind us into safety. About 5 o/c 'Hookey' Walker took us out of the trench and we advanced to the Damstrasse. Ordinarily he has a languid sort of bearing that would give one the impression that he was rather dull and unobservant but he led us across that open, shell-holed country that only two hours before had been held by the Germans since 1914 as if he knew every inch of the ground. He didn't hesitate for a moment and took us straight to the dugout in which the 124th Brigade Advance Signals had established themselves. The Damstrasse is 1200 yards in front of, and overlooking, our old front line. It is a sunken roadway about six to eight feet lower than the surrounding country and therefore of considerable military advantage. At times we have imagined that Fritz has given us a tidy battering, but judging from the frightfully mutilated state of the ground, we have given him ten times as much as he has given us. His front line has been completely wiped out and is only traceable by the remains of his barbed wire, and it was only possible to find little bits of any trench.

As we went over, we passed through only a moderate barrage and met with no casualties although the dead bodies that were scattered about showed that other parties had not been so fortunate. When we reached the Damstrasse, however, we were fairly in amongst the shells for this was now our front line and Fritz was concentrating all his efforts in the attempt to prevent us from getting any further. Also many of our own guns were firing short, and spiteful 18-pdr [pounder] shrapnel was bursting all round us. The western bank of the Damstrasse was lined with dugouts, now in various stages of demolition. The one chosen for our Signal Office was fairly sound, being constructed of reinforced concrete about three foot thick. Lt Walker and Cpl Aitken went in to take over, leaving us outside in the remains of a trench which was labelled 'Engel Weg'. Col. Carey-Barnard (known as Carey-Whizzbang by reason of his rather explosive nature) came along leading the 15th Hants. Of course he wanted to know who we were, what we were, and all about us. The trench was rather cramped so we moved across to the east bank of the Damstrasse. Looking over the top, no Germans were visible but we knew they were lurking in shell holes and hiding in Ravine Wood and Pheasant Wood, both of which were only a few yards away.

We sat down on the bank waiting for orders and wishing to goodness that our 18-pdrs would lengthen their range. On my right was Dagnall and next to him was Coultherd. One of our 18-pdr shrapnels burst about six yards above our heads and the bits came hissing down viciously. I wasn't touched but Dagnall got it in both knees and Coultherd in the left knee. We ripped their breeches open and bandaged them up. I used my own field service dressing on Dagnall and subsequently got into trouble for being in action without one in my possession. We carried them across the road to the dugout where they remained till 8 p.m. before we got hold of any stretcher-bearers. It was about 5.30 a.m. when they were wounded. The Damstrasse is a slough – mud, water and shell holes. A shell burst right on top of the Signal Office and we went over expecting to find the place blown in but it was quite unharmed inside – evidence that Fritz knows how to build dugouts.

Presently the tanks came along. They had to drop down the bank about six or eight feet, wallow through the mud and climb the opposite bank. One came over the top of the Signal Office and again we feared for the safety of those inside but there was no need to worry. Another got stuck in the mud and refused to budge. At 6.30 a.m. the advance was continued for another 1000 yards to the final objective of the Division, the attacking battalions of our Brigade being the 15th Hants and the 11th Royal West Kents.

There was not much opposition except from a machine-gun nest in Pheasant Wood. The bullets came 'zipping' over our heads until the Kents stormed it at the point of the bayonet. The Signal Office was small, and with two wounded men in it and one end under water, there was only room for one operator at a time; yet at certain periods it was necessary to have two instruments working, so I took a buzzer outside and rigged it up on a mound where the trench had been blown in. The dirt gradually wore away and disclosed the bare buttocks of a dead man so I moved into the Damstrasse where the only comparatively dry spot was alongside a dead German but he was not badly mutilated. An infantryman close by me was hit in the face by a quantity of shrapnel dust and his tears trickled down his cheeks. He cried out, 'Oh my eyes, my eyes! My God, I am blind!' The sudden realisation of his blindness seemed a greater agony than the pain of his wounds. I shall never forget that terrible cry of anguish. A big German prisoner passed me with his left arm badly shattered. He begged a drink of water but I shook my head because I had only a little drop left and had no idea when I should get any more. Two other prisoners came over, one unhurt, the other wounded in the arm and side. The former scrambled up the bank leaving his wounded comrade to struggle alone. There was a yell of execration from all the Tommies round about and it put the wind up him. He threw his hands up above his head and yelled 'Kamarade', and we made him go and help his companion along.

Time passed very slowly – I looked at my watch, thinking it was afternoon and found it was only twenty past eight. I took off a message from the Kents saying that the Huns (500 of them) were massing for a counter-attack. Walker seized his revolver and went forth to meet them but soon came back as he had left his ammunition behind. This attack was repulsed by the Kents who killed twenty-five of the enemy and took twenty unwounded prisoners. We were due for relief at noon, but the relieving Division was delayed somewhere or other so we had to hang on, feeling very tired and hungry. Also we sent back several demands for cavalry as our advance had been so successful, but apparently the state of the country was such that rendered it impossible for cavalry to get up. The 47th Division on our left met a fiercer opposition and failed to take their final objective. Of course our 'lines' (telephone wires) were continually being broken – our stock of pigeons was soon exhausted – and our runners were on the go perpetually. In the afternoon I took a message forward to Lieut. Taylor. By this time things had quietened down considerably. I climbed up the bank and looked forward. With the exception of a solitary tank that had come to anchor just in front of me, there was no sign of humanity except that displayed by the general devastation, and the explosion of an occasional shell. My only guide was the 'line' which led me to a large shell hole in which Lieut. Taylor and his party had settled themselves. Fritz had ceased making any attempts at counter-attack and seemed to be content to settle down in his new position.

Lieut. Raphael, the Surrey cricketer, was up here this morning for no earthly reason as far as I can make out, other than that of souvenir hunting. He brought his batman with him and both were killed by a shell in a dugout which he was exploring. By the evening we had given up hopes of getting relieved today. Aitken and I settled down in the trench and tried to get a little sleep but Fritz started sending shells just over our heads to a spot about 200 or 300 yards away, and the shriek as they whizzed past was more than sufficient to keep us awake. He also treated us to some shrapnel – one burst just above us and a small piece hit me on the arm. It was long and thin and by a stroke of luck it struck me lengthways just where my sleeve happened to be rucked in several folds. If it had come end-on it would have gone through. I picked it up and put it in my pocket. It is the only souvenir I brought back although I could have had hundreds of belts, buckles, buttons, bayonets and such things as some men pride themselves in collecting. Outside the Signal Office was a great pile of arms and clothing together with black bread and sausages but although we were hungry we knew better than to touch any of it.

Towards nightfall Lieut. Taylor brought his men in and they found what shelter they could in the damaged dugouts nearby. We all had exhausted our supply of rations of any sort but I managed to get a drink out of a petrol can which two Hants men were taking up. I had brought a lump of bread with me but it had gone mouldy. The iron-ration biscuits are so hard that I had substituted this piece of bread and this was my reward. We were all dead beat and about 10 p.m. we crowded into the dugout to try and get some sleep. Yet one man had to be on duty so I offered to carry on till 3 a.m. when MacDougall would take over till 8 a.m. I was kept busy all the time for although things were quite quiet we were the only front-line Signal Office. Once I had to go out and find a runner and managed to slip into a shell hole of slimy mud and water. The poor wretch was, if possible, more worn out than I was but war is no respecter of weariness and I had to make him go on his journey. From the length of time he was away he must either have gone to sleep or have been too tired to find his way.

We captured a map on which it was clearly marked that Burgomasters Farm at Dickebusch was a Brigade HQ so that if Fritz had been so minded he could have blown us all to blazes at any time during the past winter, but he certainly seems to respect places where civilians are living. Also he may have wished to avoid any retaliations.

8.6.17

At 3 a.m. I roused MacDougall and lay down with my feet in water and with my steel helmet for a pillow. I slept for a few minutes only, when I opened my eyes and found MacDougall shaking me vigorously. 'Come on,' he said, 'get up. Fritz is coming.' 'I don't care,' I said, 'I'm tired', and turned over – but he pulled me up and shouted that it was our relief that had turned up. So I staggered to my feet and got my equipment on. By this time Walker and all the other fellows except Aitken and myself were out of the dugout. I seized my lump of mouldy bread, picked up a tin of jam that belonged to somebody else, poured some of it on to the bread and shared it with Aitken. We were the last two in the file and I was feeling very fatigued when, stepping on a soft patch, I slipped and went over my knees into watery mud. Aitken helped me out but I was too exhausted to stand so sat down for about ten minutes to get my breath and a little strength. When we resumed, the remainder of the party were out of sight. We only had a vague idea of the direction in which we had to go, and after passing an immense mine crater (an old one) in the forward side of which Fritz had built some strong concrete dugouts, we eventually come to Stragglers Post. We had seen numerous dead bodies in all the ghastly horrors and mutilations of violent death, men with half their heads blown off and their brains falling over their faces – some with their abdomens torn open and their entrails hanging out – others stretched out with livid faces and blood-stained mouths, and unblinking eyes staring straight to heaven. Oh wives and mothers and sweethearts, what will this victory mean to you? Yet nature very readily adapts itself to its environment and can look on all these horrors without a shudder. But I should feel sick and almost terrified if I saw a man break his leg in the streets of London.

At Stragglers Post the guard could not direct us to our Brigade HQ so we wandered here and there making scores of fruitless enquiries until suddenly we met Bill Rogers and his runners coming from the Relay Post. Of course they knew the way and took us only a short distance past Stragglers Post to the dugouts at ET10 (Voormezeele). This is the first deep dugout that I have been in since the Somme last October. It is about thirty feet deep and has two or three galleries. When we reported in at the Signal Office, Buchanan gave me a mug half full of rum but my hand was so shaky that I spilt most of it down my clothes. It was now 8.30 a.m. and for forty hours we had been on the go without food or sleep. Early in that period, too, my nerves had been badly shaken, so it is no wonder that I felt absolutely laid out. The cooks got us some breakfast and I almost fell asleep over it, and then lay down outside the entrance to the sap but was warned that it was not a safe place to go to sleep in as a man had been killed there yesterday. So I washed and shaved as well as my shaky hand would let me and went down the stairs. Sgt Oxley lent me his bed and an overcoat and I was soon fast asleep.

9.6.17
Slept most of yesterday and all last night so feel pretty fit today except that I am a bundle of nerves. Any sudden noise makes me give ridiculous involuntary starts so that I drop anything I happen to be holding. Watched some of our triplanes doing wonderful stunts such as falling headlong for 300 or 400 feet as if they had been hit, and then righting themselves. Andy McCormack returned from leave. He was lucky in just missing this 'do'.

10.6.17
My hand still shakes too much to permit of letter writing without causing people to wonder what is the matter with me. This afternoon Davidson and I went up as far as the old no-man's-land and had a look at two of the new mine craters. One solid concrete dugout had been blown up and rolled over bodily. The dead body of a German was still inside. All our own dead have been buried but there are still a few German bodies scattered about. The RE Field Companies are working hard on pit-prop roads and trench tramways. They have carried them as far as the old front line and are now working across no-man's-land. Their hardest work is now commencing. It is an extraordinary scene of animation. Wagons and lorries full of materials are arriving in constant succession and hundreds of men are unloading and carrying and putting in place, all within easy reach of Fritz's artillery but he is not being very bothersome; probably he is tired after the big counterattack he made the night before last along the whole of the new front. He was repulsed everywhere although the attack lasted from 7 p.m. till midnight. The official reports issued to the English press state that all the objectives were captured early in the morning of the 7th, but we know that the 47th Div. is still held up some distance from its final objective and it is quite likely that some of the Divisions on our right have failed to get as far as they were supposed to.

13.6.17

After breakfast I moved up with the Advance Party under Cpl Hamilton to Spoil Bank on the Ypres–Comines Canal. Our new quarters appear to be safe and quiet. Just at this spot the canal runs between two high banks or long mounds which look as if they may have been formed of the earth dug out to make the canal. Both banks are honeycombed with tunnels with additional detached dugouts here and there along their sides. Our office is known as ES09 and we are close to the old HQ of the Kents – ES29. A few yards in front of us is a lock which holds the water back so that only a little stream is leaking out and trickling along the bed. Here and there a shell hole has been utilised to collect the water for washing purposes. The saps are lit by electric light and are kept in repair by a permanent staff of Canadian Tunnellers. The general level of the floor of the galleries is practically the same as the towpath, so we have the advantage of twenty to thirty feet above us without the disadvantage of a long steep flight of steps. Four battalion signallers have joined us permanently which will make things a bit easier for us. The 47th Div. has had a very rough time and are glad to be relieved. It is rumoured that we are to take the objectives that they failed to reach. The casualties in our Brigade on the 7th were somewhere in the region of 300, which is light considering the nature of the operations. That, I presume, is why we have been selected to carry out this additional stunt. This evening Cpl Hamilton took a party up to our advance post at White Chateau. They are all men who stayed back at Voormezeele during the first attack.

14.6.17

Went on duty in the Signal Office at 5 p.m. It was my turn on the commutator (switchboard), a job that I have no particular liking for. I was kept busy by reason of the impending attack. At 7.30 p.m. the 11th RW Kents and the 18th KRRC [King's Royal Rifle Corps] operating with the 24th Division on the other bank of the canal made the attack, advanced about 1000 yards and consolidated the position before nightfall. Where the 47th Div. had failed, our troops succeeded easily; perhaps because Fritz was not expecting us. Buchanan was in the Signal Office all the time but said nothing to me, yet his presence is always sufficient to make me nervy. While the attack was in progress he sent for MacDougall to take over from me (MacD. is our best switchboard operator) and I was put on a 'Fullerphone'. This was more congenial work so I didn't greatly resent the imputation that I was lacking in efficiency on the commutator.

When I went off duty at 10 p.m., Buchanan followed me outside and stopped me in the passage. 'Martin,' he said, 'you mustn't take it too much to heart that I put MacDougall in your place. You are apt to get a little flurried when I speak sharply but you mustn't think that I am cross – I am only anxious.' I thanked him and said that I knew I was naturally of a nervous disposition and that the shock I received on the night of the 6th–7th had made me much worse. 'I know,' he replied, as if somebody had told him all about it, 'and I quite understand so now don't worry any more and don't get upset when I shout and hustle.' He smiled when he wished me goodnight and I felt that I wanted to shake his hand for it seemed so wonderful to hear him talk so kindly after all these months during which I have thought he was 'up against' me. It seems a complete volte-face and I hardly know what to make of it. He has the reputation of not taking very kindly to strangers and perhaps he counts me a stranger no longer.

15.6.17

The Kents captured fifteen prisoners last night and six of them were killed by one of their own shells as they were being escorted back past White Chateau, which seems to be a veritable deathtrap as Fritz shells it unceasingly. We are so free from shelling here that several of our fellows have been bathing in the canal just above the lock, not a very wise thing to do as Fritz's balloons look right down on it. This afternoon, after a very heavy bombardment concentrated chiefly on the front line and the White Chateau, Fritz counter-attacked, but he was dealt with so efficiently by our artillery that only a few of his men reached our trenches where they were quickly repulsed. Cpl Hamilton has recommended Dickson for maintaining communications under very heavy shellfire between White Chateau and Brigade HQ.

18.6.17

On night duty last night and as things were fairly quiet I wrote half a dozen letters and now feel as if I had removed a load from my conscience. Transport can't get nearer to us than the Brick Stack so each evening we have to go down there and carry up our rations and supplies. How the army does live on rumours! The latest one is that we are to be relieved tomorrow, but I am beginning to mistrust the lying jade and never accept any of her promises until they are fulfilled.

19.6.17

Our relief turned up today and we moved back over a km of broken country to Elzenwalle Chateau. This was not a very big place as chateaux go and now it is only a mass of ruined masonry with only one small cellar inhabitable and that is used as our Signal Office. Although the country is torn to bits it is nothing like so bad as further up the line, and there are still a few cherry trees and currant bushes growing and bearing fruit, indicating the whereabouts of the kitchen garden. Our billets are bivouacs while the officers, of course, have tents.

21.6.17

Had a bath this morning in muddy water pumped from the moat – it isn't really a moat, it's more like an artificial stretch of water that in peacetime was probably ornamental. On duty in the afternoon and for the rest of the day I have indulged in the luxury of lounging about, lying in the sun half asleep trying to make up my mind to write letters – but I didn't commence till 9 p.m. and now I've only written one (to Elsie).

23.6.17

The entrance to my 'bivvy' looks across a little grassland, now badly torn up, with a few trees scattered up and down. Up the trunks of two of them run ladders leading to little box-like observation posts hidden in the branches. About eighty yards away, the 2nd Army troops have got a canvas swimming bath about thirty ft square, and therein British Tommies disport themselves after the fashion of Nymphs in Arcady, but the distance is not sufficient to lend any illusory enchantment to the scene. We have been given permission to use this bath provided we empty it and fill it with fresh water after we have finished. A little further away, and out of sight, the Surreys' band plays nearly all day long giving the impression that some sports meeting is being held over there. I mentioned this, and then a twelve-inch gun fired close behind us and a humorous blighter said 'There's the start of the 100 yards.'

27.6.17

We have been in reserve during the last week and now, instead of going back into the line, we are going out for a rest. Hope it won't be such a strenuous rest as the last one. Although we have felt pretty safe here we are not out of danger. A couple of days ago Fritz put three HVs [high-velocity shells] in amongst our bivvies but fortunately they were all duds. If only one had burst it would have made a pretty mess of us. Ever since the 7th there has been considerable aerial activity on both side, and almost every hour we have to take cover because enemy planes are up above. The famous Red Squadron led by Baron von Richthoven [Richthofen] is in this neighbourhood. Seven planes appear to work in concert and from the manner in which they are handled we can recognise them from a considerable distance. They are a very formidable body, although speaking generally we hold the superiority in the air. Nevertheless, the German aircraft are very plucky. It has been almost a daily sight to see one of his fast scouts suddenly emerge from behind the big rolling clouds, pounce on one of our captive balloons, set it on fire and then tear back home at a terrific speed. One plane actually came down so low as to be almost within stone's throw and peppered us with his machine gun. No one was hurt on Brigade but I hear that one or two men in the battalions were hit. Although our machine gun's going, the Hun managed to escape but another plane was brought down nearer the line.

We have played primitive cricket with a bat hacked out of a piece of an ammunition case and a ball made up of pieces of rag tied round with string. It was a bit difficult to find a comparatively even piece of ground giving us the necessary twenty-two yards between wickets; the fielders had, perforce, to stand between shell holes and a step backwards generally resulted in a tumble into dirty water which was accounted a great joke by everybody except the unfortunate fieldsman.

28.6.17

Today we have seen the first civilian that we have encountered for three weeks. We left Elzenwalle this morning under the command of a young officer of the Kents who proved a veritable pig, like so many of these ignorant, incapable youngsters who, finding themselves in a position of authority for which they are totally unfitted, endeavour by bullying to atone for their incapacity. The first part of the journey was very trying owing to the rough nature of the tracks we took to Hallebast Corner, so we were pretty tired before we had got fairly started. From Hallebast we carried on to West Outre. Here we made a bad mistake by trying a short cut which proved a very heavy-going mud track and very soon most of us were stumbling along almost 'whacked to the wide'. Tom Glasspoole was in a particularly bad way and our porcine officer who was not carrying a single article of equipment turned round and snarled, 'Why don't you fall out and die?' I would rather be in the ranks and associate with scavengers and dustmen, as I do, than hold a commission and have such men for companions. The way seemed to get longer and longer but at last we saw Davidson in the distance and knew that we were now close to our destination, for he had come on in advance to make the necessary preparations.

1.7.17

Buchanan has been promoted to Captain and transferred to an Artillery Division. The night before he left he called us all together and talked to us. Without doubt he is genuinely sorry to leave us for he has worked us to a high state of efficiency. He took the private addresses of all of us and told us that if ever we find ourselves in trouble or in need of employment to appeal to him at his business address in Glasgow and he would endeavour to help us. Which proves that beneath a somewhat austere exterior he possesses a good heart for he knows that many of the fellows when they get home may have difficulty in getting settled in civilian life again.

With our improvised bat and ball, and with pick handles for wickets, we played a cricket match this afternoon – Signals v. Rest of Brigade HQ. We won by 91 to 51. The ball performs many queer movements for it bears only a remote resemblance to a sphere, with bulges and dents and protuberances all over it. Received a parcel of cakes from Elsie and a letter from Mama. Shared out the little cakes between the members of the victorious team, together with the umpires and scorers and a few others who declared they had vociferously supported us. The weather is delightful and as I sit writing outside my tent the only sign of war is a feud between two hens who have kept up a kind of guerrilla warfare for the last hour and a half.

8.7.17

Heavy thunderstorm last night and much rain this morning. There was to have been a medal parade but when we lined up the rain came on again so the show had to be postponed. Sgt Oxley, Cpl Hamilton and Cpl Daquell have got the MM. Incidentally, I got into trouble for going on parade with my hat a bit sideways. The Commander-in-Chief has sent round a letter thanking the Signals generally for their very excellent work etc etc and so on and so forth in the recent advance. Very nice but we would prefer an armistice.

9.7.17

In accordance with orders, Brady, MacDougall, Enticknap and I this morning proceeded to Berthen by cycle to Div. HQ for a course in Wireless. We have to go each morning this week. The distance is only a few kms but we have to be over there before 9 a.m. When we were returning this dinnertime Enticknap and I called in a little café on the outskirts of Berthen and had some coffee, leaving our cycles outside the window. My luck was out for up came an MP and demanded our names, numbers etc. We could see the cycles from where we sat but that isn't good enough for the army – you must have your hand on it – so now I'm 'for it' for 'wilful negligence of Government property'.

10.7.17

Received a parcel of books from Elsie and have resumed my office of distributing librarian. The field in which we live slopes downwards towards Flêtre and at the bottom of the dip a Hants Corporal is making a model of the ground over which the next advance is to be made by our Brigade. It is really a work of art consisting only of earth, bits of stick and pieces of stone and wire. All the trenches, both ours and the enemy's, are shown, the whole model being constructed from a large-scale map.

12.7.17

Our new officer arrived – Lieut. the Hon. H. M. Sylvester – with the accent on the 'ves' if you please – and I was immediately pulled up before him to answer the serious charge concerning the bicycle. As it was the first case brought before him I was dismissed with a caution. He appears to be a merry sort of fellow and we both had rather a job to treat the matter seriously but Sgt Twycross stood by looking very austere. He has a big realisation of the dignity and importance of a Sgt RE.

Since Monday I have taken a new route to and from Berthen. I take the road over Mont des Cats – it is harder going but the views make the climb worthwhile. From the top one gets a really wonderful panoramic view over the plain stretching right up to the line, where on clear days we can see the shells bursting. Here are a number of roadways, sandy, stony tracks curling round and up to the monastery on the summit which is now being used as a hospital. And there are numerous paths running hither and thither, leading apparently to nowhere in particular, and little cottages dotted about looking so secluded and quiet, and though they are not so pretty as English cottages they are quite passable in their rusticity.

13.7.17

Continually we can hear the guns roaring in the distance and every day (generally in the morning) Fritz 'plonks' a number of HVs in Bailleul, distant about 3½ miles as the crow flies. Played Div. Signals at cricket this afternoon. They sent a lorry over to fetch us, gave us a feed and brought us back afterwards. They thought they would beat us easily but we won by five runs. I stonewalled for ¾ of an hour while Mr Sylvester knocked spots off the bowling. As we returned along the main road between Bailleul and Meteren, I saw one of the most pitiable sights it has been my misfortune to witness – a number of civilian refugees whose homes had probably been destroyed in Bailleul were trudging along pushing handcarts or carrying bundles containing all that they had been able to save of their household goods. Old men and women, little children and babes in arms, with no home left and no knowledge of where they would sleep that night. It made my heart sick, so that I had to turn my head for I was impotent to help them; but I thanked God for the strip of sea that makes England an island. This upsets me much more than the ghastly sights of death and injury up the line – a point of psychological interest.

Just eight weeks after the successful assault at Messines, the British attacked again, this time in front of Ypres. Unlike Messines, which had had a single objective, the offensive at Ypres would have a much wider remit. Furthermore, there was a move away from the previous preference for joint

Anglo-French attack such as at Loos in 1915, and the Somme; this one would be made by British and Empire troops almost entirely alone.

Throughout 1917, the Germans had adopted a policy of unrestricted submarine warfare. This caused havoc among British merchant shipping as vessel after vessel was sent to the Atlantic floor. The danger was very real that Britain might be starved into submission on the home front and starved on the Western Front of imported guns and ammunition from the USA. Field Marshal Haig had become convinced that the German army was itself close to breaking point and one more major assault would hopefully bring it to its knees. He also saw the chance of sweeping out of the Salient to the north and attacking the submarine pens on the Belgian coast.

The offensive was set for 31 July and would be preceded by a ten-day, 3000-gun, 4.25-million shell bombardment before the infantry went over on a twelve-mile front. In the event the initial assault went reasonably well, in places, and the Germans were driven back several miles. However, within hours of the men going over, a light drizzle had started which had turned into a heavy downpour. The rain lashed down and turned the ground over which the men were fighting into a quagmire, making further movement nigh impossible. Nor did the rain stop. For much of the next two weeks it continued and only on 16 August were any further large-scale attacks made.

It is a battle that has become infamous: official images capture the scene of a lunar landscape, knee-deep mud and incalculable suffering. It was the last great attritional battle of the Great War and put enormous strain on relations between the senior British command who executed the campaign and the politicians back home who saw little gain for the prodigious loss of life. In the end the Germans were remorselessly pushed back in a series of assaults until, in worsening weather, the campaign was brought to a close on Passchendaele Ridge in November, less than seven miles from the start line. If the British Army had suffered then so too had the Germans who had contested every inch of the ground.

22.7.17

This is the last day of our rest for we have received orders to proceed towards the line tomorrow morning. It has been quite evident that we were only recuperating and preparing for another attack. Apparently we are a 'shock' division which, I suppose, the military mind would consider a matter for self-congratulation and pride. The rest has been a good one although Fritz has not left us entirely in peace for his planes have been over nearly every night directing their attention chiefly to the town of Hazebrouck but frequently they fly quite low and hover about as if they are searching for any kind of a target. Sometimes they hang about most persistently for two or three hours but on only one occasion have any bombs been dropped uncomfortably near us. It was about 9.30 p.m. so we hadn't turned in and we were ordered to scatter and get what shelter we could from the surrounding trees and ditches. Several bombs dropped within a few hundred yards of us, the nearest one being close to the Kents' HQ. No damage was done as far as our Brigade was concerned although it was reported that the 20th Durham Light Infantry suffered heavily.

A matter of some interest has been the frequency with which we have had rabbits for dinner. This is assumed to have significance in regard to hopping over the top.

24.7.17
Continued the march through Dickebusch and then across broken country to our old tunnels at ES09 (Spoil Bank). There has been a lot of shelling here since we left. Close to the Brick Stack a dump of 9.2 shells had been blown up and the hole was almost the size of a small mine crater. We took our old path by the side of the canal and noticed a peculiar smell in the air and, incidentally, we were all seized with fits of sneezing. We learned that this was due to a new kind of gas which Fritz has been putting over during the last day or two. We call it 'mustard gas'. It is very poisonous. One fellow who touched a piece of one of the gas shells had his arms and hands break out in most painful eruptions and had to be taken to hospital quickly. Fritz has an observation balloon looking straight down the canal and this spot is not the comparative home of rest that it was a month ago. The outgoing Brigade look rather haggard as if

they have had a very rough time. The Signal Office is the same as last time but our billets are in another part of the tunnels and it is possible to go from one to the other without going outside. Our old mess room has been appropriated to other purposes so we shall have to eat our meals just wherever we can.

28.7.17

The weather is bad and we wonder whenever the attack is to be made. Each day we expect to receive the order but it doesn't come, and nobody cares for this suspense. We know we have come to make the attack and we would prefer to get it over quickly, for we know that the sooner it is over, the sooner we shall get back out of the hell of mud and shells and gas. We know that there will be a lot of casualties, but hope springs eternal, and each man reckons that he will get back safely.

31.7.17

At 4 a.m. in spite of most atrocious weather the attack was made on a fourteen-mile front, French and Belgian troops cooperating with the British on the left. We were the extreme right, the battalions engaged being the 11th RW Kents and the 18th KRRC. The 123rd Brigade were on the left of the canal advancing to Hollebeke Chateau. Our objective was Hollebeke Village. Fritz spotted the preparations for the attack soon after 3 a.m. and shelled our front line unmercifully, so that we had suffered a large number of casualties before the attack commenced. Fortunately for me my duties did not compel me to leave the sap, although we were all standing by for emergencies. The KRRs met a very strong resistance and suffered accordingly. They should have actually taken the village but those who managed to get through at all lost direction with the result that the Kents, whose progress had been better, found themselves with an exposed flank which was subjected to fierce machine-gun fire. Col. Corfe organised an attack on the village and by 10 a.m. the final objectives were being consolidated. The prisoners taken numbered about 100. From what I can gather by reading between the lines of the various reports that have come through, the resistance has been so fierce that only in a few places has the final objective been reached. If all the attacking Divisions have been in the line as long as we have, it is no wonder that they have failed. For eight days our men have been in the trenches under the worst possible conditions regarding weather and shellfire and to expect them to make a successful advance now is asking too much. The state of the country is indescribable owing to the recent rains and the naturally marshy nature of the ground churned up into a filthy sloppy mass by all manner of shells. Rifles and machine guns are choked with mud and are unusable. All our rifles were collected this afternoon for handing over to the Kents but some others came up from the Transport Lines just in time. In the scramble I lost my own rifle but got another which was in nearly as good condition.

2.8.17
The KRRs have been withdrawn from the line and come into these tunnels. There are many tales of heroism and terrific fighting. It has rained heavily today but Fritz has counter-attacked most furiously. He gained some ground in the neighbourhood of St Julien but on the rest of the front he has been beaten back.

3.8.17
Fritz is taking it lying down, and although the country is in such a bad state that infantry operations are almost impossible, yet his artillery is particularly active, especially on White Chateau and here (Spoil Bank). To go out of the sap is to court death, especially on the canal side. On that side I limit my journeys to one a day, viz. when I get water for a wash. This morning when I went out six pieces of shrapnel whizzed down within a few inches of me, and I was out less than a minute.

5.8.17
A day of excitement and anxiety, for the Hants were driven out of Hollebeke. Our Forward Party managed to save their instrument

and gear but lost their accumulators. The Hants counter-attacked and retook the village within a couple of hours. We had been subjected to very heavy shelling all day and just before I went on duty at 5 p.m. a shell landed in an old shell hole above the Signal Office and blew the roof in. Fortunately no one was hurt and the tunnellers got to work at restoration immediately while all the men who were not on duty had to fill in the shell hole. After nightfall things had slackened down a bit when suddenly our guns burst forth with a very heavy barrage. Then we became busy on the wires for Fritz was making another attack on Hollebeke. Soon there were no means of communication with the front line except by amplifier. We have been inclined to criticise the instrument rather severely, but it has justified itself tonight. The attack was repulsed, chief credit going to Col. Carey-Barnard who handled his own battn and the Composite Battalion very ably. There is no doubt he is an efficient soldier although he must be a strange sort of man if the tales we hear are true, although these merely give evidence of the military mind. His dog absented itself without leave for a couple of days and on its return he awarded it Field Punishment No. 1. It was tied to a tree and fed only on biscuits and water for a prescribed period. He returned his cook to the company because he failed to produce an egg and bacon breakfast in the welter of the Messines Ridge battle.

8.8.17

Had a tough business to get up the rations this evening. We met the Transport at the Brick Stack and found that in addition to the rations was a large quantity of stores which would mean us making three or four journeys. The Transport drivers are generally content with dumping the stuff off whether we are there or not and then getting back out of it at a gallop. I can't blame them for this is a most unhealthy spot and Fritz has got the roadway taped to a nicety. However, this evening Driver Ashford ASC [Army Service Corps] offered to try and get his GS wagon over the shell holes up to the sap entrance. It was some game but in crossing a mixture

of trench tramway lines and shell holes, one of the horses fell, the
front of the wagon slithered into a shell hole, the rear got caught
up in a broken tram rail and one of the wheels came off, while
the rations and stores spread themselves about the country. This
was cheerful as Fritz was bumping us pretty merrily. We set to
and emptied the wagon and unharnessed the horses; then lifted
the wagon up on to fairly level ground, replaced the wheel, turned
the wagon round and put the horses in again. It was useless trying
to get the wagon up any further so it set off back again. I admire
Ashford for attempting what none of the other drivers would think
of doing. It was raining all the time and we were soon wet through.
Before we came out I took the precaution of removing my shirt
so that I should have something dry to put on when I returned. I
fell into a shell hole with a heavy box of rations and the bacon got
covered with mud.

9.8.17
On night duty last night. Sat all the time in my shirt while my
tunic hung over a stool trying to get dry. It would have dried
quicker if I had worn it. The night passed fairly quietly except for
Carey-Barnard continually ringing up for retaliation on Hollebeke
Chateau. It has been arranged that every time Fritz strafes White
Chateau we are to retaliate on Hollebeke Chateau. The Liaison
Officer got fed up with being fetched out of his bunk so he left us
to pass the orders on to the Artillery. Every time we get the code
word 'Holly' from the Hants we just ring up the Artillery and
say 'Holly' and a few more 4.5s are sent over. Carey-Barnard is a
great believer in retaliation. About 6 a.m. I went to the doorway
to remove the gas blankets and get a little fresh air. The rain had
ceased and the morning was passably clear and bright. For a little
while I stood watching the famous Red Squadron flying to and fro
over our front line, and presently I heard some footsteps behind
me and on turning round I was met by Major Hitchens, the Div.
Signal Officer, and our precious Company Sergt Major from Div.
The latter was in a state of perspiration and unhappiness bordering

on funk. He has never before been known to come within shell range. He sat on a bench in the Office, while I talked to Major Hitchens, mopping his brow and gasping for breath. We rather relished watching him.

12.8.17

The Huns have made some fierce counter-attacks on our left today but only treated us to the usual quantity of shells. This evening we have heard that we are to be relieved tomorrow. Thank God. Although we have spent most of our time in the comparative security of the saps, this period in the line has been most trying and exhausting. By day and night the Hun has kept up a continual harassing fire, mainly of HEs [High Explosives] and gas shells. The entrances to the saps are covered at night with double gas curtains which are daily saturated with some mixture intended to neutralise the poison. They give a certain amount of protection but are not much good against persistent gas shelling. Every night when the weather has been favourable Fritz has treated us to a heavy dose of gas shells and each time the gas guard has had to wake us and we have been compelled to wear our masks for a couple of hours at a stretch. We also use fans (pieces of thin wood on handles) to fan the gas out of the tunnels. Owing to the gas curtains being kept down at night and the ventilation shaft being shut, the air in the tunnels becomes most fetid. Seventy or eighty men crowd in one of these galleries, mainly with wet clothes, and all in a filthy dirty condition, breathing the same air over and over again, their bodies stewing in the close, damp atmosphere and exuding all manner of noxious odours – this alone is sufficient to make us ill. It is positively choking to enter the tunnels in the early morning, before the curtains have been raised and a draught created. You choke and splutter and gasp for breath, but if you have slept in it you do not notice the aroma; you only realise that you have got a rotten headache and feel beastly sick. But foul air is better than poison gas, and dugouts are to be preferred to shell holes.

13.8.17

Our relief turned up to time this morning. We anticipated having to carry all the stores and equipment to the Brick Stack before we could load them on to the wagon but somehow or other Lally managed to get the Maltese Cart right up to the tunnels. The shelling was not violent but there was enough of it to cause us to waste no time in getting away. I collected the last remaining articles from the Signal Office and managed to win a watch from the incoming Brigade. As soon as the cart had got safely away we were ordered to make our own way back to Wiltshire Farm, going in twos and threes so as to avoid attracting too much attention from the enemy. A party of only a dozen or so is generally reckoned a sufficient target for a number of HEs. I trudged off with Jimmy Paterson, a man with a bulldog nature who never shows any sign of fear. We got across the shell holes and along the roadway which receives the Hun's special attention each evening at ration time, and then struck off to the right along a tramway track towards Dickebusch. So far we had scarcely spoken, all our energies being taken up in floundering through the mud and shell holes and in avoiding shell splinters.

The day was fine and bright and our spirits rose with each step that took us further from the line, though we felt so weak and tired that we were compelled to have several rests before we reached our destination.

14.8.17

Cheesman and I were on duty last night. When we went to take over at 10 p.m. Davidson was on duty. He asserted his authority as an NCO by sending me with three separate messages across the fields in the dark when I could have taken the whole lot at once. This was because earlier in the evening I had refused to do a little job for him as I was not on duty at the time. It is a pity that he spoils a fine character by being malicious. Sgt Twycross thought that we would not have much to do during the night so he gave us the bicycles to overhaul and repair. They are in a pretty bad condition so all I troubled about was to get the wheels to go round and the tyres to hold air. This occupied me till 2 a.m., while Cheesman slumbered, and then I had a couple of hours in the arms of Morpheus. There were only occasional bursts of shrapnel during the night and at daybreak we roused the Camp. Told Pte Sylvester off very severely for pinching the groundsheet from my valise while I was on duty last night. During the rush and bustle of packing up, Granecome fell down in a fit. It was not so severe as some he has had, but no man subject to fits should be allowed up the line. Yet it is impossible to get him back to the base unless he is actually seen in a fit by an officer of the RAMC. This is what is called 'Discipline'.

It was a gaunt and haggard party that straggled across the duckboards and past our old dugouts at Burgomaster's Farm but it was merry withdrawal, for we were moving in the right direction. The Farm is now in artillery transport lines and an observation balloon is tethered in the field behind the house. On the whole we look more thoroughly done up than ever before. Even the robust Brady is pale and wan, while I shudder to see myself in the glass. Still, we are out of the line now and it is really wonderful how quickly Nature picks herself up again if she is given only half a chance. In less than a week we shall be looking as fit as ever.

The lorries put us down only a few yards from our billets that are the same as before. After getting settled I removed my socks for the first time in three weeks. All the time we were in the line we were not supposed to take off even our boots and puttees but we generally got these off each night. My socks have been soaked through time after time with rain and mud and perspiration so that it was impossible to take them off in the ordinary way. I had to cut them and tear them and remove them from my feet in pieces; the soles were as hard as boards. Washed my feet as well as I could in water from the pond and now, being sleepy, I lie me to my blankets and slumber.

We do not get uneasy at feeling little creatures crawling about our bodies; we are well used to them, but last night after lights out I felt a large body of them proceeding in regular order up my leg and the left side of my body. It was a rather unusual sort of crawling, and putting my hand round my side I caught hold of something large and soft and somewhat slimy. Aitken struck a match and I extracted a young green newt about five inches long – harmless but unpleasant as a bedfellow. I quickly lifted the flap of the tent and threw him back towards the pond from which he came.

18.8.17

Up very betimes and put an extra special polish on our boots and buttons as we are still suffering from Inspectionitis. Twycross was very perky and authoritative on the preliminary parade and was quite disgusted when I dropped my rifle. Of course I know it is terribly unbecoming to be awkward on parade but I'm too old to make a thoroughly efficient soldier. Put me in the Signal Office and leave me to run the show and I'll do it easily, but ask me to slope arms or form fours and I bungle over it. We proceeded to the parade ground as before and in accordance with usual military practice arrived there 1½ hours before the appointed time for the inspection. At last Sir Hubert Plumer, the 2nd Army Commander, arrived by motor car. He marched on to the ground in true military fashion making right and left turns and going round two sides of a triangle instead of taking a short cut along the diagonal. He was radiant in five rows of ribbons and a monocle which was very refractory. He inspected each man in the whole Brigade and spoke to all those who had ribbons up, asking for particulars of how they had won their decorations. He had a short conversation with General Towsey and then took his departure, much to our relief.

After tea, three or four of us got tin bowls of water and had a bath by the side of the pond. The others were more than half dressed but I was in the middle of it – not even a fig leaf for clothing – when the gallant Twycross came rushing out in the usual mad shouting manner which he adopts when he wishes to assert his authority, and yelled out 'Fall in, fall in, fall in, fall in everybody, just as you are; never mind your clothes.' He made a mistake if he thought I was going on parade like that. Something or other had displeased him

in our behaviour at the inspection this morning so he determined
to let us have an hour's squad drill, but he didn't take us himself
– he told Davidson off to do it. I saw what was on so I proceeded
leisurely to dry myself and get dressed although to all appearances
I was bustling round very smartly in my eagerness to get on parade.

A bombing pit has been built at the bottom of our field and
whenever it is being used fragments of Mills Grenades come
whizzing amongst our tents. This afternoon some of the Surreys
were down there and one of them got a splinter in his right eye.
The Brigadier is rather enthusiastic about bombing just at present
and to encourage it Brigade HQ offered hundreds of prizes from
twenty francs downwards. I got a consolation prize of one franc,
but as there were twenty of these I am not likely to be marked as
a first-class bomber. The day before yesterday I received a parcel
from Elsie containing my wrist watch for which I am thankful as
Sgt Twycross has spruced me out of the one I won at Spoil Bank to
make up for one he has lost. There are very few watches amongst us
– we follow the simple primitive method of dividing the twenty-
four hours into two periods – light and dark – and trust to our
stomachs to tell us when it is meal times.

20.8.17

Reveille 4 a.m. Breakfast 5 a.m. and at quarter to six Davidson
and I started to cycle to Le Nieppe leaving the rest of the Brigade
to follow on foot. At La Brearde we crossed the Hazebrouck–
Steenvoorde Road just as the estaminet on the corner was being
opened, so we had a coffee and continued on our way rejoicing. We
had not gone much further when MacDonald overtook us on his
motorcycle. Davidson was feeling full of beans and started to race
him but his haversack swung round and caught his handlebars,
fetching him over a beautiful cropper. I had to swerve violently
to avoid riding over his neck. He lifted up his bike – all except
the pedal – that remained peacefully in the roadway. Otherwise no
damage was done and Davey was unhurt: but we were only halfway
on our journey. Alternately we walked and then mounted our cycles

and I pushed him till I was tired. He is no lightweight – thirteen stone at the start and about 113 after pushing him 200 yards. Reached Le Nieppe at 9.15 and found a 2nd Army lineman waiting to connect us up. This was quickly done and then I lay down on a tarpaulin and went to sleep in the sun for half an hour. The Signal Office is in the harness room attached to the Coachman's House belonging to the Chateau but our billet is in a barn at the other end of the village. At 2 p.m. I went out and met the Brigade and directed them to their quarters. Later in the afternoon I lay down in a meadow to have a sleep but watched some air fights instead. Turned in at 8 p.m.

24.8.17

Rose early this morning and got 'poshed up something extra'. Marched to a parade ground (a large turnip field) where the whole Division was inspected by Field Marshal Sir Douglas Haig. It was blowy and rainy and therefore not an ideal day for such an inspection. 'Duggie' arrived on horseback with his bodyguard and a retinue of staff officers. His arrival was heralded by the hauling up of the Union Jack on the temporary flagstaff and the band obliged with appropriate music – whether it was 'God Save the King' or 'See, the Conquering Hero Comes' or 'He's a Jolly Good Fellow' I can't remember. He rode round the lines and then took up a position at one end of the field with his satellites behind him and we did a military march past.

25.8.17

This being an official 'off' day with me, I went with MacKay and McCormack by bus to St Omer. The buses are being loaned to the Brigade to give the troops an outing. Some of them are going to Boulogne. When we were passing through the outskirts of St Omer, we saw some English Girls (WAACs) [Women's Army Auxiliary Corps] – the first we have seen since we have been out here. It was something of a shock to us and we had a funny feeling inside which forced tears into our eyes so that we turned our heads away from each other, reminding us that our nerves are still very shaky. MacKay, who cannot be accused of being sentimental, was the first to speak. 'Fair make a lump come in your throat, don't it, Joe?'

26.8.17

The Scotsmen are decidedly clannish and it was several months before they really accepted me as a comrade. Gradually and almost imperceptibly I overcame their aloofness – with the exception of Paterson. He is a very hard nut to crack and all my advances of friendliness have been churlishly rebuffed, but this evening while a few of us were kicking the football about he and I came in contact. I don't know how it happened because I was studiously avoiding him because I anticipated that he would barge into me rather viciously. But he did nothing of the sort – laughed and invited me to tackle him and was generally sportive and kittenish. Later he told me that he had found me out, which being interpreted means that he had discovered I was genuine and was not a rotter. His manner was blunt and raucous and uncouth – 'You didn't know it but I was a-watching ye up there on the Damstrasse. I said to myself "Now I'll see if the damned Englishman has any guts" and ye didn't funk it, Joe.' He held out his hand and of course I took it. All this surprised me greatly for I had given up the idea of making friends with him, as he is the most stubborn and obstinate man I have ever met.

2.9.17

Last night the mail came up about 10 o/c after I had put out my light, but I soon put it on when I found there were four letters for me – all birthday ones – from Elsie, Lil, Ada, and Edith. During the night I felt a small strange upheaval underneath me. My first thought was of rats, but I soon discovered that it was a mole working away under the canvas on which we lie. A molehill in the middle of your spine is not conducive to comfort so I had to move myself one pace to the right.

3.9.17

This morning (33rd birthday) I received two parcels from Elsie and one from Mother and Lil and one from Nellie. I unpacked them and stood all the good things round me – looked like a canteen. Was doing visual on the church tower first thing this morning. This has been a regular business for the past week and looks like continuing. We take heliographs and flags and other minor paraphernalia, get the keys from the priest's house adjoining the churchyard and climb up inside the belfry. Pigeons live up there and the place is filthy dirty. The stairs are rickety, broken in places, and long stretches of banisters are missing. One of our runners nearly fell down the whole flight when the clock suddenly struck as he was passing the bells. At the top of the stairs we creep through a trap door on to the balcony that fortunately has a substantial stone coping all round. The views are fairly extensive but uninteresting.

4.9.17

At 10 p.m. last night Glasspoole and I proceeded on night duty with my parcels. There was too large an assortment for us to sample everything but we started on a chocolate cake which Lil had made, with 'Jack' on the top of it in little silver balls. Then we tackled a bottle of preserved mixed fruits with grape nuts and condensed milk. This was so delicious that we finished the lot. Glasspoole said he would take the first watch so I rolled into my blankets till 3 a.m. but he was asleep on his chair in about two minutes. I roused him but I believe he went to sleep again although he woke me very promptly at 3 o/c. However, there is nothing doing here during the night so it doesn't matter much. Between 3 and 7 I wrote six letters and got the messages ready for despatch at 7.30. Then I washed, shaved, and fetched my breakfast having persuaded Billy Gould as a very special favour to make me some coffee which Elsie had sent. Kicked Glasspoole eight times before he would wake up. Davidson relieved me at 8 a.m. and as soon as I had got nicely settled down for a sleep the Sergeant sent for me. I told the runner what I thought of the Sergeant, what I thought of runners, what I thought of the

British Army, the British Nation, the British Empire, mankind in general, and the whole universe. And I rolled over to go to sleep. What the runner told the Sergeant has not transpired but in less than a minute he came rushing down shouting out 'Where's that fellow Martin?' although he knew where I was quite as well as I did. I closed my eyes and breathed heavily and when I thought he had shouted at me long enough I slowly opened my eyes, stared vacantly and mumbled something that was intentionally unintelligible.

There has been a competition open to the whole Division for a design for the Divisional Xmas card. George Thompson sent one in representing a Soldier, a Sailor and a Munition Girl all going arm in arm to Victory. While it was considered as showing the greatest merit of all the designs submitted, the subject was rather too allegorical. General Lawford wanted something with more blood in it. So George was commissioned to execute something descriptive of the attack on the Messines Ridge. This design has been accepted, although artistically it is inferior to the first one, but he has got the prize money, and that is the chief thing.

11.9.17

A relief model of the ground over which our next advance is to take place has been made in an orchard on the other side of the road. I have been and had a look at it. We are going to the north of the Ypres–Comines Canal and our objective is a spot called Tower Hamlets. The ground sinks down to a little stream, then rises again, and our task looks pretty formidable. We expect to get our orders to move at any time. We have had a good rest and can't grumble although the weather has not been so good as it might have been. But the return to the line is always viewed with certain misgivings and forebodings, but no man shows his heart to another and we forcibly thrust ourselves into an appearance of carelessness and nonchalance.

13.9.17

We leave here tomorrow morning. Brady returned from leave this afternoon which is rather unfortunate for him. We have been out at rest during the whole of his leave and now he has got back just in time for the wretched march back to the line.

14.9.17
Up at 5 a.m. Dismantled our bivvy, rolled it up and returned it to the RFC [Royal Flying Corps] rather the worse for wear but we tucked the damaged parts inside so that they should not be readily observable. Gobbled our breakfast and packed up in the usual rush; then commenced our march back to the line. Skirted St Omer and passed through Arques where le Street has been renamed 'Rue de Nurse Cavell' and so on to Le Nieppe. We are billeted in the same barn as before and the Signal Office is in the same Chateau.

15.9.17
Cheesman and I were on night duty last night, not a very enviable job when we are on the march. We each tried to get a little sleep but a hard cold stone floor is not a feather bed and we were not sorry when it was time to rouse the troops. After breakfast we moved off. It was a long and tiring jaunt. Brady nearly crocked up just after we passed through Flêtre but he managed to stick it to the end. We arrived at our old billets about 4 p.m. and I feel thoroughly tired out. O'Brien calls this 'the jumping off place for Ypres' and there is no doubt we are going back into that sector again. There have been no big attacks made while we have been out at rest so I suppose we shall be 'in for it' again. After we left the line on 14 August there were a few small local advances made up to the 26th but since then both sides have been content with continuous bombardment and occasional raids.

18.9.17
Had a good breakfast (goodness knows when we shall get another) and then started off for Hedge Street Tunnels. The number of derelict tanks lying about is surprising. They can go practically anywhere, but this mud is one too many for them, and, once they stop, restarting is impossible; they just settle down slowly in the

mud and Fritz 'plonks' them until the last vestige of hope of their recovery is gone. At one point we thought we had arrived 'home' but it turned out to be Canada Tunnels; we had to go further on for Hedge St. Fritz was keeping up a fairly brisk bombardment with the black heavies but not one fell near enough to us to be dangerous. These tunnels are in a large bank which may be a spur of a low range of hills (not much more than a 'rise'). There are several entrances and the galleries are more extensive than at Spoil Bank. Fritz was in them only a little while ago so he knows all about them, in fact I believe he built them as we are in territory which he held up to 31 July last. The tunnels are narrow and crowded with troops, the 15th Hants being quartered here as well as troops belonging to other divisions. The only resting places are narrow wooden benches running along one side of the tunnels. I secured one of these; it has three boards nailed up in front of it reaching from floor to roof and I have to crawl in between these. It's like a cage, but I can't fall out. We are all rush and bustle in preparation for the attack which we expect will come off in a day or two.

19.9.17

This morning I came up out of the tunnels and had a wash in a shell hole. Then I went to the top of the bank and had a look round. It was not safe so I didn't stay long. Looking towards the enemy (the front line is only 400 yards away) the land dips down into a slight valley, and on the hill beyond stands Gheluvelt which at this distance appears hardly to be touched. Tower Hamlets, our objective, is this side of Gheluvelt but on the other side of the valley. I counted a dozen derelict tanks and we call this neighbourhood 'Tank Cemetery'. Looking backwards over Zillebeke Lake, Ypres stands out grisly and white like a ghost of a city, and really that's all it is. This spot is certainly a vantage point. No wonder Fritz pays it so much attention. With the exception of short bits of trench at the entrances to the saps, the only shelter is to be found in shell holes. And half of each of these are filled with water. The Kents are lying back at Larch Wood. They were supposed to take over the tunnels there but when they arrived last night they found them crammed full of men of other units, so they had to remain in the open and have consequently suffered a good many casualties. The horses with the rations cannot get right up here so each night all men not on duty have to form a ration party and go and bring them up. After dark this evening we had to see the party off and help them a part of the way with their signalling equipment. It was pouring with rain and shells and I got wet through. Returning, I had got into the trench and was almost up to the door of the sap when a shell burst on the parapet and I was covered in mud and dirt, one piece giving me a whack on the top of the shoulder, but it was not sufficient to call for notice and I thought no more about it until later in the evening when something caused me to put my hand to the spot and I found a long scratch, no worse than a kitten would give. I am rather surprised because all I felt at the time was a thud as if a heavy clod of earth had struck me, but there must also have been a sharp little piece of something or other to go through my clothes and give me a scratch like this. Thank God it was no worse, though at times the strain of this existence makes one long for death.

20.9.17

I was awake when the attack started at 5.40 a.m. so I went up on top to watch it, but the barrage on both sides was so heavy that it was impossible to see any movement because of the smoke, but along the line of attack shells were bursting dozens at a time. It was safe enough now where I stood as the Hun was concentrating all his efforts on the line a few hundred yards in front of me, so I shaved and washed in a shell hole and about 8 o/c climbed to the top again to have another look at the attack. It was evident that things were not going so well as anticipated – the line had moved forward but it was still far from the final objective, and there was no doubt that Fritz was putting up a very fierce and stubborn resistance. The battalions making the attack were the Hants and the KRRs followed up by the Kents and the Surreys. On our left is the 23rd Division and on our right the 124th Brigade. I have been on duty in the Signal Office a good deal during the day and little bits of information have been trickling through regarding the progress of the attack. Putting them all together, the situation seems like this. Fritz had occupied some of the derelict tanks lying in no-man's-land and had made strongpoints of them. He fought desperately and disputed every inch of ground and his snipers remained at their posts, hidden in tree trunks etc, even after our troops had passed them, and continued to shoot our men from behind. One of them was captured badly wounded, and Col. Carey-Barnard, coming up, raised his revolver to kill him but seeing his terrible wounds refrained, and the wretch then pointed out where one of his sniping comrades was hidden. A machine-gun post in a pillbox held our men up for a long time. Our artillery played on it but could not get a direct hit. The Hants could get no further. They had lost all their officers and a great many men. Col. Corfe of the Kents tried to rally the men but was soon hit by a bullet in the shoulder, but he held on until the post had been outflanked. Then he collapsed.

20.9.17 cont.
It is now apparent that the attack has fallen considerably short of what was expected, but what can you expect from men who are tired and hungry and wet through? To say nothing of the fierce opposition they have had to face. Our Advance Signals when they went up last night tried to establish themselves in a dugout but were peremptorily ejected by Col. Carey-Barnard who wanted it for himself. So they settled themselves in a little lean-to shelter behind the dugout. A stray dog that has somehow or other got up the line also tried to get in the dugout. He wouldn't stop in the shelter because it was only covered with corrugated iron and a few handfuls of dirt to camouflage it. During the morning Percy Mayne was wounded in the arm while bringing a message to Brigade HQ. He delivered it and then had to be carted off to the dressing station and so down the line. An American doctor who is attached to the Kents performed the operation of amputating a man's leg in the midst of the attack. I expect that tomorrow the English papers will

be shouting the news of a great victory, but it has been a ghastly and murderous failure. A reinforcement arrived for us this evening – a young fellow just out from England. It's ridiculous to send a new recruit up to a place like this.

I was surprised to see some Military Police in these tunnels. They are the warriors who infest the rest areas and spend their time in 'running' poor unsuspecting Tommies who leave their cycles unattended for a few seconds. Their business up here is to prowl round the tunnels looking for men who have taken shelter when they ought to be outside. A miserably ignoble trade!

21.9.17

At 8.30 this morning the Sergeant sent for me. He directed me to take Cochran (the new man) and go to Sgt Jordan, who is in charge of the Signal Dump in Canada Tunnels, and bring back two drums of cable. It was wanted urgently as all our lines had been blown to smithereens and our supply of cable was exhausted. Immediately we got out of the sap I saw we were in for a rough journey as Fritz was giving us a most terrific shelling. Every conceivable type of shell was bursting all around, whizzbangs, HEs, HVs [High Velocity shells], liquid fire, gas shells and all manner of shrapnel, the latter bursting a dozen at a time. It was evident that Fritz was endeavouring to prevent any reinforcements coming up. When we got to the end of the little bit of trench I scrambled out, but Cochran lost his head and shouted out 'Don't go, don't go, we shall all be killed!' It was no time to be nice so I told him not to be a fool but to come along and I caught hold of him and pulled him up on to the parapet. A shell burst a little way away on our left and out of the smoke emerged two men, one supporting the other who had been badly hit. Another burst on our right and Cochran threw himself behind a pile of duckboards – I fetched him out and he hung on to my coat and tried to pull me into a shell hole. I coaxed him and cursed him but he hadn't a ha'porth of nerve and I literally had to drag him along. It was a thousand times worse than going by myself. When we got inside Canada Tunnels he recovered himself somewhat. I found Sgt Jordan, an old soldier, and he refused to let me have the cable because I had not brought a demand note signed by an officer. He actually wanted me to go back and get it. I thought many strong things but I didn't say them – I talked nicely to him, pointed out the urgency and told him what a nice fellow he was. Eventually he agreed to let me have the two drums if I promised faithfully to bring back the demand note at once. I was in the mood to promise anything though I had not the slightest intention of keeping any promise I might make.

The drums weighed half a hundredweight each which is quite as much as any man would like to carry over this churned and muddy country. Before we left the tunnels I gave Cochran a good talking to and told him that we had got to get back to Hedge St. in the quickest possible time; therefore he had better not act the giddy ox but keep close behind me and only duck into shell holes if he saw me do it. I glanced back two or three times and saw that he was following although gradually the distance between us was increasing. After jumping over a fragment of trench I proceeded for about fifty yards before looking round and then Cochran was nowhere to be seen. I dumped the cable and was just going back to find him when he scrambled out of the trench, trembling and blubbering worse than ever. In his fright he failed to jump over the trench and dropped down right on to a dead body. It was some job to fetch him along after that but at last we got into the tunnels. The distance was only about 300 yards each way but it had taken two solid hours. While we were out Tom McLachlan and Alec Robertson were mending a line when a shell landed between them. McLachlan was killed outright and Robertson was wounded. In the afternoon the violence of the shelling had abated and I went out to have a wash. While I was dipping into a shell hole a piece of shrapnel hissed viciously past my ear into the water. I wonder how many scores of times sudden death has missed me only by inches, and yet other fellows get done in by almost the first shell that comes their way. One cannot help becoming fatalistic.

22.9.17

Last evening Fritz treated our front line to a hurricane bombardment and developed a counter-attack. Our men were quite exhausted and it is no wonder that some of them started to retire without receiving orders to do so. Col. Carey-Barnard and Major Pennell (KRR) drove them back at the point of the revolver. For some time the position was extremely critical but our artillery managed to stop the counter-attack. The troops are all mixed up, men of different units and even of different divisions are huddled together in the same shell holes. The Brigade Major has been up the line and has sent a secret report into Division. There is no doubting the seriousness of the situation for on the phone I overheard a most amazing conversation between our Brigadier and the Divisional Commander. The Brigadier was very firm in his insistence that our Infantry is thoroughly exhausted and totally unable to make any resistance if the Huns attacked. They would break right through our line if once they got beyond our artillery barrage. The Div. Commander tried his hardest to get the Brigadier to say that we can hold on for another twenty-four hours but General Towsey wouldn't take the responsibility of making any such statement. Lawford, of course, is looking to the laurels of the Division and the honour that will fall to him. When Gen. Towsey told him that the men could get neither rations nor water he merely replied, 'Let them take the iron rations from the killed and wounded.' This conversation lasted about half an hour and I expect it will result in a speedy relief. This morning Dickson found McLachlan's body and took from it his pay book and personal property. The latter will be sent to his relatives in Blighty.

23.9.17

Late last night word came through that our relief was on its way up. We were to clear out before daylight but although we tried to get away about 3 a.m. we were subjected to various hindrances and dawn was breaking before we had got our stores loaded on to a trench tramway wagon. It was a slow procession as the tramway track was blown up every hundred yards or so and we had to lift the wagon loaded with stores across shell holes. After about six of these adventures we met a very bad hole and decided to unload the wagon, carrying the things on our backs across the country till we should meet another truck. Fritz shelled us all the way but fortunately there were a large number of duds, the ground being so soft that the percussion was not sufficient to explode the shells. There were more stores than we could carry in one journey so we had to go back a second time. The distance was not far and just as we had put down the first load and were going back for the second a shell burst close to the wagon. A man who was making his solitary way down the line was very badly hit in the face and side and arm, his fingers were only hanging on by bits of skin. Two stretcher-bearers happened to be close by and they quickly carried him off. Just as we reached the wagon and were all crowded round it grabbing at the things in our haste to get back, another shell burst in the same place. The pieces flew all round us and over us and in between us but not one of us was scratched, whereas the other poor creature, making less than a twentieth of the target that we did, got so badly wounded. Such are the fortunes of war.

We lost no time in getting back and loading up on another truck. We were amongst the guns and we hurried to get beyond them because we knew that they were going to start a heavy strafe at 7.10 a.m. but we didn't quite manage it. Jackson was standing quite close to a 4.5 howitzer but didn't know it till it suddenly blazed forth and he jumped about three feet into the air. After wrestling the wagon over a few more shell holes we arrived at Jackson's Dump where we found the limber waiting for us. McCormack and Jamieson, who we had left behind to carry on the visual till 6.30, were also there. They had not been impeded with a wagon-load of stores and had taken a shorter route along the duckboards. We now began to breathe and our spirits rose for the going was easier and every step was taking us away from Hell. We got to Ridge Wood where we rested for a few hours and had some grub. When the cooks had cleared out from their cookhouse, one of them went back to look for a tin of milk

only to find that the place was completely blown in. In the afternoon
we were left to rest in a field for two or three hours. Lieut. Sylvester
found a little shop, bought a lot of cigarettes and distributed them
among us. We trained to Castre where we found the Transport had
already arrived and had erected tents for us. Thoroughly worn out, it
did not take us long to get to sleep albeit our only covering was our
overcoats and Cochran didn't even have that as he had thrown it away
in his fright in going up the line.

24.9.17

It was nice to wake up and find oneself breathing fresh air instead
of the vile putrid solid stuff of the tunnels, to say nothing about
the absence of shells and bullets. Apart from attending a clothing
and equipment parade and taking an idle turn of duty in the Signal
Tent we have been left to spend our time in resting and in getting
passably clean. Not having been able to write any letters for nine
days, my first duty was to sit down and write to Mother and Elsie.
Tomorrow I shall write some more.

26.9.17

The Staff Clerks tell me that we are going to the coast, to a place
called La Panne. It sounds good but we can't tell what it will be like
till we get there. 'The Crumps' (Divisional Concert Party) erected a
stage and gave a performance this evening in the field in which we
are billeted. It is now 9 p.m. and we have received orders to move
tomorrow morning. We are going by bus.

27.9.17

Up very early, as usual when we are on the move; marched through
the little town to a spot just beyond the railway station, where the
whole Brigade embarked. It was two or three hours before we got
under way but the day has been fine and we had a really enjoyable
ride through Cassel and Berques (where we saw some 'Abdullahs',
i.e. French North African Native Troops, who look very picturesque
in their peculiar dress) and so to Leffrinckhoucke where we are

stopping for one night only. It is only a small village and I have found nothing of particular interest in it. We are quartered in a barn and I have got hold of a wire-netting bed. Still feeling pretty weary, as soon as it got dark I retired to rest. Presently the anti-aircraft guns got going and we heard the drone of an aeroplane overhead. The searchlights managed to pick it out and the other fellows called me to get up and see it, but it would take more than that to fetch me out of bed now. The journey tomorrow is to be continued on foot but the distance is not very great.

28.9.17

Today we can hardly believe our senses. Five days ago we were in the most horrible hell man ever created, and now – well, the difference is almost the difference between hell and heaven. We marched by a road running parallel with the coast to Adinkerke where we turned sharp to the left and so came to La Panne and the open sea. The morning was beautiful and sunny and the march was quite enjoyable. Along the road low sand dunes (and a canal) separated us from the sea; and little whitewashed cottages were dotted about here and there looking so bright and clean and cheerful, in such remarkable contrast to the filthy, dirty, gloomy condition of everything in the Ypres area. Arriving, we marched straight to our billet which is a hotel right on the seafront. Our wildest dreams had never pictured us coming to such a delightful spot as this. Of course there are no beds or easy chairs; not even lino on the floors, but pleasure and happiness is only comparative and this is bliss after our experiences of the last twelve months. We got here soon after noon. Aitken and Glasspoole had come on in advance and opened office. By 12.30 we had discovered a patisserie shop and Glasspoole and I stuffed ourselves with delicious French pastries and coffee. We don't mind this sort of warfare.

29.9.17

Strolled around the town this morning. It does not appear to have suffered any damage at all from shellfire or bombs and is fairly well populated with civilians. It is essentially a seaside resort but of course it has done nothing in that line since 1914 – consequently all the hotels and large boarding houses have been vacated by their tenants and are now occupied by troops. Our billet must have been quite a swanky place. The room I am in is in the front looking out to sea and has a small verandah where we can go and sit during the day. At night of course we have to obscure the windows thoroughly. The sands are most extensive, stretching north and south as far as one can see. When the tide is out it is almost a Sabbath day's journey to the water's edge. The ordinary seaside landladies and fleecing tradesmen have adjusted themselves to the changed condition of things and now cater for the simple wants of Tommy Atkins. McCormack, Dickson and I found a place this evening where we had eggs and chips and coffee. There are several such places about but most of them are perpetually crowded. This one, however, is in a back street, out of the usual run and therefore is not so heavily patronised.

30.9.17

Sat on the sands this morning and wrote some letters. The Crumps have started open-air performances on the beach. This evening they were selling rather elaborate souvenir programmes. Bought one to send to Elsie. Turned in about 9.30 p.m. and just before 10 o/c Veitch came in and started to congratulate me. I didn't know what it was about until he explained. I appear in orders, having been promoted Sapper from 1 June, which means that I've got a bit of back pay to pick up, and also that Buchanan must have put me forward when I was still believing myself to be under his frown. Roughly I shall draw about £3 back pay and that will be very acceptable in a place like this. The leave allotment has been considerably increased and I begin to feel that with a bit of luck my turn will soon come.

3.10.17

Have written lots of letters during the past three days as there is very little else to do. Am 'sweating' on leave very violently. At the rate the men are going, my turn cannot be far away.

4.10.17

Leave fever has reduced me to a frightful state of fidgets. Can't keep still for two minutes together. The public baths here have been taken over by the British troops and this morning I enjoyed the luxury of a real bath, with a Belgian soldier as my own particular attendant. We had to leave our clothes in an ante-room and I put my purse in my gas mask, but while I was soaking the Ypres dirt out of my skin, somebody pinched my purse. Fortunately there was not much in it, about 15/-, mostly English money which I had been collecting in anticipation of leave. My wallet with about 300 francs in notes I had left behind at the billet.

A few stray thoughts scribbled down at various times, often in moments of peril:

It is generally true that after passing through a period of suffering we remember the little bits of pleasure which attended it more than the suffering itself.

What are the frownings of Fortune compared with her favours?

Obscurity and happiness are enough for me.

Home is where the heart is.

Reunion – the bright star towards which we look with so much confidence.

Love belongs to the infinities, those things which in this life we can only vaguely grasp.

The language of the army is a psychological study. It is not a question of bad language as such – it is more the inadequacy of ordinary language to express feelings and emotions under great mental and physical strain, and when one is up against the harshest realities of existence, the strongest words seem pale and ineffectual. Love is love, but a fondness that is founded on superficialities may turn to hate.

The postbag is the oasis in the desert of our existence.

If you see that a question has two sides, and decline to become violently partisan, people will call you weak – whereas you are really strong.

The best letters are never written on paper.

5.10.17

My leave warrant has arrived in the Brigade Office. It is dated for crossing on the 8th and according to the new regulations which came into force either today or tomorrow I ought not to have it until the 7th but Sgt Lunn says he will give it to me tomorrow morning if I call for it about 9 o/c. I shall not be late.

6.10.17

Up very betimes and packed everything up in readiness. Got away soon after 9 a.m. Tramped to the crossroads at the other end of the town and then jumped a lorry which took me very nearly to the gates of the Rest Camp where I reported to the Sergeant Major. He examined my warrant rather critically and said that he thought I should not have presented myself there until tomorrow. He was very hazy over the new regulations, so I begged him to let me go on today as I would prefer to spend the night in Boulogne. I certainly had no desire to stay at the Camp which was damp and dirty and inches deep in mud with only tents to sleep in and nowhere to go in the daytime. After some deliberation and conferring with one of his Sergeants he said, 'All right; fall in with today's party at 12.45.' I hung about watching the other men come up and noticed that there were several others with passes dated for the 8th and the Sgt Major was getting windy about letting so many go through. At 12.45 we fell in and answered our names and then the SM called out, 'Fall out all those men with passes for the 8th'. About half a dozen fell out but I didn't move. He counted them and checked his list and said, 'There ought to be another'. After a few tense and anxious minutes during which he was hunting all over the place for my name, he gave up and ordered us to move on. I breathed more freely when we got out on the road. At Bray Station the passes were briefly scanned and stamped but I managed to crush through in a crowd and so on to the train where I chummed up with a motorcyclist corporal. We left Bray about 2.30 and crawled down to Calais which we reached between 8 and 9 and we marched across the town from one station to another. Here we had to wait for a couple of hours with only a small Salvation Army canteen anywhere near. It was a regular fight to get anything to eat but we managed it; and at 11 p.m. were crowded into trucks again and resumed our journey to Boulogne.

7.10.17

The night passed with the amount of discomfort usual to this method of travelling. We were crowded thirty or forty in a truck; it was impossible to lie down, the best we could manage was to sit on the floor with our knees up under our chins. Also we were unlucky in getting an extra hour of it as Summer Time ended during the night. At daybreak we were still some distance from Boulogne but we arrived there about 8 o/c. The motorcyclist knew Boulogne and suddenly he said, 'Come on, let's jump out!' The train was going slowly across the points outside the station and by jumping out we avoided being taken a mile or two further on to a camp where they might have wanted to examine passes again, and in any case we should have had to march back to the docks. We walked along the metals through the station and out into the road. It was Sunday morning and not many people were stirring. We went over the bridge into the town and found a restaurant where we got some breakfast. Two MPs were on the bridge when we returned but did not stop us – their duty was to prevent men coming up into the town – and we were going out of it. Down on the quayside a notice instructed leave men to fall in at 11.30 so we just strolled about a bit and had a basin of porridge in Lady Angela Forbes' Canteen. The other troops were marched down and we fell in with them. Then commenced a close and careful scrutiny of our warrants by the MPs who came down the ranks. There was no evading it this time and I was ordered to fall out to the rear. About a dozen other men were in the same boat but as soon as the inspecting MP had got a little way down the line I fell in again and I expect the other fellows did the same. Then came another examination as we passed on the gangway and yet another when we stepped on to the boat. The first one was easy but at the latter we had to give up a portion of the warrant. With the help of the motorcyclist who crowded up behind me I handed my portion upside down and he thrust his own on top of it before the NCO could turn it over. We had only just got settled on the boat when the order came that we were to transfer to another boat as this one was not considered suitable for the very rough weather. There was no further examination of passes and at ¼ past 12 we started to move out of the harbour. It was a terribly rough voyage; our boat was blown right round three times. I was about the only one on board who was not seasick and we did not arrive in Folkestone until ¼ past 3. Trains were waiting and soon we were speeding up to London. As we looked out of the carriage windows it required a distinct effort to realise that the people we saw walking about were English and spoke the same language we did – so accustomed have we become to seeing only civilians of other nations who jabber in French or gargle in Flemish. Reached Victoria at 6 and Ealing Broadway before 7 p.m. To 76 Drayton Gardens where strangers admitted me, Mr and Mrs Berwick being at church. I washed, shaved and helped myself to a good meal and went down to the church and saw Mrs Berwick. On to 17 Hastings Road where I found Elsie alone – she had a feeling that I would come. Slept at no. 76 on a real bed with real sheets and a soft pillow. Thus did I arrive in Blighty a day before my time.

8.10.17–10.10.17
At Ealing seeing old friends.

11.10.17
To King's Lynn with Elsie to see Lil, Edward and Peggy.

13.10.17
From King's Lynn to Dunmow with Elsie. Was glad to see my mother again.

15.10.17
Returned to Ealing with Elsie. The time is passing quickly.

18.10.17

Up early and Elsie came to the Broadway with me. It was very hard to say 'Goodbye' but she was such a brave little girl and gave me such a bright smile as we parted. We detrained at Shorncliffe and marched into Folkestone where we were put into a quarter of the town near the harbour. The streets were barricaded and guarded so that we could not get out into the town. After several hours' dreary waiting we boarded the boat and reached Boulogne about half past four. From the harbour we were marched to St Martin's Camp on top of a hill. It is a hard pull up, especially after ten days of ease and comfort. We were immediately sorted out into batches according to the different parts of the line to which we were going, and received instructions regarding our trains tomorrow. These camps are wretched places. I shall be glad to get back to my Brigade.

19.10.17

We were kept hanging about all the morning but eventually entrained. The journey was not such a long one as when we came down and we arrived at Bray at 11 p.m. Guides conducted us to the Rest Camp at Ghyvelde. Here we were put into a stable-like building with a floor partly of sand and partly of cement. Blankets were refused us; it was cold and cheerless and the stone floor was far from inviting. I took a piece of candle from my haversack, lit it and looked around. Several men were lying about trying to sleep. I chose a place next to a man who had covered his head with his overcoat. I threw my equipment off and growled. The overcoat moved, and who should look up at me but Davidson. He is going on leave. Lay down beside him for an hour or so but was much too cold to sleep – got up, stamped about to try and restore the circulation, then lay on the sand to see if that was any less cold than the cement, but it wasn't; on the other hand it seemed to be full of small objectionable creepy creatures so I got up and walked up and down till daylight.

20.10.17

As soon as it was light enough to see, Davidson and I had a wash
and a shave in some water from which we had to remove the ice.
After breakfast, nobody seeming to take any interest in us, and
no orders having been issued as to what we were to do, I decided
to make my own way up to Brigade. Davidson told me they had
moved from La Panne to Coxyde Bains and directed me how to get
there so I jumped a lorry which took me some distance and then
I walked the rest. After Boulogne and Ghyvelde it's a relief to get
back to Brigade. I was just in time for dinner – the new cook is a
decided improvement on Gould, but new brooms sweep clean –
time will prove his real worth. I have had a look round and made
myself acquainted with the run of the place and now (7 p.m.) I feel
tired out and am going to turn in. Lieut. Sylvester left Brigade
and went back to Division a few days after I went on leave. From
what I can make out Twycross worked it, but he only stepped out
of the frying pan into the fire for now we have got Lieut. Purvis as
our officer – commonly known as 'Jessie' because of his somewhat
peculiar mannerisms.

22.10.17

Went to The Crumps this evening. They are going to England in
a few days and there is some talk of their appearing at one of the
London theatres or music halls. A most cheerless day, with leaden
skies and plenty of rain but no mud! The sandy tracks have their
advantages.

23.10.17

Coxyde Bains was evidently a rather select watering place of
modern growth. There is an old port close to the beach, consisting
of tall, gaunt, unhandsome fishermen's dwellings but the greater
portion of the village is covered with the type of house known as
'arty'. The whole place is built on sand and there are only two made
roads running through the village, the rest are only sand tracks.
The Signal Office and Brigade HQ are in the nucleus of the village

Jack Martin prior to leaving for France, September 1916

Jack Martin (*right*) aged eighteen in 1902

Elsie Kate Brewster (later Martin) circa 1910.
Jack wrote frequently to Elsie who, in turn, sent
parcels of food to Jack in France.

A typical brigade signal unit photographed near Contay, on the Somme, November 1916.

'The village of Flers is close by and a crippled, battered tank, one of the first used in war, is lying almost opposite . . . Our dugout is filthy – lice and flies by the million and the stench of dead bodies makes one sick.' The Somme battlefield as it appeared to Jack Martin after his arrival in the autumn of 1916.

East of Arras: transport passes along a road built by Canadian Engineers. This panorama gives a remarkably detailed impression of a Great War battlefield as Jack Martin would have known it.

Imperial War Museum Q13396

'Every time he [Lt Buchanan] comes into the Signal Office he watches me most intently and if I make any little error or slip I hear all about it. But I don't let it worry me – I am not in the army to make a living.' A Royal Engineer signal exchange in a captured German dugout under Fricourt Chateau on the Somme.

The cramped interior of a forward wireless station.

A Test Panel beneath a farm in the Ypres salient. Jack Martin's job of maintaining communication between the front and rear lines relied on a complex system of wires and junction boxes that had to be kept intact.

Soldiers look down on the hairpin bends typical of roads in the Italian mountains. The effort needed to pull the regiment's transport up here was both monotonous and exhausting.

An enemy DFW two-seater airplane, one of half-a-dozen German and Austrian aircraft destroyed or forced to land after a surprise raid on an Allied aerodrome, 26 December 1917. Jack Martin watched the entire attack from the mountains above.

Men of the Royal Engineers bringing dirty linen to Italian women for washing in a stream. Jack Martin was astonished at how industrious the women were, in contrast to the men.

Imperial War Museum Q10798

'We were met by a continuous stream of retiring troops, fatigued almost to the point of absolute exhaustion . . . Hot, tired horses pulling guns of all calibres while, on the gun limbers, artillerymen, who had been firing their guns for three whole days and nights, slept a precarious slumber . . .' March 1918: The British army in full retreat after the launch of the long anticipated German offensive.

The Army of Occupation: Jack Martin (*seated second from left*) and the men of 122nd Infantry Brigade Signal Company outside their headquarters in Rösrath, Germany, prior to demobilisation in February 1919, Seated third from the left is Sergeant Twycross while back right is Jack's great friend, Tom Glasspoole.

Jack and Elsie on their wedding day, 6 June 1919.

where the houses are clustered a little closer than elsewhere; the Transport Lines are near the beach, while our billet is in a pair of semi-detached villas at one end of the village, and is connected to the Signal Office (about 300 yards away) by one of the sandy roads which makes the journey seem four times its length. We also have telephonic communications between the Office and the billet. This has advantages but it also has drawbacks. The village has suffered a certain amount from shellfire, particularly in the vicinity of the Signal Office, but the majority of the houses have not been irreparably damaged and still contain articles of furniture which were left by their owners when they fled hurriedly earlier in the war. It is a criminal offence to move any piece of furniture even from one house to another.

When the Brigade moved in here, about two days before I got back, the Signals were given a billet close to the Office. The runners had a house which contained real beds and they congratulated themselves. But during the second night there was a little shelling and one seemed to give the house rather a shaking but Fisher, Southwood and Co. were comfortably in bed and wouldn't get up for anything. In the morning they found the dining room out in the middle of the road. A small shell had come through the window, burst in the room and blown the wall out. The Brigadier ordered a move and so we got our present billet which, being the last house in the village, is as safe as anywhere could be, as Fritz gives his attentions only to the main road, the 'nucleus' and the Transport Lines. He does a ten-minute strafe every evening at dusk and sometimes also at 10 p.m. Such regularity is commendable – we know what to do – but occasionally he breaks forth at a different time and so catches us on the hop. I share a small room on the first floor with Hamilton and Rogers. Our room contains a table, a bureau, an overmantle and a couple of chairs. A French window opens on to a little verandah from which we can safely watch the shells dropping on the beach or in the village. Two or three civilians (including one woman) still remain in the place but they are looked on with suspicion as the whole neighbourhood is chock full of spies. I understand the 123rd Brigade caught seven in the fortnight they were stationed here. Every night we can see rockets go up from the German lines at Nieuport and answering rockets ascend from lonely spots on the dunes and marshes behind us. The country by its nature lends itself to this method of espionage. It is all marshland or rough sand dunes and a person knowing the land would stand a good chance of evading any pursuers.

26.10.17
Wrote to Mother telling her that I am trying to get Separation Allowance for her. She is distressed over my wangling an extra day's leave, is afraid I shall get into trouble! Played the piano in the NCOs' Mess this evening.

28.10.17
A day of great excitement. Our move forward has been cancelled, all men on leave have been recalled and we have had to pack up in readiness for moving off at a moment's notice. Rumour is very busy, but the only thing that is definite is the secrecy regarding our ultimate destination. Played the piano for nonconformist services this morning and again this evening.

29.10.17
Roused early this morning with orders to pack the wagons at once. Things very lively with all the bustle attendant on a hurried move. Transport got away early. The 15th Division is relieving us. MacDougall met one of their advance party who asked him what Division we were. 'Forty-first,' said Mac. 'Lord,' replied the other, 'the blood and lust division!' So now we know what our nickname is among the rest of the army. It appears that we have the reputation for making things so unpleasant for Fritz that he retaliates strongly, and other divisions do not like following us in the line. General Towsey is on leave. The Acting Brigadier is Colonel Pennell of the 18th KRRC who at the beginning of the war was a corporal in the Regular Army. Sgt Twycross and I were left to close the Office and

early in the afternoon walked about a mile to a spot where a motor lorry was waiting for us. We arrived at St Pol adjoining Dunkirk about 5 p.m. having caught up the rest of the Brigade HQ. Cpl Erith had been looking round for billets which he said were very hard to obtain, so we didn't expect anything great but what we got is even worse than we foreboded.

Situated in the main street running from Dunkirk along the coast towards Calais, trams pass the door every quarter of an hour. Houses and shops on each side of the road are closely built and yards are entered by large double doors always kept closed, a smaller one being cut in them to allow of individual passage. Such is the entrance to our billet and it will be difficult to find in the dark. Inside the doorway the upper storey of the house extends and forms an archway as in the old posting houses in England. Beyond is a pebble-paved courtyard with the entrance to the house on the right, next door wall on the left and our billet at the far end. A chicken run occupies one corner of the yard but cannot be described as ornamental. The inside of our billet, however, is the great feature. It is a cowshed with a gangway down the middle and ox stalls on either side. Certainly it has been swept out since the last cow died but chickens have had free access – we drove half a dozen out when we came in. There is a loft approached by a shaky ladder and the roof is far from watertight. I managed to settle in one of the least draughty corners on the ground floor and then Dickson and I went out to look for grub. After a little searching we found an estaminet up a side street where apparently they serve dinners every evening. This is fortunate.

30.10.17

Rumours have been many and varied as to why we have been taken from the line so abruptly. At first we were rather inclined to think it meant Ypres again, as we seem fated to spend much of our time in that area, but I don't think we should have been brought here if we were going back to the old sector. Egypt, Italy and Ireland are all strong favourites in the Rumour Race, but I think Ireland can be struck out and, as regards the other two, I am rather inclined to think it will be Italy, in view of the big reverses the Italians have had lately. On the other hand, we only know what is published in the papers and it is quite possible that trouble has arisen in Ireland or Egypt or some other part of the Globe which has not been allowed to get into the papers. Yesterday was a glorious day but today is wretched.

On 24 October 1917, in response to repeated Italian attempts to break through Austrian lines in the Alps, the Austrians, backed by German forces, launched the Caporetto Offensive. The assault was undertaken with limited objectives, primarily to curtail any future Italian ambitions in the region. However, the attack, supported by a four-hour preliminary shell and gas bombardment, was far more successful than expected. The Austro-German force, which included a young Lieutenant Erwin Rommel, advanced against thinly held enemy positions. Overwhelmed and exhausted, the Italians broke and began a headlong retreat of over 60 miles, crossing to the west of the fast-flowing River Piave on 10 November, just 30 kilometres north of Venice. Some 300,000 Italian soldiers were lost, including 270,000 prisoners, breaking the Italian army as an effective fighting force.

The Italian government quickly requested Allied help to stem the enemy advance, and a Franco-British force numbering eleven divisions was sent. The first two British divisions to arrive in early November were the 23rd and 41st, quickly moving up into the line. The enemy offensive was continued at various points along the front but, with little appetite for the fight and with rapidly diminishing returns on the battlefield, operations were halted before the end of the year.

The German army had its own eye on a proposed decisive offensive on the Western Front and soon withdrew its divisions, leaving the Austrians too weak to countenance any further operations alone.

1.11.17
From today leave is increased from ten to fourteen days – wish it had been dated from 1st of last month. Also I hear that those men who have been recalled from leave and who have not had four

days at home will be allowed to go back again. The Italian rumour grows stronger.

4.11.17
Our destination is Italy. While I was on duty Jessie had a parade of the Signals and told them that the part of Italy to which we are going is inhabited by a very poor peasantry and we must be kind to them. From what I can make out we have got to raise the morale of the Italians as well as fight the Austrians.

7.11.17
General Towsey held an inspection of the whole of Brigade HQ. He told us that the situation in Italy is very obscure and what we are going into cannot be forecasted so we must be well prepared for any eventualities, and no matter in what circumstances we find ourselves to carry on unflinchingly the noble traditions etc etc etc. He also emphasised the poverty of the country so we cannot look forward to buying food or tobacco when we are short, as we can in France. Received from Elsie copies of the photographs I had taken on leave. They are quite good but I shall never look really martial.

10.11.17
On night duty last night with Jack Carter. Overheard General Lawford tell General Towsey that Lieut. Moore [15th Hampshire Regiment] has been awarded the VC for his work on 20 Sept. The Sgt who was with him gets the DCM. Had a practice stunt on the dunes repelling imaginary Austrians. I was running a Visual Station and of course we had divested ourselves of our equipment but the runners had to keep theirs on. Presently the Brigadier came along and after a few enquiries said, 'A shell has now dropped here and killed those men who are wearing their equipment. So they can get back to their billets at once.' So we had to carry on without them. We leave here on Monday (the 12th) but I haven't heard any details yet.

I think Fritz's aeroplanes have been over every night except one, when it was too stormy for flying. He hasn't bothered us much,

however, as he gives his attention mainly to the harbour and town
of Dunkirk. But one evening when Jamieson and I were having
dinner in the estaminet some bombs were dropped close by and
two or three civilians were killed. The people of the house got the
wind up badly, the lights were turned out and we all were bundled
down into the cellar, where the beds are, until the danger was past.
We had only just commenced our meal and of course it was cold
when we returned.

12.11.17
About 10 o/c last night we had all gathered at the billet for the
single reason that there was nowhere else to go. Some of us lay
down for a while but without the blankets or any other covering
save our overcoats it was too cold for sleep. So one by one we rose
and stamped up and down to restore circulation. The cooks had
cleared up pretty thoroughly (they had left with the Transport)
but we found a few pieces of wood and made a little fire and sat
around it talking until time to fall in. At 3.30 a.m. we moved off,
our steps making a hollow clang in the silent streets. It was a fine
night and soon we were in the country, glad of the warmth that the
movement was giving us.

Only two trucks had been allotted to Brigade HQ. As this meant
over thirty men in each truck, we felt dissatisfied. For twenty-four
hours we would have endured it but the prospect of being cramped
like this for four or five days was far from pleasant so we got hold
of Jessie and protested. He adopted a high and mighty attitude
– 'Oh you'll have to put up with it – there's no more room.' Our
temper then became what is described as ugly and we demanded to
see the General. The result was that in less than five minutes other
trucks were available and now we are only ten or twelve in a truck
and shall have plenty of room to lie down. Bundles of straw have
been issued to us together with our packs and blankets. We have
scrounged a brazier and some wood and a few lumps of coal and
trust to our foraging tactics to keep us well supplied with fuel en
route. We proceeded in the leisurely fashion customary with army

trains and had not got far beyond Abbeville when night fell and we closed the doors, wrapped ourselves in our blankets, spent an hour in talking and smoking and by 8 o/c were all fast asleep.

13.11.17

We woke this morning passing through a strangely peaceful country. We stopped for half an hour or so, miles from any town or village, to let an express go through. Stretched our legs up and down the length of the train and learned from the engine driver that we are a hundred kilometres south of Paris. Very disappointed at having passed through the Gay City during the night. We all would have liked a glimpse at it. Got some water and had a shave before the train moved on. The country we have passed through today is pastoral and agricultural, containing no features of any particular note so far as I was able to observe; but it is not at all satisfactory to travel through strange country without a map and without even any definite knowledge of the route that is to be followed.

14.11.17

Passed through Lyons during the night. Soon after rising we were shunted into a country siding to make way for another express. A farmhouse stood close to the line so several of us scrambled over the fence into the garden and went to the door and asked for water for a wash. The people didn't understand soldiers' French but our soap and towels spoke for us and the farmer conducted us to a little rushing stream at the end of the house. The engine whistled before we had all finished and we had to rush back.

Perhaps the thing that has struck me most during yesterday and today is the sparsity of the population in the rural districts. We have travelled for miles at a time and our vision has scanned thousands of acres of field and road without seeing a single individual. Long stretches of well-engineered roads, with apparently fine surfaces, seem deserted, but we can only assume that it is their normal state. In fact it is quite an event to see a motor car or a horse and cart. The stately rolling river too suffers in the same wise. I cannot guess for how many miles we ran parallel and close to it, but it was a good many, and throughout the whole distance, the only traffic on it was one steam boat.

There has been a strong cold wind today which somebody says is the Mistral, but I must confess to complete ignorance. On the other hand I have got a much clearer idea of the geography of the country than most of the fellows. It is really astounding what a lot of people know a very little! We travelled fairly well all day and anticipated passing through Marseilles during daylight but our pace gradually slackened and at dusk we found ourselves among a mass of railway lines which a shunter informed us was the outskirts of the great Mediterranean port. It was smoky and dirty and uninteresting and soon after dark we closed the doors and smoked and talked till 9 o/c when we turned in and went to sleep.

15.11.17

Rising as usual when the breakfast feeling was getting strong, we found that we had made very little progress during the night – in fact Marseilles was only a few miles behind us and we were moving eastwards towards the Riviera. The morning was bright and clear and we soon found that the brazier was unnecessary. We had managed to keep it going all day long up to the present. We are adept at snatching lumps of coal, or the little egg-shaped 'coal-bricks' which are used a lot on the continental railways, from engines or trucks as we pass them, providing, of course, we are not travelling too fast.

Soon we took off our coats, the sun was so warm – and only three days ago we were shivering in the cold, damp misery of Dunkirk! Steadily we rolled through orchards of mulberry trees, maintained we were told for the breeding of silkworms, with a low range of hills on our right effectively blocking out the view of the sea. All eyes were eagerly strained to catch the first glimpse of the Alps and of the Mediterranean.

Kept an eye on the position of the sun and managed successfully to judge the bearing where the Alps would first come into view. It

was about 11 a.m. when the snow-capped pinnacles of the Maritime
Alps reared themselves above the horizon on our left front. We
were all excitement but soon turned our attention to the other side
as it was becoming apparent that we were nearing the sea. The
hills that had blocked our view were getting lower and craning our
necks till we nearly fell out of the train, we raised huzzas of delight
as we caught sight of the sea shining and glittering in the bright
sunlight. Now we are really on the Riviera – the famous winter
resort of the wealthy. Never did I think that I should actually see
this beautiful stretch of coast. I always regarded it in something
of the same light as Moses must have thought of Canaan – a fair
country which I had very small prospects of seeing.

Today, undoubtedly, has been a great day and I don't know how
to begin to record events. Yesterday at various stations, individuals
gave us chocolate and cigarettes and apples but today we have been
overwhelmed with gifts including bunches of flowers. Enthusiasm
was very high – almost the whole population turned out to cheer us
and wave flags and patriotic emblems; houses were decorated and
bands were playing the National Anthems of the Allies. From St
Raphael to Ventimiglia, a distance of 90 kilometres (56 miles) the
railway and the road follow the coastline very closely, sometimes
the one and sometimes the other being the nearer to the sea – the
beautiful Mediterranean which differs from the North Sea or the
English Channel as the sunshine of June differs from the fog and
murky clouds of November. Yet this is November and here we have
sunshades and gay frocks, and bathing in full swing. At one spot
people were having sunbaths in an enclosure overlooking the beach.
So close did we approach the sea in some places that we could look
down into it almost perpendicularly, and the water was so clear that
we could see the rocks and seaweed at the bottom, a depth of ten
or fifteen feet. Then besides this wonderfully clear blue sea there is
the sky, which is clearer and bluer and seems further away than ours
in England. And then the trees and the foliage! Earlier in the day,
the mulberry trees had attracted our attention but here on the coast
grow palms and cacti and oranges and great tall ferns and grasses

ten or twelve or more feet high – and everywhere a sense of dryness and cleanliness.

Before we reached Cannes we were sidetracked to allow a train-load of artillery to go by. A few yards away big ferns, palms and other plants were growing in profusion. We plucked great armfuls and decorated the whole length of our train on both sides, the bunches of flowers that had been given us making splashes of colour here and there. And so we rolled along in state towards Nice. We stopped in Cannes station. The civilians were kept at a distance but they threw biscuits and cigarettes at us, and some amateur photographers were busy taking 'snaps'. The train was pulled up before we got into the station but we were well inside the town with its tall white buildings gaily decorated in our honour, and waving, cheering people at every window. We had stopped in a shallow cutting where great bunches of maidenhair fern were growing on the rocky embankment. I jumped out and picked a piece to send to Elsie. A road bridge spanned the line a dozen yards from our truck and it was crowded with cheering, gesticulating people who ought to be hoarse for the next month. Children peered down at us with wide-open eyes as though we were strange creatures who might be friendly or not. But the centre of the picture was taken by a rather stout lady, with no hat, who, leaning so far over the parapet that we feared she would lose her balance, waved both arms frantically and shouting repeatedly 'Bravo boys!', her whole frame shaking and wobbling like a blancmange.

15.11.17 cont.

Arriving in Nice station, we found that our fame as a decorated train had preceded us and the people were on the lookout for us. We were greeted effusively – English ladies who would scorn to look at us in civilian life now waited on us, bringing us tea, coffee, biscuits, chocolate, cigarettes etc, conversing amiably the while. Then followed the most glorious experience of this most glorious day. Leaving Nice as day was merging into night, with Venus twinkling brightly over the sea, we continued on our way twisting and curling along the irregularities of the coastline, forward and back along little jutting peninsulas, through numerous short tunnels and skirting the most delightful little bays that one could expect to find anywhere save perhaps in the islands of the South Pacific, each little bay containing a charming little town, white and clean, with houses sprinkled about up the steep thickly wooded hillsides.

And so through Menton to the frontier where we were held up for some time at a platform which did not seem to be a station, and then on to Ventimiglia, the first town in Italy, where there were opportunities of changing our money. Here we had to put our watches forward one hour from 7.30 to 8.30 to bring us into accord with Italian time. Typewritten Italian vocabularies had been issued to us before we entrained and we had managed to learn a few words, and now we began to air them, but we found that in the next truck which contained machine gunners was a man who, although born in England, came of Italian parents and could speak the language perfectly. He will be useful.

16.11.17

About daybreak the train was standing still when somebody from outside tried to open the door. We all immediately set up a horrible shouting and growling and the door was slammed shut again to the accompaniment of some Italian jabbering. Later on when we got up we found a number of packets of cigarettes had been thrust into our truck so we passed a few mental apologies back along the line to the man we had greeted so surlily early in the morning. Our progress today has not been so heroic as yesterday, but nevertheless it has been quite satisfactory. We gave some Italian soldiers a tin of jam.

They regarded it dubiously but we endeavoured to assure them that it was quite good to eat and at last one of them put it in his pocket. Probably he threw it away when our backs were turned.

At the station where we had our 'halte repas' this morning we were able to buy bread and later in the day, when we were pulled up right out in the country, we found a house where we were able to get some more. Two little children came up with baskets of apples. We gave them pennies and they ran home delighted and soon after their parents and big sisters came along with large baskets of fruit and indignantly refused to take any payment. Presently we noticed a lady and a little girl hurrying towards us across the fields. They brought us boxes of flowers. We hadn't much use for flowers but we appreciated the motive that prompted the offering. But we soon discovered that the flowers only lay on top of a neatly arranged selection of nuts and fruit. Each box contained a postcard inscribed with a greeting in Italian. None of us could read it with certainty but our collective brain deciphered it to mean 'To those who have come to fight by the side of our fathers and our brothers'.

At 11.30 p.m. we detrained at Asola, a small town in the plain of Lombardy, light being supplied by Italian soldiers with torches. A party was told off to help unship the transport, the rest of us were led up into the little town which we were amazed to find was illuminated by electricity. Flags and other decorations lined the streets and the clatter we made roused the slumbering inhabitants; on all sides windows were opened and heads popped out to see the newly arrived Inglesi. One or two sour-looking gendarmes patrolled the market square, and we were led straight to the local 'theatre' or opera house which was to be our billet for the night. It was past one o'clock before we turned in.

General remarks on Italy, compiled at various dates, and entered here by way of preface to the record of our remarkable march:

Our march was in the nature of an Elizabethan progress. We passed through no large towns, only villages and townlets, but all the way along we were objects of great interest. All work, commerce, enterprise of every description were suspended while we passed; school children left their lessons and were ranged along the road cheering and waving flags and handkerchiefs, while old women wept copiously – a form of emotional display which rather amused us. A little of this sort of thing is all very well in its way but I soon began to feel as if I formed part of a circus procession or peripatetic menagerie. It is to be noted in this connection that enthusiasm for the war is greatest in parts furthest removed from the fighting; but it gradually diminishes to nothing the nearer one gets to the line.

The immense plain over which we marched is as flat as the floor of a room, and the light effect at dawn and sunset differ from those in Blighty – I cannot describe them adequately. After the sun has gone down there is often a soft peculiar light pervading the upper air. It tinges the little white flecks of cloud with a delicate rosy tint and the sere and yellow leaves of tall trees glow faintly as if lighted by a beamless searchlight. And it is a fine sight, when everything nearby is almost in darkness, to see the rising or dying sunlight picking out the snow-capped ridges in the distance.

The architecture of big houses and mansions is plain and solid-looking, though frequently ornamental statues are placed on the gateposts and along the outside walls and on the sort of balcony that runs along the front of the house. One striking feature that I have seen nowhere else is the decoration of the outside walls of houses with paintings. This will last for many years owing to the clearness and dryness of the climate. Sometimes a frieze runs right round the house just under the eaves and sometimes figures are painted here and there in convenient spaces. The most outstanding example of this kind of decoration that I have seen was on a house in Campo Sampiero, a quaint old town that I would have liked to have seen more of, but we only passed through it. This particular house was literally covered with paintings. Under the frieze and between the small upper windows were large panels with paintings of nymphs and gentle swains, and underneath these and between the upper and lower windows ran another border strip of cherubs flying and flitting hither and thither. As far as we could see, these paintings were carried all round the house which otherwise was a plain rectangular building.

As regards agriculture, the soil is too fertile. Crops grow without any trouble, and consequently the people are about the laziest one can imagine, at any rate the men are. Most of the work is done by the women. They are buxom and strong and are trained from the earliest days to labour while boys spend their time in play, and men in idleness. I have seen little girls struggling along with pails of water so heavy that their little legs quivered but no boy or man would condescend to help them. The women take a pride in their copper water buckets; these are always kept beautifully clean and brightly polished and are carried in pairs on the ends of a slightly curved piece of timber which is placed across the shoulder, the bucket at each end making a proper balance.

Oxen are the beasts of burden. Great heavy ponderous beasts they are, of a dirty creamy colour, with long horns and waddling gait; they look almost too lazy to walk. Slowly they pull the antiquated wooden plough to the accompaniment of much excited shouting and continual thrashing by their driver. Wearily they drag the equally antiquated harrow, and lazily they draw the rickety cart. They seem to be a distinctive breed and there is very little variation either in size or colour; some are almost white and some are slightly tinged with grey but the majority are inclined to a dreary shade of cream or fawn.

An English farmer would have no patience with them, they are so frightfully slow and although they may look quaint in pictures, in actual life there is nothing graceful, beautiful or entrancing about them. Yet with all this slowness of motion they exude warmth. You can feel it as you pass them in the road and to go into their shed at night is like entering a hothouse with the addition that they give off a most objectionable odour which grips your throat and makes you gasp. The natives, however, suffer no ill effects – custom has inured them to this strange smell and frequently in the cold frosty evenings the family sojourns to the stable for warmth and comfort, for be it understood that Italy has no coalfields and peasants rely entirely on wood for their fires, and this they have to gather for themselves. Hence fires are used only for cooking, never for comfort.

The farmers apparently only keep horses for the purpose of driving to market, and they are poor, miserable, skinny creatures that in England would soon be marked down by the Inspectors of the RSPCA. Possibly they are very hardy – well, they need to be. A few asses and diminutive mules are also to be met with occasionally. They appear to be owned by dealers and very small farmers who require only one 'general service' sort of animal. These poor brutes have to pull the most extraordinary loads. For carrying hay and straw a cart is used fitted with extensions in the front as well as the back, stretching almost over the animal's head and bending down over his sides pannier fashion, but of course not touching his body. So you can get the rather laughable spectacle of a large mass of hay moving along the road with a horse's or donkey's head poking out of the front and four hoofs pattering underneath.

The men particularly are the most indolent creatures I have ever met and they seem quite satisfied to do the smallest amount of work sufficient to supply them with the coarsest of foods for the next twenty-four hours. Their chief delight is to stand gloomily at street corners, wrapped round in their big cloaks or capes, muffled up to the nose and wearing broad slouch hats. They look just like villains from melodrama, fit for treason's stratagems and spoils, and one cannot help suspecting the presence of stilettos and daggers beneath the cloaks.

The interior of the houses, as a rule, is spotlessly clean and every morning the bedclothes are hung out of the windows to air in the beautiful sunlight. We were struck by the whiteness of the sheets and pillowcases; and we were more surprised still when we witnessed a native washing day. This is quite a picturesque affair. They don't have tubs and baths and steaming coppers – they don't even have soap. On the plains there are many streams of the clearest water imaginable; and although the country is so flat the streams run fast for they get their energy from 8000 feet up in the mountains. In these streams, in the big rivers too, and even in stagnant pools, the women do their washing. They have a board eighteen inches or two feet wide and four or five feet long; one end is placed in the water, the other is on the bank, and they kneel at that end, soak the clothes in the stream and then whack them vigorously on the board. They wring them and roll them and smack them repeatedly

until the garments are white as snow. Such treatment makes one
wonder how long the garments last; they must be made of stout
material to survive the second wash. There is no denying, however,
that it is a quite efficient way of getting them clean. Whether there
is some peculiar property in the water that renders soap unnecessary
is more than I can say, but beating and battering may of themselves
be sufficient to remove the dirt if plenty of energy is exercised. Soap
is not only expensive but very difficult to get and this may be the
cause of this strange custom.

My previous knowledge of Italy only extended to vague picturings
of isolated incidents and of odds and ends of people. I could point it
out on the map and I could write a little essay on its musical history;
and in my schooldays I could draw the map of Italy from memory
because it was easy. But now I am taking a greater interest in it.
I had heard of Garibaldi [1807–82, credited with unifying Italy]
but I had no idea of what an important individual he was. There is
no doubt that he is the national hero. Every town and almost every
little village memorialises him in some way or other if only by a Via
Garibaldi or a Piazza Garibaldi. If the municipal coffers can afford
it they have his bust stuck up in a prominent place; in wealthy
districts they erect a full-sized statue, and in places where money is
no object they have been known to raise a whole building, a town
hall or something of that sort, and dedicate it to his memory.

When wrestling with the Italian language, the thing that strikes
one most is the great number of words having vowel terminations,
about 95 per cent, I should think. One day I counted the number
of words in a magazine paragraph. There were ninety-eight and
ninety-four of them terminated with a vowel. Of course the troops
were quick to apply the gentle art of imitative caricature; therefore
we go on dutio or have a smokio or do sentry-goio. For three or four
weeks the Italians could not make us out. They couldn't understand
any hilarity amongst men going to war. This particular type of
wonderment we found all the way along the march. It has been said
that an Englishman takes his pleasures sadly, but it should also be
remarked that he can take the serious business of life jocularly.

17.11.17

At Asola we were roused at 6 a.m. with orders to get packed up ready to march off at 8.30. Found a baker's shop well stocked with bread — white bread with a soft interior but a cast-iron crust. The town was extremely clean. Notices had been posted on the walls calling on the Italian citizens to give the British troops a hearty welcome. It was market day and the square was crowded with stalls bearing all sorts of odds and ends to induce people to part with their money. As we were moving off, an old beggar man endeavoured to sell us bootlaces but the crowd pounced on him and dragged him out of our way. There was much gesticulating and shouting but we turned a corner so could not see what transpired.

The Brigadier stood on the steps of a hotel and took the salute as we marched past. Crowds of children ran along beside us for miles. We marched cheerfully although we soon felt the effects of five days lazing in the train, and eventually arrived at Guidizzolo. In the town we were not quite certain of our way and called to some Italian soldiers. They didn't attempt to understand us but set up a hue and cry which resulted in the finding of a soldier who could speak English, or rather American. Our billet is a respectable loft and the Signal Office is in the centre of the town. Rumour says that we have five days' marching in front of us. This evening Dickson and I had sausages and potatoes in a Trattoria just outside the billet. Don't know what the sausages were made of and perhaps it is as well not to enquire. Distance marched today = 17½ miles.

18.11.17

Thousands of retreating Italians passed through here this morning. They looked a pretty rabble. Had thrown away all their equipment; the only things they retained other than what they stood up in were their overcoats and these were loaded in piles on little mule- or donkey-carts, strange looking vehicles to our idea of transport. The men were straggling along rather than marching, albeit their pace was rather fast. There was very little order, they only seemed intent on getting away from the line as quickly as possible. In the afternoon Jessie S. held an inspection of all Signal Stores and our own personal equipment. He gave us a lecture on the arduous nature of the march in front of us and said that nothing was to be taken unless absolutely necessary; therefore he condemned the football to be dumped but I bet it turns up when we want it. A quantity of signal stores was packed into hampers and sealed down; these are to be left here until we can send back for them. The Post Office men are billeted in a Trattoria near the Signal Office and this evening Dickson and I joined them in a supper of stewed hare and polenta. We enjoyed it. The polenta stuff seems quite harmless and is filling. English rations have not arrived so we have been issued with Italian. Wrote several letters but Corporal Smith says he doesn't know when they will go away.

19.11.17

Roused early to get cleaned up so that we may make the necessary impression on the civilians. Jessie made me take the piece of rag off the muzzle of my rifle as it was very unsightly. Put it in my pocket and replaced it at the first halt. It may not be ornamental but it keeps the damp and dirt out of the barrel and is therefore a labour-saving device, reducing the amount of cleaning to a minimum. At midday we had an hour's halt and discovered a remarkable difference between the temperatures in the sun and in the shade. We were very hot with marching, and immediately sought the shelter of some trees but it was surprisingly cold, dangerously so in fact; so we emerged into the sunshine again and nibbled our biscuits and bully by the side of the clear little stream running merrily by the roadside. We were very tired when we arrived at Mozzecane where a lot of Italian soldiers were billeted in a place that may be a barracks. Our home for the night is a farm at the north end of the town. We were marched into the yard and left standing for several minutes when the Brigade Major came up and told Mr Jamblin to order us to remove our equipment and to fall out, it being necessary in view of possible heavy taxes on our energies in the near future, that we should be given every

possible opportunity to rest. Distance marched today = 17 miles.
Total = 34½ [miles].

20.11.17
Last night I was on night duty with Enticknap. The Signal Office
was in a stone-floored room which was part of the farmhouse and
was half filled with a heap of wheat. On this we each managed to
get about two hours' sleep but we had to start rousing the troops at
4.30 a.m. Today's march was very trying.

It happened today that one of our ten-minute halts occurred
in a small hamlet. Of course the inhabitants crowded out to see
us and one of them suddenly had a brainwave. There was a little
jabbering and then a rush indoors and in a few seconds the women
returned with, not just glasses or mugs, but buckets of red wine;
and when they were emptied they went back and were refilled.
Jessie got the wind up. He was afraid we should all get 'cut',
but a few buckets don't go far amongst a crowd of thirsty men.
We were feeling whacked when we arrived at Isola della Scala,
an unpretentious little town with no features of outstanding
interest. We knew this to be our resting place for tonight and
as we marched through the streets we kept our eyes open for
restaurants. As soon as we were settled, Hamilton and I made our
way into the town, found a Trattoria and had a feed of macaroni
and horseflesh. It was a strange dish but we were starving and had
to fill ourselves up with something or other.

For a long while this afternoon, General Lawford and General
Towsey were earnestly engaged in conversation in the road outside
our billet. On Brigade HQ we have been grousing heartily about
marching on short rations but the men in the battalions have been
shouting a bit louder and things had arrived at the point when
Regimental Commanders begin to wonder whether their authority
will be recognised for many more hours. The Surreys, who had to
proceed a few kms beyond this town, halted here for an hour to
have their midday meal consisting of bully and biscuits. Breakfast
had consisted of similar articles and they had marched ten or twelve

miles. While they were halted, who should come along but the Prince of Wales. The men recognised him and greeted him by holding up the bully and biscuits and shouting, 'How'd you like to do twelve miles on this with a full pack?' Of course those Staff Officers who are doing the journey in motor cars and having three or four good meals a day are quite ready to move on, but it looks as if there will be trouble if we don't soon get a little rest or some substantial meals or both.

Rumours kept flying about that we are to have a day's rest but the official order did not arrive until 9.30 p.m. We raised a cheer of thankfulness for I don't think any of us feel fit for another march tomorrow. Incidentally, I think it has averted the possibility of trouble in the battalions. Men can be driven and bullied a long way under a military system that continually holds out the 'FP No. 1' and 'Shot at dawn' threats, but there is a limit to human endurance of despotic government, and we have nearly reached it. Distance marched today = 13 miles. Total = 47½ [miles].

21.11.17

Walked in the town and bought some picture postcards. By the way, we are now allowed to tell our people at home that we are in Italy, but for my part I had already sent word by Tom Glasspoole when he went back on leave just before we left Dunkirk. Even the most severely enforced restrictions can be surmounted or undermined where one has the will to do it – just like Acts of Parliament – none has yet been framed but that a coach and four horses could be driven through it. Went inside the church and had a good look round; it is ornamental in a costly and rather gaudy fashion. The local bakers have been working continuously ever since we arrived yesterday but they cannot cope with the demand. British soldiers are lined up in hundreds outside every baker's shop waiting for the next batch of bread to come from the ovens. The cafés have all been crowded out all day long – they can never have done such a trade in the whole of their existence.

22.11.17

The day's rest has done us good and has soothed the spirit of unrest so we did not grumble much at having to get on the move again early this morning. We marched well and at midday crossed over the huge iron bridge spanning the Adige into Albaredo. On the move every day, it is not an easy matter to keep in touch with all the units and we all have to take turns assisting the DRs [Despatch Riders] to find them. Our directions are generally vague and the maps we have are far from reliable. So it happened this afternoon that I was sent with a message to the Field Ambulance. The only direction I received was that the FA had been seen to turn to the left at the end of the street. I soon came to another T-road and took the most likely looking turning to the right. Crossing a stream, the road divided and I didn't know which fork to take. A Corporal of the RAMC came up and I thought I was lucky. He said, 'Oh it's up this way.' So away we rode together, turned into a side road and struck the 124th Brigade HQ. He had to admit he had taken the wrong road so we set off again and eventually arrived back in Albaredo after a circuit of ten miles or more. It was quite a pleasant ride in beautiful weather and interesting country. Passing through the town, we crossed the little bridge again and took the other turning and soon came to the Ambulance billeted in a farm. After dark I had to go out there again and on the return journey bore to the side of the road to avoid a heavily laden farm wagon and ran up on to a great heap of stones and came a cropper. Grazed my hand and bruised my shin a little.

Taylor was trying to find his way this afternoon when he came to a road fork that was not indicated on the map. He accosted an Italian soldier – held his map out, performed a variety of extraordinary deaf and dumb show (he had given up trying to make himself understood by talking) and after a few minutes the Italian said in English, 'Well now, what the blankety blank do you want?' Distance marched today = 15½ miles. Total = 63 [miles].

23.11.17

Resumed our march in good spirits although some of the fellows complain of blisters on their feet. I take as much care of mine as possible, wearing only the socks that Elsie knitted for me. As soon as a hole develops I put on another pair and pack the old ones away for washing and darning at the first opportunity. The inaccuracies of the Italian maps led us to trudge two or three miles further than we need to have done. We turned along a good road which seemed to be the correct one but after nearly a mile it gradually deteriorated into a lane and finished up by landing us in a field. We just had to turn round and work our way back again. We have travelled in a north-easterly direction today and the mountains have become appreciably nearer. We halted for ten minutes in Lonigo which is Corps HQ. It is the largest town we have entered so far and was merrily decorated with flags and bunting and huge notices placarded on the walls greeting us with:

Good Health at the Allies
Bravo L'esercito Inglesi
Good Health at the England
Welcome at the Allies and co

Lonigo lies at the foot of the Monte Berico, a small spur of the Alps. A reasonably level road cuts through them to Vicenza but our route tomorrow is to be over the top. After leaving Lonigo we began to climb – a good road and not very steep but a decided change after the extreme flatness of the country which we have traversed up to the present. Passed through the little village of Sarego to a chateau standing on the hillside. Arriving at the entrance to the carriage drive we halted to get a little breath and energy to enable us to climb to the chateau which was almost straight above us. As we rested, the Surreys passed us toiling up the hill to the next village. The Brigadier was standing with us and of course the Surreys' Officer Commanding started to call his men to attention but the Brigadier waved his hand and said, 'No, no, let the men march easy.' Some

of them seemed to be getting done up and I noticed one officer
carrying four men's rifles. Our final ascent to our billet was by a
winding drive between trees and tall shrubs. It was short but it was
severe and it made us puff and perspire. Fortunately Lally managed
to get his mules up with the stores so we were saved the trouble of
carting them up. Our billet is a granary containing plenty of straw.
A lot of chickens were running about; they belonged to an adjacent
cottage, probably the gardener's home, so I went up there and
tried to get some eggs. Although I used my finest Italian accent in
pronouncing the word 'uova' it was quite impossible to make the
old lady understand. She tried me with a chair, then a table, and
finally offered me her whole sitting room. I gave it up and returned
to find that her husband had taken a basket full of eggs and was
selling them to the men at the billet. Jessie took MacDonald's
motorcycle and went off to prospect the road we have to travel
tomorrow. He came back with a tale of frightful mountains, narrow
roads and steep precipices. We know he is given to exaggeration;
still, there is no doubt that we are in for a very stiff time. Distance
marched today = 15 miles. Total = 78 miles.

24.11.17
Reveille at 4 a.m. Packed the limber. Breakfast at 5.30 consisting
of a plate of porridge and biscuit and cheese. The heavy transport
left at 3 a.m. taking the longer but more level road – only the
light limbers accompanied us. We had to carry full packs including
overcoats. I sorted out all the heaviest articles, including half my
ammunition, and packed them in my blankets, but even then I
suppose I was carrying about 80lbs on my back. We moved off at
6.45 a.m. and the going was fairly easy for the first few miles until
we reached Brendola. Here we turned to the left and began the
serious ascent, and a party was told off with ropes to help pull up
the limbers. It is on hills like these that mules prove themselves
superior to horses. They will pull and pull whereas horses soon
lose heart and give up trying to do a job which really they have
plenty of strength to accomplish. Only a few yards up the hill we

passed a Surrey limber stuck by the roadside. The horse, a great strong animal, merely looked at the hill, sighed, and refused to budge even though all the weight of the load was being taken by a platoon of men pulling on the ropes. The road twisted and turned and took us up nearly 1000 feet, the summit of the hills being 400 or 500 feet higher. The hills, being of volcanic origin, are extremely irregular and consequently the road was a continuous series of twists and bends and wriggles. The morning was cold and the hills were wrapped in mist, white and damp and chilly. Sometimes we could see only a few yards on either side. In places the road ran along the edges of precipices and there was none too much room for the transport wagons; in fact it was a very ticklish job to get past some of the great lumbering oxen carts that we met. At midday we halted for an hour, having reached the highest point of the road. Our only food was the iron rations we carried – bully and biscuits again. Now we were glad of our overcoats for the mist kept sweeping down from the summits and making us shiver. Gradually and in spasms it lifted, giving us a glorious view over the country to Vicenza. We could see the long white road and the railway running side by side in the valley and in the distance rose the mountains of the Trentino, whilst nearer, nestling in the dark background of spreading vineyards, were numerous little white-housed villages with their quaint church towers. The view was worth the climb. When we got on the move again the sun had dispersed the mist and beat down on us pitilessly. The road was up and down and in and out until we came to the final descent to the plain which was by a series of four hairpin bends made necessary by the fact that the gradient of the hillside was about 1 in 1½. Now the men with the ropes had to act as brakes, for it was more than the horses and mules could do to hold the limbers back. It is reported that one or two went over but I do not know if this is true. All of ours completed the journey safely. As we reached the bottom, Divisional HQ were passing along. They had travelled by the level road that skirts the hills on the south and east. We turned to the left and sighed with relief as we looked along the level road in front of us leading to

Longara and straightened our aching backs in a final endeavour to show the natives that twenty miles with a heavy pack was a mere bagatelle. But we were in for a most cruel disappointment. Captain Reiner and Sgt Lunn, who had come on in advance, met us and told us that our destination had been altered. We had to go several kms further on. This was the last straw, but we had to carry it. So with 'Stick it, boys' we strode breast forward but it was hard work. There was no energy for singing or whistling now; gradually we got out of step, and just as the shutters of heaven were being put up we stumbled into the little village of Costozza. A voice called out, 'Keep going, it's only another hundred yards' but my eyes were getting misty, the road moved up and down trying to evade my dragging feet – MacDougall, who was next to me, shouted, 'Stick it, Joe, the Signals never fall out!' It required a big effort to keep myself from falling but I kept up until we halted in the grounds of an enormous chateau. Then we lay down full length for a few minutes until we had recovered sufficient strength to climb to our billet in some of the rooms at the top of the building. Our entrance is at the back and we ascend by a wide staircase that would do credit to a public building in London. This is just the servants' quarters; what the remainder of the house is like passes imagination.

Once our oppressive equipment was removed we began to recover and our thoughts turned to food. The cooks couldn't get anything ready for an hour and we were empty. We had marched twenty-two miles, heavily equipped, over a range of hills that would be looked on as mountains in England and our rations for the last twenty-four hours had consisted of one small plate of porridge, a piece of cheese, a third of a tin of bully and a few bits of biscuit. So with shaking knees and our belts pulled tight, Hamilton, Aitken, Rogers and I went into the village to look for grub. We went all over it but couldn't get even a piece of bread. We had nearly given up in despair when we noticed a door beneath an archway. Through the crack shone a light, so we opened it and walked into a large room containing several tables, a counter and an enormous fireplace. The latter was situated on a raised platform at one end of the room and was by far the biggest fireplace I have ever seen. On the platform immediately in front of the huge fire were two or three small tables at which were sitting the ancient worthies of the village sipping vino buono and talking, probably about us. Women were serving wine and preparing a meal but it was several minutes before anybody took any notice of us.

Then an Italian officer who was sitting at one of the tables by the fire came and spoke to us in French. We told him that we wanted food and drink and didn't care what it was or how much it cost. He spoke to one of the women who then came over to us and by various gesticulations and a few stock words we managed to convey to her that we were starving. She nodded, looked affable, went away, and appeared to forget us. We discussed whether we should stop. Things did not look very promising. Probably our hunger made the time seem longer than it was. Food was being dished up and taken into another room but none came our way. A huge cake of polenta, steaming hot and covered with a thin white cloth, was brought from somewhere or other and placed on the counter. We decided to have a lump of that even if we had to take it but just as we were beginning to feel really desperate the woman came and laid a cloth for us. Then followed a bottle of wine and presently she brought plates and knives and forks. Our spirits rose but gradually descended as nothing further appeared. Hungry men are apt to be impatient. But there was some mysterious cooking going on at a little fire in a corner, and presently, to the joy of our hearts, came along some warmed-up chicken and several chunks of polenta. Did we enjoy it? Well, I think this will stand out as one of the very finest meals that I have ever had. Apart from the fact that it was food and that we were hungry, it will be memorable for it was so extraordinary to find something other than polenta and coarse sausages.

Distance marched today = 22 miles. Total = 100 miles.

25.11.17
It was no easy task to get up when we were roused at 5 a.m. Another long march was in front of us but fortunately without hills. It was

still dark when we had our breakfast of porridge and biscuits and bully. We ought to have had bacon but during the night some thieving Italians had stolen it. They had cut all the meat off and left us the bones. We presume the thieves were some Italian soldiers who were hanging round when we arrived last night. Eight o'clock saw us on the road again but we were not carrying our overcoats. Naturally we felt the fatigue of yesterday – but it is remarkable how a few hours' rest will restore one's energies. Nevertheless we began to tire early in the day, the kms were long and the hourly halts seemed far apart and to add to our troubles most of us were suffering from diarrhoea. But we kept our spirits up, singing and talking and reminding each other that while we were marching we were not fighting; and this thought is certainly a consolation particularly in a strange land with an enemy we know nothing about except that he has chased our Allies in one of the biggest drives of the war. The number of little cemeteries that we have passed today has been noticeable. They are really the equivalent of our churchyards but they never adjoin the church. Usually they are some little distance from the village and are all of the same pattern, rectangular in shape and enclosed by a high wall. Cypress trees, generally four, stand at the gateway, mute sentinels to keep the ghosts from straying. Iron crucifixes of varying size and ornamentation take the place of our headstones, ranging from small ones about eighteen inches high to tall ones that overtopped the wall.

Distance marched today = 17½ miles. Total = 117½ [miles].

26.11.17

The Signal Office is in a small cellar adjoining our billet and as there was nothing to do except to keep awake, Enticknap and I divided the duty, each spending the other half in his blankets. I worked the shift from 10 p.m. to 3 a.m. and spent the time in writing to Elsie. Sent the letter in a green envelope accompanied by the piece of maidenhair fern I plucked at Nice. We have got hold of some English papers; they are a fortnight old, but we have heard

that there has been a British advance at St Quentin. No details have
come to hand but of course we hope it is something good. At 3
a.m. 'Enty' relieved me and I curled myself up and slept like a log.
Breakfast was delayed until 9 o/c in order to give us a little extra
rest but no one was ready to get up even then. Dickson fetched my
breakfast for me, as, having been on night duty, I was privileged to
remain in 'Kip' as long as I liked. Later I rose, tended my blistered
feet, and went out to survey the neighbourhood. Campo San
Martino is a tiny village hanging on the skirts of a great mansion
which is the summer home of Count Breda, the Italian Railway
Engineer. It is a wonderful building but we are allowed only in the
commodious cellars. The grounds are large with big glass houses
running up one side encasing lemon trees bearing ripening fruit.
The fronts of these houses are all doors which are opened during the
daytime and closed at night. There is ample first-class stabling and
plenty of accommodation for coachmen and their families. Some of
the trusted vassals are still in residence but of course Mr and Mrs
Breda are many miles away.

In one of the cellars are several tons of coal, a very unusual sight
in this country; and in the largest cellar, where most of the men are
sleeping, is a huge boiler for supplying hot water to the baths. The
Staff Officers wanted to indulge this morning so Sgt Oxley tackled
the boiler with the result that the billet got half flooded before he
had satisfied himself as to how it worked.

28.11.17

Left Campo San Martino after an early breakfast. The rest has done
us good but hasn't healed our blistered feet. In passing through
Campo Sampiero (which looks a quaint and interesting place) we
met with a reception less frigid than we have hitherto experienced.
In the town, market day was in full swing and some of the walls
were covered with huge placards inscribed similarly to those we saw
at Lonigo. Bunting and flags of various nations fluttered from the
windows and across the narrow streets while the marketing populace
stood and gazed and gabbled with amazement, occasionally raising

their hats and bowing to us. Innumerable turkeys, geese and ducks were being bought and sold, all of them tied by a string round their legs, with a small child at the other end of the string dragging the poor birds hither and thither. Many of the birds are brought into the market tied by the legs in a bundle, and hanging head downwards over the handlebars of 'comic' bicycles. They look more resigned than happy. A small pig with the ubiquitous string round its leg escaped from its owner, got in amongst our legs and caused great amusement. Immediately a crowd of excited natives started a chase and the pig gave them a good run for their money; in fact the chase was still in progress when we passed out of the town. I wish we had halted there for the night – it would have been more enjoyable than this dreary little village (St Andrea). Passed a street organ standing derelict in a field. This is the first we have seen as their public use is forbidden for the duration.

Distance marched today = 16½ miles. Total = 134 [miles].

29.11.17

Today's journey being reasonably short, we were not roused inordinately early but were on the move before 9 a.m., heading straight for the line. Passed the aerodrome at Fossalunga where the first contingent of our Air Force has just arrived. About noon we saw the first sign of actual warfare – an Italian heavy gun mounted in a meadow on the plain and firing over the hills. Every time it fired, the native women dashed about in a frenzy, shrieking and waving their arms as if they had gone mad. Soon afterwards the road gradually deteriorated until it was only a cart track across fields and it seemed that we had gone astray. So when we came to a point where the track branched off in two different directions, Lieut. Tamblin halted us and sent the MMPs [Mounted Military Police] forward to reconnoitre with the result that we ultimately reached Musano early in the afternoon without having gone very far out of our way. The closest study of these execrable maps will not reveal the actual route we have traversed. We are billeted in the hospital with a few Italian soldiers. One of them has been teaching

MacKay to count up to twenty in Italian. Managed to get three eggs which I boiled hard and ate in the hope that they will put a stop to this abominable diarrhoea. There seems to be a shortage of drinking water in this village, a state of things which we have not encountered anywhere else in this country. There is plenty of wine but it is almost impossible to get a bottle of water. I tried several of the peasants and at last found one who had a large glass wine jar full of water. He filled my bottle so I am all right for tomorrow. There is a large wooden crucifix about ten feet high and on it are carved all the emblems and tokens of the Crucifixion from the cock that startled St Peter to the spears and the sponge of vinegar. I am glad the journey has been fairly short today for I have felt far from well and could not take much interest in the incidents of the march.

Distance marched today = 8 miles. Total = 142 [miles].

30.11.17

Aitken, Mennie and MacDougall went forward by lorry this morning as an advance party to commence taking over from the First Division of the Italian army in the line. We followed later in the day, our start being delayed so that the final stages should be taken under cover of darkness owing to the superiority of the enemy aircraft. The mountains seem to be getting mighty close although actually they are some twenty miles away. The march was slow as the roads were very narrow and congested with traffic. In passing some of our big motor lorries, the limber went into the ditch. The mules steadfastly refused to pull it out. Cajolings, threatening, thrashings, all were of no avail so we unharnessed them and half a dozen of us pulled the limber out easily despite being hampered by our equipment. And these are the same mules that pulled over the Monti Berico like Trojans! We were halted in one of the narrow roads when darkness overtook us and we were forbidden to smoke or strike matches. At a crossroads nearby, our valiant APM [Assistant Provost Marshal], cavorting on his charger, was going blue, black and purple with the violence of his efforts to direct the traffic. Soon it became evident that the road we were in was impassable for transport so I was told off to accompany the wagons by another route. Turning round in a field, we journeyed back and finally linked up with Brigade HQ in Selva. Our billet is in some farm buildings on the outskirts of the village but the moonlight is not sufficient for us to see much.

Distance marched today = 6 miles. Total = 148 [miles].

1.12.17

The night passed off quietly and although we are supposed to be quite close to the line we heard no sound of gunfire. Each of us managed to get about four hours' sleep, and after breakfast, as further slumber was out of the question, we made a tour of inspection of the village and neighbourhood. On the north, the Montello Hills rise very abruptly from the plain. A road and a small river run side by side along the base of the hills and directly you leave the road and cross the river you start a hard climb. These hills form a rather curious geographical feature. In some measure foothills to the main Alps, they are nevertheless an isolated kidney-shaped bump rising 368 metres (about 1200 feet), with the formidable Piave bounding them on the north and east. From a military point of view they are of great importance, commanding the whole of the level ground for many miles to the south. The stream that runs round this side of the hills is an offshoot from the Piave, breaking away from the main river at a point north-west of the hills and rejoining it on the south-east. Thus the whole range is virtually an island, and is crossed by twenty roads running north and south and known by numbers, no. 1 being the most easterly and no. 20 the most westerly. Along the top of the range runs a connecting road from east to west. The village itself is a dreary looking place crowded out with refugees from the east of the Piave, and there is nothing to buy, not even polenta. After an early tea we started off on the final stretch of our historic march. The distance was about two miles, but what miles! In addition to our ordinary equipment we had to carry overcoats and blankets. The roads were rough and steep and by no means gradual. Frequently we dipped down into little valleys or basins, only to have a stiffer climb out of them. After going for half an hour we had to fall out for fifteen minutes' rest. The Italians, I believe, only march fifteen minutes at a stretch in this sort of country. We eventually reached the summit of Road 8 and found Aitken and Co. waiting for us at a little deserted cottage. I was very tired, so, thanking God that all the marching is over for a bit, I quickly rolled myself up in my blankets and went to sleep.

Distance marched today = 2 miles. Total = 150 [miles].

2.12.17

It is hard to believe that we are really in the line for all last night we were not disturbed by a single shell, and in looking round about the billet in all directions it is difficult to discover any signs of war, that is, the sort of signs we have been used to. I feel very weak and tired and hungry. What wouldn't I give for a piece of bread in place of these eternal biscuits that I have to crush into powder with my pliers before I can eat them. I take the jam (when we get any), chop the margarine into small pieces and mix the lot up together and eat with a spoon. It takes about half an hour to crush up sufficient biscuit for one meal.

3.12.17

An Italian Labour Company is working in our vicinity making trenches and barbed wire entanglements, and they are making them well. It is amusing to see how they scuttle for shelter at the slightest alarm. We cannot help laughing as, compared with Ypres and the Somme, this is like being back at rest.

4.12.17

A visual post has been established a few hundred yards away and all of us who were not on duty have been over there to build a sandbag hut for the operators. Killed a snake about two feet long. I believe it is the sort known as the Italian grass snake and therefore not poisonous. The sun was going down before our task was completed, and looking towards the mountains we saw their snow-covered sides glowing in a deep rose hue. It was wonderful and almost unbelievable. We ceased our work to look at it but it only lasted a few minutes. Gradually the depth of colour grew paler and finally faded away, leaving the mountains cold and grim.

6.12.17
I was wise to lay in such a stock of tobacco before we left France. None has been issued to us since we left the train and none can be bought. Many of the fellows are smoking dried oak leaves. I am getting near the end of my store but there is still one quarter-pound tin in my valise at the Transport. I must get hold of that within the next day or so. Tobacco is more necessary than ever now that the pangs of hunger never get thoroughly appeased. We could eat at least half as much again as we get and then not be overfed. What we really crave for is bread; biscuits, even if we had them in abundance, cannot replace it. We feel perpetually empty.

8.12.17
Divisional Baths have been established at Selva so this afternoon Jamieson, Dickson and I went down and had our first bath for five weeks. The sun was hot and we sought the shady side of the road only to find it bitterly cold. In the village streets the snow has been churned into thin mud about two inches deep in which the native women splash about in bare feet. Saw an icicle almost as big and round as my body.

10.12.17
The Divisional Canteen has opened in Selva. McCormack and I went down to try and get some tobacco and anything in the eating line, but it was hopeless. After waiting 1½ hours in a queue the doors were shut – 'sold out'. MacDonald has scoured the country round on his motorcycle in an endeavour to buy food but only managed to get a small slice of polenta of which I had a share. The rations are so short that the cooks have to be most careful in issuing them – as long as every man gets the same there can be no complaint. Biscuits,

margarine, cheese and jam are supplied in bulk to each room of ten or twelve men and they have to divide it among themselves. Paterson and I are the ration drawers for our room and the dividing up has to be done with the most scrupulous accuracy. The men bring in their plates; we place them in a row on the floor and then carefully give each plate its share. Before allowing any plate to be removed we demand to know if any one has any objection; thus we avoid the possibility of any subsequent criticism or complaint. It is remarkable to observe how civilisation has produced qualities in men that are not possessed by other animals, notably forbearance and self-control. Our hunger is the hunger of wolves – it glistens from our eyes when we see any kind of food – the natural impulse is to snatch – we feel the pure animal rising in our breasts, but there is never the slightest suggestion of taking more than one's proper share. This, of course, is affected by the fact that we do get a certain amount of food each day and that tomorrow's rations are reasonably certain not to be worse than today's, but possibly better. We cannot say that we are suffering actual starvation but most assuredly we know the pangs of continual hunger. For breakfast we get a plate of porridge or a slice of bacon, for dinner, bully stew but no potatoes and once or twice we have had boiled rice. For tea a 1lb tin of jam or ¼ lb cheese has to suffice for twelve men and this is where the 'doling out' has to be so exact.

14.12.17

Another big mail! Eight letters for me! But how am I going to answer them? None of us has been able to do much letter writing because of the extreme shortage of envelopes. I have managed to borrow four from MacDonald and have written two letters. The mail didn't bring many parcels. We have never before been in such urgent need of them and of course they don't arrive although we know that plenty have been despatched. For three whole weeks we had only two bread rations and they were Italian bread. Our own bakeries have now been established and we are getting a small ration of English bread for which we are devoutly thankful.

This climate is most bracing and invigorating and accordingly accentuates our hunger. The weather is beautiful and the view across the plain is marvellous. In the far distance we can see some tall towers and we like to think they are in Venice thirty miles away but I am more inclined to think they belong to Treviso. Looking over the plain with houses and villages and churches scattered over it as if shaken from a mighty pepper-box, we can picture humanity as midges toiling and moiling, striving and struggling – and all to what purpose? – while the mighty mountains before us, immovable and eternal, look down coldly and cynically, totally unaffected and unruffled by the petty struggles of the human beings on the plains.

15.12.17

We have been in the line a fortnight and tomorrow we are to be relieved. It seems a farce to talk about relief in warfare of this sort. There is a fair amount of aerial activity – the climate is conducive to it – but otherwise we seldom hear more than a dozen shells in the course of a day. We laugh and call it 'comic warfare'. On only one occasion have we had a touch of the real thing and that was a few days ago when the Austrians tried to get across the Piave both on our right and on our left, but they got thrown back so decisively that we don't think they will attempt any further attack for some time. They met French and British troops far different from the demoralised, disorganised and mutinous army that they had chased 125 miles from Caporetto. The bombardment began early in the morning and we were on the alert nearly all day. Directly after dinner, Glasspoole and I were sent to a vantage point from which we could look down on to our front line on the banks of the Piave. Our duty was to watch for the SOS signal which would go up if the enemy attempted to cross on our front. There was no shelter from the enemy's observation so we stood amongst thick undergrowth and kept still in the hope that we should look like tree trunks or oak saplings. Nothing happened for nearly two hours although we could hear the firing on both sides. Then suddenly a couple of shells burst just in front of us and made us look round hurriedly for any little bit of shelter, but we heard a voice in the distance calling my name, and looking towards the Wireless Station behind us we saw a man semaphore the 'CI' (i.e. 'come in'). We didn't wait for any more shells but hurried back to the Signal Office where we learnt that the attack had been vigorously repulsed. Another outstanding event which I have omitted to record under its proper date is the swimming raid across the river. We had only been in the line a few days when an officer and few men belonging to the Cyclist Corps one night swam across the swift, dangerous and icy cold Piave and penetrated 1000 yards into the enemy's lines, bringing back very useful information. It was a very courageous enterprise and only powerful swimmers could attempt it. It deserves recognition.

16.12.17

Returned to Selva for seven days in reserve. We are billeted in some large buildings attached to a fairly large house at the east end of the village. What the buildings are used for is more than I can tell. The entrance is like that of an old posting inn in England. We enter a door on the left of the archway and ascend a broad flight of stairs leading up to a very large chamber. I should think it is quite sixty feet long and thirty feet wide, with two archways on one side leading to another chamber about ten or twelve feet wide running the whole length of the large room. This smaller chamber contains straw and will be our sleeping quarters. A much smaller room near the top of the stairs is the Signal Office. It looks as if we shall be quite comfortable. Sent off four letters that I wrote yesterday.

17.12.17

Carrying out a tour of investigation, Fisher and I passed through a door that took us into the house proper. We found ourselves in a bedroom that had not been entirely denuded of its furniture. The people had evidently left in a hurry and had only taken the easily portable articles. In a chest of drawers we found a big pile of picture postcards of various parts of Italy, Austria and Switzerland. We shared them between us.

21.12.17

Much excitement all day long. All the men not on duty have
been engaged in preparing and decorating the large room for our
Christmas dinner. Some of them were out all the morning up on
the hills getting holly, mistletoe and other foliage. Holly is very
scarce but they managed to get a little. Tables and benches were
obtained from somewhere and a stage, with draw curtains, erected
at the far end. Oxley and McCormack brought back a good supply
of turkeys, beef, pork, cabbages, potatoes, carrots, tinned fruit,
biscuits, custard powder, tinned milk, beer, wine and syrupo, the
latter being a descriptively named beverage indulged in by Italian
teetotallers either for drinking or for quenching their thirst, I don't
know which, but it is not much good for either. Also they brought
nuts, oranges and apples. So we did well in the feeding line, and we
deserved it for it was the first decent meal that we had had since we
left France. We subscribed twelve lire (i.e. 6/-) per head but I think
there is a surplus which will be refunded in some way or another.
After the dinner came the concert. The interest centred in a sketch
– a mere eight-minute skit on the Office particularly caricaturing
Capt. Ainger (Staff Captain) and Mr Purvis (Signal Officer) and not
omitting some of the NCOs. and men. I was the author, producer,
stage manager, musical director and everything else all rolled into
one. And it was a great success. All the Staff Officers came in to
see it and they thoroughly enjoyed seeing two of their number
parodied – indeed, Capt. Reah laughed till the tears ran down his
cheeks. It was only three days ago that some of the men came to me
with the request that I should write a sketch – so it has been pretty
quick work. I have had to devote all my time to it. If I had had
longer no doubt I could have improved it considerably, for there
is plenty of material on which to exercise the gentle art of 'taking
off'. But as it was, everybody was thoroughly amused and therefore
I was quite satisfied. I must add that there was not the least display
of jealousy or ill feeling among the men. Each man did the part
allotted to him no matter how trivial or insignificant, and did it
with great zeal and interest. They realised that it was impossible

for all of them to be in the limelight; therefore they worked hand in hand for the common end.

25.12.17 Christmas Day

Today has been beautiful and very quiet. Our guns have fired a few rounds but the Italians and the Austrians have religiously abstained from any act of warfare. We live on rumours. The papers that we get are at least a fortnight old and it is extraordinary what remarkable rumours obtain currency.

Today they are strong on peace proposals from Germany. Hope springs eternal in the human breast and it is remarkable to observe how men clutch almost convulsively at the most improbable rumours if they point in the direction of their hopes and desires. But I place no faith in the lying jade. I cannot see the end of the war for another eighteen months and so I am labelled a pessimist. In reply I tell them that an optimist is a man who doesn't know what is in front of him.

26.12.17

Up this morning and on duty at 8 a.m. I had only just taken over when looking out of the window towards the line I saw an aeroplane come over. It was immediately followed by another and another and another until in less than one minute I had counted seventeen. They were flying so low, barely skirting the crest of the hills, that at first we naturally took them to be some of our own machines returning from a raid. But we soon saw the Iron Cross on their wings and suddenly all was excitement. Not a shot was fired at them because we had not had a second's warning of their approach and it was impossible to train the machine guns on them before they had passed out of reach. They went over us not more than 200 feet up without dropping a bomb or firing a shot and scattered in all directions over the plain. For two hours or more we had a marvellous view of the most audacious air raid that I have ever heard of. From our position above the plain we could look down, not only on the country that was being bombed but also on the aeroplanes. Rifles and machine guns were firing briskly. Anti-aircraft guns could not get properly into action at such short range but they had a 'pot' at every opportunity. Bombs were dropping all over the place but without doing any serious damage as far as we could see; and every now and then one of the planes would burst into flames and crash to earth. Four or five within easy reach of unaided vision were entirely destroyed and two or three others were forced to land. Later in the day we learned that thirty-three machines had been engaged in the raid, twenty-seven Austrian bombers being escorted by six German fighters. Our 'bag' amounted to eleven machines, some of which were practically intact. A few pilots and observers were taken alive. It appears that the officers of the Austrian Air Force kept Xmas with a merry carousal lasting right through the night; and when, early this morning, orders to carry out the raid were received they were all pretty well drunk. This accounts for their recklessness. The main objectives were Corps HQ at Padova and the aerodrome at Forsalunga.

31.12.17

This morning I was ordered to relieve the Visual Station. Jamieson, who was already there, was to remain and I took Glasspoole and Cochran with me. We followed a cross-country track which will hardly be safe at night but which is much shorter than going by the road. Found Jamieson not at all well and presently he decided to 'go sick'. So I rang up Sgt Twycross and he sent McCormack to replace him. And now having arranged all the duties satisfactorily, we are settling down to make ourselves as comfortable as possible. Thus ends the year of grace 1917, a year of frightful agony and slaughter, of shattered hopes and broken lives; a year when humanity has sunk to incredible depths of inhumanity; a year that has brought tears to the eyes of the Recording Angel. But here are we, with our lot fallen in comparatively pleasant places, looking forward with an unquenchable hope to the New Year. Our souls have been scorched and seared by contact with Hell and we yearn for the healing oil of Peace.

1918

1.1.18

Last night being Hogmanay, it was Andy's solemn duty to wake us just before midnight and regale us with tea and cake (jealously saved from a parcel for this occasion). Then after singing 'Auld Lang Syne' and shaking hands all round, we were permitted to resume our slumbers.

Our abode is on the west side of Road 4, not far from an Italian searchlight which at night illuminates the opposite bank of the Piave. Searchlights (up to forty-eight inches) are quite a feature on this front, both sides using them for keeping a watch on the river banks. Two, one Austrian and one Italian, are permanently trained on the broken bridge that crosses the river south-east of Nervesa. The funny thing about it is that there is no attempt on either part to knock them out!

The building we are in is a cattle shed capable of stalling two oxen. It is situated on a spur which makes it an excellent point of vantage and provides us with wide views in all directions. Inside, the shed is about ten feet square and nine feet high. The door is on the south side and the manger on the north. Our predecessors scrounged a couple of windows from somewhere or other and have fitted them so that operations can be carried on to both stations (Battalion in the front and Division in the rear at Selva) without going outside. The lamp and telescope to the battalion have been fixed permanently so that they are always ready for operation, no adjustment being necessary, unless we fall up against them and knock them over.

McCormack woke us at quarter to eight this morning. He had prepared the breakfast and it was all ready served up, so we had it in bed. Then Glasspoole and I, acting on the directions received from our predecessors, set out to get the water and wood supply for the day. Taking petrol cans, we followed a path that led us into a rough gully which eventually opened out into a wide space containing a small lake covered thick with ice. We soon found the hole where the others had drawn their water. This had ½ an inch of ice over it which we broke with our heels, revealing the full thickness of the ice to be several inches.

Having landed the water safely at the billet, we took some straps and proceeded to fetch firewood. Going across country we passed over Road 5 and through a wood into a large vineyard where hundreds of vines are growing between poles set in long straight lines. A comparatively large and apparently modern house stood on the top of the ridge overlooking the vineyard but this didn't claim much of our attention as it was the 'vino' poles that we were after. We uprooted several dozen, disentangling them from the vines and the connecting wires, and bound them with our straps into two bundles, as much as we could carry on our backs across this country. These poles are from eight to ten feet long, bone dry, and just the things for a nice bright fire.

4.1.18

Glasspoole and I continue to work harmoniously but McCormack doesn't find a kindred spirit in Cochran so they carry out their duties separately. I am not surprised at it, for personally I get very annoyed with Cochran. There is nothing to get 'windy' about up here. Anti-aircraft duds and shrapnel are all we have to worry about and there is not much of either. This morning I had to order Cochran to go and fetch the water and firewood – he was afraid to go by himself. To this extent I am sorry for him but I cannot stand his boasting. To hear him talk when he is back in safety one would think he had won the war single-handed.

5.1.18

Busy digging a rubbish pit. It was hard work for the ground was frozen solid several inches deep. Glasspoole is a fine fellow to have a 'stint' like this. Being a signaller of greater efficiency than most, he fell under the eye of Mr Buchanan and so became attached to Brigade. He is a big fellow and, like Davey, he finds a vent for his emotions in song. At least that is what he calls it. I give it another name and have told him so frequently but remonstrance, ridicule and threatening have not the slightest effect on him. Still, when there are only four men together somebody must supply some sort of mirth or liveliness and if one man gets annoyed with another, the others get a laugh at both. But I am not saying hard things about him today as he has proved his worth in a particular direction. Not only does he know his work thoroughly but he is a handy man at all sorts of odd jobs, and what is the greatest of all is that he is a cook – not by profession but by way of a hobby!

Today he has made an excellent marmalade pudding with nothing else but grated army biscuits and a little marmalade. The grater was evolved out of a tin lid with the assistance of a nail and an entrenching tool used as a hammer. The grating took a long time so I fetched the water and wood myself. When I got back, the marmalade pudding was well under way. We thoroughly enjoyed it and were Oliver Twists, but there was no second helping!

6.1.18

Another marmalade pudding today! About noon an enemy aeroplane passed so close to us that we could easily have hit it with a stone, but this low-flying business catches us entirely unawares and before we can move, the plane is out of sight. This one went off in the direction of Brigade HQ. There has been a good deal of shelling today at the foot of the hills and on the adjoining plain. We saw scores of high explosives drop in a small field on the plain. Fritz seemed to be after something and his ranging was very accurate for the shells fell in groups in each corner of the field. Towards evening he sent over gas shells to the crossroads but they were slightly wide of the mark and fell in an adjoining field. Yet the shooting was remarkable in that the shells dropped in the form of a cross, and owing to the entire absence of wind, a cross of gas rested in that field for at least twenty minutes after the shelling had ceased.

Lights of any sort are increasingly difficult to obtain and now the supply of Italian candles has given out. At Brigade the men were using home-made oil lamps – cigarette tins with a piece of 'four-by-two' (flannel) pushed through a hole in the lid. By straining the eyes one could just manage to write down a message. We are fortunate up here for Elsie has sent me a supply of good wax candles but we use them very sparingly, relying on the firelight for all purposes except the passage of messages. Therefore, being unable to write or read after nightfall, we have to pass the time in talk and song. One evening I gave a learned disquisition on the evolution of the art of music. Another evening I discoursed on the great composers, holding the interest with a good spice of anecdote. Again I gave them the story of the heaven, taking them out into the bright clear night and pointing out the principal stars and constellations. McCormack, who is a sugar boiler by trade (i.e. a maker of sweets), showed us, by the aid of different coloured clays, how the letters get into that type of sweetmeat called 'rock' which is such a favourite at seaside places and other holiday resorts. Also he showed us how to make the black and white striped 'Bullseyes'. So we live and learn.

7.1.18

Woke this morning to find McCormack looking more miserable than usual after his spell of night duty. He invited me to look outdoors and I was amazed to see the whole landscape covered thick with snow, two feet in depth. When we turned in last night the sky was cloudless and now again it is clear as ever. The whole of this snow fell in about two hours. I took a pick axe with me when I went to get the water, for when I found the pond under its covering of snow I had to break through at least two inches of ice that had formed over the hole since yesterday morning. The dazzling sunlight on the vast expanse of snow is very trying to the eyes. We have no means of measuring the temperature but the cold is intense. In baling the water out of the pond the drops remaining in the mug or clinging to the sides are frozen solid in a few seconds. Yet it does not seem as cold as all that because of the clearness and stillness of the atmosphere – we never get cold with the bitter piercing coldness of a British north-easter which no amount of clothing will stop from penetrating to your bones even though it 'makes hard Englishmen'.

9.1.18

We never tire of looking at the great mountains which, although they undergo all manner of apparent changes owing to conditions of visibility, direction of the light falling upon them etc, remain always the same, silent, unvarying, the symbol of omnipotence and of the everlasting. They seem to look down on the plains and on the puny ways of men with a dignified superiority much as a philosopher might watch the sport of kittens. And you wonder what mighty secrets these mountains may hold, what memories going back for millions of years – and you feel very small beside them. Sometimes they will frown and make you shudder and feel afraid as if you were in the presence of the supernatural. At other times they will smile and show you wonderful sights, marvellous effects of sunshine and shade and clouds.

Often I have seen photographs taken above the clouds but today I have seen the real thing. I place it as one of the most wonderful experiences of my life. The sun was getting low in the heavens and we were preparing our tea when I looked out of the door towards the plain and it was all covered with a great white cloud which reached up to within a hundred yards of so of us. The huge white mass was almost still – it moved bodily but with extreme slowness this way and that, and here and there were great billows and waves and breakers suspended in their motion like a mighty sea suddenly frozen. And away on the left rising above the common level was a great mound, white and smooth, and shaped like a woman's breast. Slowly the cloud moved up the hill towards us and then as slowly receded, revealing every now and then the cross on the top of the church tower below us. Although the sun was sinking it was still just above the cloud and touched it here and there with wonderful tints of rose and rosy-gold. It is these marvellous light effects that are so amazing and so difficult to describe. Even painting or colour-photography are little more able to convey an adequate impression than the written word. They saw nothing of this at Brigade HQ, for being at a lower level they were enveloped in the mist. Soon after sundown the cloud disappeared as suddenly as it came. Nature is a quick-change artist in this country and no mistake.

I am now on night duty. Sitting by the firelight has grown oppressive so I have lit a precious candle to enable me to pass the time in writing. I have been outside the billet and the silence is the sort that can be felt. People who live under modern conditions of civilisation can scarcely comprehend the meaning of absolute silence. And the silence of the trenches among the mountains is uncanny and almost palpable.

Outside the billet I looked towards the line and listened for any sounds of war of contending armies; but the absolute quiet was not broken even by a 'beetle's droning flight'. There is not the least sign of life or activity and the winking stars look down like cynical eyes of cruel gods ready to laugh at human suffering and misery. Yet you know well enough that away in front, men are ceaselessly watching, ready to give the alarm at the first sign of animation on the enemy's lines; and there are rifles and machines guns and trench mortars and field guns and howitzers of all kinds and sizes ready to break forth into a clamorous roaring and screeching at any moment. And there may be added the drone of aeroplanes and the rushing of wagons and motor lorries and the rattle and banging of railway trains and many other incidental noises. You know that all this noise is possible and the Silence makes you shudder. It feels uncanny. It oppresses you. You whistle for the sake of company but your own whistle makes you start and the Silence following the momentary break seems stranger and more awesome than before. So you creep back into your billet with cold shivering down your spine and a dull nervousness in your heart – And there you have a light and you see your comrades asleep, and hear their snorings and inarticulate grunting and you feel like being at home once more. Your spine becomes warm and erect – your heart steady and brave, and you say 'Bah! I wasn't afraid; I was only interested.'

12.1.18
The warm sun has thawed most of the snow, and the roads, which are now subjected to much heavier traffic than in normal times, are covered with a layer of watery mud about two inches deep. Through this ice-cold mud the women trudge barefoot while the men wear strong, substantial boots. At every step the women's feet are almost covered with the mud which squelches up between their toes. I used to think that a fishmonger's job in the winter was about as cold as one could get but it is beaten by these same women who make a hole in the ice and kneel down for hours at a time doing their washing.

13.1.18
Owing to the intense cold we have been issued with a third blanket and plenty of straw. Saw the burial of a British soldier this morning in a field opposite the Signal Office.

16.1.18
Marched from Selva to Altivole – about twelve miles. Going out for a rest strikes us as something of a joke but we take everything as it comes. We reached our quarters for the night by 4 o/c and were soon comfortably housed in a large store or granary belonging to the big house of the village. It is a clean, quiet little place and so far as I have been able to observe contains nothing of outstanding interest. We are not allowed to go into the precincts of the chateau itself as the civilians are still in occupation.

18.1.18
Our billet is a farm, of a sort. The house is a plain rectangular building with a central doorway opening into a large, bare,

stone-flagged hall or chamber that runs through to the back of the house. On the right-hand side are the farmer's living apartments. On the left is a big store room in which over thirty of us have our quarters. We have procured plenty of straw and we sleep with our heads to the wall and our feet to the middle of the room which is big enough to allow of a large table in the centre with space sufficient to walk all round it without treading on other people's feet. The rest of the men are in a loft above us. The Signal and Brigade Officers are in a small chateau about 100 yards away – just a convenient distance.

The village is lit by electricity transmitted from somewhere up in the mountains, but it is liable to disruption every now and again when Fritz gets slightly energetic. Accustomed to the English view that electricity is something of a luxury only to be indulged in by large towns and cities, we cannot quite get over our surprise at finding little townlets and villages with electric light in the streets and in many of the houses. Incidentally, we haven't seen gas anywhere. From what I can learn by observation and enquiry there are big generating stations up in the mountains which supply current to all the towns, villages and chateaux over wide areas on the plains. These stations derive their motive power from the water pouring down the mountain sides and can produce current at considerably less cost than we can in England where we have to use such expensive things as steam – or oil – engines. But what is a matter of considerable wonder to me is how the Italians managed to scrape up sufficient energy to build these big power stations and lay the enormous network of mains.

23.1.18

We have been getting eggs from some of the farms round about but now young women and children have commenced coming into the billet each afternoon with baskets of eggs for sale. It is nothing for the cooks to have twenty or thirty eggs to boil for us every afternoon. I have been in two or three of the village homes and I certainly should not care to spend all my days in them – they are so cheerless and comfortless. The people don't seem to know what an easy chair

is, to say nothing of a sofa. They are satisfied to muddle through
life – to take their meals standing up or sitting on the floor or on a
chair or stool in any odd corner. For the whole family to sit down at
a table and have a meal together is seldom thought of. Perhaps this
is because it would take such a big table to accommodate a whole
family, for however lazy the men may be in everything connected
with work they are pretty industrious in propagating their species.
Some of the houses hold two or three families and if you were to see
all the youngsters playing about outside you would think that some
benevolent society or other was having a 'treat'.

25.1.18
Perfect weather – bright and warm with blue sky and crisp clear
air. It is a spring morning. In England blackbirds and thrushes
would be singing almost to the bursting of their hearts, but here
there is only the occasional chirruping of a few sparrows. The great
mountains which have been dull and glowering in the mist and haze
of the past few days now stand out sharp and clear and seem to have
advanced ten or twenty miles nearer to us. The radiance of morning
and the brilliance of noon have passed into the golden faintly rosy
hues of evening. The sun has gone down and the western sky is
beautiful. It is still too bright for Venus to show herself, but in the
east the moon, nearing the full, has risen and is shining palely. The
mountains with their snowy peaks and sides are tinged with purple
and ruddy-brown and dark, dark green. An evening when emotions
stir in the heart and the thoughtful soul seeks solitude and the
communion of Unseen Things.

26.1.18
Yesterday afternoon we marched three miles to Riese to get a
bath. The baths are in two marquees with canvas floors which are
slippery with soapy water and mud. As I was leaving the bathroom
I slipped over and plastered myself with mud. Had to go back and
have another – amused everybody except myself. Got a complete
change of new underclothing. Today I have sent my fourth Epistle

to Elsie in the last of the green envelopes that I brought from France. No issue has been made since we have been in this country. Two bees flew into the billet and I really believe the Italian spring has commenced as today has been as glorious as yesterday.

31.1.18

On our march from Selva and in our wanderings around Ramon we have continually come across this sign WPioX. It is painted or chiselled on the sides of houses, on wayside shrines and on all sorts of buildings and bits of walls, and on such places as churches and campaniles it is deeply cut on granite slabs. Sometimes the W stands alone without the following lettering and our best surmise is that the W is two letter Vs crossed over each other, that they stand for Viva, and that the whole inscription means 'Long live Pope Pius the Tenth'. But we are left wondering why in this district there is so much loyalty to the Pope that is not apparent elsewhere.

5.2.18

Cheesman wanted me to get in touch with the 'Dickeybirds' (the Brigade Concert Party) because they are anxious to get some original 'gags', 'patter' and sketches. So after their performance this evening, he introduced me to Scotty Williams (the leading comedian) and some of the others. I promised to write a sketch of some sort.

8.2.18

This evening we heard unusual sounds of chanting and singing coming from the civilian portion of this building. It was sufficient to demand enquiry and we were surprised to find that the sounds emanated, not from the house, but from the cattle shed which joins it. The oxen were in there (a pretty smelly place at the best of times) and the village priest with candle and crucifix was conducting a service for the benefit of the families living in the house. Can't make out why the service was held in the shed unless the people wanted the warmth exuded by the cattle and didn't mind the smell, unless they had mixed up the calendar and thought it was Christmastide. I should have preferred the kitchen. I haven't often been in any of these cattle sheds and, when I have, I have always got out as quickly as possible.

9.2.18

This evening Glasspoole and I strolled down to Poggiana in the hope of buying some nuts or oranges. We discovered a man, his wife and nine children all living in one room that was little better than a shed and only about twelve feet square. We talked to the man who seemed greatly distressed. He told us they were refugees from the other side of the Piave and that their house had been blown up and utterly destroyed. They had only escaped with what they stood up in. Such are the glories of war. We bought up his entire stock of tangerines, felt sorry for him, wished him good luck and gave him a handful of tobacco – we could do nothing more.

11.2.18

Was enticed to play football this afternoon and managed to sprain my ankle. Glasspoole and Cheesman helped me back to the billet, and Davidson, ever solicitous for my welfare, procured some embrocation and gave me a little massage. Being a professional footballer, he knows how to treat sprains and bruises and he always acts as doctor when cases arise in the section. So, of course, I was glad to see him coming to help me, but there were some who smiled that peculiar 'wait-and-see' sort of smile which proclaims a better knowledge of forthcoming events. And this better knowledge was soon my own, for Davey is nothing if not thorough and he gave my ankle such a rubbing and a pressing and a squeezing that I thought I would as soon stick the evil as the cure. He continued it for several hours – at least it seemed like several hours – I kept telling him 'That will do now', and thanked him very sweetly but he took no notice. Then I said I feared I was tiring him but he only rubbed the harder just to show what a big store of reserve energy he possessed. When at last he had finished, he said, 'That will do for tonight but I will come and give it another rub in the morning.'

12.2.18

Visions of the return of Davey got me up early this morning and I put my boots and puttees on quickly; but there was no need for alarm as he didn't turn up till midday. Then he apologised for not keeping his word. I said, 'Oh, don't mensh! It's getting on all right now. I don't think it will require any more massage.' He departed and I breathed freely once more. But lo, when I was comfortably settled in my blankets for the night he turned up and 'put me through it' again.

14.2.18

If violent excitement is a sign of musical temperament then these Italians are highly musical. One would hardly credit the effect that a brass band has on them. They almost go mad. The playing of a mouth organ is sufficient to excite them so that they have to leave off whatever they happen to be doing and listen, while at the first strains of one of our battalion bands, they down tools and rush excitedly out into the road waving their arms at us and crying 'Musica, Musica! Buono buono!' and a lot more that we can't understand but which is to the same effect only more so. Of course it is not an Englishman's nature to go into such ecstatic raptures and I think the natives rather marvel at our apparent indifference. The Surreys' Guard at Brigade HQ blow the 'Retreat' every evening and this is sufficient to send the whole village to distraction. Men and women and children march up and down behind the buglers as if their very existence depended on so doing. At the Dickeybirds concerts all the children, half the women and some men crowd round the doors begging to be allowed to enter. If the hall is not filled with our own troops they come in. And then it is that the village priest is useful. He keeps them in order and even turns them out if necessary. They obey him implicitly and without a murmur of dissent. His authority is indisputable and his power absolute. There is a report, which I can quite believe, that during the great retreat from Caporetto a whole battalion refused to take the line. The Regimental Commander threatened, entreated and cajoled but all to no purpose. The Divisional Commander tried, with the same result, and so did the Corps Commander. Then at last someone fetched an obscure village priest. He talked quietly to the men for a little while and then they returned to the line without the slightest murmur.

15.2.18

Night-bombing aeroplanes have often come over but no bombs have been dropped nearer than Castelfranco, five miles away. Mount Grappa, which has already acquired fame in this war, is fifteen or twenty miles away but looks very much nearer. Without the aid of glasses we can frequently see shells bursting on its summit. One feature of this mountain has puzzled us considerably. Nearly every night we see what looks like a bright fire nearly at the summit and very often it has a tail which runs a slightly crooked course a quarter of the way down the side. The first conjecture was that it was a small volcano pouring out molten lava and certainly that is what it looks like, but so far as I am aware there is no volcanic activity in the Alps. The next assumption, that it is undergrowth on fire, cannot be accepted as it does not spread but continues night after night in exactly the same place. So we are content with letting it remain a mystery.

17.2.18

Up betimes and marched halfway to Volpago. Here we halted for a few hours at a spot which is to be our Transport Quarters. Had a talk with one of the Dickeybirds who are going to rehearse my sketch when we come out of the line. I learnt incidentally that I lost an opportunity of playing the organ in the church at Ramon. This organ, a two-manual instrument, had not been played for two years because the organist was with the army and none of the remaining villagers knew how to play it. The priest looked among the British soldiers for an organist and I knew nothing at all about it. The Dickeybirds' pianist played it on one Sunday but he knows nothing about organs. However, he got through the service all right and this little act created a very favourable impression not only on the priest but on the community in general and resulted in the village hall being gladly handed over to the concert party.

About 3 o/c we once more got loaded up carrying blankets and overcoats as well as our standard equipment and started off for Road 14. My ankle was not painful but it was weak and made itself felt when we commenced to climb. Sgt Twycross took pity on me and allowed me to put my bundle of blankets on the wagon. It was a long pull up, the final stretch being so steep that the wagon had to take it at the run and my blankets were jolted off. We passed one of our howitzers hidden in a steep hollow. It must have been a rare job to get it there, but how they will get it out again without the assistance of an earthquake is more than we can imagine.

Our position appears to be very near if not quite the summit level of the Montello. Our quarters are a farmhouse situated on the lip of a large 'devil's punch bowl', one of the most perfect that I have seen. It is planted all round with vines and a wide spiral path leads to the bottom which is a flat space about sixty yards in diameter. In the sides of the bowl the 23rd Division have made a small but very fine tunnel with two entrances. It is large enough to shelter the whole of the Brigade HQ Staff in an emergency but there are only enough beds for the officers. It is the best piece of tunnelling that I have seen. Across the road in another dell is a small spring that will supply us with water. The cooks have established themselves in a shed near to it.

20.2.18

We are running a Visual Station in a house a few hundred yards away. The Italians have a Wireless Station in the same house and they charge their accumulators in a decidedly novel way. A little generator is driven by belting off the rear wheel of a pedal cycle suspended in a framework. For a certain period every day one of the Italian soldiers mounts the cycle and pedals furiously as if he were scratch man in a sprint.

21.2.18

From a warfare point of view, this spot is even more 'cushy' than Road 8. Each evening about half a dozen shells pass over us towards some of our batteries and this is all we have to worry us except aircraft during the day, but we are getting so indifferent to them that we hardly ever go to the trouble of taking cover. It is quite a holiday. Not far from us, in a small house, is an artillery observation post and Mennie, who has been there, tells me that the view across the Piave is wonderful. With the aid of powerful glasses they can see everything that goes on, even to the civilian women doing their washing. Once a day an Austrian battery dashes out from behind some low hills, swings round right on the bank of the river, fires half a dozen shots, and then bolts back again. From the field on the left of our billet we get a good view of the bridges that cross the river to Vidor. This is a point of honour and is held by picked Italian troops. I hope they will hold it well, for if the Austrians got across there our number would be up. George Thompson is making a painting of the view from this spot.

22.2.18

Early in the morning I had occasion to go into the billet and at my approach hundreds of rats scampered away in all directions. I shone my torch round the billet and it is certainly the most rat-infested building I have ever seen. They are much smaller than the Belgian variety but they make up for it in quantity.

Our troops carried out raids across the Piave in boats, guiding themselves by ropes that have been fastened between the numerous islands. The current is so strong that they have to keep a firm hold on the ropes or they would be washed away. They usually get one or two prisoners but so far I don't think we have suffered any casualties. The quietness of this front can be judged from the fact that our front-line troops wash and shave in the Piave which is as open to Fritz as it is to us. Also, Brigade Sports are being arranged to take place in our 'punch bowl', the level bottom being the arena while the troops will be comfortably seated round the sides. A boxing ring is already in course of construction. And this is being in the line!!

23.2.18

The weather is glorious – really too hot to exert oneself very much but this afternoon I went down to the ravine at the bottom of a slope where there is a copious well of icy cold water. I washed handkerchiefs, socks and a shirt and hung them in the sun to dry while I had a bath in a tin bowl. The sun was so hot that being naked was far from unpleasant, but oh! the water! It made my teeth chatter so I didn't dawdle over my bath. By the time I was dressed, my washing was dry enough to cart up to the billet. I'm getting pretty expert at washing but it's a job I should not care to earn my living at. Every job I think has its own particular soul or spirit – atmosphere, perhaps it may be called. So it is that sometimes I feel the washerwoman instinct creeping over me and I look at the weather and say, 'Ah, I think it will be a nice drying day, Mrs Glasspoole. P'raps you won't mind lending me your mangle for half an hour so as I can get these few things dried and ironed and put away before my old man comes 'ome which he do so 'ate to see washing about of a neevin.' Mrs Glasspoole replies suitably but I can't write it down. Well, today certainly has been a beautiful drying day and I felt like a man who has accomplished something when I took in the last pair of socks. About 5 p.m. a breeze suddenly sprang up – a thing so unusual as to attract attention – but it soon became almost a hurricane. It came straight from the mighty snow-capped mountains but the remarkable thing about it was that it was quite warm. Just as it was getting dusk we observed a bright light on the side of the mountains. It grew brighter and bigger and we made various speculations as to its nature. Then another appeared and another and another, four of them altogether. They were all in Fritz's territory and a good many miles away. Eventually we discovered that they were forest fires. The sides of the mountains are covered with bracken, undergrowth and trees and these being very dry, a slight spark is sufficient to set them aflame and the high wind did the rest until four enormous fires are raging over scores, perhaps hundreds, of square miles. It is now 10 o/c. I have taken a last look at the fires and this strange wind is still blowing fiercely.

Tonight there is a rumour of an impending move. I thought this sort of warfare was too good to last.

24.2.18

Last night's rumour has been confirmed and we have orders to pack up and leave here tomorrow. Evidently we are going out of the country and the usual rumours are abroad regarding Egypt, Salonika, France, Ireland and even England, but considering the way in which the Huns are making preparations in France I bet we land back in the Ypres Salient before long.

25.2.18

Yesterday we received slips of paper to stick in our pay books showing the new rates of pay dating from 29.9.17. Through getting Separation Allowance for my Mother I am 6d. a day better off as the government now pay the 6d. a day allotment that I made. Also I get 1d. a day war pay, having done over twelve months' active service. When I have completed the second year I shall have another rise of a penny. At present my daily rate is 2/3 [two shillings and threepence] and I feel quite wealthy especially as it means picking up a lot of arrears. In the ordinary way, I am 200 lire (£5) in credit, and 7d. a day from 29 September up to today is £4.7s.7d. Now is the time that I should like a little trip to Rome or Florence or Milan – but no such luck – the betting is on Ypres or the Somme. It is a pity that we are leaving this country just as spring is coming in. We have lived through all the dead season and now Nature is just beginning to wake up. The dormant pulse of life is commencing to throb. Birds, butterflies and flowers – all are moving and stirring and there is the springtide coursing of the blood in our veins. No doubt many more kinds of birds will make their appearance, to say nothing of insects. Spiders have been numerous all through the winter and in great variety. I don't think I have seen the ill-famed tarantula but I have seen some very big ones, bigger than the palm of a man's hand. It is a messy job squeezing them!

I don't like spiders. They are interesting but have an evil, uncanny intelligence and the lady spiders eat their husbands.

26.2.18

Marched to Riese, a distance of about eight miles. Bought some postcards at a stall in the street and have solved the riddle of W Pio X. In this little town Pope Pius X was born. Apparently he was of fairly lowly origin, judging from the size of the house in which he first saw daylight. On the house is a tablet commemorating the event, supplemented by an appeal that visitors would regard the building as an object of historical interest and refrain from doing it any damage. In the street opposite the house is a monument to this pope surmounted by his bust.

27.2.18

The illustrated papers and magazines have recently published plenty of photographs and articles dealing with the extraordinary difficulties of mountain fighting particularly in the matter of transport. In one place I believe it takes twenty men to keep one man in the line. Naturally only real mountaineers can be employed in such positions. But today we have seen some of the genuine mountain fighters. Three or four of them looked rather like grizzly bears. They wore big white long-haired fur arrangements which covered them up completely except for just the front part of the face.

28.2.18

Today we have had little to do save prowl about waiting for orders. Bought two pairs of little wooden shoes or clogs, models of what the women wear. The local clog-maker has been very busy all day as half the troops wanted these little things to take away as souvenirs. The news is fairly definite that tomorrow we entrain for France.

Following the overthrow of the Tsar during the October Revolution, the new Bolshevik government speedily sought to end the nation's participation in the war. Negotiations between Russia and the Central Powers quickly brought about an Armistice in mid-December and although a final peace treaty (the treaty of Brest-Litovsk) was not signed until 3 March 1918, the Germans used the opportunity to begin withdrawing forces from the Eastern to the Western Front in order to launch a decisive campaign against the Allies in the spring.

With the Italian Front stabilised, and with overwhelming evidence that Germany was intending to embark on an all-out assault in France, Britain and France began to withdraw most of the Divisions sent to Italy in such haste in November of the previous year. The 41st Division, much to Martin's regret, was ordered to march and retrain for the Western Front.

In the first few days of March, Martin's diary largely retraces steps similar to those taken four months before by the Division. There are a number of observations of marginal interest about Verona, Milan and the long Alpine tunnels through which they passed back into France. He mentions the lack of gaiety as they cross the border once more, and he notes the train's passage through the Marne where the fighting had been so intense during the open days of warfare in 1914 and back again to Arras and then Ypres. Martin's travelogue back to France, though interesting, is perhaps not revealing enough to warrant inclusion here. For this reason I have curtailed his notes to one fascinating incident that he jotted down as the train passed through northern Italy on 2 March.

2.3.18

Presently the mountains rose up on both sides of us. They looked very stern and wild and forbidding and their tops were in the clouds. If it had been fine we would have enjoyed some magnificent scenery but we should have lost the wild grandeur of the snowstorms. We were pitying anyone who had to be out in that weather, when one of us noticed two little black figures struggling up the mountainside. We watched them for a long while and with the aid of field glasses made them out to be an Italian soldier followed by a priest holding up an umbrella. This I should think he found more of a hindrance than a help but he kept it above his head all the time. They followed a winding, tortuous path which we could not discern and they were the only animate creatures on the landscape. So it is no wonder that we immediately became intensely interested in them. They were fighting against fierce and unrelenting elements and our sporting instincts were roused. We almost got to betting as to how much further they would be able to go. A few buildings were visible here and there along their path but the travellers passed these and went winding onwards and upwards. Sometimes we lost sight of them behind great rocks and boulders and then we tried to guess just where abouts they would reappear. Still they kept going up and up until we feared that we should lose them in the clouds but at last they turned into a little tiny building, so small that we could scarcely pick it out, and we were glad to see them safely reach their destination for we felt that they were brave men to face the mountains in such weather. I wonder if they will ever know that they were watched, admired and cheered by a whole brigade of the British Army!

The sun was now sinking and we realised very forcibly that our little joy trip to Italy had ended. Our return to France was far different from our departure. Along the Riviera we were treated like heroes – we were cheered and worshipped by the crowds – but here there was only frost and snow and leaden skies, cold and cheerless and utterly lacking in sympathy. We knew we were back in France – we knew something of what we were going to meet – our gaiety was gone – we could sing 'Excelsior' no more. All we could do was to hum or whistle snatches of mournful music.

3.3.18

We travelled fairly well during the night for when we woke this morning we were some distance north of Dijon and were running through the Saône Valley. After the Alps, the scenery has not been very exciting; nevertheless it is not to be despised. It was fairly evident that we were travelling almost parallel with the fighting line and as the day wore on, evidence of the war became more and more apparent and we could hear the booming of the guns. Yes, we know we are back in France again and our spirits have dropped accordingly.

4.3.18

We progressed in fitful spasms during the night. Consequently I woke up a number of times with the shaking and jolting of the train as it stopped and started. On one occasion we seemed to be at a busy spot judging from the noise and bustle of shunting and other railway operations. I rose up and opened the door to look out and something fell from the truck. As we were just on the move again I took no further notice but rolled up and went to sleep. In the morning my namesake Martin (who joined us only a few days ago) couldn't find his boots! I was sorry for him and at the first stop I went along to the Quarter Master to see if I could get another pair. But of course it was hopeless. All the Stores were securely packed in the wagons and could not be got at. We stopped in the sidings at Montdidier when we learnt that we were to detrain at a little place just beyond Amiens.

Arrived at Longeau where we put on our equipment and got out on to the platform only to be ordered back again as our destination had been changed. So on we went again travelling northwards until we reached Doullens. Here we detrained into about three inches of nice soft mud. Martin, minus his boots, was helped across to a motor lorry that was to take some of the stores to our billet. Then we marched off through the town and up the main Arras Road for some distance until we turned to the right and came to the little village of Halloy, seven kilometres from Doullens. This is a cheerless-looking hole; cold, dull, muddy and miserable.

7.3.18

The 11th RW Kents arrived in the village today and now the Brigade is complete once more, but there is a disquieting rumour abroad that one battalion in each brigade is to be disbanded as a part of a general scheme throughout the British Army to reduce the strength of each brigade to three battalions instead of four. The reason seems to be the shortage of reinforcements and the consequent difficulty of keeping battalions up to strength. There may also be some idea of increasing the mobility of Divisions. There is also some talk of the leave allotment being increased. There is some need, as while we were in Italy leave was almost restricted to special and urgent cases. Not a man from this section has had leave since last October so it is about time we started again.

9.3.18

Divisional orders today announce a big increase in the leave allotment so we all are a little more cheery although some of our chances are still pretty remote. Received letter and parcel from Elsie – jar of potted meat was smashed, but otherwise it was OK and very welcome. All the runners attached to us have got the wind up over this disbandment rumour because whichever battalion is the unlucky one the runners belonging to it will have to return to their unit before it is split up and distributed as reinforcements all over France. Not a very entrancing prospect. Rumours on the matter are persistent but variable; sometimes they are strong on the Surreys, then they turn on to the Hants or the KRRs or the Kents, all perhaps within an hour, and spirits of the runners rise and fall accordingly. But there is nothing definite.

12.3.18

It is surprising how irritating it is when simple little questions or arguments arise which none of us can settle because we have no other source of information than our memories. *The Merchant of Venice*, which Elsie sent me, has just settled one grievous point, viz. who was in love with Portia. I was a bit hazy over most of the play but I said Bassanio. Hamilton stuck out that Bassanio eventually trotted off with Nerissa. He had got it into his head that although Bassanio and Portia were lovers in the early part of the play, the ring episode upset things and Bassanio married Nerissa. But I was correct and now I can gloat over Hamilton although really I have little right to do so for it was more of a guess than a feat of memory, but I don't admit that to Hamilton.

13.3.18

The death knell of the 11th Battalion Royal West Kent Regiment
has been sounded. This morning orders were received that this is the
unfortunate unit to be disbanded. And now the West Kent runners,
Fisher, Granecome and Kirrage, are filled with misgivings, while all the
others are heaving sighs of relief. Colonel Corfe (who is acting Brigadier
while General Towsey is on leave) reviewed the battalion this afternoon.

14.3.18

General Lawford came and reviewed the Kents today, giving a
little valedictory address explaining that it was no discredit to the
battalion that it was being broken up. One battalion had to go and
it was decided that where there was more than one battalion of the
same regiment in the Division, the latest formed battalion must
be the unlucky one. Accordingly in the other Brigades the 21st
KRRC (123 Bde) and the 32nd Royal Fusiliers (124 Bde) are being
disbanded. Endeavours are being made to retain our Kent runners
but we are not certain that it can be achieved.

*After the withdrawal of Russia from the war, the Germans transferred
around a million men from the Eastern to the Western Front, giving
them short-term but crucial numerical advantage. These men, backed by
artillery, would pursue a campaign the broad strategic aim of which would
be to divide the Allied forces, pushing the BEF back on to its coastal ports,
precipitating its defeat or at least forcing its retreat across the water.*

*Many of these men, fresh from the Russian Front, were well trained,
battle-hardened and confident. It was Germany's moment to win the war
before US troops arrived in such numbers as to irrevocably tip the balance
against the Central Powers.*

*The Allies, in turn, had long anticipated such an attack. For two months
they had prepared, utilising much that had been learnt in the previous years
of fighting as well as introducing more recent innovations in defence that
were designed to inflict as many casualties on the enemy as possible while
preserving enough troops in reserve so as gradually to sap the enemy of his
forward momentum and strength.*

Nevertheless, there was a problem. The Commander-in-Chief, Haig, would be short of troops to meet the enemy. The protracted nature of the fighting, now in its fourth year, had driven a wedge between the senior command and many politicians at home, most significantly between Haig and the Prime Minister, Lloyd George. Fearing that Haig might use any reinforcements to launch his own spring offensive, Lloyd George had ordered that they should be held back in Britain and not in France, where they would be out of his control. Such a decision would ensure that when the Germans did attack, the British line would be more vulnerable than might otherwise have been the case. For the Germans, speedy infiltration would be the key to success, pushing some of the best trained and equipped German soldiers deep into Allied lines to sow confusion. Allied strongpoints would be largely ignored in the rush to storm the entire trench system, while mopping-up parties would later be used to clear up any remaining resistance by men who were surrounded and deep in enemy territory.

The date for the attack was 21 March, an important fact gleaned from German prisoners captured in raids a few days beforehand. Even so, the ferocity of the attack when it came was overwhelming. At 5.30 a.m., after a short whirlwind bombardment had softened up the Allies' forward trenches, the Germans advanced, helped by a thick fog that hid the attackers until they were almost on top of the British trenches. The fighting was intense and it was fluid. The British, compelled to retreat, often in headlong flight, were incapable of holding their position for any length of time although they inflicted heinous casualties on the German army, losses the Germans could ill afford.

March and April produced some of the darkest moments for the Allies and in particular for the British Army. Less than a month after his comfortable sojourn in Italy, Jack Martin was thrown into the maelstrom, his diary adequately reflecting the insecurity and pandemonium of the time.

17.3.18

The German attack is expected very shortly; consequently a 'nervy' atmosphere is commencing to make itself felt. To stir up our brutal instincts and passions we have been treated to a morally disgusting harangue by a Major of the Physical Jerks Department. The whole

Brigade was marched out to a field a few kilometres away where we squatted down in a hollow while the blood-red Major (straight up from the base) delivered his oration in a strikingly melodramatic manner. He endeavoured to make us 'see red' and it is a matter for sad reflection that civilisation should come to such a sorry pass. The authorities apparently think that the civilian-soldier is too soft hearted and gentle so it is necessary to raise the spirit of Cain in him. The whole speech was utterly disgusting and I am sorry to think that England should consider such a thing necessary. It was revolting and I believe I could better have withstood a dose of the abject platitudinous piffle that deals with the 'nobility and righteousness of our cause', 'the honour of dying for England' and 'Remember Belgium'.

18.3.18

Rumours as to the German attack have been many and varied but a telegram from GHQ says it will be on 20th or 21st, most probably the latter. I have just been on duty with Bill Rogers. There was very little to do and I intended writing a few letters, but that was impossible, for Rogers was talking and telling yarns all the time. He is a Lance Corporal of the Surreys and has been attached to us ever since the Division came out. A Londoner, he is almost a typical cockney, extremely loquacious and with a fund of humorous reminiscence which seems to have no end. Once get him fairly wound up (by no means a difficult job) and he will keep going all night; we have whiled away many a weary hour listening to his stories. In 'civvy' life he is a specialist in poultry, fish, eggs and milk, so he has been of great assistance at our Christmas feasts. Although very voluble he isn't noisy like Davidson and it is very seldom that he tries to sing. Most of his tales are concerned with the inner life of fish, poultry and dairy businesses. Some of them have prompted me to suggest that he writes a book on 'How to make Money on a Milk-round' – circulation to be strictly confined to the trade. So long as he can get an audience he is perfectly content. It is quite immaterial whether they can understand him or not, so, on the Montello one day, we were not surprised to find him talking volubly to a small party of Italian soldiers (who could not understand a single word) about Lloyd George and the prospects of peace. 'Ah,' he said, 'you don't know him. He's one of those fellows who if the Germans threw up their hands and cried, "We give in, we've had enough: you can have France and Belgium and all the Colonies as well, and you can have the whole of Germany too" would answer, "Oh no you don't, we'll fight you for it." ' Davidson, by the way, is not so confident of an early peace as he was in Italy. There he was a very strong peace optimist despite several very severe reversals in that quite a number of his dates for the end of the war had come and gone and left us just as uncertain as before. But the German attack looming immediately before us provides a very efficient corrective to the unduly optimistic views that were induced by the blue skies, clear air and gentle warfare on the Italian Front.

19.3.18
There is little to think or talk about except the imminence of the German attack. Gradually we have been making the preparations necessary for our part, and as a final touch we were treated to a false alarm this afternoon for the purpose of seeing how quickly we could turn out with wagons packed and everything ready for the march. As it was we were packed up and all in line in a remarkably short time, and the Brigadier was very pleased. But we didn't tell him that we knew what was coming, four or five hours before the alarm was sounded. I am on night duty tonight and, judging from the tone of one or two telegrams that have passed, it is pretty certain that the attack will commence on the 21st.

21.3.18
Great German Attack. Although at Halloy we were well behind the lines, the sudden and terrible thunder of innumerable guns woke me at dawn. The long-expected German Advance had commenced. It had been foretold long before we left Italy, the date

being fixed about the end of March or beginning of April as, in the words of Sir Douglas Haig, 'the initiative will then have passed into the enemy's hands'. Why it should be allowed to pass is a little more than I can understand at present. But this is no time to dwell on whys and wherefores. We are in the soup and we've got to get out of it. Gaiety and mirth have been dwindling of late, and what merriment there was as we rose this morning had little spontaneity about it. But the British soldier in the mass never gets downhearted. So when late in the afternoon we were formed up and marched away, we kept our spirits up with singing and laughing. We went along the main Arras Road to Saulty, a distance of eight miles. Here were some of our long-range guns and we felt that we were getting back into the fighting arena once more. Detachments of the Chinese Labour Corps (affectionately known as 'Chinks') were straggling down the road, no two men dressed alike and all of them carrying a miscellaneous assortment of odds and ends, such as field kettles, tins, saucepans, picks, axes etc. They dearly love to get hold of some item of the British soldiers' clothing or equipment. The fit doesn't matter — jackets, trousers, puttees, even if it is only one puttee they will wear it with pride. But they are mighty cowards. The firing of one of our own guns nearby was quite enough to set them scuttling down the road like frightened rabbits. At nightfall we entrained and understood that our immediate destination was Méricourt on the Somme, a few miles behind Albert and a place that we had known in 1916. We were uncomfortably crowded in the trucks and could only squat down with our knees up under our chins. Of course all leave has been stopped.

22.3.18

Horribly cramped, I only doze fitfully all night yet it is surprising how soundly some men can sleep in any position. One by one they woke up and stretched, kicking and pushing all the other fellows around them. It was broad daylight when we opened the doors and found that already we were beyond Méricourt and were actually passing through Albert. We crawled along until we reached Achiet-le-Grand where we detrained at 8.30 a.m. There was little hope of any breakfast but fortunately there was a large Expeditionary Force Canteen adjoining the railway. Here we bought tea and cake and cigarettes and tobacco. In a little time we were ordered to fall in as we were going straight into the line. All this part of the country was held by Fritz before the Somme Offensive in 1916 and now he is bent on getting it back again, and a little bit more if he can. Naturally there is much evidence of warfare both past and present, to say nothing of the possibilities of the future. The whole Signal Section and Brigade Headquarters Staff were lined up and inspected by General Towsey who carefully noted that each man had his full supply of ammunition and iron rations. It was a rather impressive inspection with shells bursting less than a mile away and all the multitudinous sounds of warfare rattling in our ears. There was no particular ceremony about the business; it seemed more like a fatherly interview and there is no doubt that General Towsey felt considerable anxiety for our welfare. He always has had a high regard for his Signallers and now it was very evident. The inspection was brief as we were awaiting orders to relieve one of the Divisions that has been in the line ever since the attack commenced yesterday morning. I don't know how far the Germans advanced yesterday but we have heard pretty definitely that since they resumed the attack at dawn today they have come over ten kilometres, a rather terrifying rate when compared with our advances in the Ypres Sector last year, where we measured our territorial gains in yards. It also appears that the Germans are coming over equipped to stay, each man carrying a spare pair of boots and two water bottles, one containing water and the other coffee. And this is in addition to his ordinary equipment and extra ammunition.

After the inspection we ate what bully beef and biscuits we could get and then General Towsey decided that only the next two shifts of men for duty should be taken into the line. The rest were to remain with the Transport until they were wanted. My luck is in, for I was one of the last men on duty at Halloy. When the others had gone forward we looked around and found a Nissen hut wherein we installed ourselves, and before long the cooks had made some tea. At nightfall the firing slackened a bit as, apart from the weariness of the troops, it is impossible to continue an advance in the dark. We felt that we were reasonably secure for the night, so, covered with our overcoats, we went to sleep.

23.3.18

Up soon after daybreak as we knew not what was before us. The cooks were preparing breakfast, bacon was frying and tea was brewing, when we received orders to retire immediately as the Germans had resumed their alarming advance. Tea and bacon were thrown overboard, the wagons were roped up, and off we marched to Buchanan Camp (a distance of three miles) lying between Achiet-le-Grand and Achiet-le-Petit but nearer the latter. This is a tolerably large camp with several rows of good huts. Here we made ourselves as comfortable as possible, even managing to get blankets from the Quarter Master. In the afternoon, just outside our huts, we saw a parade of what was left of a battalion of the Essex Regiment. All that had come back were the Colonel, one NCO and thirty men. The Major also was there but from what I heard he had been left behind when the battalion went into the line. First of all the Major called the roll and went through other necessary routine business. Then the Colonel came forward and addressed the men. He was visibly affected and had difficulty in delivering his little speech, for emotion was half choking him and tears were rolling down his cheeks. He was tall and big, with a square jaw and a hard-cut face that had probably never felt a tear before. His words had a simple nobility and directness about them and I shall remember his speech as one of the most considerable that I have ever heard. We were not surprised afterwards to hear him spoken of as a brave and splendid man. I do not know who he was but I shall not forget him.

24.3.18

This morning we managed to get a good breakfast and then, as it seemed unlikely that we should be moved for an hour or two,

Davidson and I walked up to the German Cemetery at Achiet-le-Petit. There had been a hospital here in 1916 and amongst the enemy graves we found one to a British Tommy who had died from wounds and one to a Flying Corps Officer whose plane had been shot down. Returning, we were met by a continuous stream of retiring troops, fatigued almost to the point of absolute exhaustion, staggering along hardly knowing where they were going. Hot, tired horses pulling guns of all calibres while, on the gun limbers, artillerymen, who had been firing their guns for three whole days and nights, slept a precarious slumber in the continual danger of being jolted into the road and being trampled by the team immediately behind.

At the camp we heard that the Canteen at Achiet-le-Grand had been abandoned. The Corporal in charge had taken all the money and hurried back, leaving the Canteen to the mercy of the troops. In a very short time it was utterly ransacked and I daresay it held at least £2000 worth of stuff. We were among the less fortunate in the scramble but some of our fellows brought back two cases of whisky and numerous boxes of biscuits and cigarettes. From the top of the rise near the camp we could see the bursting shells approaching nearer and nearer but we did not get the order to move until the shells were dropping in the camp. One went clean through one of the huts that we had been in. It was getting dusk by the time we had loaded up and were ready for the road again.

Incidentally, the Quarter Master jettisoned a whole lot of stores and paraphernalia, including all the 'props' of the Dickeybirds Concert Party, amongst which was the sketch I wrote for them in Italy. So that doesn't look like ever being performed.

Along the road a little way, we passed a big howitzer that had just been got into position and was beginning to open fire again. The roads were so congested with traffic at this point that we had to make tracks across some fields only to get our feet entangled with telephone wires. These were dangerous for the horses but we had no mishap and eventually turned into a large field on the left of the road. It was 10 p.m. before we got the transport settled and looked round for some sort of shelter for ourselves. But there was none. QMS Cass doled us out with two blankets each. Wrapping these round us, we lay down on the grass against a long, low mound, the slope of which formed something of a pillow. Tired, but very thankful it was a fine night, we were not long in dropping off to sleep. I sent field postcards to Mother and Elsie but Corporal Smith (the post Corporal) does not hold out much hope of their early despatch.

25.3.18

The opening of the barrage at dawn woke us and we found our blankets and heads covered with white frost. There was a certain expectancy in the air and we rolled up our damp blankets and had a hurried breakfast. The traffic on the road was increasing every minute and soon it began to flow over into the fields on either side. Hundreds of wounded men were struggling to get back. All kinds of wagons and limbers and civilian carts had been requisitioned to carry them back to hospital but the quantity of transport was insufficient; consequently, all those who could walk or even only hobble had to do so. It was a painful spectacle but we had little time in which to bestow pity for we were marched out on to the road while our transport was ordered to make its way across the fields towards Ayette. We had no idea where we were going and I don't think Mr Edgar had either. We had only gone a few paces down the road when a gaudy colonel dressed in a regulation tunic but with light blue trousers with red stripes galloped up and stopped us. 'Where are these men going?' he demanded. 'Down this way,' stammered Mr Edgar. 'About turn!' yelled the gaudy colonel, 'Follow me!' and away we had to go, heading straight for the line. The prospect was not very pleasing and besides we had heard some strange tales of Germans dressed as British officers penetrating into our lines and trying to take command of parties of our men. So we viewed this queerly dressed officer with suspicion although from what transpired there is little reason to doubt that he was British. I was in the middle of the party (a very mixed lot from all our battalions) and after going less than a hundred yards I looked round and saw Davidson, Rogers, Paterson and Jamieson calmly drop out and cut across the field in the direction taken by our transport. 'A good example,' I thought, 'is worth following, and in any case this is no place for me.' So I promptly followed them. By this time the fields as well as the roads were covered thick with a heterogeneous mass of all conceivable kinds of transport, guns and men, and it was not an easy matter to find our own transport. Fortunately it had not been able to get along very fast and when we found it we distributed ourselves among the wagons, avoiding any suggestions of congregating as there seemed to be a number of freelance officers knocking about whose duty was to gather up all the odds and ends of humanity who were not engaged in some duty or other, and form them into scratch parties or 'composite' battalions and lead them off up the line. They are to be avoided at all costs for they are nobody's darlings, and apart from getting the dirty work they are in a hopeless position in regard to rations, doctors, ambulances etc. There are not many men made of such heroic fibre that they would willingly join a composite party in a stunt like this. We crawled along a lane that led us past Divisional HQ into Ayette. In the village there was a tremendous block of traffic at the crossroads. We halted for nearly an hour but could not get over. Then fresh orders were received and with difficulty we turned round, passed out of the village and were soon travelling along a road that we had almost to ourselves. And so we came to Gommecourt but Divisional HQ were before us and had installed themselves in the ruins of the chateau. The village had been knocked all to pieces in 1916 and notice boards outside the ruins of the church and at the entrance to an old German dugout proclaimed, in French, that the authorities were preserving these as permanent memorials of the Great War.

Near the chateau we turned into a field where we anticipated spending the night. McCormack and I scrounged the countryside and brought back some sheets of corrugated iron wherewith to make some sort of shelter while the cooks made some tea. Dickson, Blakeway and the other fellows who had followed the gaudy colonel now returned. They had been led into a hastily constructed trench to stop the German Cavalry which was expected to break through. Nothing of the sort happened, however, and soon they were left to themselves. With no one to command them and not having the vaguest idea of what they were required to do, and also being very hungry, they all decided to vacate the trench and try and find the transport. Night was falling and we were trying to build a shelter when we received further orders to get on the move again. The moon was hidden by clouds as we trekked through Fonquevillers to Souastre. Just beyond this village we were put into a field for the night. It was now drizzling with rain and a night in the open was not an attractive prospect, but with the help of some iron stakes and barbed wire we made a roof of blankets.

26.3.18

There was a tense feeling in the air this morning and strange rumours were flying about. At 8.30 a.m. orders were received that every available man was to be sent to some unnamed spot. Only NCOs and the actual drivers were to remain with the transport. Capt. Reiner decreed that all the Signals must go, so we were issued out with iron rations and a double quantity of ammunition, and under Lieut. Edgar we passed back through the village and up the road leading to Sailly-au-Bois. There was an alarming stir at Div. HQ in Souastre – Staff Officers were dashing about furiously and gallant NCOs who had never been in the firing line looked livid and scared as if they did not know what to do. We were not left long in doubt as to the cause of the commotion, for we had barely got clear of the village when we met men hurrying from the opposite direction. Lorries, horse transport and men on foot all seemed anxious to get past us. Then we met some who called out as they hurried by, 'Don't go up there, you bally fools – Fritz is in the next village!' Mr Edgar halted us, ordered us to load rifles and fix bayonets, and was surprised to find that RE Signals do not carry bayonets. Then we were lined across the field on the right of the road and quickly the word was passed round that the German

Cavalry had broken through and might be upon us at any moment. Except for a few yards of trench there was no shelter for us at all and only one of our party had an entrenching tool. We borrowed it in turn and scraped grave-shaped holes to lie in, building the earth up in front of us to form some slight protection. Other men were doing the same thing in front of us and behind us and within half an hour there were fourteen lines of resistance drawn right across the country. We kept our eyes on the horizon and waited. It was a most horrible wait. Some there were in our line who were faint-hearted – but there was no RE among them – and crept back to the security of a little sunken lane behind us. I heard Paterson say to Jamieson, 'So much for them, but I have been put here, and here I am going to stop until an officer orders me to move.' The grim determination was heartening.

The ground fell away slightly in front of us and then rose to a long line of low hills on the horizon. For three hours we lay and watched the skyline but nothing German made any appearance. A number of horsemen came over but they were British and soon we were talking to a Sergeant of Artillery who told us definitely that the rumour was false. We got up and stretched ourselves, and breathed freely once more. It is positively extraordinary how this rumour spread over such a vast expanse of country in such an incredibly short time – just like a big puff of wind. But it is equalled by the extraordinary organisation which flung fourteen lines of resistance across the country in little more than the same number of minutes. Now we only had to wait for orders, so we wandered about a bit to stretch our legs and get ourselves warm, for the wind was rather cold. Presently I noticed men coming from the direction of the village carrying armfuls of socks, cap comforters, gloves, etc. Others had new caps, tunics, greatcoats, breeches, trousers and boots. It soon appeared that Div. HQ had scuttled off in such a hurry that they left all their stores behind them. I am pretty well equipped so there was no need for me to join in the looting. All this time the scene behind us was amazing. The contour of the land dipped and rose again so that we had a view of several roads leading out of Souastre. These were absolutely choked with transport so that nothing could move for at least four hours. Every time we looked back, the same wagons were visible in exactly the same places. The afternoon was well advanced before they made any definite move. At 4 o/c we were called off and put into a barn on the edge of the village. Of course there were no rations so we started to scrounge. At the deserted Div. HQ we found all we wanted – tea, sugar, tins of milk, bullybeef, 'maconochies', biscuits and potatoes, together with the necessary field kettles to cook them in. The stores and billets gave unmistakeable evidence of the alacrity with which the Div. HQ evacuated its quarters. Blankets were lying in heaps just as the fellows had bundled out of them, and not many of the men had stopped to put their puttees on. Soap, cleaning and shaving tackle and all manner of personal odds and ends had been left behind in the scramble. We cooked a good meal of stew and tea, then collected as many blankets as we wished (I had six) and made ourselves comfortable in the loft over the barn. Meanwhile, some rough spirits of the 51st (Highland) Division had broken into the farmhouse and thoroughly looted it. Everything they wanted, they took: all else they smashed and destroyed, even tearing doors off hinges and breaking up the furniture and tearing the women's clothing to pieces. The farmer, his wife and daughter had locked the place up in their alarm earlier in the day and had gone to some friends in the village. What a nice return for them! It was not till all the damage was done (including running off all the wine from the barrels) that an officer was found to call the men to order.

27.3.18

The remnants of yesterday's tea served us for breakfast and about 9 o/c we marched to Bienvillers. Along the road there was abundant evidence of the mighty scramble the Transport had yesterday. A lot of it had forsaken the roads and taken to the fields in order to get back somehow or other. Arriving in Bienvillers, we found the place thronged with 122nd Brigade troops and, before we reached the centre of the little town, Sgt Twycross met us and we learnt that the Brigade had been withdrawn from the line during the night. What the next move was to be was not known but we were ordered to carry on with the Transport, so away we went to Berles where we found them in a field at the end of the village. We were welcomed by Davidson who fetched out a parcel he had just received and regaled us with shortbread and biscuits.

28.3.18
The Brigade has been suddenly ordered back into the line again. We had expected to be kept out for at least a week in order to collect reinforcements for we have lost very heavily. It is fairly evident, however, that we shall not be in for long. Indeed, it is impossible for the Brigade, in its sadly depleted condition, to do much in the way of fighting. Enticknap is missing. He was last seen amid heavy shelling near Bucquoy.

29.3.18
On to Couin where we arrived about midday. This area is strongly populated by the Brigade of Guards and their excessive discipline is very evident. Very 'posh', and very shiny and not often in the line but when they are, they make themselves felt. I have heard that near Achiet-le-Grand they went over in a counter-attack as cool as going on parade.

We are billeted in some farm buildings near the chateau. Troops have been here before, as wire-netting beds have been erected in one of the lofts; so we shall be reasonably comfortable tonight.

30.3.18
We have found a place in the village where we can buy candles and coffee but not much else. The 'fag issue' today has produced some tobacco for which I am grateful. The weather has been fine and not having much to do, albeit in a continual state of expectancy, I wrote a fairly long letter to Elsie. Dashing about the neighbourhood in a big car is a ferocious looking Major of the Guards with six wound stripes, his arm always resting on the side of the car for display purposes.

1.4.18

Expecting our moving orders all day but they did not come until the afternoon. So we had a hurried tea and then marched off to Marieux where we arrived after dark and were tightly squeezed into one end of a hut, leaving the remainder vacant as the Brigade is coming out of the line during the night and the other fellows must have room to lie down.

2.4.18

At 3 a.m. we were awakened by the noisy arrival of the Brigade but in about half an hour the lot of us were asleep again. There was no hurry in getting up as we were not due to move till after dinner. The German Advance in this quarter seems to be fairly well stemmed and we are breathing a little more freely. Sgt Lunn says that we are bound for the Ypres Salient again.

4.4.18

It was still dark when we were bundled out of the train at Poperinghe and tramped through the deserted streets of the dingy little town to a large building that has the appearance of being a warehouse or store. Here we dumped ourselves down to slumber but it was too cold for me to sleep, so Cheesman and I wandered out into the town. It was now daylight and the natives were beginning to stir. We have had very little bread lately so we were quite pleased when we found a baker's shop. We went into the kitchen, made ourselves comfortable by the fire and drank coffee. The baker told us that they were forbidden to sell bread to British troops, but nevertheless we both came away with a loaf tucked under our greatcoats.

6.4.18

This morning, a party of us went off to what was once a brewery but which now, unblushing, proclaims itself to be a Delousing Station. There we had a good bath, which we desperately needed, while our clothes were fumigated, which they, also, desperately needed. Later I wrote another batch of letters. The 41st Division has been specially mentioned in one of Sir Douglas Haig's despatches concerning the operations on the Somme.

7.4.18

Last night orders were received for us to move up into the line today and this morning I was told to take charge of a relay station in Ypres. So with Glasspoole, Cochran, Chappell and Dagnall, I set off through Poperinghe and straight along the Ypres Road. On the way we had to find the location of the Transport and deliver a message to Capt. Mowat. To save time, I sent Cochran forward on a cycle to do this little business but of course he was a failure. So I did the job myself. At the YMCA Hut near Brandhoek we called a halt for refreshments and then carried on through Vlamertinghe to Ypres. Our directions were vague; all we knew was that we had to take over a Signal Office somewhere in the Ramparts. There was no shelling as we passed straight through the ruined town until we came to the Menin Gate – here the Ramparts ran right and left – we took the left and were lucky in soon striking the Signal Office in a dugout. The 99th Brigade had cleared out but had left a few written directions to guide us in joining up our instruments. Just across the road are some recently erected huts which seem to declare that Ypres isn't quite such a Hell as it was before the Passchendaele stunts last year, but they don't seem to have been used a great deal.

9.4.18

Fritz leaves Ypres alone during the day but gives it some attention during the night. We have been able to explore the town a bit by daylight but as soon as darkness falls it's advisable to keep under cover. One of the first shells over tonight broke the line connecting us with the Division on our right. Before going out to repair it, I rang up Sgt Twycross in order to find out who was responsible for keeping it in order. He said it was the duty of the other Division so I took no further interest in it. I wasn't sorry as Fritz was giving us rather more attention than was pleasant. Presently in came two linemen; they had found the break just outside our dugout and had mended it. They stopped and yarned until about 10 o/c and then, as the shelling was less severe, they took their departure.

10.4.18

Sgt Twycross rang up this morning and gave instructions for Glasspoole to make his way to Zuytpeene for the purpose of undergoing a special signal course. So he packed up and was away before noon. No one is coming in his place and that means that Cochran and I will have to run the office between us all night as well as all day. Rather exhausting if it's going to last long.

11.4.18

Last night I left Cochran to take the first night shift (from 10 till 3) but before 11 I got up and went into the Signal Office and found him fast asleep. I talked to him very sweetly and I think he remained awake all right for the rest of his shift – any rate, he was quite up to time in rousing me at 3 a.m. The Brigade is in a very unpleasant quarter. The country is an expanse of soft mud and to slip off the duckboards means getting half drowned. In addition they have been subjected to continual shelling ever since they took over.

After dinner, acting in accordance with instructions received during the morning, we left our little dugout and proceeded to rejoin the Brigade at Wieltje. Near St Jean a railway crosses the road and our passage was blocked by a long train of trucks. A noise and a rattle in front of us attracted our attention and we saw a two-horse Artillery limber rushing headlong down the road straight towards the train. The driver was doing all he knew to pull up the runaways, but they had got the bits between their teeth and it looked a dead cert for a nasty accident. But the driver lost neither his head nor his seat and he very cleverly managed to pull his team sharp right along the railway track by the side of the train and then, plunging into about two feet of mud, the mad career was checked.

12.4.18

The day has been fine and as there was practically no shelling in the neighbourhood we spent most of the time out in the open. In the afternoon Johnny Aitken was wounded in the knee and has been

taken to hospital. As the evening approached we gathered in the
saps and prepared to depart. We had all got our kit on and were
climbing up the stairs when Fritz started on a terrific bombardment,
blowing in one of the entrances but not causing any casualties. This
delayed us nearly an hour, but when we set off everything was quiet.
Crossing the country we reached the Ypres–Zonnebeke Road and
continued towards the latter place until we reached Jump Dugout,
a small but very substantial German pillbox. It is uncomfortable,
dark and stuffy but its solidity gives us a sense of security.

14.4.18

The empty quietness of the neighbourhood is weird. The silence is
only broken by an occasional shell although from the south there
is a continual heavy roar. The Germans have made considerable
advances in the direction of Hazebrouck and Bailleul and they
appear to have captured Ploegsteert. Now that I am back with
Brigade I am able to see the official reports as they come through.
Our pillbox is fitted with a periscope but there is no need to use it
for it is quite safe to go outside. I don't think we have had a shell
fall within 300 yards of us since we have been here.

15.4.18

Last night we sent a lot of stuff back on the Transport wagon that
brought up the rations. We only kept what is needed for today as
the evacuation is to take place tonight. All the innumerable details
have been arranged, consequently most of the day has been spent in
waiting and watching. The whole area is to be entirely cleared by
3 a.m. So, shortly . . .

16.4.18

. . . after midnight Lally came up with the limber and we loaded
up the remainder of the Stores and finally closed down the Signal
Office with the assistance of an axe and a couple of hammers. We
smashed everything that we could not take away – it was sheer
wanton destruction that we could enjoy. McCormack put his heart

and soul into it with a vigour that won a round of applause. Leaving a party of Field Coy REs to blow up the dugout and so give it the final coup-de-grâce, we lined up on the road and commenced our retirement. It was an eerie trek through the still and almost silent night. On all sides of us was the shell-blasted mud of Flanders, familiar enough in all conscience, but now in a new guise. It was lifeless. Passing the British Cemetery at Potijze, we entered Ypres by the Menin Gate. In the first cold glimmerings of a cheerless dawn the naked, shivering ruins of the old town rose up stark and grizzly around us. The shattered tower of the Cloth Hall gazed at us silently with a reproachful wondering. Were we deserting it for ever? It was a question none of us could answer.

17.4.18

Had a mediocre bath at Vlamertinghe Brasserie this morning, and again spent much time in writing letters. The Germans have captured Hazebrouck and Meteren but from the reports it appears that the attack in that quarter has just about spent itself, which is a relief as much more of it would cut us off entirely. The Somme Offensive seems to have exhausted itself and so Fritz is trying his hand at something less ambitious.

18.4.18

Capt. Ainger and Capt. Reah have been taken to hospital suffering badly from gas. They shared a gas shell between them a few nights ago when they were making arrangements for the evacuation. The weather is pretty dismal. For several days it has been dull and cloudy, and today there is a cold wind accompanied by drizzling rain. Still, there are plenty of signs of spring in the budding hedgerows (what is left of them), and in bright intervals, birds sing and chirrup gaily. They aren't worried at all by the beastly war and these are times when I feel quite envious of them. Still, I suppose they have their little feuds and strifes, but they manage to keep pretty merry withal.

20.4.18

I have seen the German Official Report of our evacuation the other night. It is rather amusing considering the fact that the area had been evacuated for twelve hours before they discovered it and then they came over very gingerly and tentatively. The report states that the gallant Saxon troops under General von Somebody made a furious and well-directed onslaught on the British line, driving the British back to the very gates of Ypres, capturing numerous prisoners and large quantities of stores and so forth.

This afternoon we moved about a mile across the fields to Rome Farm, on the Vlamertinghe–Briden Road. My billet is a lean-to adjoining the barn. The roof is only corrugated iron perforated with numerous shrapnel holes. It is an uncomfortable looking place so I staked my claim in the least unsatisfactory corner. The Signal Office is in a small dugout, and there is a pillbox type of building for the General. Otherwise there is no shelter, so when Fritz started a gentle strafe between 5 and 6 p.m. we had to scatter over the adjoining fields and get into what scraps of cover we could until he left off.

22.4.18

We often hear about the 'Call of the East'. Flanders has no such call – on the other hand it is a part of the globe which most of us will never desire to set eyes on again once we are out of it. Just look at it today – bleak, cold, starvation cold, dull, dreary, desolate – and you will be certain that nothing but sentiment would ever induce a person to return to it.

29.4.18

I feel almost too sick to move and have had to get some of the other fellows to take my turns of duty. John O'Brien has gone to hospital but I declined with thanks – military hospitals are places to keep out of just as long as you ever can. Granecome has also been 'evacuated sick' at last. He was constantly having fits and ought never to have been sent to France; but once here we could do nothing for him unless a Medical Officer actually saw him in a fit. Today he had one when an MO happened to be in the chateau and he was quickly fetched and ordered him to hospital immediately. The German Artillery was banging away heavily all last night and this morning they launched another fierce attack stretching from Dickebusch Lake down to Locre. Reports have been coming in almost hourly and it appears that, in the main, our troops and the French have repulsed the attack.

30.4.18
Yesterday, as the reports of the battle were coming through, 'Colin' Veitch was in a state of terrible concern. His sentimental interest in Ypres was almost too great for words. 'If the Germans capture Ypres,' he said, 'I shall never lift my head again for shame,' and I really believe he will shed tears if ever we are driven out of the town. A few shells dropped around the chateau this evening and one of the Transport drivers was wounded. He subsequently died in hospital.

1.5.18
This morning, just about noon, I was lying in my bed feeling particularly rotten when the whole building was shaken by a terrific explosion. We thought that a high-explosive shell must have hit the chateau but there was no sign of anything of the sort. Later in the day we heard that a huge ammunition dump down towards Poperinghe had been blown up and hundreds of soldiers and civilians killed. The frightful shock had been sufficient to kill scores of them as they sat or walked about their huts or houses. The attitude of the bodies reveals their actions at the moment the shock struck them; all further movement was suddenly suspended; hands are still raising the glass or holding the cigarette. Tait, the driver, went nearly mad and was carted off to hospital with shell shock.

2.5.18
This morning orders came for us to return to Rome Farm. I was feeling so ill and weak that I didn't know how I should crawl even

that short distance. So I was glad when Sgt Twycross told me I could go up with the limber for then I could get all my equipment carried for me. But directly after dinner fresh orders were given and it fell to my lot to lead the advance party. This meant carrying not only full kit but a quantity of Signal equipment and a blanket (if I wanted to keep it) as well. My knees quivered under the weight and I could only go about a hundred yards at a stretch. When we arrived at Rome Farm I was dripping wet with perspiration. I did what was necessary in taking over and changing the instruments. Then I took a bowl of water from the pond, stripped, and had a cold bath in the open. Fortunately I had a spare shirt, pants and socks in my pack so I put them on and hung the others up to dry. After the main party had arrived and we had had tea I curled myself up in my blankets.

3.5.18

I slept soundly last night and feel very much better today, only horribly weak. The sweat I had yesterday seems to have taken the fever out of me. It has been a beautiful day and I have seen swallows for the first time this year. Glasspoole has returned from his Signal course rather unexpectedly. It did not turn out quite as he had hoped. Far otherwise, in fact. He had hardly got settled in at the 'School' when all available men were collected and formed into a 'composite' battalion and hurried into the line south of Kemmel. Naturally, being a forlorn composite battalion and therefore nobody's children, they had an exceedingly rotten time, particularly at Dranoutre where they took refuge in a dugout one night only to find early in the morning that they were in no-man's-land.

4.5.18

A battery of eight-inch howitzers has been installed only about seventy yards from us and there are signs that their presence is likely to make things lively for us. The gunners have got dugouts but we haven't!

6.5.18

We have had several spasms of shelling lately, obviously directed at these eight-inch howitzers. The gunners tell us that they have been very successful in knocking out Fritz's Transport nearly every evening, and they are expecting reprisals. Lively prospect. A general order has been issued that owing to the lack of reinforcements all 'attached' men, with a few exceptions, are to be returned to their units. 'Jessie' at once declared that Glasspoole, Cheesman and Sylvester must return to their battalions but of course we don't want to lose them; so Sgt Twycross has got round the question somehow or other and I don't think the General will let them go.

7.5.18

Since quite early this morning, the rain has been rattling down fiercely on the corrugated iron roof of our billet, and the pond just outside the door is filled almost to the brim. At home, if the rain leaks through the roof we get alarmed and send for the builder – it is a serious matter approaching the terrible if it actually drips down on to the bed. But here, of course, things are different. Early this morning I woke up and heard several fellows grousing and grumbling and moving their beds in an endeavour to get into a drier spot. My little corner, fortunately, was quite dry. There is no pleasure in this sort of life despite the alleged humorous sketches and funny tales published in papers and magazines. It is an easy matter to raise a laugh at somebody else's expense. This wretched weather, coupled with a queer tension in the atmosphere, has given me a horrible fit of the blues. Today I am a Socialist, an anarchist, an apostle of downing everything that's up. Here I am, pent up and imprisoned, bound down, gagged, a mere unconsidered cog in the military machine, suffering discomfort, terror, mental and spiritual agony – and to what purpose? Merely that other people may profit – the sleek, bloated capitalists and profiteers, living in luxury and sleeping every night in warm, dry, comfortable beds – the men who started the war, who have run it for their own benefit and who now are afraid to stop it because it has grown into something more terrible than ever they anticipated. For they haven't crushed the mass of the people into the servility they had hoped. They have tried all the brutality of militarism, prussianism and junkerism to reduce the people to serfdom but they have only prevailed in so far as martial law can compel a man to do a thing or take the alternative of being shot at dawn. It's a poor creed that relies on force for its justification. But they have discovered that it is impossible to kill the spirit and they find that the flame of freedom is burning all the more fiercely because of their endeavours to extinguish it. This is why they are afraid to stop the war. They don't know what the men of the nations will do when they get back to civilian life again, and they tremble for the safety of their own miserable skins. And so, being safely delivered of this screed of bitterness, I feel much relieved.

8.5.18

The Area Signal Officer, who has a Test Box on the other side of the Yard, came into the Signal Office this morning. He is young Lush, whom I knew in London, but although I could see he recognised me he would not deign to notice me! Such is the effect of a 'pip'. May the Lord preserve me from ever taking a commission if it is going to have such an effect on me!

11.5.18

At dawn this morning Fritz started a big strafe. We were wakened about 3 a.m. by a few light shells bursting near us. Very soon we were all struggling into our gas masks and then into our clothes. One gas shell dropped on the edge of the pond and the fumes drifted into the billet. By this time it was quite daylight and we were all very much awake. Shells of all sizes and descriptions were now coming over in continuous streams. As far as we could see, the whole area was covered by the shelling and no other spot could afford us any greater security than the one we were in. So we just had to sit down or walk about and wait for something to hit us. The hours passed and there was no lull or even sign of abatement.

One by one the telephone lines went 'dis' and then a big shell dropped on the 'bury' (buried cable route) just outside the first Test Box, about 100 yards away. This finished all the lines except one back to Division. Early on, all the linemen had been sent out but as fast as they mended one break, another occurred. Then the operators were called on in order of duty to go out and help in the repairs. Dickson and I were the last pair to be called, about 11 a.m. As we were preparing to go, a 5.9 shell landed right in the farmyard and gave us all a tidy shake-up but did no other damage. Sgt Twycross gave us a drum of cable and sundry instructions and we set off across the fields to pick up the 'bury'. The shelling ceased abruptly as we started and during the whole time we were out not a shell fell anywhere near us.

Shells had fallen almost as thickly as raindrops, and the whole countryside reeked with gas but, as far as we could see, the amount of damage done was extraordinarily small. Fritz has made no attempt to come over. He has satisfied himself with giving us a very thorough 'strafing'. It has been the biggest 'area strafe' that I have seen unaccompanied by any other kind of operation. Considering the intensity of the shelling and its duration (eight hours) the total number of casualties is exceedingly small. It was remarkable to see how the fellows sat about reading, writing, laughing and playing cards as if we were in a safe, deep dugout instead of a miserable little shanty that affords no more protection than tissue paper. It was striking evidence of the fatalistic instinct which is inherent in human nature. In contact with the brutal realities of life and death, the attitude of mankind generally is that of the old Hebrew who bade his soul be merry today 'for tomorrow we die'.

13.5.18

A runner of the 23rd Middlesex came into the Signal Office this evening and he told us definitely that Sgt Hancock was wounded and missing during a raid carried out on the night of 19 April. It appears that our raiding party, when they got across no-man's-land, found the enemy in greater strength than had been anticipated. Heavy rifle and machine-gun fire effectually prevented our men from getting any further and they had to scramble back as best they could. Sgt Hancock was seen to drop but a search party that went out the following night failed to find any trace of him. There is a remote chance that he was wounded and taken prisoner but the general opinion of the men who were with him is that he was killed. As a matter of fact nothing more was ever heard of Sgt Hancock.

14.5.18

A black and white kitten, about three-quarters grown, lives in our dugout, and forms a centre of common interest. While things are quiet it will run about outside but it will not go far away. It recognises the sound of travelling shells but what is really remarkable is its ability to differentiate between ours and the enemy's. Shells coming from guns behind us make a noise similar to that of Jerry's coming towards us. But this cat can appreciate the difference in direction and also understands that danger comes from one direction only. Batteries of all sizes are around us at distances of two or three hundred yards and they are tolerably active. But puss takes no notice of our guns firing nor of the sing and whistle of our own shells coming towards us from the rear and passing over us towards the enemy; but directly Fritz starts to send any over to us she makes a bee-line for the dugout. She doesn't wait for the shell to burst; as soon as she hears its whistle she is off, no matter what she is doing; she will even leave her dinner and won't come out of the dugout until the shelling is finished although none of the shells may fall dangerously near us. There is something more than instinct in that.

15.5.18

This morning I sat outside the dugout for some time in the glorious sunshine writing to Elsie. I felt so horribly dirty and grimy that I decided to have a bath, so I got a bowl of water, stripped myself, and spent nearly two hours trying to remove the incrustations, for I have only had three baths since the middle of February. But cold water is not much good and I don't feel any cleaner – what I need is boiling. The dugouts are swarming with lice. There are literally millions of them. They crawl about in companies and in battalions. Sometimes I think I would prefer rats.

17.5.18
Moved back to Vlamertinge Chateau today. My billet this time is on the main floor – a large room with big windows opening over the terrace. An up-ended duckboard acts as a ladder from the window to the terrace and so provides a short cut to the cookhouse. We are not so crowded on this occasion.

19.5.18
A football match was played this afternoon in a field in front of the Chateau and well within the view of Fritz's observation balloons.

20.5.18
Fritz took no notice of the football match yesterday. He quietly allowed the game to be played to a finish but this morning he dropped two or three dozen shells on the playing pitch and so has put a stop to any more little games.

There is no sign of leave restarting yet although there has not been very much liveliness on this front for the last three weeks. On night duty last night so wrote a number of letters.

22.5.18
The grounds of this Chateau must have been very beautiful in peacetime. Even now there are lots of flowers blooming despite the ravages of shells and gas and military occupation. This evening I gathered some broom and rhododendrons and put them in a jug to decorate the billet. Sappers are making a line of trenches right through the grounds. It seems as if our Higher Command is not thoroughly satisfied that Fritz's offensive has been wholly scotched.

23.5.18
The broom that I gathered yesterday dropped during the night but Cheesman brought in some more rhododendrons this morning

when he came off night duty. Received two parcels from Elsie. The calico wrappings come in very useful. I always cut them open at one end only and extract the box. Thus I have a bag in which to put my bread ration every morning, and any other little odds and ends in the grub line. Some of them eventually get opened out flat and serve the useful purpose of teacloths and dusters. I have known them to be used as handkerchiefs but so far I have not been reduced to that extent. Bees have been coming in to my rhododendrons. This afternoon I found some yellow irises but the ground was too swampy for me to reach them.

26.5.18

The guns were very quiet this morning so I sat outside and wrote some letters. Then found some bits of wood and made a bench to stand beside my bed. At present there are only a few nails to hang things on, and a plate, for instance, is not an easy thing to hang up. Played crib with Jamieson all the afternoon and beat him hollow, but it was pure luck.

27.5.18

Aitken returned. After leaving hospital he was at Abbeville for a few days and experienced air raids each night. He tells me that the great and wonderful doors of the Cathedral were removed before Fritz's attack in March and were taken south to a place of safety. Had a pleasant two hours' fatigue cleaning up the camp, i.e. picking up fag ends.

28.5.18

All today, every man not otherwise on duty has been on fatigue making a cable trench. An objectionable German observation balloon was gazing down at us all day inspiring us to hurry up with the work but the trench was dug, the cable laid and we had nearly completed the filling in before Fritz paid us any attention. The first few shells fell short — he hadn't quite got the range — and we speeded up vigorously — but when three or four fell almost on top of us 'Jessie' yelled out, 'Pack up and get under cover!' and led a hasty retreat to the dugouts.

1.6.18

We have not had much shelling here but this morning just before breakfast Fritz put a few over. One came through the barn which is our cookhouse; Spicer took a header into the dugout but a lump of shrapnel caught him in the buttocks. It appears to be only a flesh wound but of course he has been taken to hospital. During the morning the shelling increased but moved away from our immediate neighbourhood and eventually settled on Rome Farm, which is being subjected to a violent bombardment with HEs.

2.6.18

Climbing on to the top of our dugouts this morning we watched the continued shelling of Rome Farm. Fritz seems to have set his heart on knocking out the eight-inch howitzers, but he hasn't done it yet, for whenever there is a slight lull in his shelling, they start barking out again. We thank our lucky stars that we are not there now. Towards nightfall Fritz accomplished part of his plan for he set fire to the farm, and we hear that the Area Test Box has been completely knocked out. The fire is now blazing away and illuminating the night. We have some dogs that have been trained as message carriers. They go backwards and forwards between us and certain stations in the line. They are fairly big ugly looking mongrels and they are persuaded to do their work by the prospect of food at the other end. That is to say, a dog that is to do a journey is kept from food for a few hours. From experience he knows that he will get a meal at another certain spot, so as soon as he is released, with the message fixed to his collar, he makes a bee-line for grub.

3.6.18

Lieut. Purvis left us today to go to Abbeville as an Instructor. He seemed very pleased about it. So now we are without an officer. The shelling of Rome Farm has continued – big black blighters have been dropping on it all day and the place is well ablaze. But the eight-inch howitzers, in which we take a very special interest, are still going strong.

After night had fallen we left MG Farm and made for Vlamertinghe. We gave Rome Farm as wide a berth as possible but even then several HEs fell so near that we dived into shell holes or dropped flat on the ground. However, we got safely to the small-gauge railway siding at the back of Vlam. Chateau and found a train of small open trucks waiting for us. Into these we were packed and after the usual period of delay the 'puffing billy' engine pulled us away in the direction of Poperinghe. Above the rattle of the train frequently came the sudden shriek of a shell. Fritz was evidently trying to 'paste' the railway. One shell set fire to a small arms ammunition dump and bullets, cartridge cases and sparks were flying about like 5 November.

4.6.18
Dawn was just breaking as we set out for Sint-Jan-ter-Biezen. It was a very fatiguing march and I was beginning to feel very funny when fortunately a ten-minute halt was called. Sitting on the bank I nearly fainted but just had sufficient life in me to pull off my equipment and stretch out full length on the ground. That pulled me round sufficiently to complete the rest of the journey. We arrived about 5.30 a.m. and found Aitken had established the Signal Office in a bow hut at the western end of the village. We lay down to rest but slumber would not be wooed. I was too cold and uncomfortable. MacDougall, who has been down at the Transport, tells us that QMS Cass has been through all our packs and taken away all the blankets he could find. A very dirty trick. We are not supposed to have blankets in the summer but most of us had managed to acquire one somehow or other. And now that little bit of comfort has gone! Broke a tooth on a hard bit of chocolate that Aitken gave me.

10.6.18
General Towsey is leaving us and we are sorry to lose him. He had us on parade and gave a little farewell speech. Having been out

here since 1914, his turn has now come to take an easier post and I understand he is going to Colchester.

12.6.18
Our new Brigadier is General Weston. It turns out that he was Cheesman's employer before the war. He is a stockbroker and joined up as a private at the very beginning of the war, subsequently taking a commission and rapidly rising to his present rank. He is utterly regardless of personal danger and while in the Royal Fusiliers went through the most exciting experiences as coolly as any stage hero. He inspected our billet, enquired if the straw was clean and that is all we have seen of him. The battalions are complaining of the cold at night (the poor blighters have no chance of scrounging blankets) so he has ordered an abundance of straw to be supplied to them.

14.6.18
My faithful old pipe, which I brought out with me nearly two years ago and in which I have smoked nearly one cwt [a hundredweight or 112lbs] of tobacco, is in danger of disintegrating at any moment, so I have asked Elsie to get me a new one, for although the best briars are grown in France, the best pipes are made in England.

15.6.18
The Officers' Mess Cook has been out here for twenty-three months without any leave. On several occasions he has been very near to it but something or other has cropped up to cancel it. Now at last he is to go. When he heard the news the shock was so great that he cried like a child and nearly collapsed. He was so bad that the other fellows had to put him to bed.

17.6.18
Leave has been increased slightly, bringing my chances up from Xmas 1920 to the autumn of 1919. It is always an engaging occupation to calculate when your leave will come round at the current rate. I daresay it will be speeded up a little more later on.

18.6.18

Sent my fifth Epistle to Elsie. I finished it the day before yesterday
and while writing it I did very little else except each evening when
I took a stroll, generally with Glasspoole, in and around the Forêt
d'Eperlecques. The German prisoners who were there last year
have gone and their place has been taken by the Chinese Labour
Corps. They are an uncanny looking lot and do their washing in
an immense crater which is almost large enough for a swimming
bath. It partly intersects a small stream and so is kept full of water.
It would be an easy matter to get drowned in it. Large areas of the
Forêt have been cut down and carted up the line to make roadways
or pit props for dugouts. This evening Jamieson and I called at a
farm for coffee and hard-boiled eggs and there we met a Sergeant
who is in charge of the 'Chinks'. He can speak French and Chinese,
having spent many years out in the East. But I don't think he is
very enamoured of his job. I know I should not care for it.

19.6.18

Much ado over the Countess's Silver Spoons! A few days ago the
Staff Officers had a tea party in the Chateau grounds, a large
number of officers being invited from the battalions. The Countess
provided the necessary silver and crockery so that the business
could be carried through in good style. After it was all over and the
crockery was being returned to the Countess, it was discovered that
several solid silver teaspoons were missing. The old lady went up
in the air about it – the Brigade Major circularised all the officers
who had been present, the whole of the gardens and grounds were
thoroughly searched but all was to no avail. Then the BM had us
all on parade and, approaching the matter as tactfully as he could
without openly accusing some person or persons unknown with
wickedly stealing the things, suggested that if any of us could find
these things would we, as honourable men, remember the great
prestige of the British Army etc etc, put them into a box which
had been fixed in a certain place where absolute privacy was assured
so that no other individual could see who the conscience-stricken

person was. This appeal was the very last forlorn hope for none
of the Signals was anywhere near the tea party. It seems to be the
general opinion that some of the officer guests 'swiped them up'
as souvenirs and now are ashamed to own up to it. I am afraid the
Countess can say a final farewell to them.

Glasspoole and I, on the hunt for lettuces or any sort of fresh
greens, made the acquaintance of an elderly couple, refugees from
Houplines, near Armentières. They can't speak a word of English
but we gathered that they had kept a china shop but it was smashed
up early in the war and they had to fly for their lives. Their life
here apparently is not of the happiest for the natives regard them
as interlopers, an example of personal feeling that is always to be
found in small rural communities. They supplied us with lettuces,
spring onions and garlic, all of which went down very well with the
hard-boiled eggs from the farm.

20.6.18

Up early this morning and immediately after breakfast were taken
out for a field day in and around the Forêt d'Eperlecques. The
whole Division was in action and we were advancing against the
determined resistance of the enemy. Funny how all these practice
stunts take the nature of advances! Retreats, apparently, are left to
take care of themselves.

21.6.18

Hamilton and Davidson have just made up one of their little
differences – so everything is bright and cheerful once more.
Hamilton is a dour Scot and is one of the smartest men in the section,
but I've never told him so. Indeed, I have often told him the reverse
for we are most decidedly vituperative in our conversation, and
horrible personalities are looked on as affectionate terms displaying
a feeling of profound respect, almost reverence, for each other. On
the other hand any suggestion of politeness is strong evidence of
strained relations. Hamilton and Davidson have long periods of
great friendliness – then comes a row and after the initial outbreak

has cooled down they utterly refrain from speaking to each other except when duty compels them to and then they are mighty respectful with 'If you please, Corporal Davidson' and 'Yes, by all means, Corporal Hamilton' etc. Eventually they bury the hatchet by offering each other cigarettes. Indeed, one of the most popular ways of either one signifying to the other that he is prepared to forgive and forget is to ask for a cigarette.

Hamilton's Christian name is John and you must never call him Jack unless you want to make him very cross. He doesn't mind 'Johnny' but he has a violent aversion to 'Jack'. Sometimes he gets horribly annoyed. Then it is Davidson's chance to laugh at him and call him 'crabbit' and soon there are all the makings of a very fine row – at least it looks so if you don't know them, but as it is, we just look on with amusement and spur them to further endeavours in tongue-slaughter whenever their energies show signs of flagging. Once, in the huts at Reninghelst, Hamilton and Aitken were reading when some dispute arose. A. threw a book at H. It passed backwards and forwards several times and finally A. threw it back; H. dodged it and didn't look for anything more but Aitken followed it up very rapidly with a lump of cheese weighing about a pound and a half. It caught Hamilton right between the eyes. It was a shock to H. but the audacity of the act was a greater shock to those who witnessed it. It was one of those unrecorded acts of bravery of the war. Everybody stood in terrible suspense, ready to intervene to prevent Aitken from being too horribly mutilated. But it was such a surprise to H. that he did nothing at all and normal state of friendly enmity was soon resumed.

1.7.18

Last night orders were received for us to move into the line today to relieve a French Division, so this morning we have been busy packing up our valises. Directly after dinner Sgt Twycross came and said, 'Be ready in half an hour to go to a spot between Abeele and Reninghelst to take over "A" Echelon Relay Station. You will have to run it by yourself but I will give you an orderly.' 'Well,' I said, 'it's a pretty tall order if I've got to be on duty twenty-four hours a day indefinitely. Give me a runner who is capable of dealing with the telephone and knows how to take down a message. I should prefer to have Fisher.' And it was arranged accordingly. Proceeding through Abeele all was plain sailing to the Dreef crossroads. Our final directions, however, were not very definite and the traffic control man could not help us but we were not very long in finding the right spot and were welcomed by the 'Froggies' who were on the lookout for us. Only one could speak a little English but we soon learnt that they were very anxious to get out of this sector. It is a bit too hot for them; they are going back to Champagne where there is 'beaucoup vin' and 'beaucoup ma'mselles'. We changed over instruments and I tested the line, speaking to a Frenchman at the other end. Then they took me along part of the line and showed me the direction in which it ran and very soon they had packed up and gone, leaving a valise behind to be picked up by one of their comrades who was guiding some of our troops into the line. Less than five minutes after they had left I tried the line again and could not get through. So Fisher went out and mended it; the break was not very far away and he did not have much trouble in finding it. The rest of the Transport arrived in due course but we have been too busy to have much of a look-round.

2.7.18
Our position is map reference L34d.5.3 about 200 yards east of the Dreef crossroads, going towards Reninghelst. We are in a rectangular field surrounded by a high hedge and trees that afford considerable shelter from observation. There is a small farmhouse but we are quartered in the stables. The Brigade Transport drivers are in the big stable while Fisher and I are located in an adjoining 'apartment' – Signal Office and Billet combined. There are two stretchers, one slung up above the other and the Frenchmen left us a pile of blankets, so in that respect we are more comfortable than we anticipated. But oh, the filth!

The whole place is in a most abominable condition. There are more flies than I have seen anywhere since that German dugout on the Somme in 1916. The Frenchmen have made no attempt at keeping the place clean or even sanitary. Outside the door the rainwater has accumulated in a hollow and formed a small pond into which the Froggies have thrown all their refuse, bones, bread, rotten meat and a great lump of putrefying sheepskin. The whole mass is seething with life in the form of fat juicy maggots with long tails. Filth and rotting matter are everywhere. Inside our billet, the floor level is lower than the ground outside. Consequently water has drained in and no attempt has been made to stop it, but a number of ammunition boxes have been placed on top of the mud to form a false floor. I can see that I am going to have a busy time getting the place into something like a sanitary condition, but the job is to know where to start. There are a few other cottages nearby; the Transport Offices and the Padres are living in one, the others are deserted. So Fisher has been on the scrounge and has brought back a few little things such as chairs and plates. A small table was already here. We intend to make ourselves as comfortable as possible, as Sgt Lunn says we are likely to be here for six weeks or more. Five times last night I had to hop out of bed to answer the telephone that is at the other end of the billet. So I decided that something would have to be altered. Accordingly my first job this morning was to get another telephone out of the limber and run a pair of leads to the head of my bed so that each night I can have the spare telephone on the table beside me.

3.7.18

The line running from this office is what is known technically as a 'comic air-line' but in this case it is exceptionally comic. It runs along the roadside and across fields in a very haphazard way, trailing along the ground or slung up in hedges (where they exist) and in one place going up into high trees, while along the road close by, it is supported on short posts about eighteen inches high. It crosses three roads and a cart track and finally comes to rest at the 123rd Brigade Rear Station nearly a mile away. All this I have found out this morning as I was unable to get through and had to go out to find the 'dis'. I located it within about fifty yards but then it became very puzzling. Some Americans were billeted in dugouts and they asked me what I was doing. When I told them that I was looking for a broken wire they said, 'What, one of them things? Well, we broke one of them this morning and tied the ends on to that nail in the tree.'

They thought telephony was a very funny thing and asked many questions and seemed to regard me as a rather uncanny individual. They must have come straight off the prairie. Anyhow, this was the first time they had been near the line and I was impressed with their ingenuous thirst for knowledge. They asked the most simple questions and seemed to be quite unconcerned as to whether they appeared childishly ignorant or not. Some of them asked me quite innocently if a little shelter they had made with a few sticks and about two inches of earth would stop a shell! These men are being taken up the line in small parties in order to break them in and give them some idea of what warfare is like.

4.7.18

The line was broken again this morning and of course I suspected the Yanks, and with good cause for I found that they had cut out about twenty yards of it to use as string. They seemed quite surprised to learn that they had caused any trouble.

The Frenchman's pack that was left behind here when we took possession has not been claimed. We fetched it inside after the first night in case it should rain, but now that all the French troops have gone from the neighbourhood there is no chance of the owner turning up, so today we opened it up and shared out its contents, the most acceptable items being five shirts. Fisher had three and I had two. Fisher went down to B Echelon this afternoon and brought back my spare valise. He has also been on the scrounge again and the result is that now we have a table, two chairs, a form and sundry boxes on which visitors are invited to rest their weary bones – also a table cloth – white with red markings – certainly it is in two pieces but neither piece is quite large enough to cover the whole table so we have to lap one over the other. In the centre of the table we have a vase of small marguerites and flaming poppies with a sprig or two of honeysuckle. The vase is an old 18-pdr shell case that we have polished up and made to look very smart.

Yesterday, when searching the cupboards in the adjoining cottage, we found some stuff that looked like cornflour. It was in a paper packet and from the reading matter thereon I concluded it was good to eat. My little French was not quite sufficient to make out whether it was to be used as a food or applied as a plaster, until I came to a phrase commencing 'Employé au lieu d.Arrowroot'. Very good – but what about the milk? Some of the neighbouring farms are still occupied by the natives so Fisher set forth with a large can and in less than an hour he was back with it full of milk – about half a gallon.

The cottage supplied us with a cast-iron cooking pot – like a small witches' cauldron – and so I proceeded with the cooking. It was a great success and when it got cool it was real blancmange. We tasted it and found it very good so we issued only a very limited number of invitations to supper.

6.7.18

We did not want all the blankets that the Frenchmen left behind so we have sent them to the fellows up at Brigade. They have got some good dugouts but General Weston spends most of his time in a little tin shed utterly regardless of danger, and when shells start coming over he just looks out and says 'Um, getting interesting' and proceeds with his work.

When we arrived here, the Froggies told us that the spot is subject to occasional bombardments – we have had one – it was all small shells and shrapnel. The previous night the Hants Transport had brought back a Maltese Cart full of bricks to make a better standing for the horses. A shell dropped clean on to the cart and saved them the job of unloading it. No other damage was done as far as we are concerned although it was a bit lively while it lasted. The only bit of shelter that we have is a funk hole big enough for two men at a squeeze and just covered over with the trunk of a tree. I have spent a lot of time digging a deep pit and burying barrow-loads of the filthy mess that surrounds us, but I don't seem to make very rapid progress. There is no 'Cresol' (disinfectant) to be had. I have sent urgent messages down to the Quarter bloke but he says he is quite unable to get any.

Our position here is on comparatively high ground. Towards Reninghelst the country drops slightly and provides us with a commanding view of the Flanders Hills which Fritz has made such frightful attempts to capture. Yet he only holds one – Mont Kemmel – and from the look of it, that is not much of a sinecure. Formerly it was thickly clad with trees and crowned by a Windmill (from which General Plumer watched the mines go up on 7 June 1917) but now it is only a scorched, blasted and desolated waste. As a point of vantage it is very desirable but it is very doubtful if our artillery is allowing Fritz to use it very much. It is continuously and heavily shelled, and, viewed through field glasses, the accuracy of the shelling is apparent and it certainly does not look possible for Fritz to establish and maintain an observation post on its summit.

15.7.18

It was really very sad last night – being Sunday too! We got the custard powder, the milk and the sugar and, surmounting a few preliminary difficulties with the fire, proceeded to make our supper. After much patient endeavour the milk was coaxed to the boil and in went the 'doin's'. The stuff ought to have thickened up directly but it didn't. I tried to coax it by vigorous stirring and by uttering incantations over it but it wasn't having any. All the previous lots have worked all right and I was disappointed but I wouldn't show it. I merely said that I intended it to be thin by way of variety – thought we would like it so that we could drink it instead of eating it with a knife and fork. There was nearly half a gallon of it and now there is little more than half a pint so it must be good all the same. Fisher has just had a parcel. It contained, amongst other things, a tin of peaches, so we are going to have peaches and custard for supper. When I got up this morning my back was aching badly and I felt rotten. So after dinner I had a good sleep and now I feel quite all right. The weather possibly is the cause. It is dull, heavy and oppressive but we have had no rain today. There has been plenty of it during the past few days and the mud is up to the ankles everywhere.

16.7.18
Exceptionally violent thunderstorm in the early hours of this morning with heavy wind and rain. The day has been frightfully hot and oppressive – not a breath of wind – and what was left of our custard has gone sour.

18.7.18
This evening a parcel arrived from Elsie. Parcels make us like little children probing into the hidden mysteries of their Christmas stockings, fetching out one thing after another and wondering what is coming next. Bunny Abbott has come down from Brigade bringing a number of papers and documents with him. It seems that some military operations are toward (what they are we do not know) and it is considered unsafe to have all the confidential documents at Brigade HQ.

22.7.18
Made a blancmange – it turned out very well. But I wasn't so successful with the jelly. Something must have happened to it because I followed the instructions very carefully and used a little less than a pint of water but it wouldn't set. We also stewed some dates although I don't know that this is a dish recognised by Mrs Beeton, but it is quite good. By supper time all the things had cooled down so we had blancmange and stewed dates and poured the jelly on top like a sauce.

23.7.18
Was continually disturbed all last night either by the telephone or by people coming in wanting to know this, that and the other. A Signal Office is looked on as a place where you can get information on every subject under the sun. You have only to put a blue and

white flag up outside the office and if you are close to a road, as we are here, you will be inundated with enquiries and expected to furnish information as to the disposition of every unit within an area of twenty square miles. I'm very civil and obliging during the day but I don't appreciate these nocturnal visits. They are too frequent and sometimes, waking up suddenly and hearing a clamour at the door, I think for a moment that it is Fritz. Since 9 o/c this morning the rain has been pouring down steadily and persistently. Everything is looking utterly cheerless. It is too miserable even to carry on the war. I have only heard two or three guns fire all day and not a single observation balloon has been up.

30.7.18
Another Washing Day – cold water, a scrubbing brush and Quartermaster's soap make it pretty hard work although sometimes we are able to get at a fire. Then we boil the things, socks and all. Nevertheless, I am convinced that it is a job at which I shall never be able to earn a living. Quartermaster's soap, by the way, is a hard yellow substance that is only persuaded to lather by the exercise of extreme patience, perseverance and elbow grease.

3.8.18
Poor old Peter Brown, who ought never to have been out here (he is a grandfather!) stayed the night on his way down the line. His case provides evidence of how difficult it is for a man to get back to Blighty once he has landed in France. For many months Brigade HQ have been trying all manner of means to get him transferred to a Home Unit but every application has been refused until now. He is, I understand, being transferred to a Labour Unit stationed at Northampton. His place is being taken by Jimmy Rumsey – another man over forty!

4.8.18
Received a parcel from Mother. It should have arrived a week ago, and as a matter of fact it did, but some letters for one of the chaplains

who was on leave had been tucked under the string and his batman thought the parcel was for him, too – didn't have the sense to look and make sure. So it had been over in the chaplains' billet (about eighty yards away) till last night when he returned from leave. The tobacco situation is more serious than words can describe. I've got about three more pipefuls and it is quite impossible to buy or pinch any from anywhere. It is a matter for earnest prayer and supplication.

6.8.18

Leave is to be increased on the 9th and men will be entitled to it after five months. There are, however, large numbers of twelve-month men yet to go, and a reasonable estimate of my chances is that I ought to get home before Christmas, possibly in October, that is if the revised allotment is maintained.

7.8.18

Have finished digging another big refuse pit, the first one having been filled up and covered in. A week or so ago we got a fatigue party from the Surreys and they spent a couple of days cleaning up the mess and saving all the scrap metal. Several lorry loads of shell cases, bits of metal, wire etc have been carted away and the place is now respectably tidy and sanitary.

The corn in the surrounding fields is now almost ripe 'unto harvest'. The whole countryside was under cultivation right up to Fritz's advance in April, consequently the front-line trenches run amid the waving corn. This makes operations more difficult, as it affords shelter to creeping and crawling troops. There have been a few raids by both sides and on several occasions Germans have been found hiding in the corn well behind our front line. The farmer who owns this land came over today with his wife, presumably to have a look at the crops. I could not make out where they are living now but it seems that they cleared out from here very hurriedly last April, but the ripening corn induces them to come back to gather the harvest. Of course the government is doing all it can to persuade the farmers to reap all the corn possible and the British Army is supplying men to help.

8.8.18
The job of preparing breakfast has devolved on me in Charlie Blake's absence and I have gained a certain amount of dexterity in manipulating the bacon. But this morning I suffered a heavy reverse. I had got it going very nicely and all the world seemed gay and bright so I left it for a minute to continue sizzling on its own. What happened I cannot say but when Fisher went out the whole lot was on fire. So we had to be content with bread and 'pozzy'.

The other day we noticed one of our aeroplanes in difficulties and eventually it crashed in the next field, where we gather the poppies and the ox-eye daisies. We didn't like it because it was well within Fritz's observation and we expected he would try to knock it out, but he left it alone and after dark a lorry came up and carted it away.

17.8.18
The civilians are cutting the corn – two women and a man are engaged in the business all day long. Where they go at night is a mystery. All day long they are in full view of Fritz but he has left them alone – yet they are in the midst of Fritz's legitimate objectives – and shells are no respecters of persons. One of their carts, loaded high with wheat, broke my line where it was carried on high poles across a roadway. It was useless to try and erect the poles again so I came back for a pick axe and then buried the cable under the roadway. This comic air-line requires some attention. On average I have to go out and mend a break about four times a week; only about half of them are due to shellfire.

22.8.18
A brilliant night with a full moon and plenty of bombing aeroplanes about. One passed over us so low down that I could almost have hit it with a stone. Low flying has become very popular lately, in

the day as well as the night. It is safer for the airmen as they are on us and gone again before we can raise a rifle to our shoulders, and of course the 'Archies' (anti-aircraft guns) are helpless to deal with them. Only the other morning an enemy plane came over in this fashion and I noticed shells bursting round it about fifty feet from the ground. I thought at first that some trench mortars must be 'having a cut' but it turned out to be some 18-pdr field guns. In connection with his night bombing, Fritz also employs small balloons or parachutes that carry a bright light lasting for fifteen minutes. These light up a big area of country and enable the planes to pick out their objectives quite easily.

We have been using small balloons to carry propagandist literature into Fritz's territory. They are fitted with a clockwork mechanism that after a certain time operates to release hundreds of pamphlets telling Jerry the most favourable items of news from our point of view. Of course they can only be used in a favourable wind and good weather. One got into a calm patch near us and sprinkled its literature about our fields. I have kept one of the pamphlets as a souvenir. One morning, two German prisoners were brought down. They were quite confident about ultimately winning the war.

Lately we have had a little variation from the custard and blancmange menu. In one of the fields through which our line runs I observed large quantities of French beans. A whole field was sown with them and as I have very little compunction in regard to pinching things from the Belgians, I filled my pockets and returned to the billet. Then Fisher remembered where there was a field of potatoes so off he went with a spade and a sack and brought back enough to last for a week. So we have had several suppers of potatoes, beans and bully beef. Hear that Campbell, the Divisional Operator, was wounded in the leg while sitting outside his dugout writing letters. Also hear that General Weston and the Brigade Major (Mr Hogge) went up to the front line one night and carried on over no-man's-land and brought back a couple of prisoners. The 18th KRRs carried out a raid (I believe it was in daylight) a short time ago and they met a rather fierce opposition, Captain Taylor, who was with us in the Messines Ridge attack on 7 June 1917, being among the killed.

24.8.18

There is a strong rumour that we are to be relieved in a day or two, and I think it is quite probable as the Brigade has been in the line for eight weeks on end. Certainly the battalions have been withdrawn one at a time for a little recuperation but they have only come back to the neighbourhood of Hooggraaf and consequently the men are very tired and nerve-shaken. No relief at all has been afforded to the Brigade HQ and they have been subjected to a pretty rough time. One morning I couldn't get through to them at all. Corporal Dunlop at 123rd Bde Rear could only tell me that a heavy 'strafe' was going forward. Eventually got on to Sgt Twycross via Division and he told me that they were being shelled with eight-inch HEs.

The shelling started before breakfast and most of the fellows had narrow squeaks in dashing from their dugouts to the cookhouse, grabbing their breakfast and dashing back again. At last one dropped right on the cookhouse and entirely demolished it. The poor cook (a man who had replaced Baldock only a week or two earlier and who insisted on wearing a Salvation Army jersey) was literally blown to atoms. All they found of him was a piece of foot in a boot on top of a dugout about 200 yards away. Then poor old Jimmy Rumsby, the Bermondsey scavenger, an honest and popular man with all the troops, caught the full blast of a shell and was killed instantly. Of course the lines all went 'dis' in no time and the linemen had a rather terrible time. Sylvester and Murphy were out together and a shell burst almost between them. Sylvester was barely scratched but Murphy had a leg and an arm practically blown off besides other severe wounds in the body and head. Somehow or other they got him in and bandaged him up and now he is in hospital. And yet with all his horrible mutilation we almost envy him at times for he has finished with the war.

Such is the peculiar mentality of men under severe and continual nervous strain. But there, we are not what we were. We are not individuals that walked and talked and went about our lawful occasions in peacetime. Those persons have faded out of existence – we have reverted almost to a semi-savage state. The thin veneer of civilisation has been washed away leaving revealed primitive human instincts that at one time we would scarcely have acknowledged. I am quite certain that Man is much nearer the savage than is generally admitted. Brought up in the ease, comfort and conventions of a civilised State we accepted the veneer for the substance. But now we are up against the stark realities of existence. We have experienced real hunger, real fatigue and real horror, and we begin to appreciate the full meaning of 'the struggle for existence' and 'the survival of the fittest'. Animal instincts rise up within us in a manner almost terrifying. We feel but little removed from the wild beasts that prey and are preyed upon. A mixed multitude of primeval passions surge in our hearts. Yet they are kept in check. The social training of generations has proved effective in the main issues, but how much our self-control is influenced by the knowledge of the support of civilisation behind us is impossible to say. We regard ourselves rather as detached personalities. Sapper Martin is not the respectable law-abiding Mr Martin of pre-war days. They are quite distinct personalities and are apt to eye each other rather insolently at times. Hunger, thirst and fear are fundamental realities and the natural passions that arise from them must be experienced before they can be appreciated.

Yet there is another point to be considered and this is where our social upbringing proves its worth. There is spirit of loyalty and brotherhood animating the troops that approaches nobility. A man is measured by his acts and if a man shirks his duty or leaves a comrade in the lurch, he is ostracised. He is no longer a 'white' man – he is beyond the pale. Such men are rare. I can only remember two – one was an arrant coward, the other a massive bully who to save himself strangled a German with his hands but left his own wounded comrade to die without even a sip of water. On the other hand the spirit of loyalty is amazing. It makes one feel proud to be associated with men who, coming from all stations of life, are banded together in a common brotherhood – a brotherhood of the blood – something infinitely more potent and sincere than can be imagined by armchair philosophers and theorists.

There is yet another aspect to this amazing existence that must be recorded. Even the most materialistic cannot deny the existence of a definite spirit permeating groups or bodies of men. A small society of men, whose individual members are in close intercourse with one another, gradually assumes a temperament or personality of any one of its members but nevertheless there is no doubt of its existence in the mass. This soul, this spirit, this strange actuating impulse, is apparent to a remarkable extent in almost any unit of the British Army. It may be said that regimental reputation and traditions are handed down from soldier to soldier but there is something more than this. Battalions have been formed, annihilated and formed again time after time but the Soul remains the same no matter how much or how often the personnel be changed. If this changing process were gradual, the psychological aspect would not be so remarkable – but the changes are rapid and violent, and moreover the new men are drawn from all the social grades, the intellectual and the illiterate, the studious and the ignorant, the thoughtful and the careless, the gentle and the rough, the pampered 'Mother's darling' and the veritable gutter snipe. Truly Mankind is a fascinating study.

26.8.18

One day I shall go to the trouble of counting up how many times I have changed my quarters but I haven't time for it just now. The past two months have not been strikingly eventful although there has been a distinct liveliness at times. Apart from the periodical 'strafes', each lasting about two or three hours and occurring about once a week, there have been sundry little bits of excitement particularly when Fritz attempted, either by aeroplane or shrapnel, to bring down some of our observation balloons.

He made a great many attacks on the one nearest to us and eventually set fire to it. The observer jumped out but the parachute failed to open and he was dashed to earth. I have seen a good many hurried parachute descents but this is the only time that it ended so tragically. On another occasion, one of these 'sausages' broke from its moorings and rose to a great height. It floated off towards Fritz lines and our anti-aircraft guns tried to bring it down but failed. It got into a cross current and drifted backwards and forwards for some hours and eventually disappeared in the distance.

Strafes always meant broken lines and I don't mind admitting that sometimes I have had the 'wind up' when I have been out mending them, particularly when I got across the fields where there is a lonely stretch where a man might get wounded and lie for hours without being found. One morning heavy shelling started down in the hollow and of course the line soon went 'dis'. The break was high up in a tree and I had to scrounge some more wire before I could establish communication. Before I had finished, the line went in another place, and later in another. Meanwhile, the shelling had extended up the slope and appeared to be mainly to the right of our billet. Having mended the third break I 'tapped in' but failed to get Fisher. I cursed him for leaving the billet, slung the instrument over my shoulder and started back, keeping my eye on the line all the time. As I came up the hill a number of new shell holes told me that the strafe had been nearer home than I thought. Outside the Padre's billet the line had been blown to bits, necessitating more wire, so I carried on to the Signal Office and found Fisher just emerging from the funk hole and a 'five-nine' shell hole within ten yards of the billet. The shelling had been heavier than usual, with plenty of 'five-nines' and big black shrapnel, but with my return it ceased and I made the final joint without disturbance. About ten o'clock a man called through the door, 'Hi, do you know that there's one of your mates lying dead out here?' We went out and found an RFA Signaller lying on the bank and beside him was a bicycle. There had been no shelling so we surmised that he must have been knocked down by a lorry but neither he nor his bicycle showed any sign of damage. At first he seemed quite dead but when we had removed his equipment and opened his shirt we could detect faint

heartbeats. I rang up the Field Ambulance and asked them to send
a motor. We did what we could to restore him, when one of the
men exclaimed, 'Look here, this is what it is!' and pulled out a half
empty wine bottle from the man's gas mask. I immediately got on
to the Field Ambulance to try and stop the motor but I was too late
– while I was still speaking the ambulance arrived and carted him
away. It is the first time that I have seen a man really 'dead drunk'.
The next morning he turned up for his bicycle and told us that he
had been down to Cassel on duty, had imbibed unwisely and the
last thing he remembered was being put into a lorry along with
his bicycle. When he recovered himself in the Field Ambulance
he was hauled up before the Medical Officer and formally 'crimed'
on three points, viz 1. Being drunk on duty 2. Wilful neglect of
government property (i.e. the bicycle) and 3. Entering hospital
without just cause. What happened to him I never heard.

28.8.18

All the morning dozens of us were scouring the countryside in
search of tobacco but without any luck. I was reduced to two
pipefuls of 'issue' shag when a parcel arrived from Elsie containing
¼lb of Smiths Glasgow Mixture – just in the nick of time! At
9 p.m. the Brigade embussed at Dreef crossroads and we were
taken away in the darkness to Hallines, south-west of St Omer, a
distance of twenty-eight miles. It was between 1 and 2 a.m. when
we arrived there and put into a barn without blankets and only
Mother Earth to lie on. A little enterprising search with the aid
of candles revealed bundles of straw in a loft and these we quickly
appropriated, only to raise the wrath of the farmer who seemed to
prize this particular straw for some reason or other. He kicked up
a terrible fuss but what was one against so many! He had to retire
until daylight and we got what sleep we could. Then he returned
and continued his protests but we were obdurate although finally
we compromised and let him have his precious straw when he
brought along a cartload of another quality. After breakfast we got
our packs from the Transport. Then took the air for an hour or so

and later wrote to Elsie and asked her to order ¼lb tobacco to be sent to me every week. The whole Division is coming into this area and we expect to be here about three weeks. Arrangements are already being made to hold some Brigade Sports.

By the summer of 1918, the German army, while by no means a spent force, was no longer able to summon enough men and materials to mount an offensive of any consequence. They had battered away at Allied lines in March, then April, then May and even into June, switching the direction of attack in the increasingly desperate hope that one more push might bring about the collapse that they had so earnestly desired in the Allied resolve to fight. But there was no collapse: although at times the Allied cause looked bleak, they nevertheless held the Germans at bay, inflicting like-for-like casualties that the Allies could countenance but the Germans, increasingly outgunned, could not hope to lose and then replenish. By August, it was clear that, with American troops entering the conflict in greater and greater numbers, and with British and French forces about to take to the offensive once more, the Germans could do little but hold the ground they stood on. On 8 August even this proposition was fully undermined by an Allied offensive that tore through German lines and took such large numbers of prisoners that the German High Command privately acknowledged the war was lost. It was, as they later said themselves, the Black Day for the German army. From that moment, the German forces began an inexorable retreat, first across the battlefields they had fought so hard to win earlier that year, then later across the open, unspoilt lands that had lain behind their positions for almost the entire war. The last great defensive position, the Hindenburg Line, was stormed at the end of September and there remained little to do but to fall back, perhaps as far as Germany and the Rhine itself. The question was only when the Germans might sue for peace.

31.8.18

A day of excitement. From the official reports that have been coming through, it appears that Fritz has evacuated Kemmel Hill and the line that we held throughout July and August. The 124th Brigade were in the line awaiting the relief that would enable them to come back to this area but they have been ordered to keep in touch with the enemy and we have to go back to join them. So our three weeks' rest has promptly been reduced to three days. We have to move from here tomorrow morning and there has been considerable rushing about since the order was received to get everything packed up as far as possible.

2.9.18

So far as we are concerned the military situation is somewhat obscure and we have spent this day in hanging about waiting for orders that did not arrive until the evening. And now we know that tomorrow we go into the line almost on the jolly old St Eloi front.

3.9.18

My birthday – and some birthday too! The busiest one I have ever spent. When we were ready to march off, Sgt Twycross told me to go across to the Transport (at the next farm) taking Dagnall with me as a runner. I was to try and establish communication with Brigade as soon as they got into the line. All the morning and afternoon I was trudging about here and there, backwards and forwards, 'tapping in' on every line I could find. I discovered a Test Box but none of the terminals produced a line that was of any use to me. By teatime I was tired out and just wanted to lie down and rest but a message came down from Brigade that I was to take a cycle and meet a runner who would be leaving Brigade with an important message about 6 p.m. Lally also had to follow with some stores on the limber and I told Dagnall to accompany him. The countryside seemed remarkably quiet as I approached Reninghelst. This little town, of more or less happy memories, was practically deserted. It has been very badly knocked about and of course no civilians have lived in it since last April. Nearby I met Morris with the all-important message but as I was now within a few yards of Brigade I decided to go and see the boys; but I didn't stop long. Before I got as far back as Reninghelst I met Lally and Dagnall. Giving the message to Dagnall to take back on the cycle, I returned to Brigade HQ with Lally, unloaded the stores and had a look in some of the dugouts. A few shells were coming over but nothing to get alarmed about yet the mules were a bit restive so Lally was anxious to make a move.

When we had got back to Ouderdom I suddenly remembered a message that I ought to have delivered to Brigade from Capt. Mowat so back we had to go once more. When we reached the Transport Lines it was five minutes to midnight and I was dead beat. Earlier in the day we had dumped our kit in the Quarter Master's hut as we could find no other billet, and here I now fetched out my blanket and rolled myself up in it. The mail had come up while I was out and there was a pile of letters and parcels for me. Lying in my 'kip' I read the letters and then fell asleep.

7.9.18

A couple of days ago Sgt Pragnell came back from leave and brought up in a wagon several dozen bottles of beer for the Officers' Mess. It seemed a pity to let them go straight up the line and 'Praggy' wasn't anxious to go on any further that evening. So we unloaded the bottles and stood them in the Quarter Master's hut where we could keep our eye on them. Somehow or other that evening there didn't seem much to do after dark so we had plenty of time to keep our eyes on the bottles and see that none was stolen. And that is how the little conviviality started. By nine o'clock Frank, the store man, was telling the Quarter just what he thought of him so Dagnall and I with a little persuasion got his boots off, wrapped a blanket round him and put him to bed with a bottle by his pillow for comfort. He was very soon fast asleep and then we stood all the empty bottles around him to act as a terrible warning when he woke up the next morning. The following day Sgt Pragnall took what remained up to Brigade. How he has accounted for the missing bottles I don't know.

8.9.18

Wretched weather – rain, thunder and lightning all last night and it has been raining nearly all day. During the night Brigade moved out of the line and now we are near Lijssenthoek, about a mile or so away in a direct line across the fields but two miles by road. Spent much time in letter writing.

12.9.18
Viler than ever today – can't step outside the door without going ankle-deep in watery mud. Have had nearly a week of it now and it's about time we had a change. Last evening it looked as if it were going to be fine so I washed a shirt and two pairs of socks – now they are hanging up in the billet hoping to get dry some day. I think washerwomen ought to go straight to heaven without any examination whatever.

14.9.18
This morning, praise be, there was no rain and soon after breakfast we were on the move again and before noon were located in a barn at the north-west end of Busseboom. I was not satisfied with the place from a Signals' point of view so I strolled round to see what other accommodation was available and soon found that QMS Cass had taken up his abode in a cottage at the south-east end of the village. There was a room in it going spare so I staked my claim and returned to the Transport to fetch down the equipment. Having got comfortably settled in, the next thing to do was to try and get in touch with Brigade. There was a crowd of wires running there and everywhere and they were mostly dud.

Along the road to Ouderdom I found the 123rd Brigade Signal Office. This was a bit of luck, as they had a spare connection on their board and another line direct to my Brigade. So by cutting and joining I got a line back to my billet before nightfall and easily got through to Brigade, much to Sgt Twycross' surprise. It has been a very tiring day, but it would have been worse if it had rained so now (9 p.m.) I am going to 'roost'.

16.9.18
Received a parcel from Elsie containing tobacco (most welcome), papers and a little book of war poems called *Counter-attack* by Siegfried

Sassoon. Very good and very outspoken, revealing things as they actually are, not as they are represented to be by the daily press. They will do old Glasspoole's heart good when he reads some of them.

19.9.18

Today we moved half a mile or so to a small cottage on the road to Reninghelst, for what reason is not yet apparent. All the afternoon and evening I was trying to pick up a line that would give me a connection to Brigade but all my endeavours were fruitless and by nightfall I was thoroughly tired out, with the result that when I was standing talking to QMS Cass about 9 p.m. I fell down in a faint, hitting my head a very nice thump on the stone floor. Cass helped me up. Got me to bed and gave me about ¼ of a pint of neat rum and very soon I was fast asleep.

20.9.18

Woke up this morning feeling little the worse for last night's episode. The back of my head is not nearly as tender as I expected it to be; but I have been taking things a little easier today. Took an obscure part in hunting rats with cordite and half a dozen dogs.

23.9.18

After a few days of fine weather, we are again being treated to rain and wind. Some of the fellows got wet through trying to play cricket. Reckon I ought to get my leave in October if the present rate continues, but we can never be sure of anything and when our leave is getting within measurable distance we live in a perpetual state of trembling anxiety which meets with no relief till we are actually on the journey home, armed with all manner of passes and certificates and food coupons. I can feel the wobbly, restless condition coming on me already.

26.9.18

When we came here five days ago we hoped we were going to resume our three weeks' rest which was so rudely broken at the beginning of the month but now the signs of the times are that operations are going to be resumed against the enemy in a few days' time, and consequently we have received orders to move forward tomorrow. I suppose it will mean that leave will be suspended again just as I am beginning to 'sweat' on it earnestly.

27.9.19
Spent most of today in clearing up and packing the wagons. Then, after tea, we commenced our trek towards the line. We went by Abeele station and along the Reninghelst Road, past my old billet at Lappe near which a large Casualty Clearing Station has been built. A nice cheerful sign! Just a little suggestion of what we may be in for. At the bottom of the hill we turned off and went on to Hooggraaf. It was dark by the time we got here. The Transport had to park in a field and of course one of the GS wagons got into a ditch. Before we could get it out, we had to unload it and then as a consequence load it up again. A little matter that caused much cursing in the darkness. Our billet is in a loft, and it is a tight squeeze. The attack takes place at dawn tomorrow morning and we have to march forward immediately it is launched; so here is one who is going to get some sleep while he may.

28.9.18
At 4 a.m. we were roused and by the light of a few glimmering candles we dressed ourselves and swallowed a hasty breakfast. Then followed the pleasing process of packing the wagons in the dark and getting them out on to the road. As we lined up on the road just before 6 a.m., the roar of artillery started. The depressing spirit of gloom which always sits heavily at these times found expression in Cheesman's words – 'another hopeless dawn, Joe' he said as we looked toward the line where the livid flashes of gunfire were striking up into the sallow dawn. I fell in with the section but Twycross fetched me out to follow the limber. This was the only wagon to accompany us all the way; where the rest went to, I don't know. I didn't greatly relish the job as it made me the very last man

in the column – a very undesirable position for when Fritz starts
firing at a column on the move it is always the rear part that clocks
for the 'dirt'. We passed through Reninghelst, leaving the church
on our right, and when we got on to the open road Fritz spotted us
and sent over a few HEs. Of course they dropped nearer to me than
to anyone else but I was not hit by anything worse than a lump
of mud and fortunately Fritz was being kept too busy in other
directions to allow him to pay too much attention to us. After a
few miles we put into a camp where we established communication
with Division and learned that the attack had been so successful
that we were to move forward to Swan Chateau, omitting an
intended halt at Ambulance Farm. So on we went past a prisoners
of war compound which was getting well filled, until we got there.
We remained there for two or three hours, during which time we
heard that the attack had met with little resistance and that two or
three hundred prisoners were taken in Canada Tunnels.

In getting out from Swan Chateau, one wheel of the limber went
into a shell hole and the column had to be halted while a dozen of
us pulled it out. I had swung my rifle on the side of the wagon and
it came out covered with mud and water so I've got a nice cleaning
job to look forward to as soon as we come to rest. For some distance
a good plank road helped us along, but once off that the going
became a little more strenuous. We were now within the German
lines of this morning but there was not the amount of evidence of
recent fighting that we had expected. In fact, the number of dead
bodies that we passed could be counted on the fingers of one hand.
But dusk was shrinking over the land so our powers of vision were
limited.

29.9.19
Soon after we were up this morning, a troop of French Cavalry
passed by on their way up the line. A little later we packed up
and proceeded to Verbrandenmolen and are now located in a field
quite close to the spot we came to last night. Although we were in
this neighbourhood in Sept. 1917, I can't say that I recognise the

country at all. Hill 60 is just in front of us and Larch Wood slightly to the left with Hedge St Tunnels a little further on. We have found a dugout — it's an English one but Jerry does not seem to have occupied it as it was littered with English papers and periodicals bearing dates early in April, just before Fritz was holding this line. The number of dead is surprisingly small. While prowling round, Cpl Smith found the body of a German Signaller, and searching through his pack discovered a Signal Chart which he gave to me. I shall keep it as a souvenir. It is dreary, desolate, cold and cheerless with plenty of mud and waterlogged shell holes. We are more or less on tenterhooks as we are merely waiting for orders to move forward again. I have no telephone lines, consequently I feel cut off from events and there is nothing to do but play cards, smoke and talk. I'm going to bed, humpy and dumpy and fed up and far from home.

30.9.18
The day was miserably spent in waiting for orders which did not arrive till evening. Then we were ordered to get out on to the road by 9 p.m., ready to move off. It was a wretched business in the dark but by very carefully examining every yard of ground before moving an inch, we manoeuvred the Signal Limber between the shell holes and got on to the road without mishap. We were the first out, for the other wagons were either less careful or less fortunate and it was 11 p.m. before they were all on the road. Then we started on a most joyless trek. Still, we were thankful that there was no shelling or bombing, neither did it rain. But the mud! For miles we were trudging through thin, watery slush over the tops of our boots and in one place it came up to our knees so that we had to lift up the skirts of our greatcoats to keep them out of it.

1.10.18
As dawn broke, we discovered that our fast-stepping mules had drawn away from the rest of the column which was nowhere in sight. We proceeded slowly until it was quite light without seeing

a sign of any other living creature. At last we came to a battery of
18-pdrs drawn up on the roadside. So we halted but could find none
of the gunners. So after conferring over a map we turned off along
a road that seemed as if it might have been a private road through
a gentleman's estate and about 5.30 a.m. we struck Brigade HQ in
a farm. There was a sound of cheering when I entered the Signal
Office that I gracefully acknowledged and then said, 'Give me
something to eat and drink and then let me sleep.' 'No such luck,'
said Sgt Twycross, 'we move forward at 6.30 to capture Menin,
eleven miles away.' What I said to that I cannot remember and if
I could I doubt if I could put it in black and white. I managed,
however, to scrounge a cup of tea and a piece of bread off Freddy
Moule (the NCOs' cook) and then piled more gear on to the already
overloaded limber. It was stacked up nearly five feet high and every
jolt or lurch sent my heart up into my mouth. However, there was
no help for it, so we set off past a derelict German steam wagon
with iron-rimmed wheels evidencing the shortage of rubber. We
marched in column of route as we did in Italy, Brigade HQ leading,
followed by the Field Ambulance, the Field Co. RE and the three
battalions. The morning was fine, the roads were tolerably good
and, except for an occasional aeroplane and a little gunfire in the
distance, there was no sign of war.

And indeed we weren't expecting any just yet as the Division
in front of us reported last night that Wervicq had been cleared
of the enemy. So we passed through the ruin of Fenbrielan quite
merrily and headed straight for Wervicq. But we had barely got
round a bend and within sight of the town when we were met by
a hail of machine-gun bullets which brought the column to a dead
stop and we made no bones about diving into the ditch that ran
beside the road. It was very evident that Fritz was still in Wervicq
and that he had been watching us all the way, allowing us to get
well within machine-gun range before he gave any notice of his
presence. When the burst of firing had died down we continued
along the road while the battalions deployed across the fields on our
left took some cover from a rise in the ground. Soon I found myself

stuck with the wagon at a corner beyond which it was dangerous to go. Sgt Twycross and Cpl Aitken with the Signallers and runners on duty had gone forward; the rest of Brigade HQ and the battalion details had scattered over an adjoining field where some trenches provided a certain amount of shelter. But Lally and I with the limber had to keep to the road and the position was by no means comfortable. The road went uphill from our corner for 200 yards then took a left-hand turn. From that point for about another 100 yards was a death trap. Fritz had some heavy guns trained on it and any troops or wagons that tried to pass along were courting death. I had no desire to run the gauntlet so when Hamilton came across to get some biscuits out of the limber I asked him what I ought to do. 'Stay where you are. There is no need to go any further yet.' We nibbled biscuits and bully and as the day wore on I began to take a great dislike to our position. Several other wagons had lined up behind us and Jerry had a perfectly uninterrupted view of us. Therefore it seemed improbable that he would let us stand there for ever. His chief observation post is in Wervicq church tower from which point he commands the whole country for a radius of five to ten miles. During this time there was a steady procession of walking wounded passing us, including Major Puttick of the Hants (wounded in the back) and Blakeway, the KRR runner (wounded in the hand). From him I endeavoured to get some information as to the whereabouts of Brigade but he was in too much of a hurry to get out of danger. So I learnt nothing.

About 4 p.m. I decided to find out where the rest of the Transport was located, so taking a bicycle I rode back about half a kilometre and found them settling down in a field beside the road. Returning to the limber, I was just giving instructions to Lally to turn round when a 'five-nine' dropped in the gateway on the opposite side of the road about ten yards away. The bits flew over us and round us but nothing more than mud hit us although the tyre of the bicycle I was holding was ripped up. Apparently Fritz thought he had left us alone long enough so we wasted no time in getting out of it. In getting into the Transport Lines, one of the rear wheels of the limber dropped into a ditch and the whole load fell over to one side. Fortunately the mules were able to pull it out and I immediately set to work to unload and repack the stores. I had not finished when six heavy shells burst right amongst us. There was enough explosive mixture to demolish half the Transport but only one man was wounded, and that but slightly, so that he was able to walk away to the dressing station.

Capt. Mowat at once decided that this situation was too exposed so we had the order to move back. We blundered out of the field as quickly as we could and back along a road that was nearly a foot deep in thick, stodgy mud. How I cursed the bicycle I had brought! The wheels were choked up, my strength was almost spent and I could not keep pace with the wagons. But I was able to keep them in view till they turned into a large field. When the limber was safely settled in, I thought it was my duty to report to Brigade so I set off to go up the line. I was starving and utterly tired but I trudged along, passing some 18-pdrs that were putting shrapnel round Wervicq church tower. Up to 6.30 p.m. our artillery had not been allowed to fire at the town because of the civilian inhabitants and even now they were limited to a few rounds of shrapnel at the church tower.

After plodding along for almost a kilometre, I glanced between some huts and who should I see but Hamilton, Davidson and Sgt Lunn. I was now just about exhausted and sank down on to a duckboard, and remained there stretched out at full length while they talked to me. They said there was no need for me to go up the line so I returned to the Transport. We had not had a meal for over twenty-four hours, and had been on the move the whole time so what we said when we heard that there were no rations for us must remain unrecorded. However, there was a sudden rumour that the Officers' rations were in a certain wagon. The driver was enticed away and the rations were ours – bacon and bread and tea. A fire was soon kindled in a hollow and before the loss of rations had been discovered, they were where it was impossible to find them.

2.10.18

Strictly speaking, as there were no rations last night, there ought
to have been no breakfast in the morning; but somehow or other
tea and sugar were 'procured' and each of us managed to produce a
little grub. So at 9 o/c we had a passably good breakfast. The day
has been uneventful.

5.10.18

While I was shaving this morning with my mirror on the back of
the limber, three of our scouting aeroplanes came up from the rear
and met another plane coming from the line. There was the sound
of machine-gun firing and we looked up to watch the fight. The
single plane tried to get away but one of the Scouts broke from
the formation and chased it down to earth. The bullets pinged and
zipped all round us and I dived unceremoniously under the wagon.
The plane crashed in the next field and then we found it was one
of our bombers returning from a night raid with its identification
marks camouflaged. The Scouts, not liking the look of it, gave the
challenge which the bomber failed to notice. Consequently the
Scouts took it to be a Jerry and promptly 'downed' it. There have
been several instances lately of Germans flying our machines that
they have captured at some point or other. One of the airmen was
slightly wounded; the other was unhurt.

6.10.18

Last night no spare accommodation was to be found in the dugouts
so Whittingsteel and I had to unearth a bivouac. We were much
too close to the crossroads for comfort. Fritz kept bumping them
all night and splinters were dropping all round us but nothing
worse than mud or stones hit the 'bivvy'.

During the morning, Brigade moved back, leaving us to follow
later. As I had sent Whittingsteel down to B Echelon, Fisher was
told off to remain with me. We got on the move after dinner.
Through Ypres to Vlamertinghe, where we halted for an hour. We
were thirsting for a cup of tea, and prowled about the place in

search of a canteen. Found one at last, but it only had beer and biscuits. Dusk was falling when we resumed the march to the farm at Whippenhoek that up to a week or two ago was a Field Ambulance. It was about 8 p.m. when we arrived and we found much excitement over a report that the Germans had asked for an armistice. The optimists crowed loudly and exulted over me for I am credited with being a hopeless pessimist, but it is useless to let desires override one's judgement and I doubt if anything tangible will result from the request (even if it be true). I look on it more as a sign of the beginning of the end, but how long it will be before the end of the end arrives it is impossible to say. I only hope that Germany will realise her doom is sealed and accept the fact very quickly. The march today was twenty miles. Consequently I am not overflowing with energy and shall not be long before I am in bed.

8.10.18

Have just heard that leave has been suspended again – I cannot express myself in words, but I have got the PIP in capital letters and the BLUES also. And this joyful news came along just as I had managed to scrounge a new tunic out of the QMS in anticipation of going on leave, and had paid the Brigadier's batman 3½ francs to make some alterations and sew on new chevrons!

9.10.18

The drivers are getting their leave all right but operators are less fortunate. We poor blighters are practically reduced to 'special cases only'. However, I went and pressed my sad case on Sgt Twycross and as there is only one other man away from the section, he is trying to get my leave sanctioned. I didn't have much trouble in persuading him to do this as he follows me very closely and the sooner I get away, the sooner his own turn will come round.

11.10.18

The truly joyful news has arrived! I am to cross over next Tuesday (15th). Hooray! I am as wibbly-wobbly as a blancmange. Bought a pair of breeches for five francs and made some alterations with my own hand. So I shall look passably respectable which is more than I have done lately for all my clothes were getting ragged and it has been almost impossible to get any new ones from Stores. Brigade go into the line again tomorrow but I am to remain behind as my leave is so near. This is a nice little slice of good fortune.

14.10.18

In accordance with orders, I joined a party of battalion men going on leave just before noon and we set off towards Vlamertinghe. Previously I had confirmed that this was where we were to join the train, but I didn't feel very confident. We had not proceeded more than a kilometre when we met another leave party who also had been sent to Vlam. and they reported that the station was not yet open and they had been instructed to make their way to Poperinghe. So we turned about and trudged along till we were able to 'jump' a lorry that took us to the outskirts of town and we were soon on the station where a number of troops had already congregated. There has been no opportunity this year of getting away a day earlier as I did last year. We entrained at 2 p.m. and reached Calais soon after 8 p.m., the journey being quite uneventful except that we were only six hours in the train instead of eighteen as last year. From Calais station we were marched to a camp near the harbour and put into tents for the night. This is the first time I have been in Calais and the little bit I saw of it did not impress me with its beauty. All the streets we passed through were narrow and almost squalid. Even the best of them had a very sad and mournful aspect and we were assailed all the way by a host of small children who begged for bully beef or tried to sell us oranges. As soon as we were settled in the camp we were given a meal that we needed rather badly, not having had anything since about 11 a.m. and by half past nine most of us were in our blankets.

15.10.18

Reveille was at the unearthly hour of 5.30 but our breakfast was not till 8 a.m. It turned out that there was another party for Scotland,

Ireland and the North of England who were to cross about 9 a.m. Consequently they had to have their breakfast early and with the thoroughness that characterises the army's doings, the whole lot of us were roused at the same time. Of course we had got washed, shaved and cleaned up long before breakfast and there was nothing to do but idle our time away.

Oh, these camps are dismal, desolate holes. Thank goodness we are only birds of passage and don't have to stay in them for many hours at a time. During the afternoon, in calm weather, we crossed over to Dover. There was not much delay here and we were soon speeding on our non-stop journey to London. I reached Ealing at 7.30 p.m. and went straight to Hastings Road where, in the darkness, I knocked at the wrong house. But that little error was soon remedied and I found my Elsie waiting for me.

16.10.18–29.10.18
On leave in England.

30.10.18
I was due to return yesterday but England, home and beauty are very sweet and I took an extra day without asking permission. Elsie came up to Victoria with me and I tried to make things as cheerful as possible by saying that I expect the armistice will be in operation before I get back to my Brigade. Judging from the comments in the press, it certainly seems as if there are definite prospects of an early suspension of hostilities. I don't like to be too optimistic but I doubt if the fighting will last for more than another month or six weeks at the latest. Yet this bright possibility does not seem to meet with much favour in the eyes of the stay-at-home community. Work people have been getting big wages on war work, employers have been piling up huge profits, and industrial adventurers have waxed fat out of the agony and suffering of the five million poor devils who have made the human wall that for over four years has protected the profiteer, the adventurer and the shirker from the violence and ravages of the Hun. And now they realise that this

profitable period is soon to close and they begin to squeal. What will they do if there is no war? And what will happen to them when the armies return home? They shiver in their shoes. They don't want us to come back. The attitude of England towards the British Tommy today is 'Hurry up and get killed before the war is over'.

We did not stay long at Dover. The crossing was perfect – the sea as calm as a lake – the sun shining brightly. I remained on deck to enjoy the sea air. At Calais we were soon plunged into the cheerfulness of the reception camp, but we are off tomorrow morning. Thank goodness we don't have to stay long in these places.

31.10.18

Entrained during the morning and were taken up through St Omer, Hazebrouk (badly knocked about), Poperinghe and Ypres. Jolly glad that the railway has been reconstructed right over Passchendaele Ridge. We had to travel slowly as it is none too safe. Near Passchendaele I was looking out of the truck and saw George Thompson working with a Labour Battalion. We exchanged greetings – that was all we had time to do. And so on to Roulers about dusk, eventually arriving at Ledeghem at 9 p.m. In Ypres I noticed that a few civilians have already drifted back. They are living in covered-in wagons.

At Ledeghem we were marched to the far end of the town and put into what had been one of Fritz's Civilian Internment Camps. Our reception was not the sort associated with open arms and fatted calves. We were just dumped into a large shed that was fitted with wire-netting beds and told that reveille would be at 6 a.m. No food, no blankets! We approached all the Camp NCOs we could find but were met with blank refusals to issue any blankets. We were not feeling any too happy and satisfied and soon the murmured protests began to grow until there was a very nice-sized uproar and some Haw-Haw Officer came in and tried to ride the high horse, demanding our pay books and threatening us with punishment. But he didn't get a single pay book and he had sense enough to realise the rising temper of the troops and accordingly gave orders for us to be supplied with blankets. If he had not done this I'm afraid there would have been something in the nature of a mutiny.

1.11.18
About 8.30 a.m. we turned our backs on Ledeghem and marched to Courtrai, the largest town I have passed through in Belgium. This place was captured by 122nd Brigade 41st Division only a few days ago. There is much evidence of Fritz's retirement. He has blown up all the bridges and railway station and has done a lot of damage to the permanent way. Large gangs of men were busy at work on Courtrai station. One thing that struck us as remarkable is the large number of Allied flags that are flying in every town, village and hamlet through which we pass. (It turned out that this was an instance of Fritz's business acumen. When retirement was inevitable he sent his bagman with loads of Allied flags and sold them to the natives!) At Courtrai our party was split up, men of different divisions going their several ways.

A limber went by going to 122nd Brigade so we dumped our packs on it. I also scrounged a tin hat from the roadside as I had purposely left mine at home, knowing full well that I should be able to pick one up somewhere or other before I got into the line. Jimmy Bissett arrived on the scene and told me that Brigade is somewhere near Kerkove but he could give me no definite information except that Fritz is holding us up on the Scheldt. We got on the move again and soon passed through one or two villages where chalk marks on doors gave evidence of recent occupation by some of our battalions. Beyond this we were not fortunate for dusk found us stranded near a few cottages. We were very fatigued and after a consultation with our officer it was decided to find shelter for the night and continue our journey in the morning. The march today covered sixteen miles.

2.11.18
We were glad of the abundance of straw last night for we had no blankets. So we just buried ourselves in the straw and slept well

except for an occasional disturbance by one of Fritz's bombing
aeroplanes that were busy in the neighbourhood.

Some rations had been procured from somewhere so we had
breakfast and then set off again on our search for the 122nd Brigade.
We had only gone a mile or two when we found them established
in a chateau. Had a look at Company Orders and observed that
a driver at Division got fourteen days' FP No. 1 for overstaying
his leave twenty-four hours. Just then Sgt Twycross came along
and asked for my pass. I felt in all my pockets and couldn't find
it. He said the authorities are being very severe on men who have
overstayed their leave and he asked me what day I left London.
I told him a lie without the least sign of guilt and he made the
necessary report to Division. Then I went out into a quiet corner
and burnt that pass with the incriminating date stamped on it at
Victoria and the burnt ashes I crumpled in my hands and scattered
to the winds.

Davidson is on leave. His father died a week or so ago so he got his
leave earlier than would otherwise have been the case. Glasspoole is
also on leave. He has 'clicked' for six weeks owing to his Yeomanry
Service. Aitken has gone to England to take a commission in the
RAF and during my absence I have been lifted into his place with
the rank of L/Cpl. The appointment dates from 18 October. Had
no idea that anything of the sort was in the air. Jack Carter has also
been promoted to Lineman L/Cpl.

The lid has come off the tin of cold cream in my pocket and the
stuff has got mixed up with tobacco dust.

3.11.18

Our men captured a most extraordinary bicycle from the enemy; we
have got it standing just outside the door of the chateau. It is more
evidence of the serious shortage of rubber in Germany, for instead
of the ordinary tyres the rim of each wheel is surmounted with a
number of helical springs bound together by an exterior band of
iron. (Later we saw many of these. The Belgians appropriated them,
and they made a truly awful clatter on the pavé).

5.11.18

Our progress was not very rapid as a great number of troops were
on the road. At one point somebody's transport had been badly
knocked about as several dead horses were lying by the roadside.
The first one we saw had lost the whole of one hind leg and we rather
marvelled at such extraordinary mutilation. But we passed three or
four others in exactly the same condition and we learned that the
natives had cut off the hindquarters and carted them away for food.
The afternoon was well advanced before we reached Harlebeke. Our
billet is in a quite respectable house but some distance from the
Signal Office.

6.11.18

Weather very cheerless – raining fast all day and we are glad that
we did the march yesterday. Now that we have got away from
the stretch of country desolated by four years of continual trench
warfare, we look like getting much better billets although there
is more moving about to do. In fact this open warfare is infinitely
preferable to the nerve-shattering, muddy, filthy and poisonous
warfare of the trenches. There is nothing like the same amount of
shellfire to contend with and now that we know that we have got
Fritz beaten we suffer no apprehensions, when turning in at night,
that we shall find him a little too near to us for comfort in the
morning.

7.11.18

Some of the runners discovered great piles of books in the attic
of our billet. Immediately I heard of it I hastened to the scene
and found a wonderful collection of books, mostly theological, in
English, French, German, Flemish and Latin. It was delicious to
turn over volume after volume, reading a bit here and a bit there.
Two huge, rather ancient Psalters attracted my attention but they
were too big and heavy to appropriate. Selected a French book on
physiology and Hamilton and I have spent some time in translating
it. The Huns have definitely asked for an armistice and we have had

orders to look out for their emissaries coming over with a white flag but it is not anticipated that they will cross over on our front. Operations, however, are not to be suspended and there is to be no relaxation in our attacks. This is hard luck as we are still held up on the Scheldt and now we (the 122nd Brigade) have got to force the passage. I must admit that I don't view the prospect with the least bit of enthusiasm as I shall have to take the Forward Party over.

It's bad enough attacking on dry land or in knee-deep mud, but when you have got to get across a wide swiftly flowing river on a pontoon bridge hastily thrown across, with Fritz directing all his attention on that point, you can't feel that your chances of coming through are particularly rosy.

This is a larger town than we usually get billeted in and it seems to be quite an ecclesiastical centre. There are crowds of priests and church officials and one old boy (possibly a bishop as he wears a mitre) who shuffles about town preceded by a small boy carrying a lantern and ringing a bell. On his approach, men and women go down on their knees in the muddy gutter and he mutters blessings over them. It certainly looks grotesque and it struck Bill Rogers as distinctly funny. He thought at first that it had something to do with Guy Fawkes Day! The funeral of a Belgian soldier was an opportunity for the ecclesiastics to make a brave show, four or five priests intoning Latin chants in raucous tones, yet doing it heartily withal. A detachment of British troops acted as a firing party.

9.11.18

Early today it was evident that there was something 'in the wind' and during the morning we received the order to stand by. Later we were ordered to pack up and be ready to move, and accordingly in the early afternoon we marched off a distance of eight miles. The latter part of the journey was rather rough especially where we had to pass under the railway. Fritz had blown the bridge up and we had to clamber over heaps of masonry. The greatest difficulty was in getting the wagons over but it was all accomplished without mishap. It was getting dusk when we reached the farm and we quickly perceived that the old farmer and his family did not welcome our arrival. This attitude was explained later when we learnt that last night a unit of the 9th Division was billeted here and the fellows fairly looted the place, milking the cows on to the ground, breaking all the eggs and ransacking the house. It is always a curse to follow one of these Hooligan Divisions.

10.11.18

Up very early, according to plan, and soon the news came through that Fritz had retired from the Scheldt during the night. I, for one, heaved many sighs of relief. It was daylight when we got on the move again and continued our march to the Scheldt where we found that the Engineers had already thrown across a footbridge and had repaired the demolished road bridge sufficiently to carry light transport. The approach to the river was over marshy land and we were unfortunate to get held up for a few minutes. This was sufficient to allow the wagons to begin sinking into the mud and it required the help of all available men to pull them out. The river runs swift and cold and deep and we shuddered as we passed over it thinking of what might have been our fate. Once across, however, we struck a good road and continued merrily until we reached Sulsique. It is remarkable that we have not seen a single scrap of war material except huge shells used for mining the crossroads. Fritz seems to have cleared the country of everything before he retired. We were directed to take a short cut across some fields while the Transport went round by the road. We had to jump a stream and struggle up a steep hill and so into a lane that was a foot deep in thick, stodgy mud. It was terribly hard work at the end of a tiring day and it was impossible to push the bicycles. It needed three men to pull each one. Eventually we reached a good road and lined up, a very worn and weary looking crowd. A few cheery words from Mr Bell, telling us that we were nearing the end of our day's march, put a little life in us and we plodded on to Nukerke in the moonlight, arriving there about 7 p.m., the Transport putting in an appearance about an hour later. Our billet is in an estaminet kept by two elderly ladies who seem very nervous and fearful. After getting our packs from the wagon we wasted very little time in getting into our blankets, sleeping on the straw on which Germans slept last night.

11.11.18 Armistice Day

I was sorry for the men on duty last night, especially the runners, for they were kept on the go all night long and Bill Rogers, who normally should have turned in soon after 10 p.m., had to remain on duty throughout the night. Consequently at 8 a.m. I went on duty and relieved him. We were anxiously awaiting orders when about 8.30 [the 122nd Infantry Brigade War Diary states that the signal was received at 09.08] the 'Sounder' started to tap. Campbell was the Divisional Operator on duty and as the instrument ticked I read off 'Hostilities will cease . . .' That was enough. I had to suppress the jubilation in the Office in order to give Campbell a chance to get his message off. Before he had finished, the Office was crowded with enquirers. Mr Bell came in and took the telegram while I appropriated a copy (I kept this until some months after I got home and then it mysteriously disappeared and although I have turned the whole house inside out three or four times there is no trace of it anywhere). The excitement among the troops was not great; indeed, except for a little spasmodic jubilation here and there, no difference in the ordinary behaviour of the men is to be observed. It is just taken as a matter of course. The two old ladies of the estaminet hardly know where they are. For the past week they have been living more or less in a state of terror, not understanding what was happening and spending sleepless nights because of the noise of the guns. When we told them the good news they broke down and cried. We gave them jam and cheese, luxuries that they had not enjoyed for years and in return they gave us some apples which they had kept hidden from Fritz.

The language of the neighbourhood is Flemish but one of the old dames speaks French, so we are able to make each other understood. Their chief concern last night when we arrived was whether they would be able to get a good night's sleep without the disturbance of shells and bombs. We did our best to calm their agitated feelings and they did get a good night's rest for everything was very quiet. Our orders for the day were merely to remain where we were, but the 123rd and 124th Brigades had to push forward as far as possible and not halt until 11 a.m., securing, if they could, the passage of the River Dendre. From information that has come through during the day, I doubt if they have got quite so far. There was not much gun firing this morning and what there was ceased at 11 a.m. except for an isolated gun that kept banging away until 3 p.m. I understand that this was an Australian Battery that had got out of touch with headquarters and consequently had not received the 'cease-fire' order. But I have my doubts. I fancy they were having a little bit of 'own back'.

This evening we celebrated the Event by having a little dinner in another estaminet. There were just the NCOs from Brigade HQ and our own officer (Mr Bell). It was a humble repast for there is no spare grub in the village; but Joe Laycock went on his motorcycle and brought back a few things, and the landlord dug up some bottles of special wine which had been buried since 1914. So we had a mild carouse from 7 till 10.30, after which we slept the sleep of the just.

In the end it had taken just one hundred days from the Germans' Black Day in August to defeat on the battlefield in all but name. When the Germans asked for an Armistice, their initial overtures were for a negotiated end to the fighting. This was immediately rebuffed. The terms of the Armistice would be dictated by one side and one side only. The Germans had no choice but to capitulate to all the terms set down by the Allies. Members of the German High Command might later spin the result, spuriously claiming that a lack of moral fibre at home rather than battlefield defeat was the reason the war was lost, but that was not the case. The German army was beaten and on 11 November 1918 they dutifully signed to that effect.

12.11.18

This morning I had a walk round the neighbourhood. Most of the crossroads had been blown up but Fritz wasn't able to accomplish all he intended in this direction and there are scores of huge shells, four or five feet long, standing and lying about all over the country. He was pretty thorough in his treatment of railway tracks. Every bridge and station has been demolished and all along the permanent way he has put small charges under the joints of the rails, thus twisting a few inches of each rail upwards, an inexpensive but nevertheless very efficient way of putting the whole railroad out of action. Another thing he has done was to throw trees across the roads but in this matter also he did not do all he intended for only a small portion of the trees were felled. Thousands of others, however, all along the roadsides, have been sawn through save for about two inches and only need a little persuasion to come toppling over. A good strong wind will fetch most of them down.

15.11.18

Being an NCO has certain advantages. For instance, when we arrived feeling rather worn out yesterday afternoon the people at our billet (a farm) gave us coffee and bread and butter and refused to take anything for it. Here we have truly been welcomed with open arms. The farm people are most concerned for our welfare and comfort. Our billet is in a large stone-floored building adjoining the house and the people had put down piles of straw, placed palliases on them and supplied us with clean white sheets! We looked askance at these and Carter said, 'Here, Joe, we can't go making these dirty.' 'Take what the Gods send,' I replied, 'when Fortune smiles let us bask in the sunshine.'

Before the war, English was taught in the village school, but Fritz put a stop to that and substituted his own lingo but one of the farmer's daughters (about thirteen or fourteen years old) can talk a little English. It is anticipated that some time will elapse before the peace treaty is signed and there are rumours that demobilisation will commence before that event.

One of the provisions of the Armistice agreement allowed for the advance on to German soil of four armies, one each from the principal Allied powers that fought on the Western Front: the British (including Empire troops), French, Americans and Belgians. The joint decision was not to march on Berlin but instead to seize one of the Germany's economic and commercial jewels, the Rhineland. Once across the Rhine, the Allies could wait while the provisions of the peace treaty were hammered out at Versailles, with the implicit threat that should the Germans not sign the treaty, the Allies would move on the capital. In the Rhineland, the British took control of the city of Cologne and remained there for the next six years. British troops lived amongst a generally friendly and largely law-abiding population, and many came to enjoy life there, especially as the German mark fell in value against the British pound. Jack Martin's time there was relatively short and his desire to go home to his fiancée outweighed any wish to explore to the full all that such a cultured city could offer.

17.11.18
Davidson returned from leave today and Twycross is on his way back. The signs of the times are that we are to march into Germany.

18.11.18
Marched via Grammont to Viane. Grammont is a fairly large town and the populace turned out to greet us. At the top of the hill beyond the town, the crossroads had been mined but the mine had not exploded. A guard was mounted over a couple of wires that came up from the ground, to which Fritz had attached a revolver in the hope that some souvenir hunter would grab it, pull the wires and get blown to blazes for his cupidity. The Huns seem to have played a pretty rotten game in the way of pinching food from the civilians. And the pinching was not confined to the lower ranks. Officers and men of position commandeered all manner of foodstuff and sent it home to Germany. When any of the civilians were ill, they were attended by a German army doctor who refused to take payment in money but demanded it in flour or potatoes or something of that sort. Censorship restrictions have been relaxed and we can now say where we are and where we have been.

19.11.18

Today we have been looking up maps and trying to make out our route to Germany. It looks as if we shall miss Brussels by a few miles. But this looking and searching was in vain, for about 10 p.m., just as I was going off duty, a message arrived ordering us back to Everbecq tomorrow. I went to dig out Sgt Oxley who was already in bed. To get to him I had to pass through a room where a man and his wife were sleeping in one bed and their grown-up daughter in another. It appears that the Commander of the 9th Division (who are behind us) has protested against us being given the post of honour in preference to his Division which is a good bit senior to ours. So the 9th are to go to the Rhine while we remain in this neighbourhood.

23.11.18

The last two or three days have been specimens of real miserable November weather – cold, damp and dreary with a thick fog; but today is quite the reverse – bright sunshine, a cloudless sky and no wind. A sharp frost during the night has made the roads nice and hard so Carter and I went for a good walk this morning.

The palliases on which we sleep look like coarse canvas or woven fabric but in reality they are made of paper. With a little care the strands can be unravelled and spread out into sheets of paper. String is made in the same way and although inferior to jute or hemp, it is rather surprising to find it as strong as it is.

26.11.18

In the kitchen of my billet today a big brass pot is on the fire; the iron handle is thick with rust. It is one of a number of household treasures that have been dug up from the garden now that Fritz has gone for good. Madame told me that Fritz appropriated the wool from the people's mattresses and they had to use straw as a substitute. I don't like the floors of these houses – they are tiled and therefore cold, especially as one never meets with a carpet or rug. Perhaps Fritz had them as well!

29.11.18

Up at 5.30 a.m. and walked into Grammont (five or six km) with
Twycross, Hamilton and Davidson, to catch a lorry that left at 8.30.
The journey to Brussels was uneventful except that the natives have
not yet got accustomed to British troops. Triumphal arches had
been erected here and there, flags and bunting were everywhere. We
reached Brussels at 11.45 a.m. and our first concern was to book
beds for the night as we did not want to find ourselves stranded.
A civilian who could speak English directed us to a small hotel
near the Gare du Nord and we booked a couple of double beds in
adjoining rooms for which we were only charged twelve francs all
told. But Brussels made up for it in every other way. Everything is
tremendously expensive. Only a millionaire could stay there for a
week. We each had about 120 francs (nearly £5) but that barely kept
us in food and drink for twenty-four hours. A very unsatisfactory
dinner cost us fourteen francs each – small cups of coffee are a shilling
each – boots nearly £12 a pair – ladies' cloaks about £23 – tea £4
per lb – ladies' stockings £3 a pair – other things in proportion, so
the purchase of souvenirs was out of the question although the shops
were well stocked. We had to content ourselves with guide books (in
English) and books of views. Despite the high prices, the majority of
the people are well dressed and they don't look starved. During the
German occupation America did a tremendous lot towards feeding
the people and in addition there was some sort of national committee
which provided necessitous persons with about 14/- a week. Met an
Englishman who has lived in Brussels for eighteen years. When the
Germans arrived he became a Belgian and so avoided being taken
off to Germany. We also met two Englishwomen who were nurses or
governesses or something of that sort, also a number of Belgians who
had lived in England and could speak our language fluently. It was
from these that we learnt a good deal about the conditions of things
during the German occupation.

On the whole Fritz seems to have behaved quite decently. Although
he took the brass and wool, yet he paid for it and when he took household
fittings such as door knobs, window catches etc, he replaced them with

black painted iron ones. The iron does not require so much cleaning as brass so the people haven't much to grumble at in that respect. What astonished us more than anything else was that although Fritz has only been gone about a fortnight, the local authorities have already got sundry monuments erected. They are only plaster casts that do not take long to make, but the artists must have been at work on the designs and initial preparations for some considerable time. There is one to Nurse Cavell bearing the inscription 'Hommage à l'Angleterre', one to the United States, one to King Albert, one to 'our heroic defenders' and one or two others. The Belgians seem to place President Wilson second only to their own King and Queen. This is because of the feeding business. These plaster statues are, I believe, to be replaced by bronze in due course, but I suppose the people were anxious to make a show of something or other in a hurry.

The first train to enter Brussels since the Germans left came in today and there was much rejoicing. Large batches of released prisoners straggled into the city. As Fritz retires, so the prisoners are released and left to make their own way back. They looked very rough and unkempt, garbed in all manner of odd clothes. A crowd of Russians looked particularly disreputable – no doubt they all had a very rough time. A reception camp has been established to deal with them. We tramped round the town seeing as much as possible in our limited time. It was dark by teatime and the evening resolved itself more or less into a café crawl. At 10.30 Davidson and I returned to the hotel and got to bed. Twycross and Hamilton followed about an hour later. The native girls and women are very interested in our kilted soldiers!

30.11.18

Our lorry was due to leave Brussels at 8.30 a.m. so we were up betimes and had breakfast in a neighbouring café – a little bit of poor bacon, one egg, bread, butter and coffee – 8½ francs each. When we got to the lorry, the Officer in Charge decided to postpone our departure till 2.30 so we went into the Porte de Hal, the last remaining vestige of the old fortifications of 1357. Originally it was surrounded by a moat and approached by a drawbridge. Has served as a watch tower, corn loft, arsenal and prison. Now it contains a fine museum of arms and armour, the most recent being relics of the Napoleonic campaigns. It was dark when we got back to Grammont and we did not feel very cheerful as we trudged on to Everbecq. However, a good wash and a feed have made us feel better.

5.12.18

Went with Cheesman in the Maltese Cart to Grammont to get a barrel of beer for the canteen. The man at the Brasserie couldn't speak English and my French is very weak but we managed to complete the transaction satisfactorily. On the way we gave a lift to a one-legged Belgian who could speak good English. He had lived in England before the war. Undoubtedly the natives in this district have had a pretty rotten time during the past few years. I don't think any of them have had a real wash since the early days of the war because it is absolutely impossible to get perfectly clean with the soap they have. You can't get one solitary bubble of lather out of it. If I could drop into Brussels with a train-load of Sunlight I should make my fortune. The people would pay any price I chose to ask. The same applies to chocolate and oils and candles. To give a woman a cake of Lifebuoy means getting your washing done for nothing and also making a friend for life. Perhaps.

9.12.18

The Germans divided the country into Military Areas and no civilian was allowed to move from one area to another under penalty of a fifty-mark fine. They carried out periodical inspections of the houses to see how much food the people had, and appropriated all that they considered in excess of requirements. This refers to the Grammont Area that we are now in, where the Kommandatur (one Schwartz by name) has not left a very enviable reputation behind him. He was the man who pinched the people's food and sent it home to Germany. In Grammont, an English prisoner of war died and as the funeral passed down the street some of the civilians saluted the coffin. This so incensed Schwartz that he issued an order that the civilians were to salute all German funerals under penalty of another fifty-mark fine. So they used to stop indoors or slip down side streets to get out of the way.

12.12.18

A desolate, cheerless march to Terlinden where the railway runs unprotected beside the road. Before we made the first halt, it started to rain and continued to pour all day. Billeted in the chateau. Absolutely tired out.

Today's march = 26 km.

13.12.18

Better weather and only a short march to Saintes where we have a decent billet in the chateau buildings. Yesterday's march was a long one to kick off with and we are all feeling the effects of it.

Today's march = 9 km. Total = 35 km.

14.12.18

On to Wauthier-Braine where we had a most exhausting climb up through private grounds to the chateau perched on a commanding hill. This last stretch took it out of all of us, but tomorrow being the Sabbath we are to have a day's rest. Carter and I have a little room to ourselves in the house occupied by the coachman or chauffeur. Soon after tea I was jolly glad to get my boots off for these wretched paved roads are terribly tiring. The country is getting a little more interesting but oh, I do wish the Belgians knew how to make roads. Since I came to bed I have written three letters but now I find the miserably wet weather has stuck up all my envelopes.

Today's march = 16 km. Total = 51 km.

16.12.18

Over the field of Waterloo. The whole countryside is dotted with monuments and every other house or building bears a tablet commemorating some event connected with Napoleon. A large field of pickling cabbages attracted our attention and we could only conclude that as 'roses never blow so red as where a buried Caesar bled' this must be the grave of hundreds of plebeian common soldiers. Our billet is in a loft approached by a very rickety ladder. It is probable that some of Napoleon's soldiers were billeted here on the eve of Waterloo. A little further down the road in the direction of Genappe is the house in which Napoleon slept on the night before the battle. It's a small double-fronted house standing close to the road. The glass panel over the front door bears the familiar N. The double gate at the side of the house also carries the sign on each half of it and in addition has a plate with just this on it: '17–18 Juin 1815'.

Today's march = 13 km. Total = 64 km.

17.11.18

Our billet tonight is in a barn with a stone floor so we asked the chief farmhand for some straw. He was a surly individual and refused so we took the matter into our own hands and hunted round until we found some very nice straw to which we helped ourselves liberally, much to his chagrin. He stormed and jabbered in Flemish and we answered in very direct English. As a reward for his obstinacy we took twice as much as we needed and left him muttering and grumbling. Curse him, does he think that the men who rescued this country are going to sleep on cold stones now that the war is over?

Today's march = 16 km. Total = 80 km.

18.12.18

To Sombreffe in execrable weather.

Today's march = 12 km. Total = 92 km.

19.12.18

Today's march = 14.5 km. Total = 106.5 km.

20.12.18

A long march in atrocious weather. Round about the forts of Namur the 1914 shell holes are plainly visible and Fritz had used gaps and quarries by the roadside for storing heavy ammunition – a good bit of it is still there. After leaving Namur we got delayed for about an hour, and we adjourned to some cottages and got some coffee and, incidentally, some shelter from the wind and rain. Later on the wind blew and the snow and rain came down pitilessly and we were a sodden crowd that sludged into Bierwart about 4 p.m.

Today's march = 25 km. Total = 131.5 km.

21.12.18

Marched nearly to Huy then turned off across country, where the hills 'took it out' of the Transport.

Today's march = 18.5 km. Total = 150 km.

23.12.18

Well, this billet is certainly all right. We have two beds in the same room – 'posh' beds, with spring mattresses, feather beds, sheets, blankets and fancy bed covers. And the people! Why, they wait on us hand and foot. The family consists of man and wife and two daughters, one about nineteen (Jeanne) and the other about twelve or thirteen (Laure) and they simply insist on doing things for us. We are used to washing in any old bucket or tin in the back yard but they simply won't let us do it – we have to use the toilet set in the bedroom. They have washed all our dirty clothes and even want to clean our boots but we draw the line at that, although M'sieur holds very strongly that this is woman's work. In return we give them soap and chocolate for they refuse to take any money payment. The people in this area speak good French but don't understand Flemish a bit. On the other hand some of them speak Walloon, whatever that is. They hardly saw a German soldier here until after the Armistice was signed. Then Fritz fixed up a Wireless Station in this house.

25.12.18

We have not had time to arrange the big Xmas dinner for today, but the NCOs have had a 'do' this evening, goose and a wartime Xmas pudding being the principal features.

28.12.18

Last night we had the Brigade HQ Xmas dinner and it was a great success. We finished up about 1 a.m. and the result was that I didn't wake up till 10 a.m. this morning – but I was not on duty till 11.30. A very stormy day but not quite so cold as yesterday. We have had to fill in our Demobilisation papers (Army Form Z16). These are to be sent to England where employers will be asked to confirm our statements and eventually we shall begin to dribble homewards in ones and twos. Miners and a few others have already gone and a good many men on leave have managed to 'work their tickets' but it will be some little time before demobbing gets going at anything like a decent rate. I hear that 'Slip men', i.e. men with jobs to go back to, are not to be allowed to go on leave. This is a rather hopeful sign. Have filled up a Z15 (form for officers claiming priority release or for men who have positions to go back to equal to those which officers might hold). This may hasten things a bit.

31.12.18

Goodbye to 1918 with all its excitement and horror – we are glad to see the back of it – And now for the New Year with all its hope and glowing promise!

1919

2.1.19

This evening the troops arranged a dance in the local schoolroom, inviting the native damsels. Such things have no appeal for me so I stayed at home and looked after the old lady. Laure has gone back to school at Huy, and Jeanne and her father have gone to the ball. These people have some cows so I suggested making some custard. Madame had only a vague recollection of having seen some made once upon a time, so I managed the business and fetched out a tin of pears so that we had a good supper ready when the revellers returned.

3.1.19

Regimental censorship has ceased. We now are to censor our own letters!

5.1.19

Sgt Lunn goes on leave tomorrow and doesn't expect to return so I have had to take over the Canteen business. It is reported that we are to go to Germany in a few days' time. Davidson is going on leave in a day or so. He has got a special pass to visit the grave of his brother who, since the Armistice, was killed by a motor lorry. Every week the local newspapers contain advertisements inserted by returned soldiers, renouncing their wives owing to their conduct with German soldiers during the occupation. Went into Huy and had a look round. The Meuse flows swiftly – only a few days ago some mules that were being watered ventured too far and got swept away.

7.1.19

Sgt Oxley has gone on with the Advance Party to arrange our billets in Germany. Our destination is the other side of the Rhine beyond Cologne.

9.1.19

During the night we crossed the frontier and passed through Aachen (Aix-la-Chapelle) and when we got up this morning we were nearing Cologne. We passed through the city and over the Rhine at ½ past 8 and on to Hoffnungsthal where we detrained and marched back 2½ km to Rösrath, being about ten miles east of the river. Got into our billets early in the afternoon. All the billets are in private houses. Hamilton and I had the choice of two. The first we were not taken with, but the second one was quite satisfactory. The 'landlord' (a retired tailor) was not at all anxious to have us, proclaiming that his wife was too ill to look after us. We told him that we needed no attendance and so took possession.

10.1.19

This billet is 'the goods'. The house is called 'Villa Josepha'. It is a little way outside the village and is a fairly modern construction. A rose is blooming in the front garden! When Meinherr discovered that he was not going to get rid of us by pleading a sick wife he produced a very capable daughter who is the wife of a German Officer and she waits on us. The old boy is a typical German with a round face, stiff grey hair and big round spectacles. Our bedroom is even better than the one at Foncourt. We have a double bed with sheets, pillows, quilt and eiderdown. Beside the usual bedroom appointments, we have a table and two chairs (one with a cushion) and an inkstand with pens and ink but the pens are no good. There is no fireplace but the room is heated by a radiator which we can turn on and off at pleasure. The natives generally are very docile and obliging and we look like having a good time. From Cologne to Rösrath the country is flat, but going eastwards it becomes almost mountainous. A lot of it is forest, often thick and dark, the sort of place where Erl Kings live. The Signal Office is in the Civil Post Office which we have taken over, so all messages which Fritz wants to send go via the British Army. The NCOs' mess is in a sort of small hotel in the centre of the village and the messroom bears the marks of revolver shots, made by our predecessors the Canadians, who, I think, rather put the 'wind up' the natives.

13.1.19

This morning Tom Glasspoole and I went to the Div. Canteen to buy stores. Found the Canteen and transacted business and then decided to have a look at Cologne. So we trained back to the city, had some grub and looked round the place. Got confused between the different stations and so lost the last train back to Rosräth. (By the way, we do not have to pay any fares on the railway or State tramways.) Now the army does do sensible things sometimes and one of them is that British soldiers on applying to the APM of Cologne are given billeting tickets that entitle them to sleeping accommodation in one of the hotels. It was past 9 p.m. and the hotels were all shut up, but we banged violently on the door and then the proprietor let us in. He spoke perfect English and told us he was a Frank, not a German. We had separate rooms at the top of the building and locked ourselves in which was a good thing for later on some giggling maids came trying our doors!

14.1.19

Caught the first train back to Rösrath and then Hamilton wanted me to go to Cologne with him. So we caught the next train back. The great Cathedral is very fine outside but the interior is disappointing. There are a few other good buildings and the museum is moderately interesting, but except for the exterior of the Dom and the wonderful Hohenzollern Bridge the place does not come up to Brussels in any single respect. The Guards Division in Cologne is mightily regimental with their double sentries and their route marches when all civilians have to salute the Union Jack. Any failing to do so are pulled into the rear of the column and have to finish the march and then receive a lecture on how they should behave towards their conquerors, and are then allowed to go. Curfew is at 10 p.m. and any civilians in the streets without passes after that time are taken into custody by the Military Police.

15.1.19

Very busy with Canteen affairs. It's not exactly like running a Harrods Store but the nuisance is the various currencies we have to deal with. When we got here I spent a lot of time and mental effort in changing all prices and accounts from francs to marks. I had just completed this task when the bank rates changed and I had to do it all over again. The retail business is quite headaching for the number of calculations one has to make are beyond counting. For instance, a man buys ten or twelve marks' worth of goods and then offers payment in a mixture of francs, marks and shillings! And in addition to English, French, Belgian and German money we often get Italian, Portuguese, Argentinian, Rumanian and sundry other sorts of coins. Fortunately none of the purchasers is as au fait with the exchange rates as I am, so they accept what change I give them without a murmur. Hamilton and I were busy till after 1 a.m. devising a system of accounts. It's necessary to balance up every night or we should soon be in a hopeless pickle.

26.1.19

The Canteen business has kept me very busy so that I have had no time for anything except grousing about demobilisation which has seemed utterly hopeless for us who are in the Army of Occupation. This afternoon I wrote a letter to Elsie bewailing our fate and had just sent it off when the Demobilisation Clerk came into the Signal Office and said that two of the Signals were getting demobbed but I was not one of them. He wouldn't say the names, yet I knew that there were only two who could possibly have a prior claim to me and as they are the two Sergeants it was unlikely that they would both be allowed to go at once. Later on I found out that it was to be one of the Sgts and a Sapper. This meant that somebody was getting an advantage over me so I began to make a noise in the land with the result that half an hour later the Clerk came back and told me to prepare to leave the Brigade on the 29th and proceed to England for demobilisation. I danced round the Signal Office and behaved, generally, like one slightly demented, for at last I could see Blighty and Freedom within a reasonable distance.

30.1.19
At 9.30 we paraded, marched to the station and entrained, leaving Cologne at 11 p.m.

1.2.19
We were delayed for several hours last night owing to the inability to obtain water for the engine as all the pipes and pumps were frozen. On through Tournai and Bergues to Dunkirk where we arrived at 11 p.m. tired, cold and hungry, only to find that all the Camp Orderlies had retired for the night. Consequently we had to wait about while they got dressed and then we were put into tents. Our temper was not very good and we demanded food. We clamoured at the door of the big dining hut and a Sgt told us we could not get a meal unless we first obtained a ticket. Then a gentle stirring and commotion grew into a howl – 'We don't want no blankety tickets' – and then a mighty shove pushed the Sgt clean through the door of the hut and we swarmed inside. Very soon we had hot tea, sausages and bread, but it was a near thing for a general riot.

3.2.19
Up at 4.30 and washed myself with a lump of ice and also tried to have a shave. I was unfortunate in being included in the second party for breakfast and there was not enough grub to go round. So I only had half a meal. Marched to the Docks and embarked at 7.30 a.m. It was very foggy and there was some doubt as to whether we should cross over today but by 10 o/c we got away only to come to anchor in a bank of fog just outside the harbour. We were stopped for two or three hours not merely because of the

fog but chiefly because a number of floating mines were reported in the neighbourhood. Soon after noon we began to crawl down the coast and then the fog gradually lifted and we reached Dover seven and a half hours after embarking at Dunkirk. Up the hill we marched to the Dispersal Station close by the Castle and here we went through the really wonderful and elaborate process of demobilisation. It took just about two hours (from 5 until 7) and then we were told that we should have to stay in the camp that night. Dirty, tired and very hungry, we lined up for a hot meal but just as we were going into the dining hut there was a shout, 'All the men for London come this way at once!' We grabbed the sandbags containing our belongings and rushed across the parade ground. A lump of bread and cheese was handed to each of us and we were thrust forth from the barrack gates into the wide, wide world. Free men at last! The feeling was a queer one after so much restriction and discipline. It was a thoroughly undisciplined rabble that slithered down the hill (the road was covered with ice) singing 'Mademoiselle from Armentières'. The townsfolk gazed at us as they would at a menagerie but we were soon in the station and at 8.35 p.m. the train steamed out from Dover and rushed us up to London where we arrived at 11 p.m.

And now we dispersed, going our several ways, other travellers looking on us with suspicion and even shunning us. We were sneaking home – that's all that can be said for it. Evidently the stay-at-homes did not welcome our return. Where were the flags and the banners and the laurel wreaths and trumpets? Let it be recorded for all time that the men who fought and suffered and won had, in the end, to sneak back to their homes like convicts released from gaol. But what does it matter? At last I am home with those who love me.

It was past midnight when I reached Ealing, and 17 Hastings Road was in darkness but my first ring brought Elsie and her father out of bed to welcome me. Oh, it is good to be home once more.

ACKNOWLEDGEMENTS

I would like to thank everyone at Bloomsbury, particularly Bill Swainson, the senior commissioning editor, for his belief in the project and his unwavering encouragement. I am also grateful to Nick Humphrey, who is always thoughtful and encouraging, and Anna Simpson for her editorial advice and support as well as Richard Collins for his excellent copyediting. I would also like to thank Anya Rosenberg, Colin Midson, David Mann, Ruth Logan, Penelope Beech, Lisa Fiske and Polly Napper, all of whom have worked hard to produce and market this book.

I should like to thank Rosanna Wilkinson, research assistant at the Imperial War Museum Photograph Archive for her generous help and the Imperial War Museum for permission to reproduce a number of images from their library.

Thank you to my good friends Jeremy Banning, who originally brought my attention to the diaries, and Peter Barton who originally discovered their importance. As always, I am grateful to Taff Gillingham for his help and expert knowledge of the Great War, and to my superb agent, Jane Turnbull, for her continued enthusiasm and encouragement throughout this project.

Thank you, as always, to my wife, Anna, for all her understanding as I disappear to my study to write. A special thank you to my mother, Joan van Emden, whose unstinting support and expert advice is always more appreciated than I can say.

I should also like to thank Peter Martin for the private family photographs he kindly supplied for the plate section as well as for his first hand memories of his father that proved so useful during the writing of the introduction. I am also very grateful to Laurence Martin for his unfailing help and encouragement as I edited his grandfather's memoirs.

Acknowledgement from the Martin family:
Jack Martin's family would like to thank Peter Barton for being the first historian to discover this material and confirm its quality to the family.

Their thanks in equal measure also go to Richard van Emden for having such faith in Jack's narrative and making it 'a book'.

A NOTE ON THE TYPE

Linotype Garamond Three – based on seventeenth century copies of Claude Garamond's types, cut by Jean Jannon. This version was designed for American Type Founders in 1917, by Morris Fuller Benton and Thomas Maitland Cleland and adapted for mechanical composition by Linotype in 1936.